Theoretical Analysis of

Information Systems

Börje Langefors

Theoretical Analysis of Information Systems

Fourth Edition

Studentlitteratur · Sweden
AUERBACH Publishers Inc. Philadelphia, Pa., 1973

Library of Congress Cataloging in Publication Data

Langefors, Börje, 1915—
 Theoretical analysis of information systems.

 Includes bibliographies.
 1. Management information systems. 2. Electronic data processing. I. Title.
 T58.6.L353   001.5   72-8124
 ISBN 0-87769-151-7

© Börje Langefors 1973

First published in the USA in 1973
by AUERBACH Publishers Inc.,
Philadelphia, Pa.

Fourth edition
First printing
Printed in Sweden
Studentlitteratur
Lund 1973

ISBN/Studentlitteratur 91-44-08154-5
ISBN/AUERBACH 0-87769-151-7

Contents

PREFACE 11

ACKNOWLEDGEMENT 15

PART 1. SYSTEMS THEORY 17

Chapter 1. Basic Problems of Systems Theory 17

11.1 Needs for a Formal Systems Theory 17
11.2 Common Faults in Systems Design and Analysis 20
11.3 Different Kinds of Systems Study 21
11.4 Systems Engineering 21
11.5 Structural Systems Theory, Electric Networks and Elastic Systems 25
11.6 Mathematical Systems Theory as a System 30
11.7 Other Kinds of Systems Study 33
11.8 Elements of a Systems Theory 34
11.9 Usefulness of our Concise Definition of Systems 37
11.10 The Systems Analysis Approach 48
11.11 The Fundamental Principle of Systems Work 51
11.12 General and Special properties of Systems Problems 53
11.13 System, Subsystem, Parts and Boundaries 56
11.14 Structure Types of Systems 60
11.15 System Partitioning 64
11.16 Systems Partitioning of Outer Boundary 66
11.17 A Sketch of a Basic Theory of Systems Analysis 66
11.18 The Suitable Number of Subsystems in a Subsystem 84

Chapter 2. Systems Algebra 87

12.1 Algebraic Tools for Describing Systems 87
12.2 Precedence Operator of a System (or Graph) 88
12.3 The Precedence Matrix of a System 98
12.4 The Precedents of a Set of Parts 101
12.5 Use of the Precedence Matrix P to Determine the Precedents of a Set of parts 102
12.6 Connection with a Linked Data Structure 106
12.7 Matrix by Matrix Composition. p^n, n-th Precedents and Paths 108
12.8 Succedence Matrix P_T 112

12.9 Generalization of the Precedence Concept 116
12.10 A generalized Matrix by Vector Operation 118
12.11 Generalized Matrices 120
12.12 Matrix Operations as Processing of Data Structures 120
12.13 Other Kinds of Algorithms for Processing Data Structures 127
12.14 P^{11}, the 1-dimensional Precedence Matrix 128
12.15 P^{01} and P^{10}, Precedence Matrices for Mixed 0-1 and 1-0 Dimension Respectively 134
12.16 Relations Between P^{01}, P^{10} and P^{11} and P^{00} Respectively 136
12.17 Definition of E^{10}, the Incidence Matrix 136
12.18 Boundary Operation on a System and the Incidence Matrix 137
12.19 Co-boundary Operation and Incidence Matrix 141
12.20 The Coincidence Matrix M^{10} 143
12.21 Data Structure Representation of Incidence and Coincidence Matrices 147
12.22 Illustration of Boundary Operation in Accounting 152
12.23 Built-up Systems and Gross Systems 155
12.24 System Connections, Boundary Operation and Cycles 163
12.25 Positional Operator for the System Graph 164
12.26 Simple Paths and Closed Paths in a System Graph 166
12.27 Transposed Positional Operator, Forward Positioning 169
12.28 General Positioning 171
12.29 Requirements Computation and Scheduling 172
12.30 Determining the Boundary Operator from M^{10} and the Part Boundary Operator R^T 188
12.31 Boundary Operator for Generalized Systems 189

PART 2. INFORMATION SYSTEMS THEORY 195

Chapter 1. Information Systems 195

21.1 Information System Design 195
21.2 Formalization of Information System Design 195
21.3 Component Problems of Information System 196

Chapter 2. The Function of an Information System 199

22.1 The Function of an Information System 199
22.2 Two Tasks of an Information System 200
22.3 Operative Information Requirements. An Example. 202
22.4 The value of Directive Information 205
22.5 Effect of Time for Decisionmaking. Executive Decisions 208

22.6 Transient Decision Situation. Satisficing. 211
22.7 Information Needed in a Simplified Model of a Manufacturing Shop 212

Chapter 3. The Economic Quantity of Information and Processing 221

23.1 The Economic Quantity of Information 221
23.2 Information Value as an Information System Design Parameter 222
23.3 Information and System Control 227
23.4 The Meaning of Information within a System 229
23.5 The Value of Information in a System 233
23.6 Data Representation of Information in a System. Volume of Data 242
23.7 The Information System for a Simple Inventory 249
23.8 Operative versus Directive Information 252
23.9 An Example of Optimum Reduction. Information Processing for a Simple Inventory 256
23.10 Information System for a Simple Work Station 258

Chapter 4. Some Problems of Information Systems Design 265

24.1 Complexity of an Information System 265

Chapter 5. Precedence Relations between Information Sets in an Information System 277

25.1 Data Structure of an Information System 277
25.2 On the Definition of Elementary Files (e-files) 293
25.3 Inference Problems in Information System Design 296
25.4 A Further Illustration to Information Precedence and Elementary File Definition; Computation of Weekly Wage 298
25.5 Cost Distribution of Job Costs as Another Illustration of Discussing Elementary Files 304
25.6 Identification of Precedence Information 306
25.7 Use of the Information Precedence Matrix P^{00} for Compatibility Checking 306
25.8 Some Other Uses of the Precdence Matrix P 309
25.9 The Precedence Structure and the Dynamic Flow of Processing 311
25.10 Completeness Theorem of Information Precedence Analysis 312
25.11 Systematic Design of a Directive Information System 313

Chapter 6. Data and Information Files 319

26.1 Data and Information Files 319
26.2 Size of Data Terms and Precision Required 320

Chapter 7. Files, Computations and Processes   324

27.1   Files and Processes   324
27.2   The Size of a File   329
27.3   File Volume and Transport Volume, Processing Period   338
27.4   Transport Factor   350
27.5   Topological Transport Factor   359
27.6   Grouping of Computations into one Process   360
27.7   Incidence Matrix of Processes and Files   366

Chapter 8. Effect of Process Grouping   371

28.1   Effect of Process Grouping on the Transport Factor   371
28.2   Memory Requirment Associated with Process Grouping   373
28.3   Computer Programs and Memory Space for a Process   375
28.4   Example of Process Grouping with Memory Limitation   379

Chapter 9. File Consolidation   387

29.1   Reducing the Number of Transport Equipment Units   387
29.2   The Effect of File Consolidation in Direct-access Stores   393
29.3   Effects of the Size of File Blocks (Physical Records)   398
29.4   The Effect upon CPU-time   402
29.5   Conclusion about File Consolidation and Choice of Block Sizes   403
29.6   Adaptation to Hardware System   404

Chapter 10. System Design Computation Using Matrix Algebra   413

210.1   Information System Design Computations   413
210.2   Joining Rows in E^{10} to Represent Grouping of Processes   415
210.3   Representing Process Grouping by a Generalized Matrix Operation   417
210.4   Matrix Operations to Compute File Transport Reduction and Memory Space   418
210.5   Calculations for Minimum File Transport Design   424
210.6   Procedures for Aiding the Intuitive System Design Phases   426
210.7   Defining File Consolidation by Matrix Operation on E^{10} 433
210.8   Influence on Programming Language Development   437

Chapter 11. File Storage Considerations   439

211.1   Files in Systems Using Mass Memories of Pseudo Random Access Type   439
211.2   Direct Processing versus Batched Processing   441

Chapter 12. File Organization 443

212.1 Record Layouts 443
212.2 Record Organization 445

Chapter 13. System Reliability 449

213.1 Reliability of an Information System 449
213.2 Means for Checking Input Data 450

Chapter 14. The Problem of Optimum Grouping of Information Processes 453

214.1 The Problem of Optimum Grouping of Information Processes 453
214.2 Special Case: Grouping Processes in Pairs 453
214.3 The Problem of Optimum Pairing Without Memory Constraint 453

PART 3. SOME DATA PROCESSING PROBLEMS 457

Chapter 1. Relation Between a Process and its Files 457

31.1 Relation Between a Process and its Files 457
31.2 Some Basic Problems of File Processing 457
31.3 K-Progressive Process 461
31.4 Rectangular File Processing and Group Access 462
31.5 Retrieval of File Records for a Process 464

Chapter 2. Influence of Word Structure 467

32.1 Influence of Word Length on Tape Recording Speed 467

References 471

Index 477

Preface

This book is about systems. Systems which collect, store, process and transport information. Information systems. Different components are used to provide these activities. To emphasize the *system* aspect is to stress that it is the *combined effect* of the components that is important. How the properties of the parts are used to generate those properties of the whole that are desirable and important. To design good systems is different from designing good, individual components. It requires understanding of how the components interact and may be brought to cooperate. To design a good system also requires to understand how to define what properties the whole system must have to be good. Good to the users, not just fascinating to the designers.

Information systems handle *data* to provide *information*. An information that any user in the whole system might find useful. — Provided he is authorized to use them. — The data processing systems of yesterday — and, alas, of today, still — do not allow this. They were designed as isolated systems, fragments of the information system. They also worked as isolated. Most people in the user system who could have used the data could not get them. They could not even know whether they were there. The names given to data by the designers of data processing "routines" could not be guessed at by others. And it was rarely possible to guess what information was involved. Information systems design must be based on information — not merely the symbols, the data — and it must be oriented towards the system, the whole.

To design a system is to take a set of decisions each of which imposes some constraint on the design. When so many constraints have been added that only one alternative for implementation is left open then the design task has been finished. In its first stage. Modifications will usually have to be made before it really works.

The important problem for system design is to find a good sequencing of the individual design decisions. Technical people, such as computer specialists, tend to specify the technical constraints first or to formulate the users constraints in technical jargon so they are unintelligible to the users. To guarantee that the users needs are given enough consideration one must specify user oriented (and usage oriented) constraints first and introduce technical constraints as late as possible. To be able to do this we need to find out what can be specified at each stage trying to have no technical constraints at all in the early stages and as few and as broad ones as possible in between, leaving technical details — such as programming — until last.

The need to design the system for the right information for the users calls for doing early analysis in terms of overall system structure and information relations while then successively specifying more details of data structuring and process programs.

In this book the analysis of system structure and modelling the structure for determination of system properties by computation or simulation, based on structure and component properties are studied. Information analysis, data structuring, system structuring and specifying the "external properties" of processes are considered extensively. We have thus a separation of data design from programs not only in the implementation of the data base of the system, as has become common lately, but right from the early stages of system studies. We took, from the beginning, a relational approach to data base design and, what is more, an informatological approach as one of the basic points, all from the first version of the present book in 1963. The book is very much about how this can be done, from early explorative system analysis to the implemented, computerized, company system. The book also is aimed at providing an understanding of the importance of designing the systems that are wanted or needed by the users — to have the organizations get the systems they want and not just get the systems they get.

Finally the book is about how all this might be achieved combined with efficiency. To design large systems one must tackle problems which appear so simple as to be trivial at the first view. For instance stringent methods are needed to identify and name the elements. Formal methods are needed not only to identify the elements. Formal methods are needed not only to compute properties but even to document analysis and descriptions. We treat elementary mathematical methods to handle this. We borrow from abstract algebra, topology and graph theory. But we need only some simple tools. Much of what is commonly treated in these fields could be avoided. Instead we needed to introduce some generalizations into the known mathematical tools. In this way we present a "system algebra". This is sufficient to document most system descriptions in a formal way. This description can then be the basis for advanced computations which can be handled by other people than those who did the analysis. We illustrate how such algebraic computations can be developed to compute performance estimates of varying information system design alternatives using varying data consolidation and groupings of computing processes.

By using strict formal methods the analysts can avoid getting bogged down in complicated computations while doing design lay-out. He can handle them over to computing specialists or even to computers. Thus improved possibilities for cooperation between distinct groups such as users, analysts, system architects and programmers are obtained. The system experts can use the same formal tool to document the analysis, the design attempts, the project schedule, software design and the computational procedure for treating project networks and structural computations such as e.g. parts requirements computation for production control systems.

In this book we concentrate on information structure and the data and their relations associated with the information. In this kind of study the information processes appear as isolated islands in the total structure. The relations between the processes are established by the information relations. The data structure of the system establishes some of the important properties which are to be specified for the processes, i.e. they specify input and output. We have not considered details of process description as this is the main theme of the vast literature on programming. We would have liked to say more, however, about how the system analyst could specify processes. This will have to be left for later work, however. Leaving it out here does not mean that we would not consider it important.

The present book on different, basic, problems of analysis and design of information systems got its starting impulse when the author was invited to give an one-week series of lectures at an advanced course on business data processing at Regnecentralen, Copenhagen, in 1962. This course was a pioneering effort in Schandinavia and was one of the many examples of the forsighted and progressive activity of Regnecentralen of Copenhagen. After a repetition of this course at Norsk Regnecentral, Oslo, in 1963 the author gave an extended series of lectures at the Institute for Business Administration, Lund University, spring 1964. Based on these lectures and on a series of articles published earlier in BIT (Nordisk Tidskrift för Informationsbehandling) the first draft of this book was worked out in the spring 1964, containing the main substance of the present version and was mimeographed. This first issue has been used then at two-week courses at Saab Aircraft Company, Linköping, Sweden, and at Lund University. When this material is now made available to a wider public it is in a third wersion which differs from the first one (of 1964) mainly by additions made to enhance readibility.

The author's interest in information for system control dates back, at least, to 1943 when he was led to designing a small system where an analogue computing network was integrated to an instrument for dynamically balancing rotating machine parts, thereby automatizing the decisions as to the weight and location of counterbalances. In connection with a series of sudies and implementations of analogue networks for engineering structural analysis and analogue computers using negative feed-back amplifiers for studying aircraft flutter problems and work on a digital contour control system of a milling machine (completed in 1955) and a digital computer (completed in 1957) the author started in 1950 to use electronic punched-card machines and then digital computers for engineering analysis problems. In 1954, after having studied some of the plans for using digital computers in business data processing in UK and USA, he worked out a proposal for introducing digital computers both for data processing as then done by punched-card machinery and for management control. The plan suggested that work should be started on two lines. One should be a short range project to automatize present procedures whereas the other should, according to the proposal, set high ambitions and be planned for a longer range and should be worked by a group containing people from management, production, engineering analysis and mathematicians and computer specialists and it should have liberty to design an electronic total management control system. While to management was interested in the project part of the middle management was not very enthusiastic and the project was accepted only after considerable modification. This can now, on afterthought, be highly deplored for it has now turned out to be the way one needs to attack present-day ambitious total management systems projects. The author had occasion, however, to continue on a limited scale in the direction indicated by generalizing other systems-theoretical work and by automatizing much of the planning and control of his own department which employed a large group of computer specialists and was running a computer for engineering calculations.

Stockholm i april 1972

Börje Langefors

Acknowledgement

It is natural that the amount of work put into this volume could not have been done without a lot of encouragement and assistance from many people. It is not possible to mention them all but my former employer, Saab Aircraft Company, and my colleagues there, especially those at the ADP Systems Development Group at the Computer Department, as well as different members of the Swedish Society for Information Processing and the Swedish "IDP-gruppen" and many business leaders and organization directors of Swedish companies and researchers in engineering and business administration and mathematicians in Sweden have deserved my thanks.

I thank my wife Eva who has so patiently and inspiringly encouraged my writing and research work over all the years.

During the years, since 1964 when this material was first put into educational use in university courses in information processing (or business administration), a lot of mistakes and misprints have been detected all of which were not accordingly corrected. A large number of corrections and modifications have been proposed by courses. These have been introduced here and this work put into it is hereby acknowledged. Special thanks go to miss Agneta Olerup, Lund University, and mrs Anita Kollerbaur, Stockholm University, who have done very thorough and skilful work in this connection and to mrs Marianne Swendsén, Stockholm University, who has done a great job correcting many misprints for the new type-setting of the book, as well as making many language refinements.

Part 1. Systems Theory

Chapter 1. Basic Problems of Systems Theory

11.1 Needs for a Formal Systems Theory.

We attempt a formal theory in order to be able to obtain useful guidance to systems work, which is much needed. To do this will of course take a long time as we must start from the beginning. Our goal here is to treat the subject in a way which will further, as efficiently as possible, the establishment of a systematic theory.

We try to do this by presenting formal methods at least for the statement of problem. Rather than spend too much time in this early stage on establishing formal algorithms for solutions to specific problems we shall often be satisfied with a formal description only. The reason is twofold. First, once a formal statement is made of a problem then a solution procedure may well be worked out by any skilled numerical analyst. Secondly so many important parts of the theory are still not formalized at the description stage. In our opinion they deserve more of our present attention.

When we do not find any formal description or statement we still attempt some degree of precision. We also try to emphasize problems which we think important though not treated so far in the literature (as far as we know). We try to achieve precision by defining, when procedures are not available, at least which empirical information should be collected. If even that is not yet possible we insist that estimates, even guesses, be made explicitly, and be documented during the system design work. This is a basic requirement for rational progress. We also emphasize the importance of making it possible to obtain missing information from the system itself. This means that the system should be designed in such a way as to be self-instructing.

Finally we try to support statements by drawing analogies from other systems theories, for which precise solutions to the specific problems, or techniques for solution, have already been devised.

When these analogies cannot be used directly to establish solutions they will give, at least, some precision to the guide lines presented, thereby illustrating some kind of a proof of feasibility.

One result of the use of our approach to some actual systems design projects has been to reveal, at a very early stage, that the system lay-out was not compatible with the memory size planned for the computer. These problems have been solved by restructuring the processing system into a greater number of "smaller" runs. As this was made clear before any programming had been done the restructuring could be made relatively easily. It was also of great advantage that the resulting increase in total processing time was detected early so that it could be considered in the planning in good time. In some cases the solution has instead been to order a larger memory size. This again could be done without trouble as the need for it was detected early. If our approach had been followed from the start these problems would probably never have occurred for we build the system "from small parts" while watching out for equipment requirements continuously. In another practical case a production scheduling system, which had been in use for some time, was found to have a subsystem for parts requirements computation which was unnecessarily complicated, having an unnecessary time-consuming tape sorting operation. The interesting point was that a simpler solution was immediately obvious to anybody familiar with the systems algebra presented here. Also the documentation describing the method used in the actual system was extremely complicated and it took a thorough analysis before it could be demonstrated that the procedure was in fact logically correct. The corresponding documentation for our solution is, by contrast, simply by a couple of matrix algebraic formulae. These are some practical examples of the advantage of a deeper understanding of the underlying principles and of using a concise definition language. It should soon repay the cost of study in order to be mastered appropriately. The really important advantages are still to come. They will come through better use of information processing equipment in the improvement of management, when a better understanding and a suitable language for discussing its real needs have become more widespread and, on a higher level, the balance between information value and information processing cost will be optimized. This is one of the most natural paths for further research along the lines presented here.

People who have been working with business data processing

systems before will probably find, at first sight that the way system analysis and design is approached here is so different from what is common today, that the systems they have designed could not have been obtained by our method. This is a mistake. In fact our detailed description of file consolidation provides the most natural explanation of why business ADP files look as they do. Every system which is a correct solution to the information systems problem at hand can be obtained as one feasible solution of the present approach. The difference is mainly that we do a more systematic breakdown of the system. This makes possible a more systematic utilization of the different possible combinations and hence chances are great that our approach will lead to a more "nearly optimal" solution. This is to say that we might well come to define the same solution as is in use today — but at the same time would probably also find other solutions which offer other advantages.

Our approach also has the definite advantage that it is a step toward automatic solution of information systems design problems. Present-day ways of designing information systems are far too unsystematic to be suited for automation.

During the decade that computers have now been used for business data processing, a great majority of the computers used have not been very suited for their purpose, and the purpose has seldom been chosen appropriately. Memory need and logical speed required have been vastly underestimated both by manufacturers and users. Such misjudgements would be almost completely eliminated if design were based on such an insight of the basic problems as is given by our theoretical analysis. It is interesting to note that such an analysis could in principle have been done even ten years ago, for it is *not* dependent on practical experience other than that available after the first use of computers for scientific purposes.

It has also been typical of business data processing that almost no use has been made of one of the most efficient tools for automatic computation: standard computing procedures. The reason has been the apparent dissimilarity between the business routines of different companies, even in the same branch. By using the detailed breakdown of files and processes described in this book the basic generality of the elementary processes and files comes to indicate great possibilities for using standard procedure for most business data processing.

It must therefore be stated that world wide it has been very expensive not to have used scientific methods for analyzing business ADP-problems from the start.

11.2 Common Faults in Systems Design and Analysis.

1 Resource and activity allocation is almost always unbalanced. Some questions are given too much consideration, while others get too little. As cost functions involved are mostly progressively non-linear this makes for losses.

Countermeasure: More planning and analysis following a true systems approach. Use of cost statistics. Supporting general research.

Example. Extensive resources allocated to design work on insufficiently analyzed premises.

2 Cost, time and resource consumption are mostly severely underestimated. Remedy: Detailed analysis and listing of all parts of the system. Often the unexpectedly high number of parts makes it clear quite early that previous estimates were too low (very often by 50 %)[1]).

For each part in the list establish or estimate — or even guess in the first case — the requirements.

3 Subsystems and goals for them are not clearly defined.

4 Subsystems are not given directives or boundary conditions suited for approximating total optimization. It is overlooked that this cannot be handled *within* the subsystem. (For instance a department head needs a set of directives computed on the basis of overall system goals.)

5 Subsystem definition is not used to eliminate redundant control information flow. This tends to saturate both subsystem and system control channels.

---

[1]) The author has seen this proved in several occasions from his own experience. Similar results have been published by Rand and by Harvard Business School, as referred by 1 Mi 1963.

6 Subsystems are not specified well enough to permit separate testing of subsystems before total tests. Subsystems must also be defined with an eye kept on the efficiency of a testing system by a rationally designed sequence of subsystem tests.

7 Documentation is unsatisfactory so that a) management has neither a complete nor an understandable set of descriptions of all decisions taken during design of all decision functions built into the system, and is thus unable to use the system and to know it is doing what is wanted and b) replacement of the system staff people becomes almost impossible.

11.3 Different Kinds of Systems Study.

The word system is very frequently used in our time with fairly distinct meanings although all are more or less related to the same concept as we use it here. We therefore give in the following a brief survey of some of the different fields of systems study. In some of the fields a fairly formalized systems theory exists or is in the state of being developed. This is true for instance for systems engineering and control systems theory, where mathematical methods for the analysis of the dynamic behavior of systems is in the center of interest. It is also true for the structural systems theory, as developed in electrical engineering and in structural mechanics, where mathematical models are used to describe how systems are built up by joining parts. Also the formal systems of mathematical logic are examples of this kind. On the other hand there is a set of systems studies which are not formalized but where a general philosophy is more or less related to systems theory in its intuitive interpretation and which are presented under names such as "systems analysis". In this class are economic studies related to decentralized decision making or sub-optimization or biological systems or "general systems philosophy" studies. Some general properties of these different "theories" are presented briefly in the paragraphs to follow, after which we take up the basic systems theory as we are going to use it here.

11.4 Systems Engineering.

The systems engineer is concerned with the problem of designing a system of mechanical, electrical and other physical components, such as machines, motors and instruments, in a way which assures that these components will work together in a manner which, at least, satisfies minimum conditions of feasibility and compatibility, and, at best, does this in an optimal way. Interaction between man and the mechanical system is also of great importance to the systems engineer so that in fact human beings are also components in his total systems.

There is one theoretical aspect of all systems problems and one practical one. The theoretical problem of systems engineering has been to develop, in mathematical terms, the dynamic properties of a proposed mechanical system ("mechanic" used here in its broadest sense). Thus systems engineering theory is concerned with demonstrating, at least, that the system will have a stable dynamic behavior in the environment where it will have to work. At best systems engineering expects to be able to determine how the components are to be designed and interconnected so as to work as a system in some optimal way as determined by some economic, or other criteria.

To reach his theoretical goal the systems engineer uses mathematical tools such as systems of differential equations. In trying to find the solutions of these differential equations and how these solutions are influenced by the design parameters of the system, that is by the properties of the components and their interconnections, the systems engineer developed tools such as block diagrams and transfer functions. Laplace transformation has been one of the typical mathematical aids used in this context.

The analog computer has been a valuable tool: System components are simulated by electronic feed-back amplifiers and system build-up is simulated by interconnecting these amplifiers. Some effort has been made to make the analog computer work in real scale because this will enable the connecting of real systems components where these are difficult to simulate. The real-time requirement for analog computers poses the problem of slowing down the computer, contrary to the situation with a digital computer.

The practical aspect of systems engineering has to do with the problem of constructing the different system components separately, supplied by different companies for instance, and then put them together, to work as a system. Early experience (World War II) showed up so many cases where this approach did not work. The separate components would not work together — or would not even enable their proper interconnection. *System incompatibility* (or component interphase difficulties) became the hard fact of life of practical systems engineering.

In the author's opinion this seems to have led the development in the profession of systems engineering and — as a consequence — that of other fields of systems study in an unfortunate direction.

Thus to avoid the practical systems incompatibilities it was said that systems engineers have to control the design of all systems components. The resulting requirement then would be that the systems designer has to be an expert on all the components designs — an impossible requirement indeed. A consequence of this philosophy has been that text books on systems engineering[1]) — and as a consequence those on other systems as well[2]) — tend to be mainly compendia on collected subjects — leading to superficiality and lack of unity. The true *systems concept*, which has to do with the problems of the whole and the interconnection between the components rather than the components proper, became lost in these kinds of texts.

Of course, this way of handling systems problems cannot work, simply for the reason that it is impossible for human beings to be sufficiently expert in sufficiently many component fields. In practice, therefore, this philosophy could not be adhered to completely. This meant however that practical systems engineering work came to lack the guidance of suitable theory. This has been the case, then, also for other fields which have tried to take up systems philosophy such as the ADP systems work for business data processing.

In the author's opinion (supported by what he believes to be fairly conclusive theoretical as well as practical experience) the problem of practical incompatibility of systems should be solved in another way which is more in line with a systems philosophy. This is to develop a technique which concentrates upon the main systems problem — that of the interaction of the parts. If such a technique — where the systems analyst is not trying to be an expert on everything but is truly an expert in this genuine systems concept — is followed with full consequence, incompatibilities are detected early and thus avoided in the implementation while each component

---

[1]) 1 Go 1957.
[2]) 1 J K 1963.

type can be handled by the proper specialists. The systems analyst will, of course, have to have a general knowledge of the "external" properties of the different system components in order to handle correctly the interactions problems[3]).

This point-of-view has obtained increasing support as experience has accumulated and it is an interesting observation that only after it has been well enough understood — to be given all the effort needed to follow it fully — have we obtained the full benefit out of it. There is an explicit theoretical background development, running parallel with implementation experience, to the development of this view. This theory will be one main part of the present writing so we will return to that soon. Some comments about some experiences may deserve their place here. Following a growing awareness of the potential benefits of the systems approach advocated above, the author has tried to guide his associates, working on projects of such diverse kind as machine design, aircraft analysis, ship design, computer-type equipment, computer programming systems, or administration procedures, to define subsystems and implement them separately while giving due consideration to compatibility questions and total systems goals. Earlier, when confidence was probably not firm enough, it seemed reasonable to let the different project leaders do it their way and thus compromise with the systems principles of modular design, which were believed to slow down implementation because of the detailed analysis and planning which they require. Later on, when theoretical arguments had become more distinct and experience had shown the drawbacks of earlier compromises, and in situations where very strict cost and time conditions called for the highest degree of efficiency, the adherence to strict systems technique, and thus to modular design, were insisted upon.

And now the confidence springing from more insight and experience turned out to be the right background for persuading and motivating project leaders. Success as measured by time and money was often even better than hoped for, and it has turned out to be possible to avoid incompatibility problems (interface problems between modules) almost completely by very careful attention.

---

[3]) In fact one of the important problems of systems analysis is to find out how the "external" or "interphase" properties of different components should be defined. When this is done these properties are mainly what the systems man needs to know about distinct components.

As the general trend of systems and projects work has been along the same lines as those advocated above it is probably not necessary to argue this point any more. It will be a basis for what is to follow in this writing.

It should be added that we have taken a somewhat narrow view here on the concept of systems engineering as practised in the past. On the whole, systems engineering has the same goals and basic philosophy as our concept of information systems together with the management systems or other systems for the control of which they are used. Also the fact that systems engineering typically works with control systems or communication systems brings the subsystem information system also within its scope. However, we are mainly interested in finding a formal theory so that efficient guidance for doing systems work can be given. From that point-of-view we concentrated above, as we do in the sections to follow, on what formal tools are available or typical in the different systems fields. It must be assumed that in the long run systems engineering and management systems work will come to use increasingly similar tools and approaches[4]).

11.5 Structural Systems Theory, Electric Networks and Elastic Systems.

Electric networks and elastic structures are often such big and complicated systems that the derivation of their properties or behavior will have to rely on numeric computation of quantitatively specified systems. This makes it natural to shift the main interest from analytical-mathematical deduction of dynamic behavior to systematic construction of computation schemes — from dynamics to structural questions. A valuable by-product of this approach therefore is that attention is focused on one of the genuine systems problems — that of taking care of the interactions between systems parts. This kind of systems analysis, which has gone in parallel with that of systems engineering, is not an alternative to the dynamic analysis of systems engineering. It is rather a complement, and drawing from both areas is one of the most natural means for advancing systems theory.

---

[4]) Such a trend is clearly visible for instance in Zadeh and Desoer, Linear System-Theory (1 Za 1963).

The treatment of electric networks as systems in a true sense was to a large extent started by the great works of Gabriel Kron[1]), although it can be said — in retrospect — that already the works of Lagrange and Maxwell are based on a systems philosophy. Kron's method treats electric networks in their two dual aspects. In one of these, the "mesh analysis", branch currents of the electric network are the basic variables; in the dual approach, the "junction pair analysis", electric potentials of junction points are instead basic. In the mesh analysis meshes are defined in the network in a way introduced by Maxwell.

Kron then sets up equations which express the mesh currents (I) as combinations of the branch current variables (i). Using matrix algebra he thus obtains

$$I = C\, i$$

C is then interpreted by Kron (in one of the basic steps in his analysis) as the *connection matrix for the network*. In so doing Kron introduces the important insight that the interconnections of the system parts define the mathematical relations between the system entities: mesh currents; and the part-entities: branch currents; and that therefore these relations reflect the systems interconnections or the structure of the system.

(Those who are not familiar with the concept of matrices but happen to know data processing may interpret the matrix equation above, and some to follow, as stating that the data set symbolized to the left (I in the above case) can be produced by a processing routine which takes the data sets C and i as input, where the data sets C and i are collected to describe the known properties of, and conditions for, the network studied. It is also worth noting that this interpretation in terms of data processing is more general in that it does not require that the data and the procedure are restricted to those of matrix algebra.) Kron then shows that if z_{ii} is the impedance property of the i-th branch of the network, then the system impedances Z associated with the meshes can be obtained by the routine procedure

$$Z = C^T (z_{ii}) C$$

---

[1]) 1 Kr 1942.

where C^T is the transposed matrix C and (z_{ii}) is a diagonal matrix of branch impedances. (Again the data processing interpretation of this symbolism can be to regard it as a computer run using the files C and (z_{ii}) and outputting the file Z.)

For the dual analysis, using node voltages, similar procedures hold.

If we go over to elastic structures we find that instead of a branch current we will have a beam force. This, however, is characterized not by one value but by six component values. What is more, the force components (moments) may have different values at different ends of the beam. Kron[2]) made (the first part of) this observation, and established a part of the analysis similar to electric network analysis, the analysis of elastic networks. There were three restrictions in this work of Kron: firstly, it only applied to elastic networks, that is, structures consisting of beams only. Secondly, stiff joints not "pin-joints") only are presumed. Thirdly, he was not able to obtain the counterpart to his mesh analysis in the electric case but only the junction pair analysis. Langefors[3]), [4]), [5]) obtained solutions to all these problems and thus eliminated the restrictions. Similar solutions using matrix algebra but with less appeal to systems theory were obtained by Falkenhainer[6]) and others. Kron's method, and that of the work on applications for elastic structures as well, uses as a basis for development of the system equations energetic principles such as that of least work or virtual work or virtual displacements. Langefors[7]) explored the possibility of obtaining a more general analysis and therefore redeveloped and extended the theory by omitting the energetic basis. The advantage was threefold. Firstly, the energetic principles were useful, in the pre-matrix era, by enabling a systematic (non-intuitive) procedure for analysis. With matrices available this was no longer made use of as the analysis used matrix algebra which is routine anyway. Secondly, the ener-

---

[2]) Kron, G., Tensorial Analysis and Equivalent Circuits of Elastic Structures, Journal Franklin Inst. Vol 238, No 6, p. 339 Dec. 1944.
[3]) Langefors, B., Improvement in Electric Computer Network for some Elastic Structures, Saab TN 1 (1950).
[4]) Langefors, B., Structural Analysis of Sweep-back Wings by Matrix Transformation, Saab TN 3, 1951.
[5]) Langefors, B., Analysis of Elastic Structures by Matrix Transformation, Journal Aeoro Sci. Vol. 1952.
[6]) Falkenhainer, H., Le Calcul systématique des caractéristices elastiques des systémes hyperstatique. La Recherche Aéronautique No 17 (1950).
[7]) Langefors, B., Algebraic Methods for the Numerical Analysis of Built-up Systems. Saab TN 38 (1957).

getic principles restrict the applicability to such systems (physical mainly) where they make sense and also obscure the insight into the basic mechanisms of the systems. Omitting the energetic (or kinetic) basis would for instance make administrative systems or production systems come within reach for the theory. Thirdly, it turned out that the theory could be developed from the junction properties and element properties alone. As these were also inherent in the energetic approach, the omitting of the latter can be regarded as eliminating a redundant element. In other words, we can say that the same analysis procedures could be obtained without the need for proving energetic or kinetic theorems first, and at the same time more general applicability and, also, more guidance for intuition was gained.

Some interesting by-products of the development towards more generality and abstraction were obtained. One is that an explanation was given as to why the attempt by Kron to obtain both dual analysis methods failed in his elastic application. Another was that a further decomposition of the systems analysis work into more, and simpler, steps was obtained. This was an important advance towards the concept of system technique, as we are going to advocate it here, of treating the system component by component and using formal procedures for compiling results for the whole.

The additional system-theoretic decomposition can be explained with reference to the above mentioned equation of Kron: $Z = C^T(z_{ii})C$. In this, Kron had established a decomposition of the work needed into three separate phases. Thus the connection matrix C could be set up as a separate work done by analyzing the mesh currents in the network, or the static equilibrium of beam forces in the elastic structure, respectively. The branch impedances z_{ii} can be determined quite separately (and indeed for each branch separate from the others).

Finally the composition of C and z_{ii} can be obtained in a third, separate phase. We have, in fact, here a *strict theoretical proof* of the feasibility of the true systems technical procedure, as well as precise guidance for its performance.

The further advance in this direction now lies in the fact that the systems connection matrix C (or its counterparts) can be split up into a product of two matrices[7]). Only one of these two factor matrices has to do with the physical (or geometrical) properties of the system. And it turns out that this, like (z_{ii}), can again be split up into one smaller matrix for each system part. The other factor matrix will be the only one where the genuine systems aspects enter. And on the other hand it will not be concerned at all with physical properties (and it will not be concerned at all with component properties). It is constructed very simply from the structural, or topological, properties that tell how each component is joined to the system (or interacts with it). And that is all. We shall meet it later on under the name of co-incidence matrix for a system..[7])

In the way described we have, for the class of systems covered by our theory (and it may turn out that a part of it will encompass all systems) *obtained a strict theoretical decomposition of systems work into separate component tasks and one purely structural or system-theoretical work phase which alone is concerned with the whole system.*

Within the kind of systems theory we are discussing here some other, important, mathematical systems analysis techniques have been developed. These are the technique of "analysis by parts" inherent in Krons[14] earliest work and the technique of "solution by parts" introduced by Langefors[5]) and later on studied extensively by Kron under the name of tearing. In the analysis by parts the system matrices are set up from those of subsystems if those are already at hand. In the solution by parts even the solving of systems equations is partly eliminated by use of solutions of equations for subsystems[13]).

The author has later on followed the search he has started for more generality by reworking the theory using algebraic topology as a basis[8]), [9]).

A study of this kind has also been done by Samuelson[10]). It may be mentioned that algebraic topology itself may be regarded as a kind of systems theory and the objects studied in this discipline of mathe-

---

[8]) 1 La 1959.
[9]) 1 La 1961.
[10]) 1 Sa 1962.

matics, such as complexes or sets of interrelated homology classes, are typical of systems as discussed here. See for instance[11], [12]).

11.6 Mathematical Systems Theory as a System.

Before we go over to study some other fields where systems are discussed let us show how theory itself often can be a natural example of a system. In our brief discussion of systems theory for electric networks or elastic structures we have seen how the latter appears as a generalization of the former. It was not a very simple generalization however, although this happens to be the case in important specific restricted cases. This was reflected slightly in the discussion when we mentioned some obstacles that were omitted only after some time. One reason for a difficulty in the generalization, in our specific example of networks, is that in the more general area where branch flows are vector valued (have several components) — as is the case in elastic structures — then degenerative phenomena may occur which cannot exist when branch flows are scalar entities.

A consequence of what we have said is that if we want to have one theory only, general enough to cover both problem types, (and there are more systems that could be so covered) then we must have the general one in full. This however would always be an annoyance to analysts who are only interested in an applications area which does not need all the generality. (If generality would not have meant added complication this problem would not have arisen. This is the case in many practical circumstances.)

It is also an annoyance, however, to repeat large similar parts in presenting theories for two different applications when in fact one theory would suffice.

The reason for this problem, in the case of our present discussion, is that regardless of important differences between the general and

---

[11]) 1 Ax. 1957.
[12]) 1 Hw. 1960.
[13]) The class of methods called by the author *"solution by parts"* has been extended to cover also systems problems where linear programming is used. This was done by e.g. Danzig and Wolfe and is usually referred to as *decomposition methods*.
 1 Da 1960.
[14]) 1 Kr 1942.

the special theory they turn out to lead to exactly the same type of system equations. Thus the later part of the analysis is not more complicated for the more general theory.

A solution to this problem is to split up the theory into two levels. One level is the more detail-oriented one. It analyses the properties of the systems parts, the system variables and the connections. On this level the differences between the more general theory (applicable in elastic systems and others as well) and the restricted theory (sufficient for instance for electric networks) are big enough to justify distinct theory development. In this connection we can still draw on similarities in philosophy.
On the upper level, on the other hand, we need only one theory. This amounts to a true decomposition of the theory work in a true system technique sense.

The lower levels of theory, i.e. the systems parts oriented ones, appear very naturally founded from an intuitive point-of-view. Thus theories are based (in the author's work) on propositions which state such natural properties as that, for instance, when several systems parts are connected to make up one system point, they all have identical values for one of their states which is associated with the connection to that point or, as an other example, state that all flows in a junction add up to zero.

The upper level theory, the one common to two (or more) fields of application, does not have available such natural elements, for it is concerned only with the systems equations and other concepts associated with the system as a whole, that is, with the *gross properties* of the system. Thus for this theory the basic propositions (or axioms) are to identify those gross properties which exist within the system. This brings up the problem: How do we know that the system we want to study will actually possess the properties postulated? One answer is that the detailed, lower level theories may have theorems which state such properties. In the network and elastic structure problems the similarity of some equations can be stated as just such theorems for the lower level theories and axioms for the common, upper level theory. Alternatively the answer may be that it is known a priori that the system has such properties or it has been found during experiments.

We see, on second thought, that the gross theory is not such an unnatural construction as might appear at first. Also, in fact, for

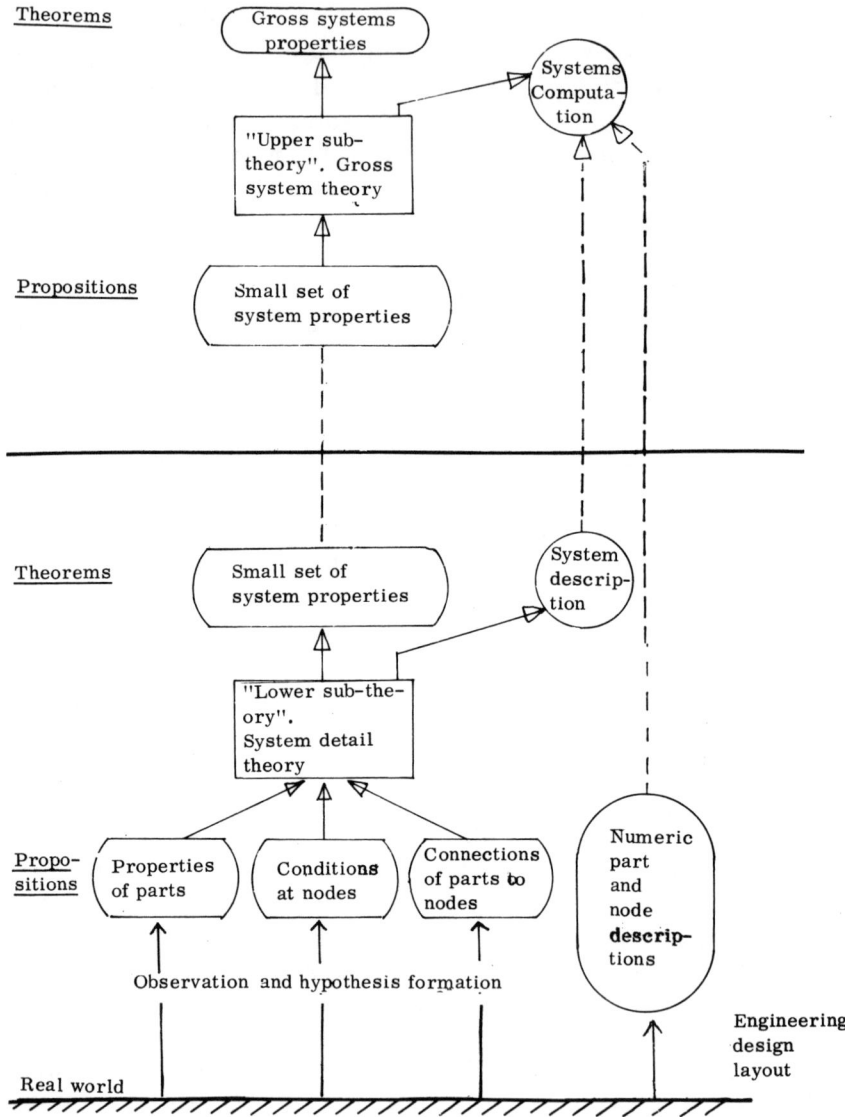

Fig. 1. Total systems theory as a system of subtheories of an upper subsystem treating gross systems properties and a lower subsystem of build-up properties. By replacing the lower subsystem by another which has a sufficient set of identical theorems we obtain a new system theory without changing the overall structure.

every elementary part (or primary) of the system we have to state some properties which are, for that part, exactly gross systems properties.

This discussion may also serve to illustrate why in modern mathematics we often encounter theories which are founded on rather intricate axioms which look more like "deep" theorems. It also indicates that the geometry of Euclid, in fact, is a systems theory.

We shall take up the concept of gross analysis of systems later.

It is worth noting that the treatment of a theory, as the one for electric networks and elastic structures, as a system of subtheories where a lower subtheory can be replaced and thus giving rise to a new theory, is an example of the use of "solution by parts". We save the work of redoing the theoretical analyses for those parts where solutions are already available.

In this section we also have to mention the "logistic systems" which form a subject of study within mathematical logic. Thus for instance "deductive systems" are described by Copi[1]) in this way: "The ideal of science, then, cannot be a system in which *every* proposition is proven and *every* term defined, but is rather one in which a minimum number of propositions suffice for the deduction of all the rest, and a minimum number of terms suffice for the definition of all the others". This is seen to be a statement quite in accordance with the true systems concept of considering a system as built-up from well defined parts in a well defined way and therefore amenable to strict analysis. For a modern, concise ,account of "formal systems", based on a definition of "logistic systems" and defining "deductive systems" as special cases of logistic systems see Porte[2]).

11.7 Other Kinds of Systems Study.

In addition to the kinds of systems study treated briefly above, there is a set of areas where the system is often referred to although no formal systems theory is used or developed. In this area we can mention the "General Systems Theory" which is concerned mainly with classifying different systems into a sequence of classes with increasing complexity so that systems falling in the same class might

---

[1]) 1 Co 1954.
[2]) 1 Po 1965.

be treated in similar ways or using the same tools. L. von Bertalanffy and K. Boulding are names of some of the authors of this field. It is not very closely related to our interest so we do not give any detailed account. We refer instead to other work[1]).

Another school using the word "system" in its name usually talks about "Systems Analysis". It is to a great extent concerned with criteria problems. The main association with true systems questions of this school is through its emphasis on definition of problems of suboptimization, subgoals and decentralization of authority. All these questions are, of course, concerned with subsystems of a system. As both the criteria questions and the other problems mentioned are of great importance for systems design, work in this school is a valuable complement to the more formal systems theories referred to above — as well as developed below[2]).

In connection with data processing it is also common, of course, to see the word system. Again there is seldom much formal systems theory or formal technique used. However the recommendation to do the studies in stages, starting with feasibility studies, does represent an approach typical of systems work. The growing emphasis in this field on the interconnections among different "data" processing of the organization (often in association with the term "integration") are examples of a systems philosophy, but in themselves also illustrate the need for more formal tools. It is of course in this class of systems problems that most of the interest in the present work will be focused.

11.8 Elements of a Systems Theory.

The concept of systems.

1 Before attempting to present a systems theory it is of course desirable to make an attempt to define the concept of systems.

Much has been written to-day about "systems" but nothing like a formal theory has been presented, except for some specific cases. This is only to be expected as long as not even an attempt to give a strict definition has been made.

---

[1]) 1 JK 1963.
[2]) An important reference in this context is Mc Kean: Efficiency in Government through Systems Analysis.

Even when one is attempting to obtain a general treatment of systems, one would do well to see what has been achieved in the limited special cases where a theory has actually been established. This possibility always seems to be overlooked. When we talk, for instance, about "business systems" or "management systems" and try to talk, at least vaguely, in terms of general concepts, we should not neglect the possible advantage of looking into what people working in the older fields of engineering systems have learned. As long as we neglect this opportunity, the most obvious advantages of generalisation would not be realized.

It should not be without value that some systems theories have been cultivated for a long time, and for this reason, have achieved a fairly thorough state, although limited in scope[1]).

2 The first we can learn from the theory of physical systems mentioned above is that it is practical to define:

Definition. A system is a collection of objects, called parts, which are correlated in some way.

In the physical systems it is common to have the correlation between the parts in the form of some sort of physical connections. In the mathematical model of such a system however, the connections occur just as relations, and as all kinds of relations are usable we have chosen to state the definition in the more general way from the beginning.

3 Note that this definition implies that a mathematical model of a system is, itself, a system.

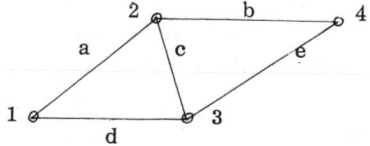

The diagram depicts a system consisting of a set of lines, a, b, c, d, e and a set of points, 1, 2, 3, 4.

---

[1]) See sections 11.3 to 11.6.

4 These sets make up the set of parts from which the system is made up. The system correlations here are given by the connections of the end-points of the lines with the points of the diagram, such as the connections of "a" and "b" to the point "2".

Example. The lists a, b and c below constitute a system.

a. lines: a, b, c, d, e
b. points: 1, 2, 3, 4
c. correlations: a with 1, 2
                b   2, 4
                c   2, 3
                d   1, 3
                e   3, 4

This system is seen to have a complete similarity with that of example in 3, if considered in a sufficiently abstract way.

The relativity principle for systems.

5 *Every system which is subject to influence from its environment is a subsystem of some larger system and every system part is potentially a system.*

This relativity principle follows, in its first part, from the definition in 2 because the influence from environment is equivalent to a correlation with other systems so that they can all be regarded as parts in some "supersystem". The second part follows from the experience in physics and philosophy. Rather than attempt to prove the second part we assert that if one wants to state that it would not be true, so that all parts of the system would not possibly permit a further break-down, one will have the burden of proving this — or take the risk of using it without proof.

6 The most typical systems problem arises from the definition with the additional assumption that the system has some complexity. This leads us to expect that the correlations between the system elements may imply that in the design of a system or in the operation of a system we easily come to a conflict with such correlations — that is a *system incompatibility*. During design we may define different parts so that some correlation between these cannot be satisfied. The cost for this will be a necessary redesign. During operation we may come to make resources available at some point in the system too early or too late. This is associated with costs of too much or too little inventory holding and lost utilization possibilities of productive capacity.

7 It is interesting to note that one and the same kind of difficulty is the reason for all the incompatibility losses mentioned. This is the *difficulty of forecasting*. In the design problem it is the difficulty of seeing in advance all implications of decisions taken at every step of the design work, *although this is in principle exactly predictable*. In the operative problems it is the difficulty of predicting every event which is going to happen. This, in most cases, is not possible to do exactly, even in principle.

8 We can see from this discussion that *one problem in all systems work will be to make as good forecasts as possible*, which in its turn brings the problem of *gathering information relevant to the forecast*.

9 Another problem which is again common to all systems work is to specify corrective action when forecasts indicate that incompatibilies are to be expected. This brings up the decision problem.

10 In the systems design area there is another general principle for reducing incompatibility costs. Knowing that it is natural to have to iterate several steps of design work because incompatible ways of design have been followed one can plan the design analysis so that incompatibilities are detected as soon as possible *so that the re-iterations involve as little work as possible*.

11 Further, incompatibility problems can be eliminated or reduced by consistent use of exact and detailed specification of all interphases between subsystems which are to be worked out and documented before subsystem design is started.

12 In the study to follow we shall make constant use of the simple principal facts about systems work that we have now disclosed.

11.9 Usefulness of our Concise Definition of Systems.

1 The definition of a system as merely a set of objects which are interrelated in some way appears surprisingly short and general at first sight. It seems natural to ask whether one can make any use at all of such a general statement. It is also not uncommon to find more specific (and, therefore, more lengthy) definitions in literature. The reason that we are proposing this very concise definition is that we have found that most of what can be said of one system

holds true for any system. One then, naturally, tries to find what these systems have in common. It is often found that the fact that the systems do consist of parts which are interrelated is the underlying reason for many of the system properties. Therefore the concise definition combines the advantage of being short and clear with the advantage of allowing the formation of a strict and very general theory, which holds for very many systems of the most different kinds. As a consequence is saved a lot of work when going from one class of system problems to another. Those system problems that are of the most general and fundamental kind are already solved in connection with the first class of problems. For each specific class of systems one will then, of course, have to perform a specific analysis concerning such system properties which stem from the further specifications. That class of systems can be defined as a subclass of the general family of all systems which satisfy our definitions.

What we have to do is to show that if an object (which we may want to refer to as a system) consists of a well-defined set of parts with defined attributes and which parts are connected together in a well defined way, then we are able to define and even compute a set of attributes of the system as a whole. The attributes of the system thus are strictly determined by the attributes of its parts and its connections, and nothing else.

Les us choose an illustration which is very simple and of such a kind that it will not be hard for the reader to see that it is an example drawn from a class which contains also less trivial cases.

Example.

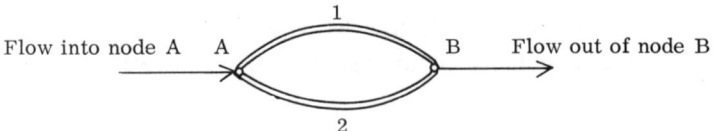

Fig. 1

2 We assume that we have a system consisting of two channels of some sort (denoted by "1" and "2" in Fig. 1) which meet at two nodes A and B and that through each channel a certain quantity of pieces of some sort can flow. Thus we may assume that channel no. 1 has the property that it is capable of carrying a flow of f_1 units/second and that channel no. 2 can carry a flow of f_2 units per second. It is,

of course, natural to regard the configuration consisting of the "input junction A" joined to the "output junction B" by the two parallel channels "1" and "2" as a system which has properties that are analogous to those of a single channel with flow capacity f_s where we must have

$$f_s = f_1 + f_2$$

This shows that the system itself may have a property (f_s) which can be determined from the properties of the parts and the way these are connected. We see already that our short definition of systems can, in fact, be applied to obtain both theoretical and practical results. In order to avoid the idea that the property of a system would in general be just the sum of the properties of the parts, as happened to be the case in our simple example, let us consider the system of Fig. 2.

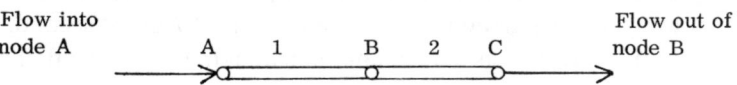

Fig. 2

3 In Fig. 2 the part no. 2 has been connected to the other end of part no. 1 so that a sort of "connection in series" is obtained. If we let again f_s denote the capacity of the system it is natural to assume f_s to be

$$f_s = \min (f_1, f_2)$$

meaning that f_s is the smallest of the flow capacities f_1 and f_2. (This, of course, is an instance of the saying that a chain is no stronger than its weakest link.)

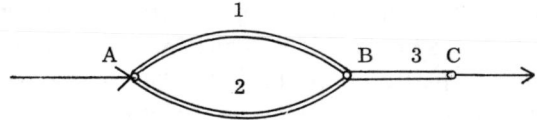

Fig. 3

Exercise. What would be the value of f_s for the system of Fig. 3, assuming the capacities of the parts to be f_1, f_2 and f_3 respectively?

5 In order to study the application of the definition to some other kind of system properties let us suppose that we feed into point A of the system shown in Fig. 3 a flow of 10 units/second. We may assume that some of this flow goes through channel no. 1 and some goes through channel no. 2. We may ask whether it is possible to determine how much goes through each of the two channels. The answer is, of course, that we have not yet said enough about the system to be able to answer the question completely. In fact we shall see immediately that unless more is specified about the system, there is no unique answer. There is one assumption which it is very natural for us to make: if 3 units/second flow through channel no. 1 then 7 units may be assumed to flow through channel no. 2 and in general, if f_1 flows through channel no. 1 then $10 - f_1$ may be assumed to flow through channel no. 2. We find it natural to assume that if 10 units/second flow towards the system at the junction point A then the different branch flows within the system, away from junction A, will sum up to 10 units/second. This may also be stated as an assumption that the sum of all flows at any junction point in the system will be equal to zero, if flows towards the point are taken with opposite sign as compared to those flowing away from the point. This zero-sum property is, in fact, valid for many physical systems. Thus if the flow is that of a fluid, water for instance, the zero-sum property is the law of continuity of flow which is of basic importance in fluid mechanics. In the theory of electricity this same zero-sum flow property is one of Kirchoff's laws.

6 We see that if we assume the zero-sum property to hold at each node; we know how much flows in one branch in Fig. 3 as soon as we have determined how much goes through the other. We know nothing about the latter, however. The system may be such that someone is able to control how much is to go through one branch. He is then not free to decide how much is to flow through the other, if the input at the junction is prescribed. It will instead be determined by the zero-sum law. Thus in this case the flow through the system is partly controllable (or "it can be partly administered"). A system of this sort may be a factory with two production lines, both handling the same kinds of objects.

7 Now that we have discussed how an input flow at node A of Fig. 3 can be distributed in different ways through the two branches of the system, let us discuss what the flow will be at the other ends of the branches (channels).

It is natural to assume that if the inflow of 10 units/second at A is distributed so that $f_1 = 3$ units/second flow into channel no. 1 and $f_2 = 10 - f_1 = 7$ units/second flow into channel no. 2, then there will be an inflow to node B of 3 units/second from channel no. 1 and 7 units/second through channel no. 2. Then according to the zero-sum law (assumed to hold at each node, hence also at B), there will flow 10 units/second from B into channel no. 3. This will probably appear so natural that one may easily overlook the fact that this reasoning is based on an assumption about certain properties of the channels or branches from which the system is built up. It is, however, exactly this dependence of the behavior of the system upon the properties of its parts that we want to illustrate here. It will also be important for the analysis of more complex systems to be able to define those properties of the parts that do in fact determine the system properties that we want to study. For this reason we have to make explicit what assumption about the properties of the channels that we were making implicitly above. Obviously the tacit assumption we made above was that if the inflow at one end of channel no. 1 was f_1 then the outflow at its other end would likewise be equal to f_1. If we let the flow into one end of a branch have an algebraic sign that is opposite to that of an outflow, we see that our assumption about the flow property of a branch can be described as a zero-sum property: The sum of the external flows at both ends of a branch equals zero. This is, actually a reasonable description of the property of many different kinds of channels for instance of electric conductors, transport lines, or hydraulic tubing. There are, however, also many real systems for which the flow properties of the branches are not that simple. We shall give illustrations of this fact later in the book.

We have seen that our simple flow system of Fig. 3 (when it is assumed that the zero-sum property for its internal flow holds both for its nodes and its branches,) will behave in such a way that if an inflow of f_s is introduced at node A and is distributed so that f_1 flows through branch no. 1, then one will obtain a flow of $f_2 = f_s - f_1$ through branch no. 2. Further, at node B these flows will converge and add up to f_s. The flow through branch no. 3 will thus be f_s and the outflow from the system at node C will likewise be f_s. It is seen that in this case the external flow at the system end, nodes A and C have the same zero-sum property as the flow in each of the individual branches. We have thus obtained a simple illustration of the fact that some property of a system as a whole can be deduced from the properties of its parts together with the properties of the connections of the parts. We may also notice that the property of the system in this case was something less trivial than just "a sum of its parts". The system property that we found in this specific example means that the system as a whole has properties as "seen from outside" which are similar to those of a single branch. This is to say that this whole system might, itself, be inserted as a single branch in a larger system. We may say that it has *external properties* similar to those of a single branch.

8 We assumed above that the distribution of the flow at node A into the branches no. 1 and no. 2 was determined in one way or the other, (while always obeying the zero-sum law at the node). Often there are properties of the flow of the branches in the system that uniquely determine this distribution. This is the case, for instance, with the flow of fluids or electricity. Thus in order to make a fluid, like water or oil, flow through a tube one will have to apply pressure at the input end or suction at the output end, or both. We see that it is natural to assume that the flow through a tube will be determined by the difference of "static pressure" at the two ends of the tube. More precisely it may be the case that the speed of the flow through a tube will be approximately proportional to the pressure difference (pressure drop) over the tube (or, perhaps to the square-root of this number). In an electric line one finds similarly that the voltage drop over the line determines the flow of electricity through the line.

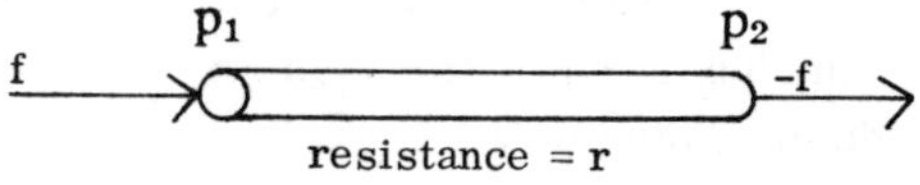

$$\xrightarrow{f} \bigcirc \underset{\text{resistance} = r}{\overset{p_1 \qquad\qquad p_2}{\rule{6cm}{0.4pt}}} \bigcirc \xrightarrow{-f}$$

Fig. 4

In the most simple case where proportionality holds between flow and difference of pressure or difference of voltage, we get

9 $$f = \frac{p_1 - p_2}{r}$$

where p_1 and p_2 are the pressure (or voltage) at the two ends, and r is the factor of proportionality.

We see that it is natural to regard the factor r as a property (called resistance) of the line or branch. In fact it is found in real cases that the factor r varies with the geometric (and other) properties of the line. The property r may be said to be a *responsive property* of a system part. It describes how the system part *responds* to an applied condition of one kind (here the pressure difference or the voltage difference $p_1 - p_2$) by generating a certain state of another kind (here the flow f). Thus the branches discussed here respond to a pressure or voltage) by generating a *flow*. It is equally reasonable to say instead that the branch will respond to a *flow* f by generating a *potential drop* $(p_1 - p_2)$. This follows from 9 which is seen to be equivalent to

10 $$p_1 - p_2 = r \cdot f$$

11 We have now discussed two distinct kinds of properties of the branches which are the elements of our system, pictured in Fig. 3. The *responsive property* just described and the property described earlier, which implied that if the inflow at one end of a part was equal to f then it was equal to -f at the other end. We may call the latter a *transference property*. The transference property is a characteristic of a system part (or a system) to transfer one value of a certain state variable (the same value, as is the case here) to the same state variable at the other end of the part (or the same system). Thus a response property generates one kind of state as a response to the application of *another* kind of state, at the same place in a part (or "over the part"), whereas the transfer property generates a state of the same kind but at another place.

We can now apply our findings about the responsive property to our discussion of a system such as may be represented by Fig. 3. We found before that if a flow of value f_A is introduced from outside at node A then the flow into branch no. 1, at A, may be f_1. Then, by the zero-sum law, the flow in branch no. 2 will be $f_2 = f_A - f_1$.

Now we assume that the responsive property "resistance" has the values r_1 and r_2 in the branches no. 1 and no. 2 respectively.

We further assume that the potential values in the system nodes (pressure or voltage, for instance) are P_A, P_B and P_C respectively. The pressure drop in branches no. 1 and no. 2 will be

12a $$\Delta p_1 = f_1 \, r_1$$

12b and $\quad\Delta p_2 = f_2 r_2$

respectively.

13 There is now one further assumption we have to be specific about and that is how the potential (pressure or electric voltage, for instance) will behave in the nodes. The most natural assumption, is perhaps, that there will be one unique value of the potential, at each node. This means that when we connect an end of a branch to a system node we assume that the potential value of the branch end will equal the potential value at the node it is connected to. This property is the common one in for instance the theories of electric networks or hydraulic networks. We may call this a *coincidence* of the potential *property* at the nodes, because it means that when a branch end-point and a node point coincide then their potential values coincide.

Making use of the assumption of potential coincidence at nodes we find that the potential values at the first end-points of the branches no. 1 and no. 2 are both equal to p_A. Because of the potential drop generated in the branches by the flows f_1 and f_2 respectively, we obtain the potential values at the other endpoints of these branches as:

14a $\quad p_{1,2} = p_A - \Delta p_1 = p_A - f_1 r_1$

14b $\quad p_{2,2} = p_A - \Delta p_2 = p_A - f_2 r_2$

where, for instance, $p_{1,2}$ is used to denote the potential value at the second end of branch no. 1.

As the branches no. 1 and no. 2 both have their second end-points connected to one and the same node B, their second end-point potentials must be equal, if the potential coincidence property is to hold at node B. Thus we must have

15 or $\quad\begin{aligned}p_{1,2} &= p_{2,2} \\ p_A - f_1 r_1 &= p_A - f_2 r_2\end{aligned}$

Thus

$$f_2 r_2 = f_1 r_1$$

16 and $\quad f_2 = \dfrac{r_1}{r_2} f_1$

As we also found earlier that we must have

17 $$f_2 = f_A - f_1$$
(f_A = flow input at node A)

we find

18 $$f_A = (\frac{r_1}{r_2} + 1) f_1 = \frac{r_1 + r_2}{r_2} \cdot f_1$$

so that

19 a $$f_1 = \frac{r_2}{r_1 + r_2} f_A$$

19b and $$f_2 = \frac{r_1}{r_1 + r_2} f_A$$

(We may verify that $f_1 + f_2 = f_A$ as it must be.)

20 Thus we have established that in a system such as shown in Fig. 3 the flow distribution over the branches no. 1 and no. 2 respectively is uniquely determined if

> the *system parts* have the tranference property for flow and the responsive property between flow and potential difference as assumed

and if

> the *system nodes* have the zero-sum property for flow and the coincidence property for potentials.

Now that we know the distribution of flow we are also able to determine the potential value p_B at node B. p_A (at node A) is given. In fact it follows from our discussion that

$$p_B = p_A - f_1 r_1$$

so that

21 $$p_B = p_A - \frac{r_1 r_2}{r_1 + r_2} f_A$$

It is then also easy to compute the potential value p_C at node C, recalling that the flow f_3 through branch no. 3 is equal to f_A. We find

$$p_C = p_B - f_A\, r_3$$

or

22
$$p_C = p_A - (\frac{r_1 r_2}{r_1 + r_2} + r_3) f_A$$

We can now see that the potential drop over the whole system, from node A to node C is determined. In fact

$$p_A - p_C = (\frac{r_1 r_2}{r_1 + r_2} + r_3) f_A$$

and we see that the system behaves as a single branch with resistance value r as computed by

23
$$r = \frac{r_1 r_2}{r_1 + r_2} + r_3$$

The system can be said to have the *external property* or *gross property* (i.e. the property as looked from the outside where only nodes A and C were visible) r as computed by the formula.

Thus we have another system property that could be computed when we know how the system was built up from parts if we knew the properties of parts and relations between parts.

It should be clear now that quite a lot could be stated about the system studied, assuming only such things to be given as are mentioned in our very general and yet concise definition of a system.

The reader will probably find it natural to expect that the results we have obtained for the very simple and specific system depicted in Fig. 3 will hold for general network systems where the same general properties of flow and potential in branches and nodes are valid. One of our objectives is to show that by reworking our mode of analysis so that it becomes a more systematic and somewhat more abstract, formal, algebraic systems theory, we will be able to fulfil this expectation. In order to indicate already now what kind of generalization will be necessary we point out that the system of Fig. 3 had only one input node and one output node, just as is the case for any branch. It was therefore possible to show that properties of the system parts (or branches) had direct counterparts for the whole system e.g. zero-sum flow at the two end-points, taken together, or the resistance r as the quotient of potential drop over the two end-points divided by the flow at either end-point. Obviously a network will in general have more than two external connection points and the number of input points may be different from the number of output points. This makes it necessary to define the properties of the system in a more complex way. Fortunately there are algebraic tools which make it possible for us to obtain precise solutions to such problems. A set of these algebraic tools are presented in subsequent chapters and called here "systems algebra". The elements of systems algebra are very simple and yet sufficiently comprehensive to formally describe a large number of systems problems.

As such a description is a strictly formal one, it makes it possible to hand over the description to mathematical or numerical experts if more sophisticated mathematical manipulation is judged to be of value in subsequent system design work phases. The algebraic description can also be input to an automatic computer. The system-algebraic systems descripition is often a disciplined and powerful tool for communication between the systems analyst and other expert groups or between the analyst and the computer.

Among the classes of systems that satisfy our general definition, and therefore will lend themselves to formal description and analyses based on the definition, are management control systems, information systems, and various data processing systems such as for instance production scheduling systems as well as computer programs. One must therefore expect our general definition of systems to be an important basis for design and implementation of such systems. This is especially true because these systems are often very complicated and, therefore, strictly formal methods are necessary for an efficient handling of them. In addition the systems analysis and design work itself is a complex system and the efficient planning of this systems work is also a problem in systems design, which needs formal metholodogy. This system (the system which is the project plan for the system design work) satisfies the general definition of systems and will therefore, also be able to profit from formal systems theory based upon the general system definition. Such a theory will therefore be similar to the analysis we have done upon the very simple examples above. The management of an organization also can be regarded as a system according to our definition.

It is obvious that a data systems analyst will find very useful a formal methodology of systems analysis and design which is so general that it can be used as a tool both for designing the systems work to be performed (e.g. by using planning network methods) and for designing the different subsystems and the whole system including the systems of computer programs and administrative procedures to be included in the system.

Many other kinds of systems exist for which formal systems analysis can be based upon the definition of systems. In some of these classes of systems mathematical methods have been developed on this basis and have made it possible to use automatic computers, for more than a decade, as an important analysis tool. Among these are the fields of electrical networks, hydraulic networks and elastic structures in civil engineering, housebuilding and aircraft design.

11.10 The Systems Analysis Approach.

Fundamental problem of design and administration of an operating system.

The system is, typically, much more complicated than a man can grasp in one viewing. Only a piece at a time can be tackled. You can try to deny that and will likely fail; you can admit this and try to do the best about it. This means that you must accept not being able to consider everything. It also means that you must check that you have not neglected any critical aspects.

To adopt the systems analysis approach is to take the position that the analysis or design work starts from the idea that the object to be studied is to be viewed as a system. This must then be based on the definition of a system, that is it must consider the existence of a set of systems parts and the set of relations between them.

The system definition means that in studying an object we must make clear if it should be regarded as a subsystem of a larger system. If that is the case it is often assumed that the systems approach then means that only by studying "the system as a whole" can we design it efficiently, and to design the object separately would lead to the impossible task of connecting it with other unknown parts of the system.

1 We want to advocate another approach. We state instead that one of the most fundamental techniques for systems analysis and design is to define a set of subsystems — i.e. a set of intermediate boundaries — and then try to define the conditions that the system imposes on the subsystems in such a way that it will then be possible to do much (although not all) of the analysis and design on the subsystem itself.

2 Our first argument in favor of this approach is that even if we try the "total systems" approach it is impossible to adhere to it. This is because as soon as we use more than one man for the work we impose some sort of subdivision of the systems work. It is easy to see that this corresponds to a subdivision of the system worked on as well. The same is true if only one man handles the work but needs several days.

Knowing that a subdivision must be done it is easy to conclude that it is better done in an organized way which considers natural subdivided properties of the system.

3 Other arguments are that often systems possess properties which make specific subsystems natural to work on, and which in their turn can be subdivided.

By working on a well chosen set of subsystems (and the same for each of these) we will be able to obtain a so much better result, as far as the subsystems are concerned separately, than would else have been possible — if at all possible — that even if some deviation from the exact relations between the different subsystems is unavoidable the total result is nevertheless better than would have been possible in any other way.

4 It is also very often the case that our failure to consider the interdependence between subsystems in a correct way stems not from the difficulty to do so but from ignorance of techniques which make this possible.

5 We see that once we accept the technique of choosing a good set of intermediate boundaries within the system as one basic working principle for systems work, we immediately come to the basic problem of defining the outer boundary and its conditions which are to be subject to estimates or forecasting, and the inner boundary, that is the smallest subsystems or parts from which we have to consider the system as built up.

6 Another natural working principle now emerges. We want to be able to define the properties of the parts and to deduce the properties of the subsystem from these, derived from the definition of the connections building such a subsystem. This means that for the parts we need only their properties as a gross system[1]).

From this we then conclude that when we are able to deduce "gross system properties" for subsystems we are in a position to repeat the process until the "total" system properties are deduced.

7 Not only the system worked on is a system for us to consider. Also the system work itself is a system. Hence it also has to be divided in an optimum way into subsystems. One natural subdivision of the work is, of course, to subdivide it in analogy with the subdivision of the system itself.

However the systems work will have at least one more subsystem which is the work to connect the subsystem works to obtain results for the system as a whole. Thus, while system work basically has to profit heavily from system subdivision and the possibilities for separate subsystem work this offers, it has to have at least one echelon which has to cover the whole. This echelon also benefits from the technique of subdivision, freed from the problem of analyzing the properties of the subsystem, it can concentrate on the connections for the total system.

From this introduction of subdivision by echelons — and not only by subsystems — which are defined by subsets of the system parts, we go on to observe that the echelon subdivision also should be done in a well-chosen set of several echelons[2]).

---

[1]) See section 12.23.
[2]) See also section 11.13.

11.11 The Fundamental Principle of Systems Work.

The argument presented above, as well as experience from different kinds of systems analysis and design, suggest the use of a fundamental principle for all systems analysis, design, or management. We give a precise statement of this fundamental working principle here and we then take it as a guiding rule for our further discussions.

1 Partition the systems work into separate tasks, a through d,

   a. *Definition of the system as a set of parts.*
      List all parts from which the system is regarded as built-up.

   b. *Definition of system structure.*
      Define all interconnections which make up the system by joining its parts together.

   c. *Definition of the systems parts.*
      For each single part (or group of similar parts) separately define its properties as required by the system work at hand and do this in a format as specified by the way the systems structure is defined (in task b).

   d. *Determination of the properties of the system.*
      Use the definitions as produced by the tasks a, b, and all separate tasks c, all taken together. Compare with specifications wanted for the system and repeat a, b, c, and d until satisfied.

2 Notice that the working principle, as laid down in 1, subdivides into one set of tasks which are concerned with the whole system, i.e. the tasks a, b, and d and another set of tasks of which each can be treated separately as each is concerned with a single part and its properties. Several advantages follow from these facts. A natural way is obtained for dividing the systems work among several people (or at least over separate time periods). Further, very different skills are required for the different tasks as defined in the fundamental principle. So, for instance, detailed knowledge of very different kinds may be required for the different parts and the separation of the work to be done for each makes it practicable to use people with specific knowledge and experience for each part. This is a further advantage because such separate parts work can be done in the same way as before the systems approach was taken. In this way the central systems team does not need a very extensive

experience regarding each separate part and its functions. It can therefore be composed in a way that makes it more suited to the true systems tasks a, b, and d. Again a subdivision of labor, and therefore a specialization of skills, can be done also in the true systems tasks. Thus the task b can often — and should whenever possible — be formalized by means of mathematical methods (such as the Systems Algebra presented in chapter 2) and can use computers. A special team handling this task can therefore best be staffed by people having a background in mathematics or computation.

3   The most efficient way in which the Fundamental Principle can be applied is, of course, when it can be mathematically formalized in most of its tasks. This has actually been done in the fields of systems such as electrical networks and elastic structures. In these cases it has proved efficient to have separate groups define separate parts properties, using mathematical methods or laboratory experiments, while the task d has been solved by using matrix algebra and algebraic topology, and where computers have then been used to do the bulk of the work associated with task d. Again in the Systems Algebra we shall meet some of these methods.

4   It is important to notice that also in cases where a mathematical formalization of the working principle has not been possible, a strict adherence to the principle led to successful systems work, making extensive distribution of labor possible and yet leading to no incompatibility problems when connecting the separately designed parts — a problem that is otherwise very common. This has been successfully done in a number of cases, examples of which are the design and production of a compiler system for a programming language[1]), the design of integrated data processing systems, and also computer hardware.

5   **Principle of the complicated middle way.**

The greatest complications in systems analysis almost always arise with systems (models) of mean complexity. While it is obvious that less complexity will imply less complex analysis it is worth noting that also when complexity grows beyond a certain limit simplification possibilities will present themselves to the analyst. This follows because for complex systems some kind of aggregating of

---

[1]) La 1964.

analysis will be required and will also be natural. This will reduce analysis to average complexity which then takes the place of some sort of maximum difficulty which is not increasing when system complexity grows.

11.12 General and Special properties of Systems Problems.

A question that is often encountered in connection with systems work is whether a certain problem would best be handled by the specialists in its field or by people who are not very familiar with that field but do instead know the total system — or even, on a still more general level, do not either know that system but are experts in basic systems design methods. The answer should be fairly obvious — but is yet most often missed — a balanced cooperation between different groups is what gives the best promise of success. In smaller systems work it cannot be used but whenever large work with many people involved is to be done it should be the natural thing to do. A basic problem of systems theory should be to find out the best way of subdividing the work between different groups of specialists.

Experience shows that different groups in organizations tend to neglect the importance or the difficulty of the other peoples' field[1]). For instance central systems teams work on ADP-implementation tend to regard typical subsystems problems, such as the local problem of each user group which has to provide input data for the "integrated" ADP system, as something that has to be handled or supervised by the systems team. From a veritable systems point of view this should rather be looked upon as a component problem where the users and the systems team have to work out detailed specifications for what the users shall produce as system input, whereas the actual production is then a management problem which could best be handled by supervisors of office work — rather than by systems experts.

On the other hand specialists within a field often ignore the fact that many of their problems are of a systems type and might well be better solved by methods known within other fields or within the area of general systems theory. Thus for instance people working

---

[1]) Cf. Theorem 1. Underestimation, section 11.17.

with payroll routine seem to find it hard to believe that some of their most intricate problems fall within a general class of systems problems for which methods may have been devised by non-experts of payroll operations. A close analysis should instead envisage other problems which are not mainly of a general systems (or a logical) type but appear to be rather specific to the field of specialty.

As another example it is obvious to many mathematicians or information processing researchers that many of the intricate problems associated with medical diagnostics and treatment planning are of a very typical information processing type and are also very similar to much advanced engineering work.
The part of the problem which has special medical characteristics seems mainly to be concerned with the information to be used and how it can be gathered and — most of all — the actual operation of gathering it and of performing actions involved in the medical treatment process. Contrary to this most physicians, while admitting that electronic experts or computer programmers could help in making some progress toward automatization of routine parts of their work, seem to be completely convinced that no mathematician or information processing expert could do anything which could be of value in developing methods for part of the medical work.

What could be done to improve matters in this difficult but important problem of co-operation? It seems that systems theory could clearly show how problem areas could be subdivided into subareas of which some are concerned with the general properties of structure involved, some concerned with the special properties of structure within the field, and some others are mainly concerned with the specific problems of meaning and property for that specific field only. This is one of the most basic objectives of all systems design — to define subsystems in a proper way and to take advantage of such subsystem definition.

A set of simple diagrams will help to make this idea clear.

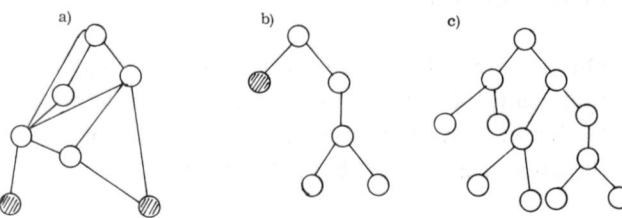

Fig. 1

In Fig. 1 three diagrams depict three systems a, b, and c. A general systems theory, from which all three could draw, would be one which studies properties common to all systems consisting of lines and points in the way shown. A less general systems theory could then be used to obtain more detailed knowledge for such systems as b and c which have in common a property not shared by a, e.g. of having no closed paths, that is, of being "tree like".

Instead a and c might draw from theoretical analysis regarding big systems which would be of no interest to b because it is small (the reader should imagine the difference in size to be very much understated by the Fig. 1). Again for system b some special properties, such as being small plus being tree-like plus some more special properties may be useful. These properties, which are specific to b only, might be best handled by "b-experts" while the more general ones could perhaps better be handled by general systems experts.

Finally the properties of different objects, like the circles in Fig. 1 may be very different, even within the same system (within b for instance). Then each of them may pose problems best handled by people working within each narrow field. On the other hand one circle in b might have its properties shared by a circle in a so that people working on one or the other might find that they have several common interests. (See shaded circles in Fig. 1.) Such similarity of tasks or goals for subsystems — as far as they exist in one company — may sometimes be displayed in a table (or "matrix") as shown in Fig. 2[2]).

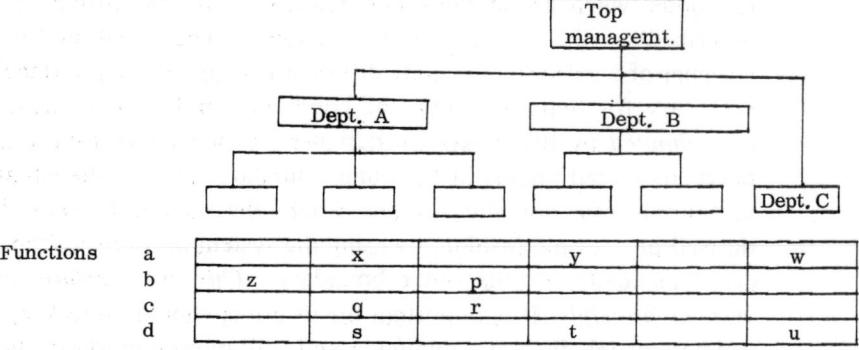

Fig. 2 Notice that, for instance x and y do not imply a duplication of effort even though both are associated with the same function a. x and y may use slightly different procedures and completely distinct data. Nevertheless some specialist knowledge may be of value to both as they have similar problems.

---

[2]) See for instance 3 Mn 1965.

11.13 System, Subsystem, Parts and Boundaries.

1 Although, as follows from the relativity principle[1]) for systems, every system acts as a subsystem in some — or several — greater systems, it is a task for the systems design work to define what is to be regarded as the total system to be designed. This means that one problem of systems design is to describe the boundary for what is considered, for that design, "the whole system". We may call this boundary the *outer boundary*.

In a analogous fashion a problem of systems design is to describe the *inner boundary* for the system, by which we mean the set of subsystems which from the design point of view are to be regarded as parts. The determination of the inner boundary, i.e. the parts used as building blocks, is a matter of decision by the design team. The "parts" may be small and simple or very complicated. For instance a computer will usually occur as a part in this sense, just as may a simple punch-card lay-out. The boundaries to other subsystems will be called *intermediate boundaries*. The importance of making these distinctions stems from the fact that the problems to be solved for the outer boundary differ completely from those at the intermediate boundaries, and also for the inner boundary. It is also important to observe that defining the intermediate boundary, i.e. the subsystems to use (conceptually at least) is one of the most efficient tools for systems design — and also for planning this design work itself.

What makes the outer boundary specific is that the conditions or functions which act at the outer boundary must be estimated and described by the designer of the system[2]). The situation for the designer of a subsystem is quite different because at the intermediate boundary for that subsystem the conditions or functions must *not* be *estimated* by the subsystem designer whenever they follow from decisions already made at the outer boundary. Instead the situation of intermediate boundary is one where the conditions should be derived in a formal fashion, by using the system properties, from the decisions made for the outer boundary. *This we declare as a systems principle*. It is important for its effect should be to keep the estimations involved at a minimum and, still more important, should guarantee consistency to hold throughout the system. In actual systems this principle is seldom adhered to[3]). When it is stated here

---

[1]) See section 11.8-5.
[2]) Or by its manager, during operation.

that in those actual systems, improvement would always result by changing policy to follow the principle, this means a requirement to give a proof or at least present sufficient support for the thesis. *We state therefore that this is one of the objectives of our systems theory.* Another is to provide formal methods of deriving intermediate boundary conditions from outer ones. (Example Pd^0. etc. or $\delta b^0)^4$).

The observation that the boundary conditions for a subsystem are not to be determined independently by the subsystem management itself, does not mean that the manager (or management) of the subsystem should have no opportunity to make his own estimations. Instead all questions which are to be regarded as internal to the subsystem are subject to evaluation and decision-making at the subsystem.

For the moment we only give some examples where it is obvious that this systems principle leads to optimum systems. One example is the system of a production firm. The outer boundary of that system is, for instance, concerned with sales to customers. The estimate for the whole system concerning sales is the sales forecast. There will of course always be errors or deviations in actual experience. On the basis of the forecast a master plan is worked out as an activity within total system design (dynamically).

Thus for instance the subsystem "Production" has to be given directives from higher level management — or simply from any level management associated with its "precedence information" (Sales Forecast). Production must not be free to decide on its own goals, for if that is permitted its operation will not be compatible with that of Sales. Losses will then occur by too much inventory or undercapacity.

This requirement for directives does not mean that there would be no means by which Production would be able to influence the plan to be followed. On the contrary this is made distinctly possible either

---

[3]) This is especially true for management systems. It is however also true because processing information to make decision takes cost and some simplifications are required. Thus realistic optimization will reduce inconsistencies where ideal optimization would eliminate them, cf. section 22.5.

[4]) See sections 12.9 and 12.18.

by establishing a feed-back from Production to Sales or by having a function which takes the Sales forecast and the relevant information from Production to generate the optimum (or satisfactory) master plan which then is the goal for Production to follow.

For the rest Production can manage to optimize autonomously its operations by following the directives given to it.

Assigning prices to products or services is also a function where the difference between the situation at an intermediate boundary and that at the outer boundary is significant. At the outer boundary of the firm prices are the market prices which are set by competition or by judgement regarding the market situation. At intermediate boundaries, e.g. between departments, "transfer prices" are sometimes used as a basis for controlling the departments[5]). This is another example of derivation of conditions at intermediate boundaries from estimates made af the outer boundary.

2 In almost all systems design work there is a type of economic balance problem which states the basic fact that almost always when one property is desirable its realization induces a cost. The economic design problem is thus to find an optimum — or a reasonable — balance between the value of the desirable property and the cost. We can state this problem by saying that to the degree that we do not realize the maximum of the desirable property we are admitting a "loss", while to the extent we have realized it, it has taken efforts to which corresponds a cost. We then have the problem of minimizing the sum of cost and loss, i.e. the "total cost".

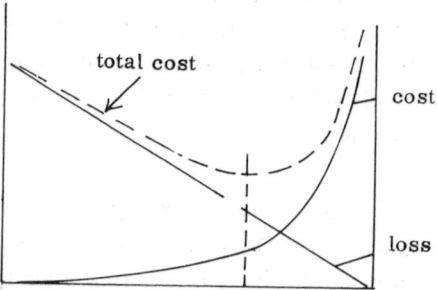

Fig. 1

This situation is depicted in Fig. 1. Let us consider some typical situations where this problem is inherent.

---

[5]) See for instance 1 BJ 1964.

3 One of the most well-known problems of this type is the economic order quantity calculation connected with quantities to buy or to manufacture. We may think of the cost curve as representing set-up cost or order cost. In this case the right-hand side of the diagram would correspond to ordering one piece. Increasing batch sizes ordered corresponds to moving left, leading to a decrease in cost per piece. The loss curve would then correspond to the losses incurred by having to hold pieces in the batches ordered in inventory. These costs are increased when we move left, i.e. when batch sizes increase.

4 Another problem of this type is associated with the utilization of some capacity for production or service, be it a single service station or a whole factory. In this case "loss" could be thought of as associated with unused capacity, while "cost" would correspond to the cost for queues accumulating in front of the service station. This queue grows indefinitely as we approach 100 % utilization. We find that the goal is not maximum utilization but an optimum utilization which must be well below maximum.

5 Finally, we take the problem of delegating authority. When authority is not delegated it is because of a feeling that this would incur risks of different kinds. We can imagine that the left side of Fig. 1 corresponds to the top level of management, and moving right thus corresponds to moving down in the hierarchy (to smaller and smaller subsystems). The risk cost associated with delegation would then be depicted by the "cost" curve. However, there is also a cost associated with centralization of authority (which has to do with queues) and the "loss" curve can be associated with that cost. We find then that when the cost function for risk cost for delegation and queue cost for centralization are known (or estimated) for a certain kind of decision, then we can define an optimum level for decision authority for this kind of decision.

6 It is seen from these examples, and from all kinds of experience with systems, that often the designer or the management of a subsystem faces a desire to maximize some value and therefore "sees" a loss function associated with a degree of deviation from this maximum. The balancing cost, on the other hand, will often belong to another subsystem — or to the total system. Therefore, only if this cost is made visible to the first subsystem designer will a possibility for achieving an optimum balance exist. Thus we have brought out, quite clearly, the need for an outside directive to the

intermediate boundary circumscribing a subsystem. We have, in fact, good reason to regard this situation as a typical one, for when we talk of a subsystem we are already stating the existence of interdependence within a larger system. This interdependence means, exactly, that we cannot make a change in the subsystem without affecting the larger system, and we cannot in general make changes in a system without influencing its properties such as efficiency or economy.

7 A type of subdivision by echelons or work phases concerned with coarse models of the whole system rather than by subsystems consisting of subsets of the system elements is of quite general interest in systems work. It is concerned with cost-loss relations of the type indicated in Fig. 1, but it also has to do with the complicated balance situation in most system designs. When we have to find an optimum economic balance we often ask for the value or cost function as expressed in money units. This is often unavailable (and is called "intangible"). It is therefore important to observe that in general this problem can be resolved only during the work of systems analysis. It is often practical to use one work phase for the analysis of ADP systems during which hardware is considered constant. Then the economic balance during that phase is no longer concerned with costs, as they are fixed, but with alternative use of resources[6]). Thus the "cost" function will be interpreted in terms of the alternative uses of a resource. In a second work phase a similar analysis is then made for another hardware proposal. Only when in this way we have obtained optimum solutions at different costs do we have to tackle the problem of an evaluation of these solutions, in terms of their costs, (which are known) and the money value of their performance in order to make a final choice. This money evaluation may be a lot easier to do, in this final stage, because the alternatives will as a rule also have money costs associated with them.

11.14 Structure Types of Systems.

Although it is important to have recourse to a completely general systems theory, which makes no assumption or only the minimum of assumptions regarding the structure of the system, it is also of interest to try to define specific system structure types, which have

---

[6]) We can also state this fact by saying that we are concerned with opportunity costs.

special properties and, hence, permit more detailed results to be obtained from theory[1]).

Several concepts which have to do with the type of structure can be listed, some of which are nonexclusive, so that a system can have more than one of them. Such are the network, the cellular type, and the planar type.

It is also feasible for a system to be of different types when analyzed by parts or by subsystems of one level or another.

Of special interest from an information system point-of-view are, of course, those properties of the system to be controlled (or managed) that will impose similar properties on the associated information system. When interrelationships of this kind are well understood, we will often know from the beginning some of the important properties, or problems areas, of the information system to be designed. A system can be regarded as of network type — or as a network — if we model it as consisting of a set of parts which have a linear character i.e. that to each such part is associated two ends and the linear parts are connected to other parts of the system only through its ends. The linear parts of the system have their ends joined at "junction points" or "nodes". It follows from this description that networks are representable by linear graphs[2]).

Practical applications (which have led to considerable theoretical work) of network models have been made in engineering where electric networks and elastic networks are common[3]). Network models are also used in economic system studies, for instance in connection with transportation problems[4]).

In all the network models, for engineering as well as for economic studies, a kind of system state called *flow* is assumed. Flow in a network is characterized by the property that all part flows joining at a node, together with the external flow to that node, sum up to zero. It can be shown[5]) that this zero-sum property (or node-flow condition) implies that the system has a natural boundary operation.

---

[1]) It is also important to make use of special properties of a system in order to reduce computation in its numerical analysis.
[2]) 1 Be 1958.
[3]) 1 La 1959, 1 La 1961. See also section 11.5 above.
[4]) 1 Ff 1962, 1 Ga 1960.
[5]) 1 La 1959, 1 La 1961. See also sections 11.9 and 12.23.

The boundary operator is obtained from simple matrices describing the network. It is common that a network flow is assumed to take on one single, scalar value in each network branch (linear element) and that it is constant along the branch. For elastic networks this simple model does not work. A theory for the more general case where the flow has several component values (or a vector value) at each branch (and varies along the branches) has been worked out for this case[6]. It is general enough to be applied also for production systems for instance[7]).

By *cellular system* we mean a system which is more general than a network in the sense that its parts may have more than two ends, that is it can be joined by more than two groups of node values to the rest of the system. It is also more restricted than a network in that it is only connected to its "neighboring cells", where we still have to define what we mean by "neighbor" in this connection. In the general case this is not a trivial question and we leave it for later research work — it is certainly of interest to systems theory. In the more restricted case where the system has intuitive geometrical associations, as is often the situation in physics or engineering systems of "field" problems, "neighbor" can be taken in its intuitive sense and we can then easily describe what we mean by cellularity.

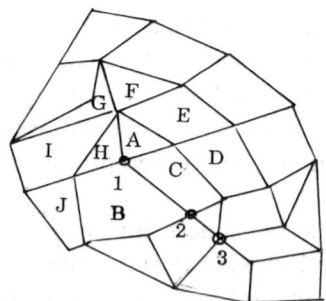

Fig. 1

If we take a 2-dimensional, geometric system as in Fig 1 where we have subdivided the system in a set of cells, we can see that the cell A for instance has an intuitive neighbor relation with the

---

[6]) 1 La 1961.
[7]) See section 12.31.

cells C, E, and H in that it has one boundary line in common with them. It also has neighbors of a different kind, i.e. B, D. F, G, and I which have, each, only one point in common with A. Depending on the application we have in mind for Fig. 1 we may define as the class of neighbors for the cell A (and analogously for all other cells) either the first set (C, E, and H) or the second set (B, D, F, G, and I) or the union of both. Whichever is chosen it is seen that the cellular system has the property that every part is connected (or directly related) only to a few other cells (its neighbours). This has consequences for the numerical analysis of the system, for it has the consequence that systems of equations for a cellular system will have special, simple, numerical properties (band matrices). Band matrices are known from the numerical analysis of field problems of mathematical physics. Such fields are of a cellular systems character and we see that it is thanks to their cellular character that they lead to such simple matrix representation. This property of cellular systems, also has another consequence, which is of a systems theoretical, rather than numerical, character. This can be seen in the following way. Let us assume that in the cellular system of Fig. 1 a flow q_1 is imposed from outside into one of the system points, such as point 1 for instance.

We assume that this flow has the common zero sum character. This means that q_1 will be split up into four flows, one in each of the cells A, H, B, and C. If the cells are reasonably similar in character, that is if the system is fairly homogeneous, and if the boundary conditions for these neighboring cells are also fairly similar, then the flow into every one of the 4 neighbor cells will be roughly equal $1/4\ q_1$. Each of these cell flows will then be split up into one component for each of the remaining boundary parts of the cell, and will thus enter the other neighboring cells with a still more reduced magnitude. It is intuitively seen in this way that a cellular system will have the property that a disturbance entering one point of the system will have a rapidly diminishing effect as it spreads out from this point. It is also fairly obvious that this property could be demonstrated in a rigid way for any cellular system satisfying some well specified conditions of a very plausible kind. Again however, we leave this for later research but pointing out only that the kind of effect that we have discussed is known from the theory of elasticity under the name of Saint-Venant's principle. As this has not been formally proved, a formalization of this kind for cellular systems theory in general would also mean a logical improvement within elasticity theory.

The system theoretical, and information theoretical, significance of this latter property is that as in a cellular system distant parts have small effect, information about them could be given with less precision — and thus smaller records — and could be transmitted less often, thus reducing data transport in two ways. It should also be possible to use this property to reduce the computational work of taking this information into consideration.

11.15 System Partitioning.

Partitioning of a system into a set of subsystems, or blocks, is an important method of systems analysis. It has to be done in such a way that each subsystem (or block) has simplest connections with its *complement*. "Complement" of a subsystem here is used to denote those parts of the system which are not contained in the subsystem.

Gross system diagrams should exhibit the blocks only and for each block a diagram exhibiting its partitioning into smaller blocks should be given, down to parts.

Notice that subdiagrams should be made to be consistent with system partitioning.

Example. Subdiagrams for the subsystems shown in Fig. 1.1 have been made in a wrong way in Fig. 2 a and Fig. 2 b. For instance Fig. 2 a contains some parts of B (Fig. 1) in addition to all those of A.

Gross diagram

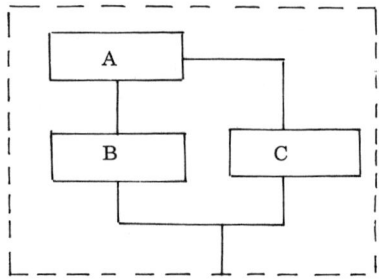

Fig. 1

incorrect subdiagram 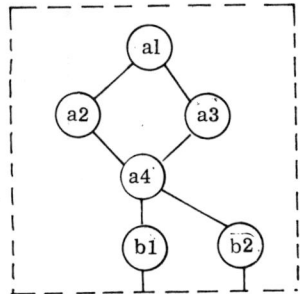 incorrect subdiagram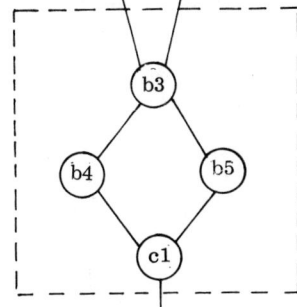

Fig. 2 a

Fig. 2 b

Example. Two steps of increasing detail of representation of a point in the systems graph. (point C)

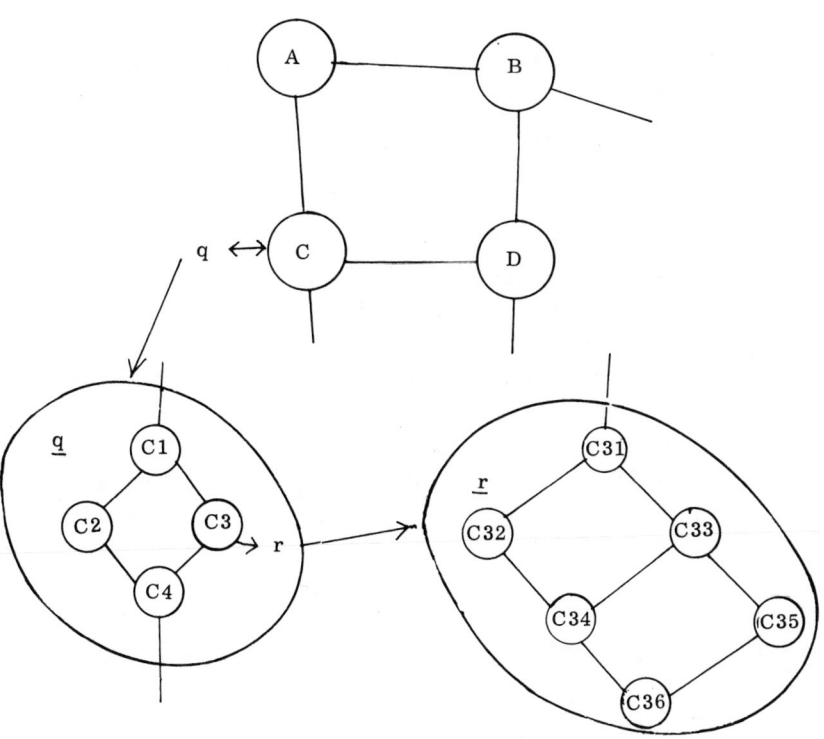

Fig. 3

Example. Two steps of expansion of a line element in the systems graph. (line A)

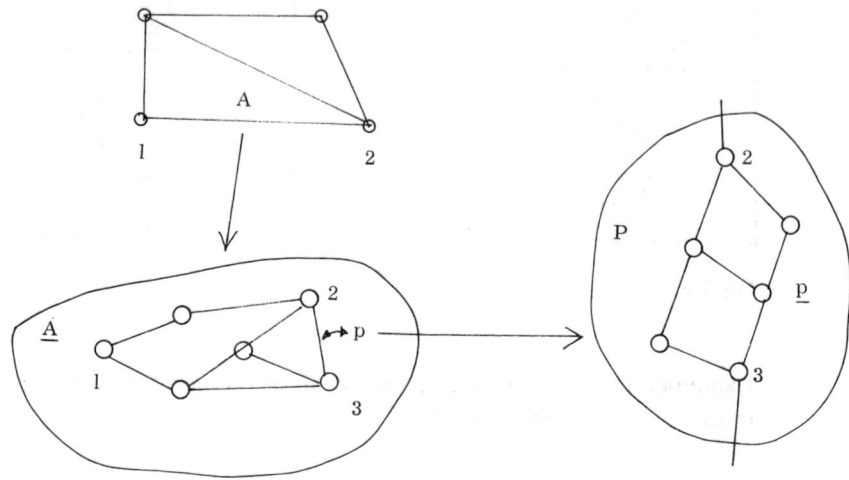

Fig. 4

11.16 Systems Partitioning of Outer Boundary.

When subsystems have parts of their boundary which coincide with the outer boundary, then estimating associated with that part of outer boundary may be included in the field of the subsystem. This is the case for instance if a department of a firm is developing a product of a sophisticated kind which is new to the firm. Evaluating the market potentiality for that new product may require the assistance of the development department for this specific product, even if the department does not take part in such evaluation regarding other standard products it may be working on. These other products may be well understood by the regular marketing department (which is, certainly, charged with outer boundary evalution on a regular basis). The boundaries of the developing department is by and large an intermediate boundary of the system (e.g. the firm) but in regarding the new product it touches the outer boundary of the firm, by participating in the market evaluation.

11.17 A Sketch of a Basic Theory of Systems Analysis.

There is a set of performance rules for the systems analysis stage of systems design work which is implicit in much of the literature associated with systems work and much of such works as done in practice. An example is the recommendation (or requirement) to *do systems work in a set of stages starting with a rough survey stage, making each successive stage more detailed than the preceding one.* By the way, the subdivision of production planning into a set of increasingly detailed phases reflects that planning is a systems work although not often called so. This technique of subdivision into phases is mostly proposed on the argument that this is the way systems works has been done before. This is, of course, not a very rational argument especially since it is seldom that an ex post facto analysis is presented to find out whether or not the systems work has indeed been efficient or not. Also no guidance is obtained in this way for how to define the scope of each phase. *Another, commonly quoted rule*, (closely related to the one above), *relates to the use of an hierarchical systems structure.* This is often suggested on the ground that natural systems are often (or even always) built on a hierarchical structure. Again this is not a very satisfactory state of affairs, because it does not provide an answer to the question "why" it does not give a sufficient insight. Also, although a set of rules or principles is fairly generally accepted, not only does the literature lack good arguments for their support, but also an explicit listing of them is still missing and the rules are seldom operatively precise enough. The result of this vagueness appears to be that even accepted rules are not adhered to consistently, and thereby inconsistencies in the systems work and design follow and cause losses — sometimes heavy losses. In fact the main trouble with systems work is lack of courage and imagination in following the rule, of giving full attention to planning before implementing. There are also some rules which the author has found very valuable and which do not appear in the literature.

In view of the facts mentioned it seems desirable to give an explicit list of rules and to present, in addition, all theoretical support and empirical evidence available. However it seems plausible that most of the useful rules are founded on a few basis principles or propositions. If that is so this fact should be used to provide both improved understanding and a more suitable basis for remembering all rules.

After a lot of hesitation the author has decided to try to set up a set of postulates, and from them to deduce other rules and principles as theorems thus leading to a basic theory. It is believed that although this could be done only as a first draft, needing much refinement, it does in fact provide the advantages sought — and also produces some additional rules and added precision to the reasoning on systems analysis and on how to do systems work.

Many people may be surprised to see the idea proposed that axiomatic arguments might be feasible and useful in this non-quantitative context. It is, however, the author's personal view that this will become a necessary development not only in technical systems design but in social sciences and even in political analysis. It will, of course, take one or two decades before this becomes widely recognized, however.

PROPOSITION 1. People tend to neglect the importance or the existence of things they are not able to see or perceive.

>This proposition is partly very obvious, for it is a truism to say that you can only ignore what you do not see or perceive by inference. This is not all there is to the proposition though. For it could also be possible that people would imagine the existence of things which they do not see — and indeed this often happens. Of this our proposition then states that such imagined things are given less weight or consideration than things perceived. This part of the statement may seem reasonable but we do not know of a means for proving it by logic. Such a proof, by the way, would have to be based on other propositions. We do not know such propositions which could be more conveniently used as primaries in our discourse. Not being able to prove the proposition we like some arguments to support our using it as one basis for our theory. This is a matter of psychology.

There is much empirical evidence to support proposition 1. Most of it, however, is more directly associated with some theorems we derive from it below. We therefore give reference to it below, in connection with these theorems.

PROPOSITION 2. Every detail in a system and also in the systems work of describing it has a positive cost associated with it.

This proposition is fairly obvious, to put it mildly. However, it might be possible to find systems where proposition 2 is not true. By taking it as a proposition (axiom) we point out that our theory will not be applicable to such "strange" systems.

Remark. There is a tendency for a reader of any theory to think that the fact that a certain statement is a truism, would mean that it is also useless. In fact, if it is taken as a statement about the world, it is of little interest, but when taken as a proposition or axiom from which more interesting statements (theorems) are to be deducted, the opposite is true. As an axiom it is only intended to make explicit what is taken as a premise, and in this connection its being obvious means an argument in favour of the applicability of the theory.

Indeed, by taking a proposition as an axiom we do *not* claim it to be universally true. On the contrary, we rather indicate thereby that it might be found to be false in some case and *therefore* it is important to make it explicit by an axiom formulation, that in such instances the theory is not applicable[1]).

Definition 1. Imperceivable systems. We define "*imperceivable system*" to mean a system such that the number of its parts and their interrelations is so high that all its structure cannot be safely perceived or observed at one and the same time.

For practical reasons we shall often say "systems" when in fact we mean "imperceivable systems".

Theorem 1. Underestimation. People tend to underestimate the complexity of an imperceivable system, i.e. the number of parts and relations it contains.

---

[1]) There are indications that this very elementary fact still is often found hard to understand so readers are recommended to read this carefully.

Proof. This follows from proposition 1 and from the definition of imperceivable systems. Thus according to that definition there are details in the system not perceived. Then, according to the proposition 1, they will tend to be neglected from which the theorem follows.

Theorem 2. *Underestimation of systems costs and costs of systems work is likely to occur when the system is imperceivable.*

This follows obviously from the theorem of underestimation and the proposition 2.

There is a fairly extensive empirical evidence to the validity of theorem 2. We must admit, of course, that it is *this empirical evidence* which is the strongest support for the idea of making explicit the statement of the theorem. This is because our proof is based on propositions 1 and 2. Of these, proposition 2 can fairly easily be tested for a system where we want to apply it, but proposition 1 is rather relying on likeliness because it is frequently found to be true. In fact the empirical evidence of the theorem 2 can be referred to serving as a support for proposition 1. (Psychological research has perhaps empirical support directly for axiom 1.)

Empirical evidence is given by extensive experience by the author himself. He has found that he consistently tends to underestimate his own jobs by about a factor of ½. Several studies of project works under his responsibility have also revealed the same factor: projects normally cost twice as much as estimated. Also studies made at Rand[2]) and Harvard[2]) have shown a factor of about 2 for the cost of large projects and about 1.5 for the time duration of the project.

Theorem 3. *Underestimation of manual work is likely to occur.*

To prove this theorem we would actually need a proposition stating that a person's job is likely to be a complicated system (of different activites). As this theorem is somewhat beside our main line here we do not state the proposition.
Also this theorem has a strong empirical support and, again, therefore projects backward to support the proposition 1.

---

[2]) 1 Mi 1963.

Empirical evidence is mentioned above. Also there is much evidence that the installation of punched card machines or computers for business routines have often run into difficulty by severely underestimating the existing manual work procedures. See for instance Wallace[3]). Studies of manager behavior (by Sune Carlsson and by IMAR-Consult, Stockholm, Sweden, etc.) have also revealed facts which support this theorem.

On the other hand it is also easy, again in accordance with theorem 3, to neglect the economic advantage that one machine has over another by eliminating some manual work. Thus, for instance, on comparing a computer system with mass memory of the magnetic tape variety with one having a direct-access memory (disc for instance) it may well be the case that the latter does not only reduce turnaround time for some processing but also eliminates some complicated manual operator routines. The latter is hard to evaluate but, by theorem 3, will most likely be underestimated.

We are going to replace strict logical arguments (true or false) by the weak argument: *possible* or *not possible*.

We are either sure of no success or we only have reasonable *hope* for success. We cannot be sure of success[4]).

If we are in the situation of studying a system we may either be contemplating the design of a new system or we may be regarding a system already designed and implemented.

If we are about to design the system we must start by making clear what our purpose is and thus what properties the system ought to have. This is concerned with the system as a whole.

When we talk about the properties of the system at this preliminary stage we must, of course, limit ourselves *to a perceivable set of properties*. We have at once the problem of how to check whether the properties assumed to be desirable are the ones actually desirable. It is wise to make clear to ourselves that the final check

---

[3]) 3 Wa 1961.
[4]) It appears that our replacing of the strictly logical arguments "true" or "not true" by "potentially possible" or "not possible" will be found to be generally appropriate as we go from *natural science* to *systems science*. The reader should beware of believing that the weaker form used here would be "less scientific". Natural science is too narrow to be sufficient here.

on the suitability of the specified properties can only be through practical use of a system having the specified properties. Thus this check must await implementation, unfortunately. However, preliminary testing can be done — and should be done — by analyzing the effect of hypothesized situations. Only after such tests have been done are we justified in taking the next step. It is natural that in the testing of the specified properties we face the probability that they will not stand the test and, therefore, modification and re-testing may have to be done, one or several times[5]). Scenarios or simulation are useful tools in this connection. Thereafter we set out to design the system so that it will have the properties desired. This necessarily brings in the concept of subsystems, for we can only design a system as the result of combining subsystems (or cutting away subsystems as in woodcutting). We state this fact in a proposition:

PROPOSITION 3.
> The only possibility of designing a system so that it will have specified properties is by combining a set of subsystems which have necessary properties and interconnecting them in such a way that the resulting system contains the specified properties.

Definition 2. A *subsystem structure* given to a system is a partitioning of the system into a set of subsystems together with a set of interactions between the subsystems.

Definition 3. A *workable subsystem structure* given to a system is a subsystem structure such that the properties of its subsystems together with its interactions result in the properties specified for the system as a whole ($=$ the global properties of the system).

Definition 4. A *realizable subsystem structure* is one where each of its subsystems and its interactions can be realized (implemented).

---

[5]) Properties desired$=$external properties. For a simple illustration of the latter see page 40.

We can now rephrase proposition 3 as

PROPOSITION 4.
> The only possibility of designing a system to have specified properties is to design a workable and realizable subsystem structure for that system.

We see that we very soon come to the question as to how the system is to be built-up from subsystems, and what properties these must have in order that the system as a whole will have the desired properties. There is also the question as to whether or not the subsystems may in their turn be realized.

If the properties of the subsystems and the interconnections are all defined then it may be possible — by mathematical operations or by a finite sequence of logical steps, each concentrating on a perceivable set of parts and connections — to deduce or compute the properties of the system resulting.

Definition 5. A *constructive subsystem structure* of a system is a subsystem structure so defined that its properties can be deduced (or "constructed"). Such a subsystem structure will be said to be *constructive*.

Theorem 4. A subsystem structure can be checked for workability if, and only if, it is constructive.

The proof is obvious — we can, by definition 5, construct its properties and having done this we can compare them with the specified properties. If it is not constructive it cannot be checked.

Theorem 5. A subsystem structure can be said to be a workable subsystem structure if, and only if, it is a constructive subsystem structure and its constructed properties satisfy the specifications.

The proof is immediate.

Remark. The reader is asked to make clear to himself the basic importance — in fact necessity — of constructibility, for it alone makes it possible to design systems which are so complicated as to be imperceivable. Notice also that it is exactly by satisfying this condition that the mathematical method is such an important tool in development work. *One thing will always have to be done, at least, to achieve constructibility: to document precisely each subsystem structure.* Thus, to talk about documentation as something that could be done afterwards — and that could even be skipped — is to misunderstand completely what systematic systems design really requires.

Examples of constructive subsystem structures are the mathematical formulations used in control systems engineering or in the electric or elastic network systems theory as explained earlier. For some simple illustrations see section 11.9. Also computer programs where the subsystem structure is a set of subprograms, is of course constructive for the computer will construct its properties. In order to show that, even if no mathematical calculation scheme is available, a constructive subsystem structure can be found, let us indicate that our present system of propositions and theorems (as any of the kind) are supposed to be constructive in the sense defined here. But how do we know which subsystems to use in the build-up and how do we determine the connections giving desirable properties? The system being imperceivable we cannot do this — at least not with any reasonable chance of success — if we have set out to design the system.

The advantage of a clear theory model to guide the management of complicated projects has become obvious to the author during many years of managing system development projects. In this connection a continuous refinement of the management methods has brought them into successively closer agreement with the above theory model. The compiler design and implementation project for the first general-purpose programming language, Algol-Genius[6]), can, in retrospect, be viewed as a successful application of this sort of systematic systems design. After the first publication of the model above in the first issue of this book, in 1966, other published works (Dijkstra[7], Randell[8]) indicate that models of a somewhat similar kind will soon be widely recognized as necessary tools for efficient management of large software design and construction projects. Thus, the value of precise theoretical foundation for practical systems design work is clearly gaining recognition in different areas of work.

---

[6]) 3 La 1964-1.
[7]) 1 Di 1968.
[8]) 1 Ra 1968.

If our problem were instead to determine the properties of an existing system, we might be able to do this. Then we could, experiment with alternatives to the system. If the system is not designed, however, we must start by defining a perceivable set of subsystems. Being a perceivable set it is possible that we might have a reasonable chance to guess at the properties to be *required* of the subsystems in order that from them the system with desired properties may be obtained after a reasonably small number of modifications and iterations. Once we have defined the required properties, to be specified for all the subsystems, we may be able to determine which properties the system would have, if built-up from these subsystems. This would be done in a finite sequence of steps, each adding a perceivable set of connections.

If the properties thus demonstrated do not agree (enough to be acceptable) with the original specifications we may modify subsystems or connections and, after a finite number of iterations, may arrive at a system design which we can accept (perhaps after having modified our requirements).

Definition 6. A *perceivable step* of systems analysis is the addition of a perceivable set of subsystems, or a perceivable set of interactions to a subsystem structure of a system.

By saying that a system to which we have not yet given a subsystem structure has a subsystem *structure although* it is *empty*, we find that definition 6 implies that any subsystem structure can be obtained by a set of perceivable steps of systems analysis. In each step we may either be adding a perceivable set of subsystems or we may add a perceivable set of interactions.

Theorem 6. If a system with specified properties can at all be designed then it can be given a workable and realizable subsystem structure and this can be done through a (finite) sequence of perceivable steps of systems analysis such that a constructive subsystem structure is obtained.

First, it follows from proposition 4 that the system must have a workable subsystem structure. Second, such a structure can always be split up into a set of perceivable sets of subsystems and a perceivable set of sets of interactions and this, in turn, corresponds to one or several sequences of perceivable steps of systems analysis. Third, each of the subsystems must certainly be realizable. Finally theorem 5 provides the last, necessary step of proof.

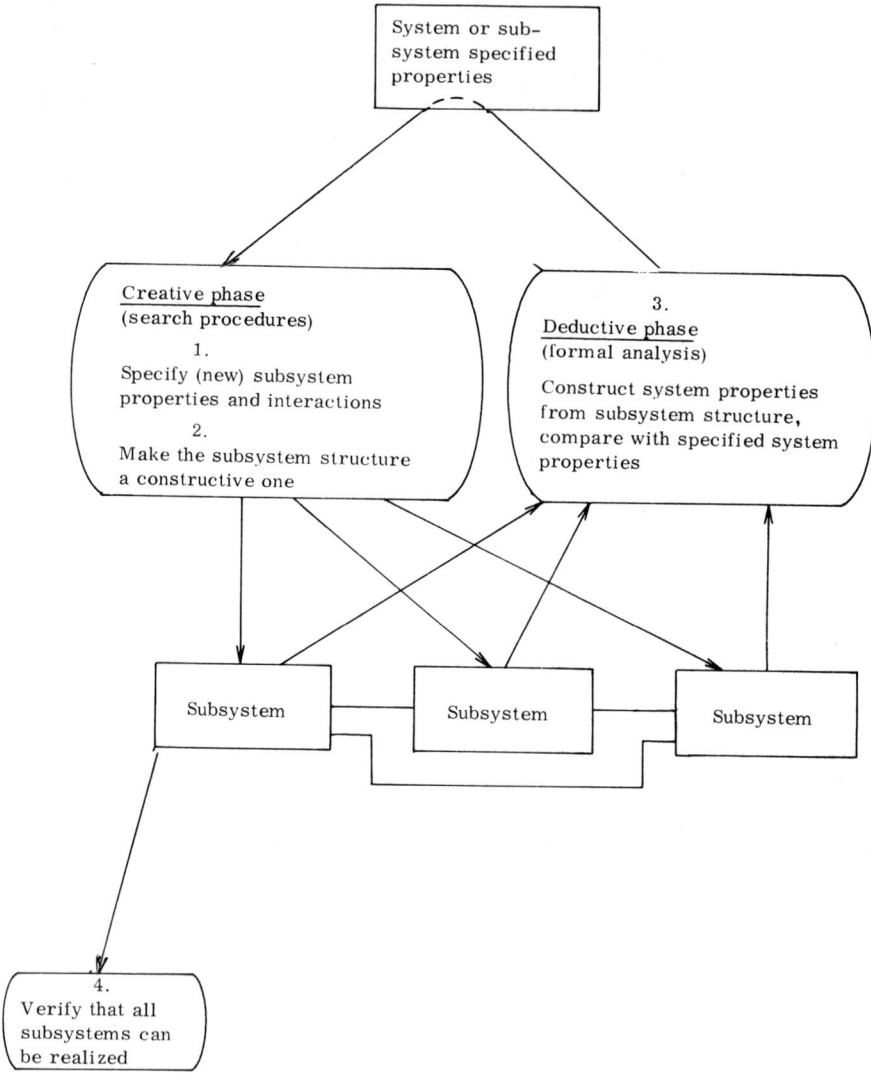

Fig. 1 Designing a feasible subsystem structure by "downward specification" and "upward construction" (and iteration until constructed properties sufficiently equivalent to specified ones), cf theorem 7.

Example.
Cf. sections 12.18 and 12.23.

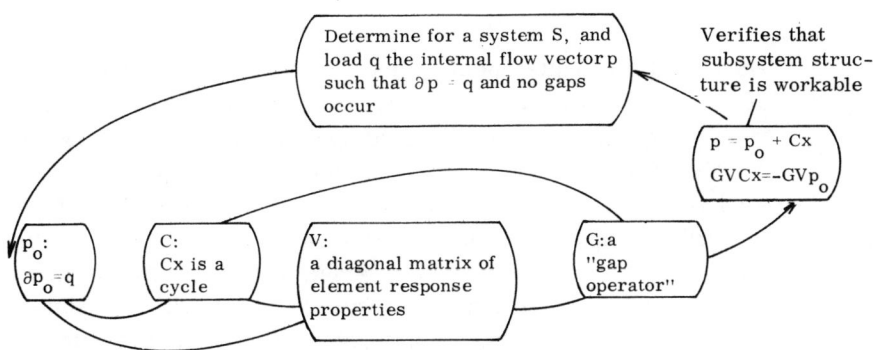

Realizable if processes for determining p_0, C, V and G can be designed and equation $GVCx = -GVp_0$ can be solved.
In this case the subsystem structure is constructive strictly, by means of algorithms.

The importance of the concept of a "perceivable step" makes it desirable to have a less vague definition of it. We do not attempt to solve this problem here. We point to the fact, however, that if design procedures of the kind discussed would be implemented with an electronic computer, then a perceivable step would have the well defined meaning of a process which can be done on one loading of the main memory of computer.

Theorem 7. In the design of a workable subsystem structure it is likely that a set of iterations have to be done on the scheme (see Fig. 1):

1. Perform some perceivable steps of systems analysis to obtain (a new version of) a constructive subsystem structure.

2. Construct the properties of this subsystem structure.

3. Compare the properties (from 2.) with those specified. If a sufficient similarity of constructed properties to specified properties is obtained go back to 1.

4. Test each of the subsystems for realizability.

5. Repeat 1 thru 4 for a number of alternatives and select one of these (or some) for further study.

Having (if fortunate enough) defined the desired system in terms of the subsystems, we still have the problem of whether or not these subsystems can be designed to have the properties we have deduced for them from the requirements on the total system. If we know that such subsystems already exist (for instance because of earlier design of similar systems or as a result of independent research) we have solved our problem and the design is finished. If this is not the case but the subsystems are sufficiently similar to existing ones this still does not solve our design problem but it may have solved the problem of a feasibility study. We may then have a basis for judging the feasibility of designing the subsystems as required. For the design problem we can only repeat the procedure as described for each subsystem for which a design did not already exist. This is also true for a feasibility study if not all subsystems in the workable subsystem structure are sufficiently similar to existing subsystems. Each such recursion brings in more, and smaller, subsystems and all the time it may happen that some of them may be identical to existing designs. It may also happen, however, that some subsystems always turn out to be of a new kind. Then we may finally end up with a set of subsystems which, in a feasibility study, are sufficiently similar to existing ones, or, in a design work, can be regarded as perceivable systems and therefore can be constructed with reasonable confidence. We call these subsystems (as well as the already existing subsystems) the parts of the system[9]).

From the parts we try to construct the subsystems in the nearest superordinated level and again we may have to iterate and modify before we succeed (and, alternatively, we may fail completely). If successful we may repeat level for level. Only when in this way we reach the total system after a finite number of steps of "*upward construction*" have we succeeded in designing the system. We still have to test it in practice before we are sure it works, however.

---

[9]) As pointed out by Ackoff et al. (Scientific Method, Optimizing Applied Research Decisions, John Wiley 1962) it may — in the general case — be an illusion to believe that lower level subsystems will be "smaller" or "simpler". However only when the latter is true — for the specified properties — can the system design be finished.

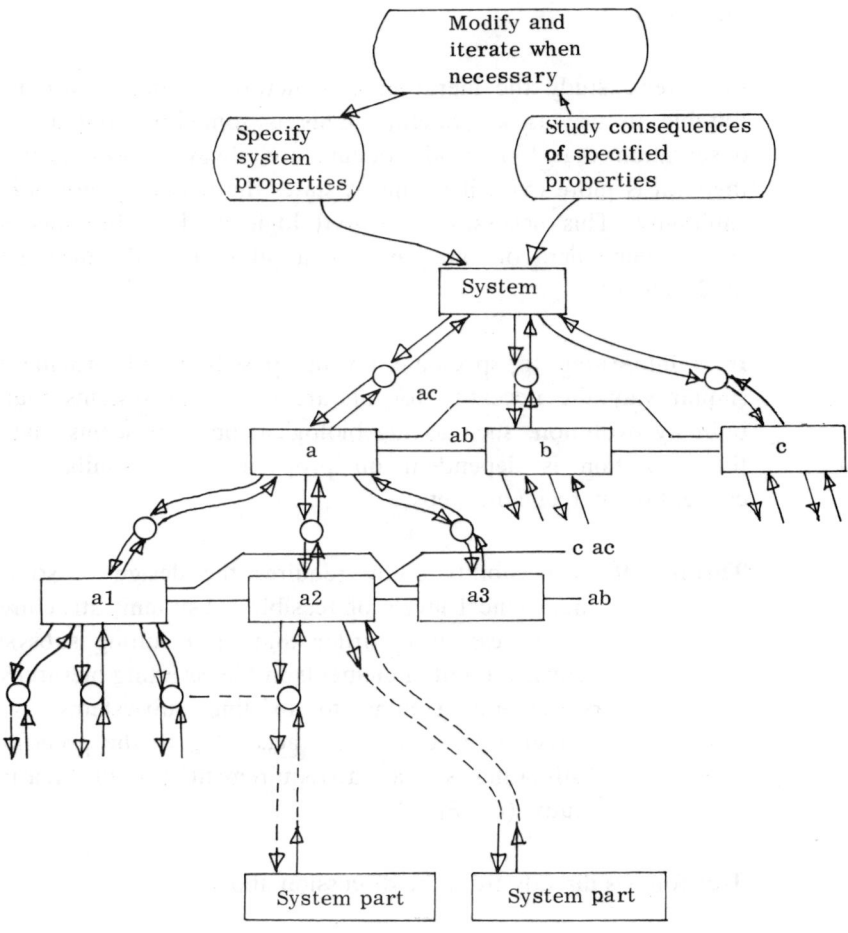

Fig. 2 System designed as an hierarchy of subsystem structures, each with a downward specification and an upward construction. Each subsystem with its subordinated subsystems, as shown in Fig. 1, is here simplified by indicating only one circle between each pair of subsystems. Above the main system is indicated the iterative procedure needed to "certify" the system properties, before breakdown is started.

Theorem 8. A system can only be designed to specified properties through an hierarchical system of design processes, in each of which every subsystem specified in a previous process is designed by organizing a workable subsystem structure for it and the system so designed will itself have an hierarchical structure.

The proof follows from theorem 5 and from the text following theorem 7.

In systems study the hierarchical structure is often mentioned as suitable to use as a guideline. This is sometimes based on the observation that biological systems are always hierarchical. Our theorem is more explicit in that it states the necessity, not only the suitability. This necessity is proved logically here but this is, of course, dependent on our basic assumptions (i.e. the propositions made above).

It is interesting to speculate on the possibility of proving in a similar way the necessity for hierarchy also in systems that are built by evolution, such as the biological ones. It seems plausible that evolution is dependent on properties very similar to our concept of "perceivable steps".

Theorem 9. A feasibility study requires the design of so many hierarchical levels of feasible subsystems structures as are necessary in order that all resulting subsystems which are initial elements in the resulting hierarchy are sufficiently similar to existing subsystems or are perceivable subsystems, according to the precision of estimating set as a requirement for the feasibility study. (Cf. Fig. 3)

This follows directly from the discussion above.

Theorem 10. An efficient way of designing an imperceivable system is by testing each subsystem's structure for feasibility before any subsystem contained in it is designed (by giving, in turn, its subsystem structure).

Proof. From theorem 7, iterations are likely on each phase of designing a subsystem structure for a certain subsystem. In each iteration one or more subsystems of the subsystem to be designed are given modified properties. If they are designed, the design has to be changed, if they have only their properties defined, only definitions need a change. On the other hand such subsystems which are not designed down to the "part level" (i.e. the "bottom") and then built up again are not known to be designable. However, if we would think this to be a reason to do such design down to bottom, we must remember that by so doing we would prove the possibility of designing a specified subsystem but if this then would have to be modified during the design iteration we would have no advantage of having proved the possibility of designing it.

We have said above that if our task is only to do a feasibility study for a proposed system design then the breakdown to a sequence of perceivable subsystem structures may stop well before we have come down to well-known subsystems (Fig. 3). This is because in a feasibility study we have limited time and resources and therefore have to accept certain risks. The problem then is to decide how far we have to go in the break-down sequence, given a rough, subjective estimate of the risk to be accepted. The answer is, roughly,

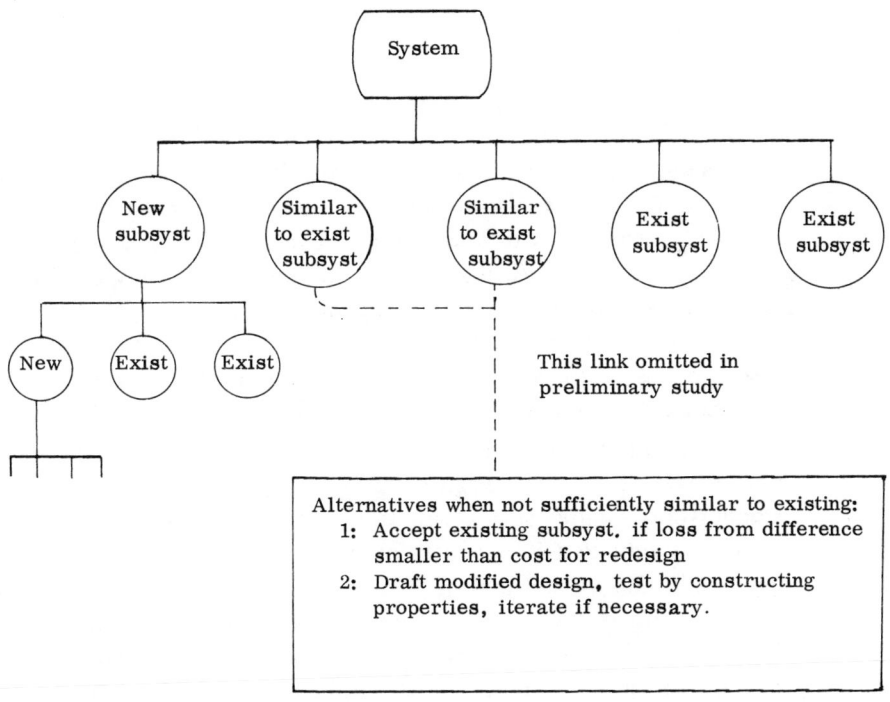

Fig. 3 It is seen that the extent to which system break-down is required depends on:
a) existence of desired subsystems
b) access to information about existing subsystems (design and properties)
c) possibility of modification of existing subsystems (flexibility of design)
Research can contribute to b) and c) by finding procedures for designing flexible subsystems.

that we may stop when all the lowest subsystems that we have reached in the break-down process are sufficiently similar to known ones, so that a subjective probability estimate of the chance that they can be implemented in a way similar to that used for the existing, similar, subsystems matches the margin of risk that is to be accepted.

In deciding on the risk tolerance to accept for a feasibility study, we must consider the time and resources that are allocated to the study. We must then make some sort of optimal balance which considers that the total risk for the project may be smaller if a larger risk is accepted for each specific study. This is so because *by accepting a greater risk we may stop the break-down earlier which means that within a given budget we may be able to test more alternatives, which reduces the risk of having chosen the wrong alternative design.*

The chances of finding, in the break-down process, subsystems which are already known depends, of course, on how many systems with similar goals have already been designed. That is not all however, for it may also depend on scientific research which may have established a set of known facts or theorems which correspond to a large class of known subsystem designs. These may have been generated separately, without being dependent on earlier applications in embedding larger systems. This is the way mathematical research has often been found to have produced results useful for applications without having been created with such intentions.

We have mentioned that in the feasibility study or other study phases we reduce the design work by stopping the break-down to smaller and smaller subsystems fairly early. The system work will thus be subdivided into phases of increasingly more detailed analysis. A further subdivision of the systems design work can be made by designing different subsystems in different work phases. This kind of subdivision of systems design work can also be applied in the phase of final design and implementation. Thus for large systems it will often be most efficient to implement one subsystem after the other. In this case our method of starting by defining upper level constructive subsystem structures and checking their properties against specification will be a useful planning tool. In this way it is ensured that when successively new subsystems are designed and implemented, they will fit into the total system as intended. This is often not obtained with presently used methods.

The method last described can be seen to correspond closely to the diagram of Fig. 2.

We are now in a position to look with increased understanding upon the statement of theorem 1 (of "underestimation") in view of theorems 7 and 2 and also to state another theorem which shows how underestimation can be reduced. The hierarchical structure implies that, at least from a certain level on, an imperceivable system will have an imperceivable subsystem structure. By proposition 1 therefore some subsystems will tend to be ignored, which then means that the subsystems of each of them, down to all levels, are also ignored. Further the subsystems not ignored will, in general, have lower imperceivable subsystem levels which, again, implies that subsystems on lower level will be ignored, in early project estimates, before systematic break-down has been done.

Theorem 11. By testing for workability, an increasing number of hierarchical levels of an imperceivable system, going down from the top level (i.e. the whole system) we reduce increasingly the number of subsystems or parts ignored.

It may be worth noting that our model does not exclude a sequential definition of the system. This can be seen in the following way, see Fig. 4.

Exercise. Show how this theory can be used to guide the reasoning which is called for when we are required to estimate how far to carry the analysis of a specific stage of an ADP systems project. It is assumed that one of the specifications for the stage of analysis is that it shall provide cost and time estimates for the whole project with a certain degree of accuracy.

Exercise. An alternative to the approach described in the above exercise is to determine, instead, how much work is to be invested in each stage. Especially for the first stage this is often the case. Show how arguments similar to those above can be applied to this situation

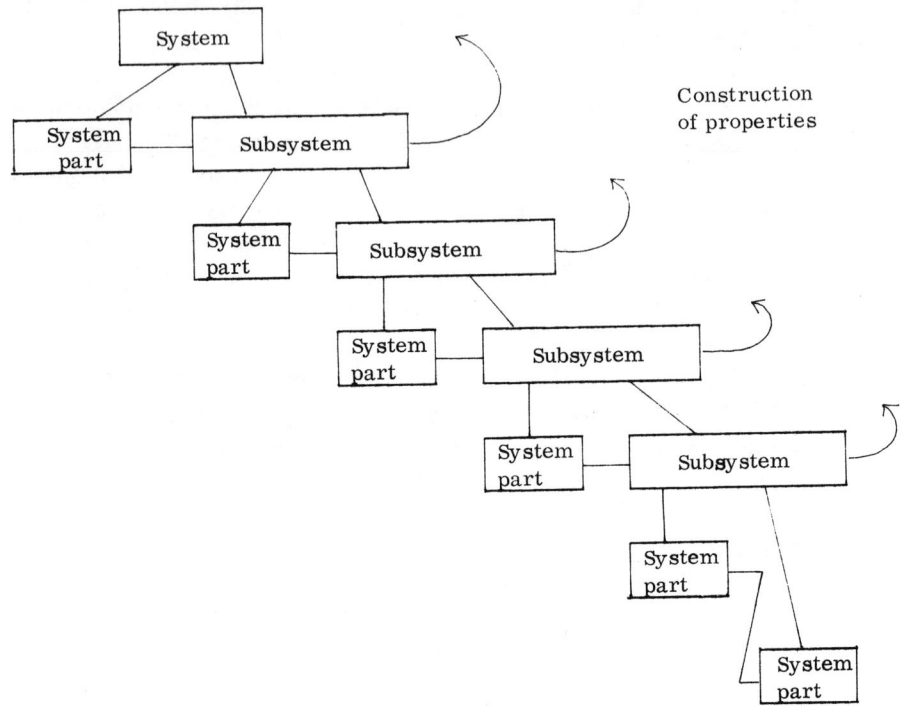

Fig. 4 In the first perceivable step of analysis one part of the system is defined together with the remaining (or "*complementary*") subsystem. The subsystem is then in the second step again defined as one part and one subsystem, and so on.

11.18 The Suitable Number of Subsystems in a Subsystem Structure

The question as to how many subsystems can there be in a perceivable structure seems to have a fairly precise answer: *not more than 10 — and not less than 4* (The author and his co-researchers have found this to hold in a large number of cases. Also, the literature often suggests 5 or 7 — and sometimes 2 — as the number of facts that decision makers can consider). It may be asked: what to do if the "logical" number is higher than ten — or smaller than four. The answer is that there is no logical, larger number. One rather has to decide how much information one wants to present in one stage. This has been verified in practical systems analysis studies over two years by Mats Lundeberg[1]). He found

---

[1]) 2 Lu 1970.

that he never was forced to exceed ten as the number of subsystems in one structure. Also it seems that often, when one thinks one has only two subsystems in a structure, it is suitable to partition some of them to increase the number of subsystems. In that way one is giving more information in one stage. On the other hand there are cases when there does exist a *logical* reason for having only *two* subsystems. One example: the task of designing an information system seems to contain strictly two logical components: 1. To determine what information to have in the system and 2: how to provide that information. These can than be partitioned so that e.g. 5 subsystems occur in the next stage, but the first stage turns out to be exactly two, for logical reasons. Our argument for having not less than four subsystems in any subsystem structure, when not logically necessary, is that because we are able to handle four to ten we do not use our capability efficiently by using fewer. For instance we would get unnecessarily many levels to handle.

Because the subsystem structures we work with have to be kept very small, so that they are perceivable, it is important to use a work method which allows covering as large a part of the system at a time as possible (that is in one work stage or one subsystem structure). *Fortunately there is a simple work principle which makes this possible in general: Focus on one single aspect of the system at each stage of work.* Thus when information sets and their relations are being studied one may leave aside the algorithms involved. Instead, when the algorithms are studied, they can be taken one at a time, each together with its information precedents (inputs) and succedents (output), leaving out the other information sets and the other algorithms.

Another example of the use of the principle of minimizing the number of entities used in each description of a subproblem, in order to enhance overview, is when mathematicians use very short symbols (e.g. x, y, z, a, ε etc.). In this way they make it possible to cover by one perceivable formula more mathematical structure than would else have been possible.

The fact that a human being can only perceive — and make use of — very limited structures (or sets of facts) at a time is, of course, observed by many workers in the field of psychology of decision and problem solving. Among such studies are: 4 MS 1958 where the "bounded rationality" of decisionmakers is given an important rôle. (See also Schroeder, paper presented at MIS symposium, Cologne 1970, 2 Sr 1971, where it is demonstrated that decision-makers can make use of five facts at most in making a decision, a number which could not be improved by training).

Chapter 2. Systems Algebra

12.1 Algebraic Tools for Describing Systems.

In order to be able to analyze a system we need a method of describing it. According to the definition of a system that we have given at the outset this means that we want to describe how the system has been built up from its parts. We are interested in ways of describing a system which are suited to the *determination of different properties of the system*. We also want a method of *description which can be handled by computers*. This means that we are interested in algebraic description methods, rather than, or at least in addition to, graphic methods. (It may be well to add here that it may be possible to have computers read diagrams, but the techniques for storing the information thus fed into the computer will again rely upon algebraic means. These, by the way, turn out to be the same as we will develop.)

1 As we shall find, the *descriptions of system build-up that we shall propose, will work directly as operators which, when given property of the system or some situation* (a loading for instance) *in which the system finds itself, operate on this property or situation to produce another one.*

2 It is seen that in this way one will expect different operators to be descriptive of the system in different ways and therefore be of interest in different contexts. We shall see that this is actually the case.

3 We are of course also interested in graphic ways of depicting system build-up and we are going to use tree-like diagrams or network-like diagrams for this purpose. This is to say that we are going to use "linear graphs" to depict system properties. Linear graph theory then also provides us with some of the algebraic, descriptive tools that we want. We shall however extend the list of such tools beyond what is presently available from graph theory.

4 Definition of Set Union and Set Intersection
  Let A denote the set points enclosed by the contour A. Similarly for B.

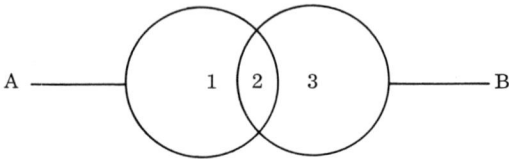

  Then, if 1 denotes the set of points inside of A but outside of B we have

  $A = 1, 2$ (that is the set A is made up by the sets 1 and 2).
  $B = 2, 3$
  $A \cup B = 1, 2, 3$ (*Union* of the sets A and B.)
  $A \cap B = 2$ (*Intersection* of the sets A and B.)

5 Set inclusion
  $2 \subset A$ (The set 2 is included in A.)
  $2 \subset B$
  but $3 \not\subset A$ (The set 3 is not included in A.)

6 If x is an element of the set 2 we denote this fact by $x \in 2$.
  From $2 \subset A$ and $x \in 2$ it follows that $x \in A$.

12.2 Precedence Operator of a System (or Graph).

The very simple — and therefore very generally applicable — definition of a system as a set of objects (of any kind whatsoever) and a set of relations between the objects was shown above[1]) to be enough to make it possible to define systems of different kinds with enough precision that the properties of the systems as "wholes" can be computed. While such mathematically "complete" treatment of systems is possible only for some classes of systems and while many of the most important kinds of systems are much too complex and ill-defined to permit a complete mathematical analysis of their properties, it is nevertheless useful to study some simple systems and their mathematical descriptions and analysis. This makes us familiar with the meaning of the systems concept and thereby aids us in applying a system-analytic approach also to such complex systems where we are able to use informal, conceptual reasoning only, because of too complex or undefined properties of the system. Thus, it is easy in mathematical analysis of simple systems to define

---

[1]) See section 11.8, Ch. 1.

and compute meaningful gross properties of a system. In studies of general system theory authors often have difficulty in defining system properties as something less trivial than just a sum of part properties. Even simple mathematical systems analysis might help them overcome this difficulty, as we have already shown[1]). We are giving further illustrations below. It is also possible that systems which cannot be analyzed in a closed mathematical form may well be treated by numeric calculations or data processing operations and then a precise description of the system structure will be necessary. Thus, also for such applications of systems analysis will it be useful to have done some formal exercises on simple, mathematical system models.

Finally, to use computers for the management of systems or for planning the production of complex products (i.e. systems) it is absolutely necessary to be able to describe the systems or products in mathematical terms (although this may be referred to as data about the systems or product structures).

Formal description of a system.

It follows from the definition of a system that to describe it one may describe the objects and the relations which together form the system. It often appears natural to describe a system by using

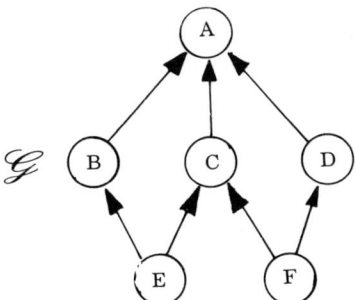

Fig. 1

a diagram, in which each object is symbolized by a circle or a point and each relation between two objects is symbolized by an arrow connecting the corresponding circles. (It is obvious that this kind of description is only sufficient when it is not important to symbolize differences between the distinct objects or relations.) We use arrows to symbolize relations which only go in one direction. (If the relations are not unidirectional we use lines (or double arrows) instead of arrows.) A system diagram of this sort, see for instance Fig. 1, is often called a *graph* or a *linear graph*. The points or circles are called *nodes* of the graph and the lines or arrows are called *edges* or *branches*. When it is desired to emphasize the unidirectional character of the relations indicated by the use of arrows, rather than just lines) in the graph, one sometimes uses the term *directed graph* or *digraph*. We shall often use the term *precedence graph* instead, because we have found it useful to have a term which associates both with the relation itself and with the elements that are joined by the relations. Thus we talk about the directed relation as a *precedence relation* and we say that a set of system elements or subsystems are *precedents* (or *predecessors*) to another system element if they are related to the latter by precedence relations. Thus in Fig. 1, B, C and D are precedents of A. Likewise F is a precedent of C and also of D. The word "precedent" is chosen as it is easy to remember that if one follows in the system graph (like Fig. 1) a path by a sequence of arrows, one will arrive at a precedent of a system part A before one arrives at A. When B is a precedent of A we also say that A is a *succedent* of B (or a *successor* of B). When a precedence graph is used as a representation of a real system, the relations in the real system that correspond to the arrows in the graph may or may not be of a kind that is "naturally" a precedence relation. An example of a simple kind of systems analysis where the relations will correspond naturally to precedence relations is when the graph depicts a project plan where each node corresponds to an event in the work on the project. (The project itself may be the building of a house, the construction of a computer program or the planning of a sales campaign, for instance.)

The graphical description of a system (as in Fig. 1) is very illuminating and helps getting an overview over its elements and relations. One must remember however that when one is concerned with large systems, the number of elements and relations in the system may be in the hundreds or even thousands. This is not uncommon in everyday life. Then a graphic picture loses much of its advantages. It is therefore somewhat dangerous to develop diagram-assisted methods using small test examples (like Fig. 1) and then expect to realize all the advantages that are encountered in such experiments also in real, large scale applications. It appears for instance that a lot of mistakes in the use of graphs as "planning networks" to large projects have occurred for this reason. This kind of mistake may be guarded against if we can develop formal, mathematical methods for analyzing the system or its graph. The reason we might have for such an expectation is that *we may test out a mathematical method on small examples (like Fig. 1) and then prove the method to hold true for any similar system, regardless of its size*. This is an important difference between the mathematical method and the sole use of diagrams. *Thus the main usefulness of the diagram or graph may be as an aid in developing a mathematical method.*

As we shall see, very simple mathematical methods suffice for many fundamental analyses of large systems or for their treatment by an electronic computer. The mathematics needed for formal description and the most basic analysis of systems are so simple that they appear well justified for anybody who wants to study or use systems methods — even if only as a philosophical tool — to get familiar with it. A familiarity with the elementary systems description and analysis tools also *has a special advantage exactly for those who do not want to get involved in mathematical intricacies* (even though these might (in some cases) be of advantage in later design optimization attempts) *but prefer (wisely) to delegate such work to specialists*. Thus the formal description is the ideal instrument for communication with the specialist. *Also those who expect to avoid mathematics by using system simulation will need a basic knowledge of formal description and analysis methods for systems. To simulate we must, of course, describe our simulation model.*
The simple mathematical descriptions and calculations on systems that we shall study have to do with symbols or data. As there will be data about the system elements and data about the relations, the data themselves will form a system which we will often call a *data structure*. (Notice that this is a suitable kind of description regardless of whether we have in mind the use of a computer or not. We therefore may call it an *abstract data structure*.)

The mathematical treatment of a system will normally be formed as an *algorithm* (or scheme for data-processing) which will operate upon the data structure to produce a set of new data or a new data structure. Thus, for instance, if the data structure contains one data set representing an object A (or a *record* representing A) and another data set representing B then the latter data set (the "record B") may contain data that tell that A is a succedent of B. It will then be a very simple algorithm that will "compute the succedents of B" and give A as (part of) the answer. In this way the *data structure together with an algorithm* may give information about the structural properties of the real system of which the data structure is a description (or a model). It may be stated that most formal analysis of systems and also most data processing can be seen as an elaboration of this basic scheme *data structure/algorithm*. *Notice*. The reader should convince himself that the data structure and algorithm concepts are relevant to the formal analysis of systems regardless of whether or not we have in mind to use a computer. Thus the *data-logical* and the mathematical treatment of systems are very closely connected indeed.

Let us see now the simple system depicted by the graph of Fig. 1 can be represented by a data structure. We denote by $\mathscr{P}$ (A) the operation of pointing out the *immediate precedents* (or *direct precedents*) of A. Then it is seen from Fig. 1 that we may write

(a) $\mathscr{P}$ (A) = B, C, D;

We notice that the equation (a) as written down is, itself, a data structure which contains the data A, B, C, and D each of which names different objects in the system (or different nodes in the graph). It also contains the data $\mathscr{P}$ ( ) which are used to indicate that B, C, and D; have precedence relations with A. Obviously an algorithm for identifying the precedents of A, given access to a store where (a) has been stored, would have to search only the store trying to find a data set (or record) where the identifier A occurs in the position with respect to the data $\mathscr{P}$ ( ) indicated in (a). The algorithm then only would have to fetch the data recorded between the signs "=" and ";". It is, of course, natural to assume that for the storage system there are available functions or algorithms which are able to locate the records for the objects A, B, C, and D (etc) when given the names A, B, C, and D respectively. Thus the algorithm locating precedents will normally use the service of other algoritms which will save the trouble to scan all of the store. An alternative type of data structure, which is very common, is one where the addresses in the store of the locations of the records for A, B, C, and D are given instead of the names.

We may refer to a list such as $\mathscr{P}$ (A) = B, C, D; as a precedents list for A. We may now write down the set of precedents lists for all the objects of the system or graph under study. If the graph is named $\mathscr{G}$ then we obtain the *list of precedents lists* of $\mathscr{G}$. (We may symbolize this by $\mathscr{P}$ ($\mathscr{G}$). We may use the same symbol $\mathscr{P}$ ( ) also for the list of precedents lists as long as the name of a graph can be formally distinguished from a name of a node for instance by using different typographical symbols²) as we do here. We now have

1
$$\mathscr{P}(\mathscr{G}) = \begin{cases} \mathscr{P}(A) = B, C, D; \\ \mathscr{P}(B) = E; \\ \mathscr{P}(C) = E, F; \\ \mathscr{P}(D) = F; \\ \mathscr{P}(E) = \mathscr{P}(F) = \emptyset \ (\emptyset \text{ is used to denote the empty set}) \end{cases}$$

It is easy to see that one can also use a more compact form for representing $\mathscr{P}(\ )$:

2
$\quad\quad\mathscr{P}(\mathscr{G}):$ A (B, C, D) B (E) C (E, F) D (F) E (ø) F ø;

An object which is a precedent of a precedent of an object is also regarded as a precedent of the last mentioned object. It is said to be a *second order precedent* or a *2nd precedent*. Thus in Fig. 1 B is a 1st precedent of A and E is a 2nd precedent of A. Likewise we say that A is a 2nd succecent of E. In a similar way we may define n-th precedents and succedents.

We also use the notation $B \ll A$ to indicate that $B \in \mathscr{P}(A)$. Further if $C \ll B$, $B \ll A$ we say that $C < B$ (C is a precedent of B) and, also if $D < C$, $C < B$ we say that $D < B$. We likewise say that if $B \ll A$ then also $B < A$. Thus $\ll$ denotes precedence relation of the first order (direct precedence relation) and $<$ denotes precedence relation of any order.

3 **Exercise.** Describe verbally how an algorithm will have to work in order to establish the names of all the 1st precedents of any named object in the data structure $\mathscr{P}(\mathscr{G})$ given in 1 above.

4 **Exercise.** Describe verbally how an algorithm might work to find the names of all precedents (of any order) of a named object in 1. How would it be extended in order to tell also, for each named precedent, which order it has?

---

²) Thus by using here $\mathscr{G}$ rather than G we have indicated that we are referring to another class of concepts. Thus G might denote an object or a node in the graph while $\mathscr{G}$ denotes the system or the graph.

93

5 **Exercise.** Discuss how an algorithm might work upon the data structure 1 in order to find the names of all the succedents (of any order) of F.

6 **Exercise.** Construct a succedents list of lists (denoted $\mathscr{S}(\mathscr{G})$) for the graph $\mathscr{G}$ and repeat the exercise 4 for this new data structure.

7 **Exercise.** Is there anything about the system which can be seen from the graph of Fig. 1 but not from $\mathscr{P}(\mathscr{G})$? In the graph it is as easy to follow succedence paths as precedence paths. Is this also the case with $\mathscr{P}(\mathscr{G})$? It is the case with $\mathscr{P}(\mathscr{G})$ and $\mathscr{S}(\mathscr{G})$ together?

8 **Exercise.** Write a data structure similar to $\mathscr{P}(\mathscr{G})$, which contains the information of both $\mathscr{P}(\mathscr{G})$ and $\mathscr{S}(\mathscr{G})$!

9 **Exercise.** The system under study may be a set of integers. If the square of the value of an element in the system is defined as its 1st succedent, which are the 2nd succedents of 5? Which are the 1st precedents of 16? Which are the 2nd precedents of 16?

Data structure representation of a system.

We have seen how precedents lists and succedents lists can be regarded as mathematical descriptions or as data structure descriptions of systems. The data structure description of a system can easily be extended to tell more about the system. This is not so with the mathematical description, that is if we make such an extension it will no longer be natural to regard the data structure as a mathematical description. (We are willing to admit that this may be stated as merely a matter of opinion, because we do not want to go deeper into this argument here.)

The extension of the system description that we have in mind is a very natural one for it will, of course, often be required to say something about the attributes of the objects of the system and not merely to give their names. It may also, of course, be required to say something about the relations between the objects.

In order to introduce, in a natural way, extensions to the data structure associated with a system, we notice that the structure $\mathscr{P}(A) =$

B, C, D; may be designed as a record[3]) associated with the object A.

Thus we may use the record format, Fig. 2.

```
Record A;
   P; B, C, D
```

Fig. 2

as a representative for $\mathscr{P}$ (A) = B, C, D;

We may now add a subrecord for A, containing a set of data or a data structure which describes attributes of the object A. We do not need to discuss here how this subrecord is designed. We now have a record format as in Fig. 3.
(It may be a text or natural language, a table, or any kind of formatted document.)

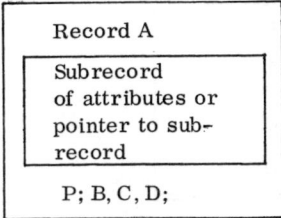

Fig. 3

If the data system where the record is used contains a function or an algorithm for retrieval by name, i.e. for locating any record in the data store, when the name of that record is given to it (i.e. the name of the system object associated with that record) then the names B, C, and D in the record act as *links* or *pointers* to the records for B, C, and D. We may call them *name links* when it is necessary to distinguish them from other types of links which we shall talk about later.

We may depict the data structure constituted by the records, (similar to "Record A", for the system of Fig. 1) by drawing arrows to indicate the role of pointers played by those terms in each record which name other records (or their associated system objects) Fig. 4. Notice carefully that the arrows do *not* represent the links directly

---

[3]) By "record" we denote any group of symbols stored together or "data terms" (words for instance) which are used to carry information about some object or some event. (In recent publications of CODASYL the word "entry" is used for this concept.)

but indicate the combined effect of the link data and the retrieval algorithm using them. This is an important difference between a data structure and a graph.

10 **Exercise.** Modify the data structure of Fig. 4 by adding linking data and the corresponding arrows, so that succedents of system objects may be found by "retrieval by name", without the need to scan the whole store!

11 **Exercise.** Is it possible in the structure of Fig. 4 to retrieve by name the other 1st precedents of A when one starts at B?

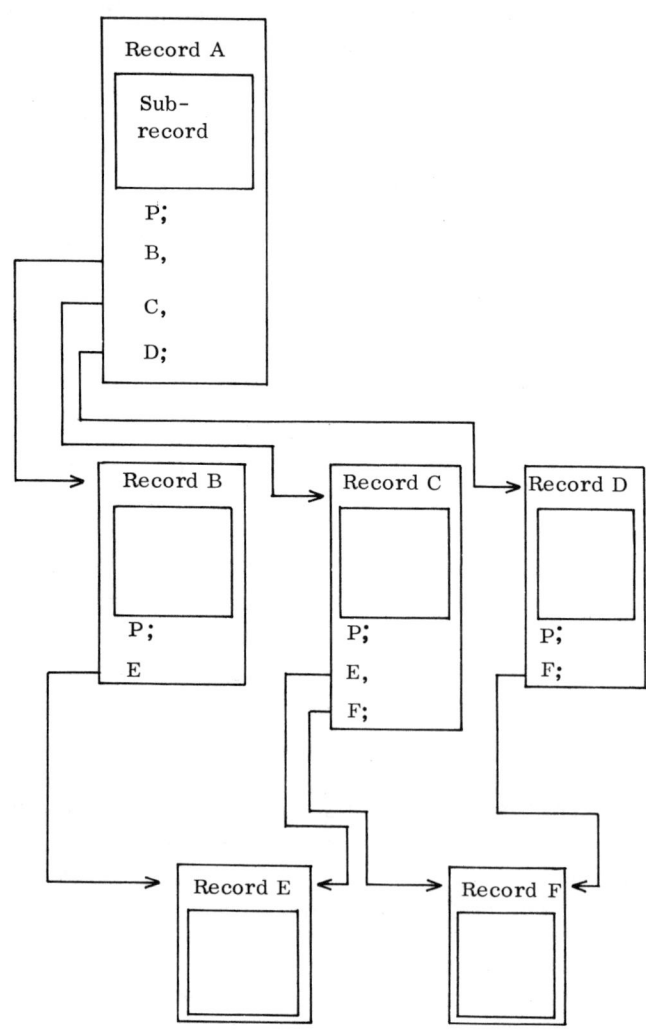

Fig. 4. Data structure corresponding to the system of Fig. 1.

Is it possible in the structure according to Exercise 10?

12 **Exercise.** Modify the structure of Fig. 4 so that when starting at any of the 1st precedents of A one can find all the other 1st precedents of A in a simple sequence of at most three steps of "retrieval by name"!

13 **Exercise.** One will get a feeling for how a computer would work upon a data structure if one writes each one of the records on a separate card where each card carries the name of its record. Do the exercises 1, 2, and 3 using such cards!

14 **Exercise.** The use of arrows in diagramming may be misleading in the sense that it may give the impression that following the links from one record to another is trivially easy. Draw a diagram analogous to Fig. 4 but with no arrows. Use numerical "addresses" for records and a table which translates from record names into "addresses".

The *concept* of "finding the precedents of A" indicated by the *conceptual* mathematical symbolism $\mathscr{P}$ (A) has *its datalogical* counterpart in P (A). $\mathscr{P}$ here stands for the concept of finding the precedents, i.e. just what we have *in mind* when we think of finding the precedents. P, instead is the name of an algorithm which we may have represented by a set of data written on paper or stored in a computer, as a program for how to work upon the data structure. Notice that there may be several distinct algorithms, P_1, P_2, ... that could represent the concept $\mathscr{P}$. For instance different sorts of data structures may be used to represent the system to be analyzed and, of course, when we change the data structure we must change the algorithm, in order for it to correspond to the same concept of operation $\mathscr{P}$ (cf. the exercises above).

$\mathscr{P}$ corresponds to what we speak of when using the word *information* while P corresponds to a *data representation of $\mathscr{P}$, given a data structure for the system under study.*

"$\mathscr{P}$ ( )" may be referred to as an *abstract operator* (or *conceptual operator*) whereas P ( ) is an *algorithmic operator*. P ( ) is an *algorithmic realization* of $\mathscr{P}$. (In this specific case $\mathscr{P}$ ( ) is a "precedence operator" as it determines the precedents of its argument.)

We shall now take up another way of establishing an algorithmic realization of $\mathscr{P}$ ( ).

12.3 The Precedence Matrix of a System.

1 We have already mentioned that the concept of identifying the immediate precedents of system elements, i.e. the operation symbolized by $\mathscr{P}$, can be realized in different ways. The way we illustrated above used the precedence lists for all the system elements together with simple rules (algorithms) for using the data structure given the lists. The precedence lists have the advantage of being intuitively natural, which manifests itself by the simplicity of the algorithm which finds the precedents. A disadvantage of the precedence lists as a systems description is that they are somewhat unsystematic. This, for instance, makes itself felt if ones looks in $\mathscr{P}(\mathscr{G})$, as given in 1 (section 12.2), to find all elements for which F is a precedent, that is if one searches for the *succedents* of F. One will have to scan all the lists in order to make sure that the elements asked for are D and C. It would obviously have been easier to do this search if all occurences of F in the data structure would have been aligned vertically. One would then only have had to search one column corresponding to F. We shall now study how another kind of data structure (together with other algorithms) can be designed, which will have some interesting properties, one of which is the one mentioned as desirable when we looked for the succedents of F.

We notice that if we list the set of all system parts, the *base set* of $\mathscr{G}$, depicted in Fig. 1 as a column

$$\begin{array}{c} A \\ B \\ C \\ D \\ E \\ F \end{array}$$

we may then write another column to the right of it, heading it by "A", as

2
$$\begin{array}{cc} & A \\ A & \emptyset \\ B & 1 \\ C & 1 \\ D & 1 \\ E & \emptyset \\ F & \emptyset \end{array}$$

then this second column has been used as what we will call a *selection column* (or *selection vector*) for A (in general: for the object we indicate by the heading).

Note that the selection column must have a number of elements which is exactly equal to that of the base set, for any element in the selection vector is related to its element in the base only by its position in the column. If every element of the selection column is accompanied by a label pointing to its associated base element then blank elements can be deleted. This is exactly what is done in section 12.2.

On comparing 2 and (1, section 12.2) we find that the column in 2, headed by "A", has a "1" to the right of each of the parts which are (immediate) precedents of A. Thus the second column *selects*, out of the set of all parts within $\mathscr{G}$, exactly those parts which are members of $\mathscr{P}$ (A).

It is seen that the selection vector headed by "A" is exactly equivalent to the relation $\mathscr{P}$ (A) = B, C, D, (when the vector is associated with the base set). Thus 2 is a data structure which is equivalent to $\mathscr{P}$ (A) = B, C, D. Note that "equivalent" here means that some algorithm can be constructed such that it is able to identify the precedents of A, when working upon 2, which another algorithm can do, when working upon 1, section 12.2. If we go on and put selection columns for all the lists of 1, section 3, we obtain

3
$$P = $$

	A	B	C	D	E	F
A						
B	1					
C	1					
D	1					
E		1	1			
F			1	1		

if we use blank boxes instead of having ø to indicate no selection[1]).

---

[1]) When we want to store an array like P as shown in 3 on magnetic tape or a direct access memory of a computer we may store each column as a set of character or bit positions containing zeros or ones and head this set by a code identifying the column (like A, B. ... in 3). However we shall often have to do with large arrays of which very few elements are different from zero. Then the columns of an array are more economically stored as lists, like 2 section 12.2. Still the array form, like 3, is more convenient to use as a basis for discussion and for computing on small exercises.

4 **Remark.** We shall later on have reason to write P^{00} rather than P for this operator.

The table, or two-dimensional array, denoted in 3 by P will be called the *precedence matrix* of the system or of the graph.

The precedence matrix of a system has one column and one row for each point (or *vertex*) in the system graph. The column P^j associated with a part "j" selects, by units in its corresponding row positions, those parts that are immediate predecessors, or precedents, of the part "j". The column "j" of P may therefore be referred to as the *precedence vector* for part "j".

One interesting property of the precedence matrix P can be pointed to immediately:

5 **Theorem.** Any row P_i of P is a succedence vector for part "i", that is P_i selects the parts which are immediate succedents (or successors) of part "i".

The proof is simple and left as an exercise.

6 *Note.* The parts which have no precedents will be called *initial parts* and those without succedents will be called *terminal parts* with respect to P). The columns in P associated with initial parts are obviously empty and so are the rows associated with terminal parts. These rows and columns, which are always empty, will in general, be deleted. Parts which are neither initial nor terminal may be referred to as *internal parts*. Also, it is natural to refer to the set of 1 st precedents and 1 st succedents as the set of *neighbors* of a part. We also say that a part x is order-related to part y if y is either a precedent or a succedent of x.

7 **Exercise.** List the set of neighbors and the set of non order-related points for each point (A, B, ... F) of Fig. 1.

Answer.

Point	Neighbours	Non-related
A	B, C, D	∅
B	A, E	C, D, F
C	A, E, F	B, D
D	A, F	B, C, E
E	B, C	D, F
F	C, D	B, E

12.4 The Precedents of a Set of Parts.

In analyzing a system one will often want to determine the immediate precedents of a set of system parts rather than those of a single part only. This will be the case, for instance, if one asks for the "second precedents" (2nd precedents) of a part X. These are, of course, the precedents of all the parts which are 1st precedents of X. They could thus be said to be the 1st precedents of the set of 1st precedents of X. For instance in

$$\mathscr{P}(\mathscr{G}) = \begin{array}{l} \mathscr{P}(A) = B, C, D \\ \mathscr{P}(B) = E \\ \mathscr{P}(C) = E, F \\ \mathscr{P}(D) = F \end{array}$$

$\mathscr{P}(A)$ determines the set of parts (B, C, D) as the set of 1st precedents of A. The set of 2nd precedents of A then is the set of precedents of all parts contained in the set of 1st precedents. We may refer to it as the set of 1st precedents of the set defined by $\mathscr{P}(A)$. Thus the set of 1st precedents of $\mathscr{P}(A)$ is the set of the 1st precedents of B (which is $=E$) together with the set of 1st precedents of C (which are E and F) together with the 1st precedents of D (which is F). The set of parts which are precedents of one or more of the elements in $\mathscr{P}(A)$ contains the parts E and F. We can thus say that the set of precedents of the *set* $\mathscr{P}(A)$ contains E and F. We might show this symbolically as

$$\mathscr{P}(\mathscr{P}(A)) = E, F$$

We may also write down our definition of the precedents of the set $\mathscr{P}(A) = B, C, D$ as

$$\mathscr{P}(\mathscr{P}(A)) = \mathscr{P}(B, C, D) = \mathscr{P}(B) \cup \mathscr{P}(C) \cup \mathscr{P}(D)$$

which says that the 1st precedents of $\mathscr{P}(A)$ are determined by the union of the sets $\mathscr{P}(B)$, $\mathscr{P}(C)$ and $\mathscr{P}(D)$ that is

$$\mathscr{P}(\mathscr{P}(A)) = (E) \cup (E, F) \cup (F) = (E, F)$$

We used parentheses here to denote sets, for example (F) denotes the set consisting of the single element F. Note that (F) and F are distinct concepts although they happen to be associated with the same object.

It is, of course, natural to generalize the concept of precedents of sets to allow for the definition of the precedents of *any set*, not just a set of precedents. In general if $S=(S_1, S_2 \ldots S_n)$ is a set of n parts then we will define the set of 1st precedents of the set S as

$$\mathscr{P}(S) = \mathscr{P}(S_1) \cup \mathscr{P}(S_2) \cup \ldots \mathscr{P}(S_n)$$

12.5 Use of the Precedence Matrix P to Determine the Precedents of a Set of Parts.

The set S can of course be defined by a selection vector. If for instance we take $S = C, D$ where C and D are parts of the system of Fig. 1 in section 2 we thus obtain

1
$$S = \begin{array}{c} \\ A \\ B \\ C \\ D \\ E \\ F \end{array} \begin{array}{|c|} \hline s \\ \hline \\ \hline \\ \hline 1 \\ \hline 1 \\ \hline \\ \hline \\ \hline \end{array}$$

where s is the "name" of the column which selects S out of the base set.

2 We now want to show that we can obtain the precedents of the set S by means of a very simple computation which operates upon the selection vector s of the set S and the precedence matrix P. This can be stated as the problem of how to compute $\mathscr{P}(S)$ by manipulating upon the data structures P and s, that is upon the precedence matrix and the selection vector for the set S. It is natural to define the set $\mathscr{P}(S)$ of precedents by means of a selection vector which we may call s'. It would be very convenient if we could use a notation for specifying the operation upon P and s giving s' in the following way

3
$$P(\cup)s = s'$$

This notation brings out the fact that P and s are to be involved in the calculation and also reminds us (by using the operation symbol ($\cup$)) that s' is to define the set theoretic union of all precedents of all elements in S. The suggested form was chosen with a desire for a good mnemo-technical quality. Thus s' is to be the selection vector for $\mathscr{P}$ (S), and thus the operational notation for the data structures involved is very similar to the conceptual notation of what is to be achieved.

It is not hard to see that the algorithm to be used will have to contain a step which selects those columns of P, which belong to the system parts contained in S. We see that this first step of the algorithm asked for is a very natural one. It simply means that when we write s to the right of P then we think of s as selecting columns of P instead of selecting parts from the base set of the system. We may thus indicate our first step, in the present example as:

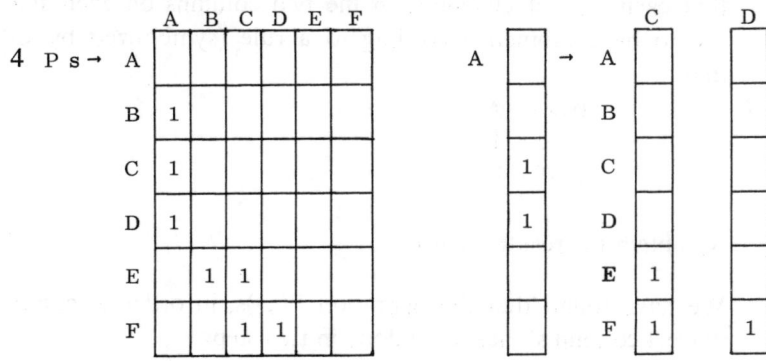

4   P s →

s selects the columns C and D from P because the elements in the positions C and D in s are = 1. The two columns to the right now define all precedents of the set s. They show that the set of precedents $\mathscr{P}$ (S) contains parts E and F because they are precedents of C which belongs to S and contain F also, because it is a precedent of D which also belongs to S. F thus occurs twice but we need mention it only once if we ask only which system parts are precedents of S and ask nothing more. We ought to have as the result:

5

s'=		
A		
B		
C		
D		
E	1	
F	1	

103

It is easy to see that if we let

6

	A						
	B						
	C		(∪)		=		
	D						
	E	1				1	
	F	1		1		1	

the operation symbol ∪, when placed between two columns, means that each pair of elements, in the two columns on each side of ∪ are to be combined according to a rule (symbolized by ∪) such that:

7
$$\emptyset \cup \emptyset = \emptyset$$
$$\emptyset \cup 1 = 1$$
$$1 \cup 1 = 1$$

we obtain the result required.

We have found that the operation P(∪)s, in order to compute the correct column s', has to be done in two steps

8a 1. P(∪)s selects those columns in
P which "belong to" the system
parts contained in S

and

8b 2. combines the columns selected in 1,
two at a time, successively, until
a single column remains.

9 **Example.**

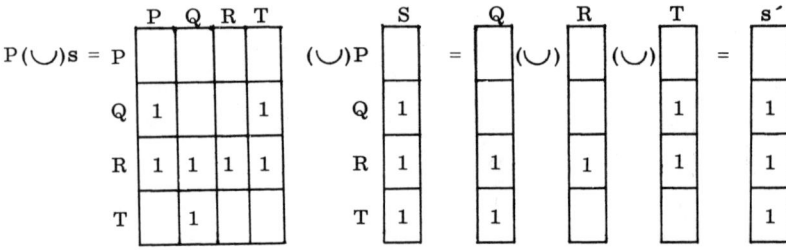

104

10 It is important to note that the *matrix-by-vector* operation P($\cup$)s has one suboperation (i.e. the column selection) which has to do with *retrieval of data from data structures* and another suboperation (combination of columns) which is, simply, a set of *simple arithmethical* (logical) *operations* on pairs of retrieved data terms of the data.

Distinct matrix operations often differ only in the arithmetic operations. This means that the same algorithm for retrieval of data from the matrices (data structures) involved can be used for many distinct matrix operations. As this part of the operation is the most complicated one this fact can be used to save a lot of programming work. It forms the basis for developing general "*data management*" systems to support computation programs.

11 The composition defined by 7 is often called *logical* (or Boolean) *addition*. Accordingly the selection vectors, and thus also for instance, precedence matrices, containing only the element values ø and 1 will be called logical (or Boolean) matrices.

We shall consider later *numerical* selection vectors and matrices. Then normal addition rules will hold for the individual elements instead of Boolean addition. In those cases we shall also see that we have reason to make explicit distinction between 0 and ø (blank or empty). In logical matrices we may use 0 to be equivalent to ø, but in general matrices this will not be possible. (In data processing we may still need another symbol for "blank" because if we use ø to denote "the empty set" then we may in addition have to signal that "no symbol" is specified.

Exercise 1. Compute the sum of the logical vectors (that is: the (union)

$$v_1 = \text{ø}, 1, \text{ø}, \text{ø}, \text{ø}, 1$$
$$v_2 = \text{ø}, 1, 1, \text{ø}, \text{ø}, 1$$
$$v_3 = 1, 1, \text{ø}, \text{ø}, \text{ø}, \text{ø}$$

Verify that $v_1 \cup v_2 \cup v_3$ selects $s(v_1) \cup s(v_2) \cup s(v_3)$, that is the union of the sets selected.

12 *In* addition to the operation of *union* ($\cup$) the operation of *intersection* ($\cap$) is a common one in set theory cf. section 12.1.

It is defined for our selection numbers by

13
$$\emptyset \cap \emptyset = \emptyset$$
$$1 \cap \emptyset = \emptyset$$
$$1 \cap 1 = 1$$

It is also called Boolean multiplication.

Based on our definition of $\cap$ for single selection numbers we now define $P(\cap)$s in analogy with $P(\cup)$s as defined in 3.

14 $P(\cap)s =$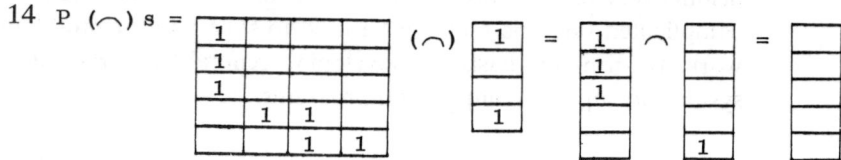

Instead we find, for example

15 $P(\cap)s =$ if $s =$

16 **Remark.** In formuias like those in section 8 we need of course a special symbol (like the ø) for blank but in an array (like P) leaving a box blank serves as well. It is therefore redundant to use ø in a matrix but we do it sometimes when we believe it will give clarity of reading. The reason we do not use 0 (zero) for blank is that, as we shall see later we often need to distinguish between zero and blank.

12.6 Connection with a Linked Data Structure.

When we discussed the precedence list $\mathscr{P}(\mathscr{G})$: $\mathscr{P}(A) = B, C, D$, $\mathscr{P}(BE) = E$, $\mathscr{P}(C) = E, F$, $\mathscr{P}(D) = F$, $\mathscr{P}(E) = \mathscr{P}(F) = \emptyset$; as data structures we found that the names listed could be thought to have the same effect as arrows pointing to the records associated with these names. It appears perhaps still more natural to let the 1:s in a selection column be associated with links (pointers) to those elements in the base set which are selected. Indeed, the selection vector appears to be equivalent to just a set of pointers in a set of records each one of which is associated with one system part.

The matrix P then appears as a set of sets of pointers. However, we found in a theorem above that the rows of a precedence matrix are selection vectors for succedents of the system parts. It will therefore often appear at least as natural to consider a *precedence matrix as equivalent to a set of double links,* such that each link has a counterpart which joins the same two records but in opposite direction.

We conclude from what we have just said that the operation $P(\cup)s = s'$ also has an algorithmic interpretation in a linked data structure. It is easy to see how this can be achieved. We assume that we have a data structure representing the precedence matrix P of the system as before, Fig. 1. The boxes in Fig. 1 represent data records which, in their turn, represent system parts.

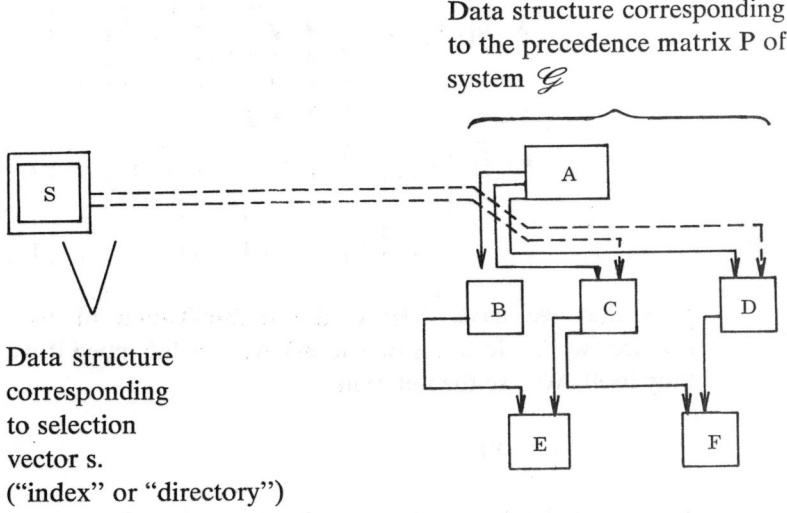

Data structure corresponding to the precedence matrix P of system $\mathscr{G}$

Data structure corresponding to selection vector s. ("index" or "directory")

Fig. 1

The selection vector s, defining the set S now is to be represented by a set of links. It is shown in Fig. 1 as a box (double lined square in Fig. 1) with the name S. This box represents a record containing links to the selected objects C and D. The algorithm corresponding to the operation $P(\cup)s$ (and thus, corresponding to $\mathscr{P}$ (S), will now consist of a step which retrieves the record S (by its name S) and another set of steps each of which retrieves link information from within record S (link to C, for instance) and then retrieves the corresponding record (record C, for instance).

107

12.7 Matrix by Matrix Composition. P^n, n-th Precedents and Paths.

The composition $P(\smile)$s studied in 3 will often be referred to as "multiplication" of the (logical) matrix "P" by the column "s", or of "s" by "P". We can naturally extend the definition of this operation to the multiplication of two (logical) matrices, A and B, say. To do this we simply let the vector "b" in the *product* $A(\smile)B$ be extended to a set of two vectors, as $[b_1, b_2]$ and then perform

$$A(\smile)B = A(\smile)\ [b_1, b_2]\ \text{as}\ [A(\smile)b_1, A(\smile)b_2]\quad \text{if}\ B = [b_1, b_2]$$

As long as there is no doubt about which operation is intended one will often prefer to write e.g. AB instead of $A(\smile)B$.

Example.

$$A\begin{bmatrix}b_1, b_2\end{bmatrix} = \begin{bmatrix}1 & \emptyset & \emptyset \\ \emptyset & \emptyset & 1 \\ 1 & 1 & \emptyset \\ 1 & 1 & 1\end{bmatrix}\left[\begin{bmatrix}1\\1\\\emptyset\end{bmatrix}, \begin{bmatrix}\emptyset\\1\\1\end{bmatrix}\right]$$

$$= \left[\left(\begin{bmatrix}1\\1\\1\end{bmatrix}\smile\begin{bmatrix}\\1\\1\end{bmatrix}\right), \left(\begin{bmatrix}\\1\\1\end{bmatrix}\smile\begin{bmatrix}1\\1\\1\end{bmatrix}\right)\right] = \begin{bmatrix}1\\1\\1\end{bmatrix}, \begin{bmatrix}1\\1\\1\end{bmatrix}$$

Now that we have defined the multiplication of two (logical) matrices we are in a position to ask what will happen if we multiply P by itself. We use the notation

2 $\qquad\qquad P^2 = PP$

If we look back to section 12.3 we see that the operator can be said to *map a set of parts onto the set of its immediate precedents*.

The column P^j of P selects the immediate precedents of the part "j" and as PP^j maps these onto their precedents the result vector selects the precedents of the precedents of "j", or the *second precedents of "j"*. If we now extend this to the operation with P on all columns of P, that is to the operation $PP = P^2$, we find that the columns of P^2 are the selection vectors for the second precedents of the parts of the system.

It is now easy to conclude that P^2, when used as an operator, will map a part (or a set of parts) onto the set of its second precedents.

In a linked data structure, with links corresponding to the precedence matrix P, P "maps" each system part onto its precedents. It does it simply by pointing to these precedents, see Fig. 1.

System with
links corresponding
to P

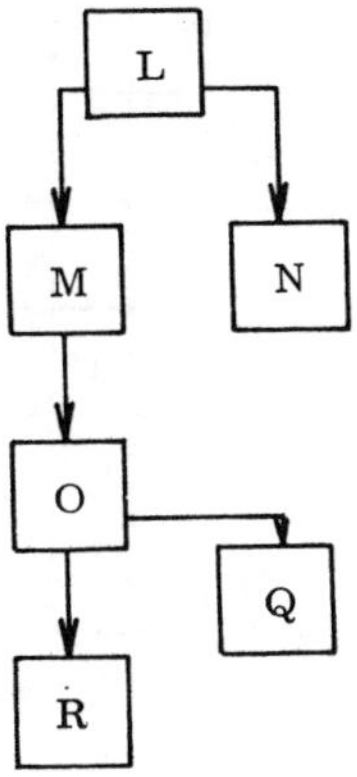

Fig. 1

It is also easy to see how the links corresponding to P^2 are to be drawn, see Fig. 2. The link from L in Fig. 1 which corresponds to P^2 has to point to the 2nd precedents of L, i.e. the 1st precedent of M which is O, and the 1st precedent of N, which does not exist, see Fig. 2.

System with
links corresponding
to P^2

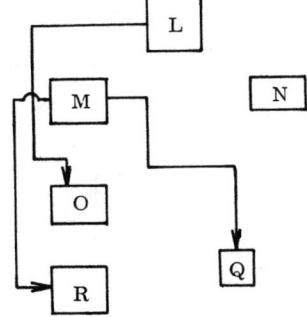

Fig. 2

3 Then $P^3 = P^2P$, $P^4 = P^3P$, ... $P^n = P^{n-1}P$ in an analogous fashion define operators for the third precedence, the fourth precedence and so on.

Further it is easy to see that if all paths in the systems graph, obtained by going from one part to one of its precedents, and then to a precedent of this one, are of length l at most, then P^{l+1}, P^{l+2}, ... will all be identically zero.

4 **Exercise.** Compute P^2 for Fig. 1, section 12.2, and interprete the result.

5 Exercise. Set up P for the system of Fig. 1 and then compute $P^2 = P(\cup)P$. Compare with Fig. 2.

$$P^2 = PP = P(\cup)P =$$

	L	M	N	O	R	Q
L						
M	1					
N	1					
O		1				
R			1			
Q			1			

$(\cup)$

	L	M	N	O	R	Q
L						
M	1					
N	1					
O		1				
R					1	
Q					1	

Hence $P^2 =$

$\underbrace{\text{L}}_{M} \;(\cup)\; \underbrace{\text{M N}}_{N \ O} \;;\; \underbrace{}_{} \;;\; \emptyset \;;\; \underbrace{\text{O}}_{R} \;(\cup)\; \underbrace{}_{Q} \;;\; \emptyset \;;\; \underbrace{\text{R Q}}_{}$

L	M	N	O	R	Q
1					
		1			
		1			

$=$

	L	M	N	O	R	Q
L						
M						
N						
O	1					
R		1				
Q		1				

The notation used indicates that on the "right hand side" we have two columns of P which are selected by the two units in the first column (column L) in the second P in P($\cup$)P. These columns are M and N and by placing L above them we indicate that they were selected by the L-column.

Obviously one can perform the operation P²($\cup$)s of identifying the 2nd precedents of a set S in two ways first by using links corresponding to P, as in Fig. 1, in combination with an algorithm which takes two steps along the link paths from every system part in the set S, or one can, alternatively, introduce P²-links, as in Fig. 2, and then use an algorithm which takes simple steps along these links. As it is so simple to indicate, just by writing P² instead of P, the use of a double step algorithm upon the set of P-links, there is normally no need to introduce the complication of adding P²-links, to the system. The fact that P²-links allow identification of 2nd precedents in one step may be of importance in the implementation of the data structure and the algorithms in a computer, because the retrieval of the records which are 2nd precedents would save one physical retrieval operation. However, we are presently only interested in a logical study and may therefore well disregard the problems of physical efficiency.

It is obvious that our study of the problem of identifying precedents is valid for any type of relation, which has been represented by links in the data structure. Thus P($\cup$)A indicates the identification of those records which are named (or otherwise pointed to) under the label P in the record for A. It is natural that we might design the record in such a way

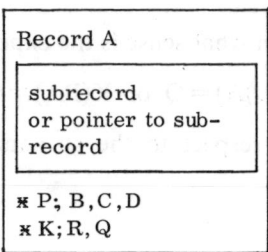

Fig. 3

that there is another label, K, which has a similar form as P[1]). We may, for instance, take these labels by preceding them by an asterisk as in Fig. 3. In the example of Fig. 3 we have

---

[1]) Obviously we may use an arbitary number of differently named links, each associated with a specific relation.

$$P(\cup)A = B, C, D \text{ or } PA = B, C, D$$

and it is then natural to say, also that

$$K(\cup)A = R, Q \text{ or } KA = R, Q$$

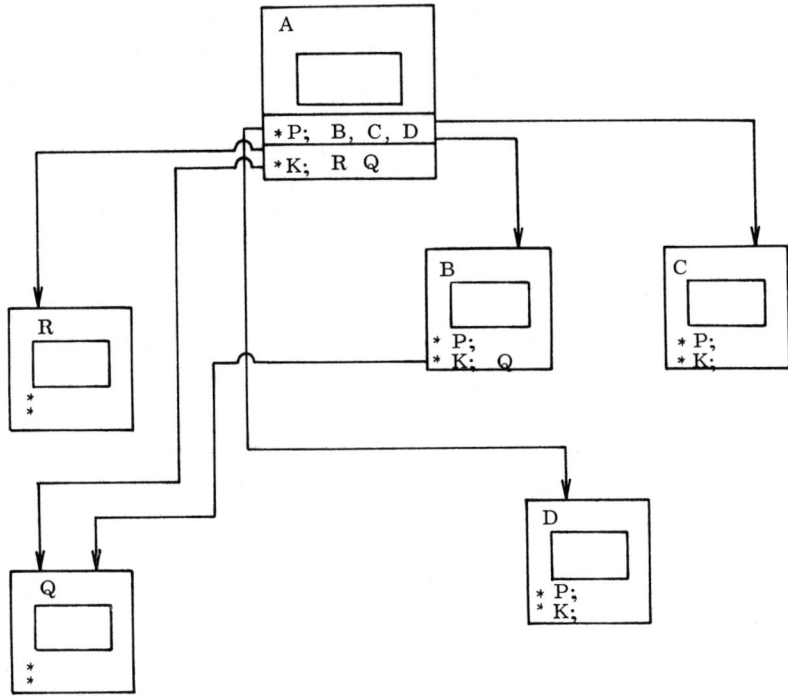

Fig. 4

6 **Exercise.** In what sense is the expression

$$K(\cup) (P(\cup)A) = Q \text{ or } K(PA) = Q \text{ or } KPA = Q$$

true, with respect to the structure of Fig. 4.

12.8 Succedence Matrix P_T.

We have seen in Theorem, section 12.3, that a row "i" of the matrix P is a selection vector for the succedents of the part "i". Therefore if we form the matrix P_T (or P^T) which has the rows of P as its columns, and which is called the transpose of P, then this matrix P_T will be a succedence operator for the graph.

Clearly P_T is an operator which "moves" in a direction that is opposite to that of P. Thus in Fig. 1, section 12.2, P maps downwards and P_T will instead map upwards.

Note that the operation P_T is not the inverse of P in that in general

1 $\qquad P_T(Ps) \neq s$

2 $\qquad P(P_T s) \neq s$

For instance in Fig. 2.1 we have

3 $\qquad P_T B = A$

4 $\qquad PA = B, C, D$

Hence

5 $\qquad P(P_T B) = PP_T B = B, C, D$

Likewise

6 $\qquad PB = E$

and

7 $\qquad P_T PB = B, C,$

However, if we iterate we obtain

8 $\qquad P_T(PP_T B) = P_T P(P_T B) = P_T(B, C, D) = A$

so that

9 $\qquad P_T P(P_T B) = A = P_T B$

Thus when P is applied to $P_T B$ then P_T is the true inverse of P (in this example).

113

10 Similary $\quad P(P_T P)B = PP_T(PB) = P(B, C) = S, F \neq PB$

or
$$PP_T(PB) \neq PB$$

so that when P_T is applied to PB then P is not the true inverse of P_T (in this example). Instead we find that if we replace B by C then P is a true inverse of P_T in this example.

11 **Conjecture.** If P is applied to a complete succedence set (or a set of such sets) then P_T is its inverse and if P_T is applied to a complete precedence set (or a set of such sets) then P is its true inverse[1]).

12 **Example.**

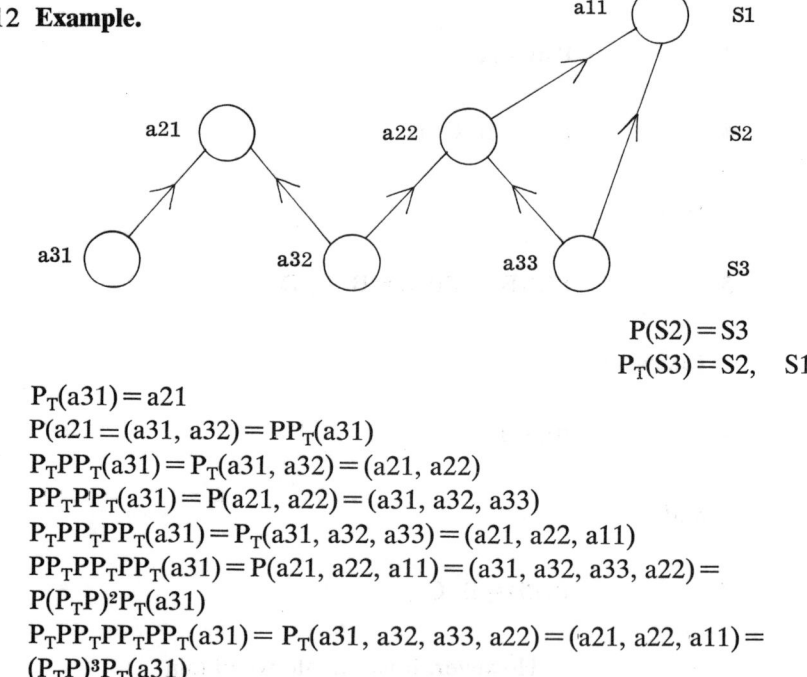

$P(S2) = S3$
$P_T(S3) = S2, \quad S1$

$P_T(a31) = a21$
$P(a21 = (a31, a32) = PP_T(a31)$
$P_T PP_T(a31) = P_T(a31, a32) = (a21, a22)$
$PP_T PP_T(a31) = P(a21, a22) = (a31, a32, a33)$
$P_T PP_T PP_T(a31) = P_T(a31, a32, a33) = (a21, a22, a11)$
$PP_T PP_T PP_T(a31) = P(a21, a22, a11) = (a31, a32, a33, a22) = P(P_T P)^2 P_T(a31)$
$P_T PP_T PP_T PP_T(a31) = P_T(a31, a32, a33, a22) = (a21, a22, a11) = (P_T P)^3 P_T(a31)$

$P_T P(a21, a22, a11) = (a21, a22, a11)$

so that P_T is a true inverse of P with respect to (a21, a22, a11). Thus (a21, a22, a11) qualifies as a complete succedence set of a31.

---

[1]) Notice that we have not defined "complete succedence set" and "complete precedence set" used in the 11 Conjecture. Show that in 12 Example the complete succedence set of a31 cannot be a21 but must be a21, a22, a11. Show that to obtain this we have to iterate $P_T P$ a number of times.

Note that starting from a32 we get

$$(a21, a22, a11) = (P_T P) P_T (a32)$$

13 Example. Literature retrieval using the reference lists given in the literature.

Let D be a given document.
Regard references given in D as precedents of D.
Then symbolically we may write: references of $D = P \cdot D$.
This is called the *reference index*. Then
inverse reference ("citation index") $= P^T D$ defines the set of documents referring to D. Then for example $(P(P^T D)$ defines other documents referred to by those documents referring to D and are therefore related to D in some meaningful way.

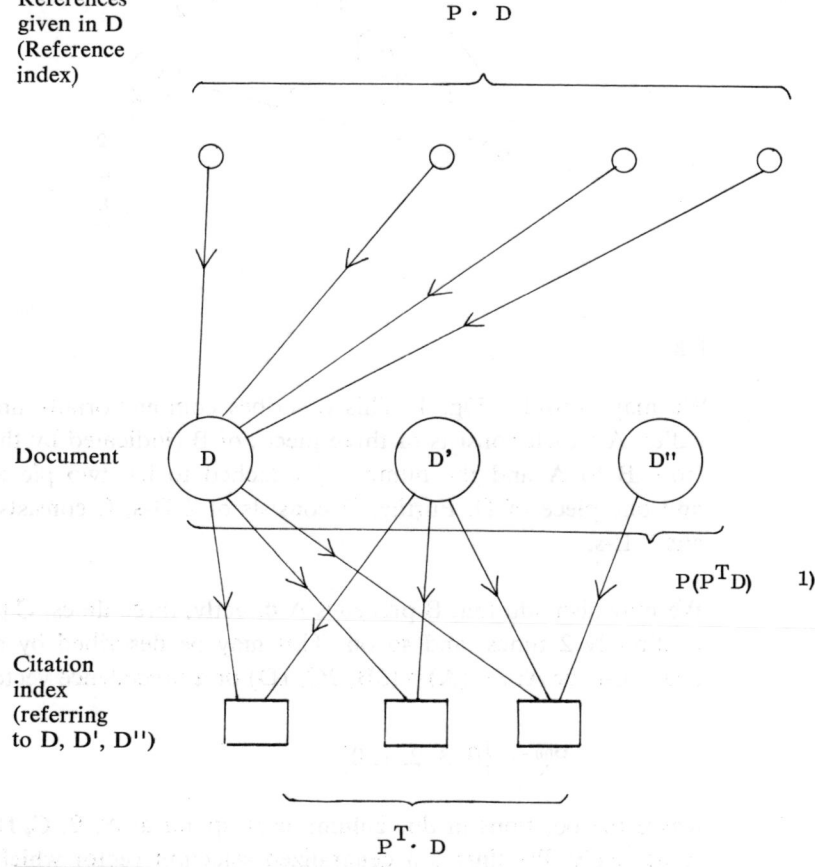

[2]) Cf. 2 Br 1965.

12.9 Generalization of the Precedence Concept.

Let us suppose that we have an object which is built up from a number of other objects. These smaller objects or subassemblies each in their turn may be built up from still smaller subassemblies or parts. The construction of the top object or final assembly can only be done after its nearest subassemblies have been completed. The latter therefore can be regarded as direct precedents with respect to the final assembly. The whole construction can obviously be described combinatorially by a precedence graph.

Example.

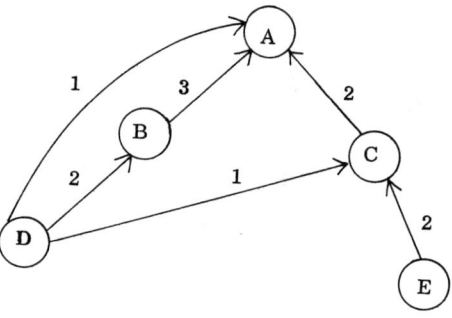

Fig. 1

We may consider Fig. 1. This describes combinatorially an object called A which consists of three pieces of B (indicated by the arrow from B to A and the number 3 attached to it), two pieces of C, and one piece of D. Further B consists of 2 D-s, C consists of 1 D and 2 E-s.

We may also add that B precedes A directly, three times, C precedes A directly 2 times, and so on. This may be described by a precedence list for A: $\mathscr{P}(A) = (3B, 2C, 1D)$ or a precedence vector for A

$$1 \qquad P_A^{00} = \{0, 3, 2, 1, 0\}$$

where the positions in this column correspond to A, B, C, D, and E respectively. P_A^{00} thus is a generalized selection vector which selects 3 pieces of B, 2 of C, and 1 of D.

In this way we can put the precedence columns for all the objects A through E together to form a (generalized) precedence matrix. This is a *numerical* or *quantitative* matrix, rather than a Boolean one:

2

$$P^{00} = \begin{array}{c|c|c|c|c|c|} & A & B & C & D & E \\ \hline A & 0 & 0 & 0 & 0 & 0 \\ \hline B & 3 & 0 & 0 & 0 & 0 \\ \hline C & 2 & 0 & 0 & 0 & 0 \\ \hline D & 1 & 2 & 1 & 0 & 0 \\ \hline E & 0 & 0 & 2 & 0 & 0 \\ \hline \end{array}$$

Remark. We use here P^{00} instead of P because we shall soon need to distinguish this precedence matrix from other ones to be defined. The double zero for upper index will indicate the fact that the precedence relations defined by P^{00} are concerned with points versus points. Points are taken as 0-dimensional parts of the graph hence the 00 in P^{00} reminds us that we have to do with relations of points to points.

Computation of precedence quantities by means of P^{00}.

In section 12.3 we have seen that the logical P^{00} matrix could be used to compute the precedents of a part, or a set of parts. This was done by means of the (logical) matrix-by-vector multiplication $P^{00}s$, where the element "i" of s, or s_i would select the i-th column of P^{00}. Now that we have a numerical rather than a logical matrix P^{00} we redefine the selection operation so it will also be a numerical one.

$$\text{if } s_i \neq 0,$$

then s_i times the i-th column of P^{00} is selected.

Further we introduce pseudo-multiplication, which we denote by "(.)" for the composition of P^{00} and s which does not involve the summation of the selected columns[1]).

---

[1]) Note that the "non summing operation" leads to a number of columns to store, which multiplies for each level. This is an important problem which will often require some measures for reduction. In practice therefore "summing multiplication" will be used as far as possible and "non summing" will be used only where it leads to significant, economic gains in the application system. This may be the case in production control applications.

3 $\quad P^{00}(\,.\,)s = s_1 P^{00(1)}, s_2 P^{00(2)}, \ldots s_m P^{00(m)};$

Then easily we can compute the normal matrix by vector multiplication by simply performing a summation of $P^{00}(\,.\,)$s.

Thus

4 $\quad P^{00}s = \sum\limits_{1}^{m} s_i P^{00(i)} = \text{sum } (P^{00}(\,.\,)s).$
$\phantom{P^{00}s = \sum\limits_{1}^{m} s_i P^{00(i)} = }\,1{:}m$

As an example let $s_T = s_T^0 = (5, 0, 0, 0, 0,)$ and P^{00} as in 2 above. Here s_T is the transposed vector s. Thus s is a column.

Then

5 $\quad P^{00}(\,.\,)\,s^0 = 5 \begin{array}{c}\text{A}\\\begin{array}{|c|}\hline 0\\ 3\\ 2\\ 1\\ 0\\\hline\end{array}\end{array} = \begin{array}{c}\\ \text{A}\\ \text{B}\\ \text{C}\\ \text{D}\\ \text{E}\end{array} \begin{array}{c}\text{A}\\\begin{array}{|c|}\hline 0\\ 15\\ 10\\ 5\\ 0\\\hline\end{array}\end{array} = s^1$

6 Then $P^{00}(\,.\,)\,s^1 = 15 \begin{array}{c}\text{A, B}\\\begin{array}{|c|}\hline 0\\ 0\\ 0\\ 2\\ 0\\\hline\end{array}\end{array}, 10 \begin{array}{c}\text{A, C}\\\begin{array}{|c|}\hline 0\\ 0\\ 0\\ 1\\ 2\\\hline\end{array}\end{array}, 5 \cdot 0 = \begin{array}{c}\text{A, B}\\\begin{array}{|c|}\hline 0\\ 0\\ 0\\ 30\\ 0\\\hline\end{array}\end{array}, \begin{array}{c}\text{A, C}\\\begin{array}{|c|}\hline 0\\ 0\\ 0\\ 10\\ 20\\\hline\end{array}\end{array},$

Here A, B (for instance) identify the column selected by element B of the previously selected column A.

7 and $P^{00}s^1 = \begin{array}{|c|}\hline 0\\ 0\\ 0\\ 40\\ 20\\\hline\end{array}\quad$ by summing (A, B) and (A, C).

12.10 A Generalized Matrix by Vector Operation.

We see now that a matrix-by-vector composition may always be denoted in one and the same general form A(op)B.

We introduce the matrix operations mentioned by way of examples. It should not be difficult for the reader to interpret the result in the most general way. To illustrate, A(op)B could mean (for instance)

$$1 \quad \begin{bmatrix} a_{11} & a_{12} & a_{13} \\ a_{21} & a_{22} & a_{23} \end{bmatrix} (\text{op}) \begin{bmatrix} b_1 \\ b_2 \\ b_3 \end{bmatrix} = b_1 \text{op}_1 \begin{bmatrix} a_{11} \\ a_{21} \end{bmatrix} \text{op}_2 \; b_2 \text{op}_1 \begin{bmatrix} a_{12} \\ a_{22} \end{bmatrix} \text{op}_2 \; b_3 \text{op}_1 \begin{bmatrix} a_{13} \\ a_{23} \end{bmatrix}$$

$$= \begin{bmatrix} b_1 \text{op}_1 a_{11} \\ b_1 \text{op}_1 a_{21} \end{bmatrix} \text{op}_2 \begin{bmatrix} b_2 \text{op}_1 a_{12} \\ b_2 \text{op}_1 a_{22} \end{bmatrix} \text{op}_2 \begin{bmatrix} b_3 \text{op}_1 a_{13} \\ b_3 \text{op}_1 a_{23} \end{bmatrix} ;$$

Thus the operation symbol (op) is a symbol for a set of three sub-operations op_0, op_1 and op_2, the first of which, op_0, is always the same. op_0 is the "selection" of the i-th column (A^i) of the matrix $A = (a_{ji})$. This is performed above by writing each vector element together with the column it has selected. The second suboperation is denoted by op_1.

op_1 will be different for each different (op) but we shall always assume that when we call an operation (op) then its suboperations op_0 and op_1 always consist of the selecting element b_i together with each one of the elements in the selected column. The third suboperation, op_2, defines how the columns resulting after op_1, are to be composed or, rather, how the elements of these columns are to be composed to form the final result. If we take (op) to be the conventional matrix by column multiplication we leave out the symbol (op). op_2 will then be the normal, scalar, addition. In this case we have

$$2 \quad Ab = \begin{bmatrix} b_1 a_{11} \\ b_1 a_{21} \end{bmatrix} + \begin{bmatrix} b_2 a_{12} \\ b_2 a_{22} \end{bmatrix} + \begin{bmatrix} b_3 a_{13} \\ b_3 a_{23} \end{bmatrix} = \begin{bmatrix} b_1 a_{11} + b_2 a_{12} + b_3 a_{13} \\ b_1 a_{21} + b_2 a_{22} + b_3 a_{23} \end{bmatrix}$$

if A and b stand for the same matrices as above[1]).

We earlier[2]) found reason to use the modified operation (.) which differs from conventional matrix-by-column multiplication only in that op_2 is put equal to "concatenation" only, by which we mean

---

[1]) Note that when Ab is computed by means of "column selection" as shown here then A is to be sorted by columns. In conventional matrix operation schemes A is instead to be sorted by rows. As a consequence, if we want also some composition $A^T c$, where A^T is the transposed matrix, we can obtain this without resorting to the matrix A if we use instead the conventional scheme for this operation.

[2]) See section 12.9—3.

that the columns instead of being added are just written one after the other, separated by, for instance, a comma. Thus

3 $A\ (.)b = \begin{bmatrix} b_1 a_{11} \\ b_1 a_{21} \end{bmatrix}, \begin{bmatrix} b_2 a_{12} \\ b_2 a_{22} \end{bmatrix}, \begin{bmatrix} b_3 a_{13} \\ b_3 a_{23} \end{bmatrix};$

or

$A\ (.)b = \begin{bmatrix} b_1 a_{11}, & b_2 a_{12}, & b_3 a_{13} \\ b_1 a_{21}, & b_2 a_{22}, & b_3 a_{23} \end{bmatrix};$

12.11 Generalized Matrices.

It should be observed that once we admit of more general operations for op 1 and op 2 then we allow for more general elements in the matrices, vectors and scalars (A "scalar" is a single element) as well. For instance the elements need no longer be restricted to numerical (or Boolean) values. They may be e.g. sets or alphabetical text or matrices or decision tables or reference links (pointers) or data structures.

12.12 Matrix Operations as Processing of Data Structures.

1 If the matrix *M and the vector v are each stored in a magnetic tape file the* operation M(op)v will call for a data processing operation involving four main steps. The first of these, the column selection, will be a file matching operation of the common file updating type, and the third will be a normal sorting operation, while the second and fourth steps are simple arithmetic procedures. The column selection operation will read one element at a time (as a record or subrecord) within the tape file carrying v, and then the file carrying M, where a record carries one column of M, is scanned until a column having the same number as the v-element is found (or until it is obvious that there is none). Then the v element is operated upon the elements in the M-column, and the result put on the output file. A subsequent sort operation is then needed to collect elements with the same row number (of M) from the different columns. Finally a composition operation of the collected elements may, or may not, have to be performed[1]).

---

[1]) Cf. also section 12.5.

It is important to note that as we may assume standard computer programs to take care of the use of file storage for handling the matrices and operations on them, we need not have these problems in mind. We can better forget about the computer and file storage in most of our problem analysis and think in terms of the much more convenient matrix algebra manipulations.

2 **Example.** Let the vector $v = [1, 0, 3, 0, 5]$ be given and have to be operated on the matrix P^{00} as shown above [2]) by P^{00} (op)v.

We have the files

$$P^{00}: A(3B\ 2C\ 1D)\ B(2D)\ C(1D\ 2E)$$

$$v: A(1)\ C(3)\ E(5)$$

We have indicated each file record by an identifier followed by a parenthesis containing the remaining items of the record.

The column selection will now run as:

a. read record from v: A(1)
   read record from P^{00}:   A(3B 2C 1D)
   operate v_i on P^{00i}:   A(1 (op_1)3B 1(op_1)2C 1(op_1)1D)
   write on output file

b. read record from v: C(3)
   read record from P^{00}:   B(2D)
      identifier B from P^{00} does not match the selecting
      identifer C, hence
   read next record from P^{00}:   C(1D 2E)
   operate with v_i: C(3 (op_1)1D 3(op_1)2E)
   write on output file.

c. no more match.

The output file now contains

A(1(op_1)3B 1(op_1)2C 1(op_1)1D) C(3(op_1)1D 3(op_1)2E)

---

[2]) See section 12.9—2.

We now sort on the identifiers within the parentheses:

a. we find no element within parentheses which has identifier A.

b. we find only in the first parenthesis an element with identifier B, this element contains: $1(op_1)3$. It is put first on the sorted file.

c. we find elements "named" C in the first parenthesis only. Perform as under b.

d. we find elements "named" D in both parentheses: Hence the result file obtains the element $D(1(op_1)1, 3(op_1)1$ (notice that this time we need a comma or some other separator between the two terms, as the first finishes with a number and the other starts with a number).

e. we find an element named E in the last parenthesis.

the output now is the file

$B(1(op_1)3)$ $C(1(op_1)2)$ $D(1(op_1)1, 3(op_1)1)$ $E(3(op_1)2)$

To proceed further let us assume that we specify

(op_1) shall indicate that the elements "joined" by (op_1) shall be multiplied *and* that op_2 then indicates that all elements within one record are to be summed. This means that (op) is the standard matrix multiplication.

Only the parenthesis after D contains two elements. These are to be composed according to op_2; hence they are to be added.

We then obtain

$B(3)$ $C(2)$ $D(4)$ $E(6)$

as the final result. (For instance $D(4) = D(1 \cdot 1 + 3 \cdot 1)$).

3 Notice that for the data processing we can have standard programs for the column selection and for the sorting, while one may use different programs for different operators (op). As a check let us compute

$$P^{00} \cdot v = \begin{bmatrix} 0 & 0 & 0 & 0 & 0 \\ 3 & 0 & 0 & 0 & 0 \\ 2 & 0 & 0 & 0 & 0 \\ 1 & 2 & 1 & 0 & 0 \\ 0 & 0 & 2 & 0 & 0 \end{bmatrix} \begin{bmatrix} 1 \\ 0 \\ 3 \\ 0 \\ 5 \end{bmatrix} = \begin{bmatrix} 0 \\ 3 \\ 2 \\ 4 \\ 6 \end{bmatrix} \begin{matrix} A \\ B \\ C \\ D \\ E \end{matrix}$$

which is seen to give the same result.

Such general matrix manipulation schemes are not available as yet. We guess that they will become standard in the future. The advantage will be that one can use the same data structure in the data files representing matrices and vectors and one can have the same basic data handling procedures. A change from one kind of matrix by vector operation to another, will need only a change of the simple programs which are to perform the operations "op_1" and "op_2". As the data handling routines are by far the most complicated ones, this is a significant increase in the flexibility and generality that can be achieved in a system for matrix operations. Such a system will therefore be of much greater help in general systems work than has been the case before.

If a direct-access file storage is used the handling of the matrix operations by computer takes on a slightly different form.

The notation for the matrix P^{00}

P^{00}: A(3B 2C 1D) B(2D) C(D 2E)

could be interpreted such that (A3B 2C 1D) would be a record where A would be a data term giving the address in the direct-access store where a record describing the item A would be stored. This data term could be called "succedent address" term. Analogously, B, C, and D would be represented by data terms working as "precedent address" terms. In this way we have a situation which is fairly similar to the magnetic tape file.

The item records A, B, C etc. will contain address terms as well which contain the addresses of the respective P^{00} columns. For instance the item record A will have a data term giving the address of the record "A(3B 2C 1D)" i.e. the address of column A of the matrix P^{00}.

A computer program will now be able to traverse the structure given by P^{00} in both directions.

4 There are some reasons why a modification of the representation of P^{00} as given above is in order. A record type such that a matrix column makes one record means that record lengths are varying. To handle varying length records on magnetic tapes is normally easy because the files are copied onto another tape in each operation. In a direct memory this is not the case and, therefore, varying record length would introduce either the drawback of having to move data, when length changes, or the drawback of having to reserve space for maximum length for each record. The common way to solve this problem is to split up varying length records into smaller parts of fixed length. In our example this could be done by having a record for each element in the matrix P^{00} rather than one record for each column. We would then obtain: P^{00}: A3B A2C B2D A1D C1D C2E.

5 However, in order to be able to use storage space wherever available in a direct store one normally uses a scheme where every record may be given any position, This, however, means that the positions of different elements of a column in P^{00} will no longer necessarily follow each other in sequence. To find them all we would therefore either have address data terms for all of them, rather than only one for the column, stored in the item record for A (which would thus be of varying length) or one will have to let one element in a matrix column point to its succeeding one by having an address term, for instance called "next element address". In this case we say that the records of a matrix column form a *chain*. The choice of alternatives will depend on the types of problems that will be most common. In some cases one method will call for fewer access operations and in other cases the other. The way which is most similar to our approach would be to let each element in a column point to the next element in the column, for in this way the concept of matrix column would retain its function in our system.

We would then obtain:

P^{00}: A 3 B next   A 2 C next   A 1 D A
      B 2 D B
      C 1 D next   C 2 E C

where the last element in each column has its "next-term" contain the column identifier. Thus the end of a chain representing a matrix column refers back to the head of that chain so that the chain forms a cycle.

Notice that to save storage space we have paid the price of allocating more space to every record. The problem is whether or not a net gain results. We have also gained flexibility, however.

6   In Fig. 1 we have shown how the *linking* address terms in the records set up connections between the records in the store.

7   It is obvious from Fig. 1 that the link from each record in a column (e.g. from [A 2 C next] back to [... col A A]) is not necessary when the records are connected to a chain. Again, whether to delete the link or not is a matter of how much it will be used. In Fig. 2 the links from column elements to the corresponding item record have been deleted. In addition the item records have been moved in the figure so as to better reflect the structure.

8   Notice that we have to decide carefully whether a link (such as the one pointing to the item with which a column is associated) is to be retained or not, for a change of a record format is not easy, once the system has been implemented. On the other hand, if only a field, sufficient for storing one link address, is held in reserve then it can always be used to set up a chain of records and the chain can have completely variable length. In fact it is not even necessary to have a special link field reserved for we can always use the existing outward pointing link to connect a chain, but this may be more awkward for the processing.

9   It is now easy to see how a column selection operation would be performed on a chained record structure such as in Fig. 2. Suppose for instance that the demanded vector v has the form

      v:A(17) . . . . .

The element A(17) of v as shown would be stored in a record with a link address corresponding to A.

The program would read A(17) and use A, to fetch the element record in the chain of column A of P^{00}, that is: (3 B, next). It would then multiply the quantity, i.e. 3, of that record with the quantity 17 of the v-record and the result. 51, would then be stored into the item record for B, pointed to by B in (3 B, next).

The program will then use "next" to fetch the next element record in the column chain, i.e. (2C, next), if during this process there will later on be generated more requirements for item B the program will either simply add these to the quantity 51, obtained above, or one may want to store each requirement separately, in which case one will also want an identifier for each individual requirement. In such a system one would rather not store the quantities in the item records but set up a chain to the record for item A.

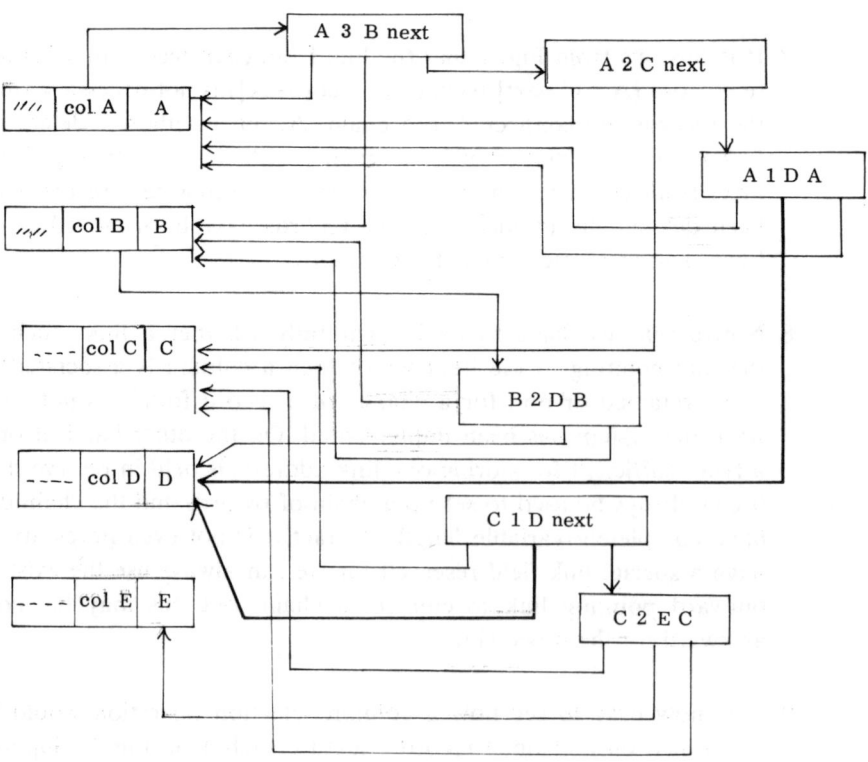

Fig. 1

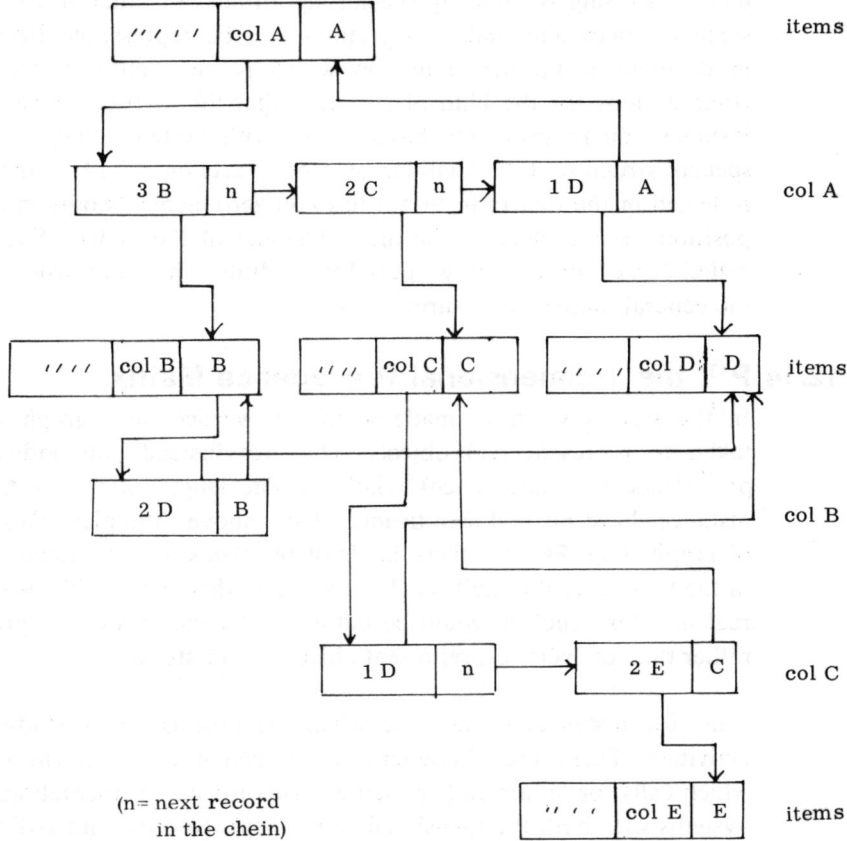

Fig. 2

10 It is important to notice, once more, that a system for handling general matrix procedures — as well as other systems analysis procedures — need only contain a single set of "utility procedures" for handling data in the data structure so that only the very simple programs corresponding to "op_1" and "op_2" need be made in different versions for a general matrix handling system to be implemented or adapted to changing needs.

12.13 Other Kinds of Algorithms for Processing Data Structures

The information about a system that can be computed by matrix operation may sometimes be computed by alternative algorithms, sometimes called "topological" ordering. These may be done faster in a computer. One may well use matrices as symbols while actual data processing is done by special algorithms. In other words, the same matrices and matrix operations can be represented by data in different ways, depending on which is most efficient for the computations for the kind of structure that the matrices have. For instance, many problems have to do with systems that have a special structure (cf. "cellular systems", section 11.14) which is reflected in the matrix in that it has non-zero elements only in such positions as are close to the main diagonal of the matrix. Such so called *band matrices* allow special procedures which are faster than the general matrix procedures.

12.14 P¹¹, the 1-dimensional Precedence Matrix.

In the studies we have made so far the vertices in a graph were taken to represent real objects. The arcs instead only indicated precedence (or succedence) relations. The length of the arcs, for instance, have no real significance in the above examples. This use of graphs (e.g. P⁰⁰) for these kinds of problems is quite dominating in the literature. We shall see, however, that there are problems from real life, for which it would be natural to let the arcs of the graph, rather than the vertices, represent objects under study.

This, for instance, is the case when the objects under study are activities. These are characterized by having a length (in time) which calls for an arc rather than a vertex for its representation.
Systems with both 0-dimensional components (0-cells) and 1-dimensional components (1-cells) are called 1-complexes. (The 0-cells and 1-cells are sometimes defined as 0-simplexes and 1-simplexes.)

1 **Example.** Suppose that three groups of people, let us call them g(a), g(b) and g(c), respectively, travel from three different places, A, B, and C. They all travel to a place D at which all people from g(a) and some of the people from g(b) and g(c) form a new group g(e) and go in common to a place E. The remaining people from g(b) and g(c) form a new group g(f) and go from D to a new place F.

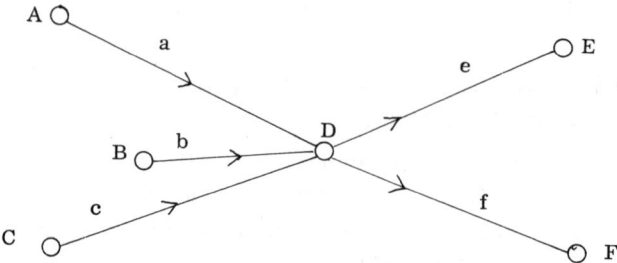

Fig. 1

When we considered precedence relations between vertices in a graph, every precedence relation was represented by an arc. In our problem here arcs are the objects we study. We may then instead consider vertices as the representatives of immediate precedence relations. In Fig. 1 the vertex D indicates a relation that any arc that is incident toward D precedes any arc incident away from D. By "incident toward/away" we mean a contact between an arc and a vertex where the arc is directed toward/away from the vertex.

2 P^{11}

We may use a precedence matrix to represent precedence relations between arcs (just as we used precedence matrices P^{00} for vertices[1]), although this has only occurred in a few cases in the literature[2]). A precedence matrix for arcs will be denoted by P^{11}. The upper indices 11 are used to indicate that both elements considered in any relation are 1-dimensional ones, i.e. arcs.

P^{11} has one row and one column for each arc in the graph. Each column in P^{11} selects those arcs which are 1st precedents of its associated arc.

3 Example.

The precedence matrix P^{11} (for arcs) for the graph of Fig. 1 is

$P^{11} =$	a	b	c	e	f
a				1	1
b				1	1
c				1	1
e					
f					

4 Basic properties of P^{11} for a graph.

P^{11} has one special property, which is not shared by P^{00}:

4a Theorem.

If $P^{11(i)} \cap P^{11(j)} \neq \emptyset$ then $P^{11(i)} = P^{11(j)}$; ($P^{11(i)}$ denotes the i-th column in P^{11}).

or: either $P^{11(i)} \cap P^{11(j)} = \emptyset$ or $P^{11(i)} - P^{11(j)} = \emptyset$

or: If there is some row of P^{11} in which two columns, i and j, both have unit value, then they have units in exactly the same rows.

---

[1]) See section 12.3.
[2]) 1 La 1962-1.

This follows from the fact that if for instance $P^{11}_{ki}=1$ (the element in row k and column i of P^{11}) and $P^{11}_{kj}=1$, then both arcs i and j are incident away from the end point K of k. Hence all arcs ending in K form the set of 1st precedents of both i and j.

5 **Example.** Fig. 1 gives a usable graphic representation of the "geographical" aspects of 1 Example.

If we are interested in planning the journeys of 1 Example, however, we may instead be interested in other precedence relations. Then the same graph is not effective any more.

When considering time we note that the journey e made by the group g(e) cannot start before the journeys a, b and c have been completed. We now may express this by saying that a, b and c are precendents of e, that is

$$P(e) = \{a, b, c\};$$

This corresponds to the precedence matrix

		a	b	c	e	f
P =	a				1	
	b				1	1
	c				1	1
	e					
	f					

We note that P violates *4a Theorem* so that P cannot be a precedence matrix P^{11} for arcs of a graph.

It is not hard to see that we might simplify the problem slightly by regarding f as being preceded also by a. In this way the precedence matrix P would satisfy 4a Theorem and the graph of Fig. 1 would map also the time precedence relations. This deviation from the true conditions may however be very disadvantageous in some cases. It would mean that in case a can only be finished a long time after b and this symbolism would make us let the start of f wait this amount of time, which would not be necessary if we follow the true constraints only.

6 **Mixed precedence of arcs.**

We have seen from 4a Theorem and 3 Example that a problem occurs when we have a kind of mixed precedence relations for some arcs. Thus when two objects have precedence sets which contain partly, but not completely, the same elements, this situation cannot be represented by a graph in which each object is represented uniquely by one arc. It can on the other hand easily be represented by a precedence matrix P. This P cannot be a P^{11} for a graph and it will violate 4a Theorem[3]).

Notice that this problem is only associated with the graph. It thus only occurs when we insist on a diagrammatical representation. In the matrix representation there is no problem.

The difficulty occurs because two arcs with different precedents sets must be incident away from two separate points. Then any object which is a precedent for both the given arcs would have to be represented both by an arc incident toward the first point and by an arc incident toward the second one thus the uniqueness of representation is invalidated.

This problem of mixed precedence for arcs can be removed by the introduction of additional vertices toward which such arcs are incident as are precedents of more than one object. These additional vertices are then connected to the initial vertices of their different successors by "dummy" arcs which are not associated with any objects. These dummy arcs only serve to indicate precedence relations.

7 **Example.** For the problem of 3 Example we have two successor arcs e and f. The arcs b and c are precedents for both whereas a is a precedent for e only.

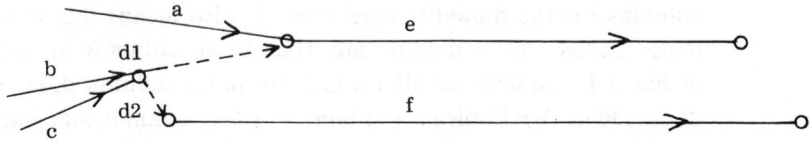

Fig. 2

In Fig. 2 this problem has been represented by a graph with arcs representing the objects a, b, c, e and f (the travels) in a unique way.

The arcs d1 and d2 are dummies. If time increases when we move to the right in Fig. 2 then time intervals associated with the travels

---

[3]) 1 La 1962-1.

are represented by the distance that the terminal point of an arc has to the right of its initial point. Length of an arc thus is taken as the length of its "horizontal projection". For the dummy arcs, length may go down to zero but it may not be negative so that all arcs must be directed to the right (or be vertical, which gives them zero length of horisontal projection, i.e. zero length of time).

In Fig. 2 the earliest time that e can get started must be the same or later than the earliest start time for f. This means that we may put d2, but not d1, equal to zero, without imposing unnecessary restrictions. Thus Fig. 2 can be simplified to Fig. 3.

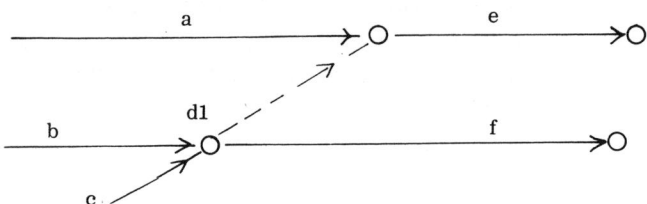

Fig. 3

Exercise. Show that now P will satisfy 4a Theorem.

8 Generalized precedence matrix for arcs $\tilde{P}^{11}$.

What the dummy arcs do to solve the problem of mixed precedence is by transforming the objects that are mixed precedents from being 1st precedents to becoming 2nd precedents. The introduction of new arcs (the dummy ones) calls for new rows and columns in P^{11}. P^{11}, as well as P^{00}, defines by its columns 1st precedence relations. We introduce now a new precedence matrix P^{11} for arcs, in which every dummy arc as a 1st precedent is replaced by the 1st precedent of this dummy. This means that in P^{11} no rows and columns for the dummies need exist. It also means that if a row d^1 is associated with a dummy arc, then in all columns in which row d^1 has a 1, are inserted all 1 s that are in the column d, i.e. column d^1 is added (by Boolean addition) to every column that has a 1 in row d^1, whereupon the column d and the row d are deleted. (See 9 *Example*.)

9 Example. Let P^{11} be the precedence matrix, for arcs, for fig. 2a.

	a	b	c	d1	e	f
$P^{11} =$ a				1		
b				1		1
c				1		1
d1					1	
e						
f						

The only column in P^{11} in which row d^1 has a 1 is e. Thus we insert into column e the 1s that are in column d^1, i.e. in rows b and c. We obtain now, after deleting row d^1 and column d^1,

	$\tilde{a}$	$\tilde{b}$	$\tilde{c}$	$\tilde{e}$	$\tilde{f}$
$\tilde{P}^{11} = \tilde{a}$				1	
$\tilde{b}$				1	1
$\tilde{c}$				1	1
$\tilde{e}$					
$\tilde{f}$					

We also check that actually e is obtained by Boolean addition (or by taking union) of the columns d^1 and e:

$$\begin{array}{cccccccc}
 & a & b & c & d1 & e & f \\
e = & \{1 & 0 & 0 & 1 & 0 & 0\} \\
d^1 = & \{0 & 1 & 1 & 0 & 0 & 0\} \\
e \cup d^1 & \{1 & 1 & 1 & 1 & 0 & 0\}
\end{array}$$

From $e \cup d1$ we obtain $\tilde{e}$ by deleting the fourth element.

10 **Remark.** For the generalized precedence matrix $\tilde{P}^{11}$ the restriction of 4a Theorem does not apply.

11 **Example.** For comparison let us use a graph in which vertices are taken to represent objects associated with the problem of 1, 5, and 7 examples.

The objects then will not be the activities (travels) but rather events (points in time) that are associated with them *in a unique way*.

We then have a planning network of the "Pert-type". We may for instance consider as events (and as vertices in the graph) the earliest instances at which one or more activities can get started. If (A), (B), (C), (E), (F) and (G) are the events defined in this way for the activities a, b, c, e, f and g, when g is supposed to be a successor of both e and f, we get Fig. 4.

Figures 2 and 3 also represent planning networks which are, however, not of the Pert type. They may be classified as activity networks.

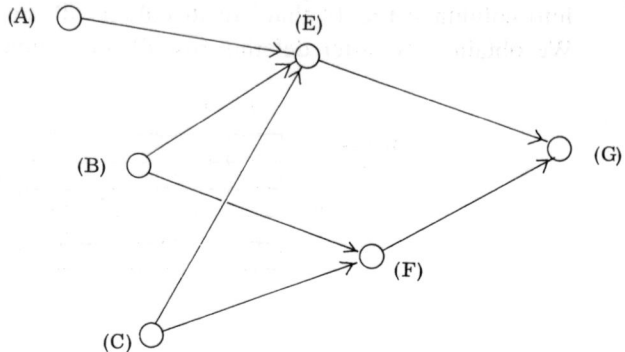

Fig. 4

In this diagram (Fig. 4) note that for instance the arc (B) (E) only indicates that (B) must precede (E) and that this only means that the start of b must precede the start of e. There is nothing in Fig. 4 to indicate also that the completion of b is to precede the start of e. If one also tries to give this meaning to the arrow (B) (E) then one actually makes (B) (E) represent the activity b, that is one has an activity graph as in 1 Example for instance. Then, however, also the problem arises that (B) (F) also would be thought to represent b while in fact we have no unique representation of activities.

12.15 P^{01} and P^{10}, Precedence Matrices for Mixed 0-1 and 1-0 Dimension Respectively.

The constructions of P^{00} and P^{11} indicate how precedence operators which specify vertices that precede arcs and vice versa could be constructed, and that these might be denoted by P^{01} and P^{10}, respectively.

1 *Definition of P^{01}, the matrix of initial vertices.*

P^{01} has for each arc one column which selects the vertex which is the precedent of that arc. P^{01} thus has one row for each vertex of the graph.

2 **Theorem 1.** Every column in P^{01} has one single element equal to 1; all other elements in the column being zero.

The element with unit value indicates by its row-number the vertex which is preceding the arc associated with the column, that is it indicates the initial vertex of the arc.

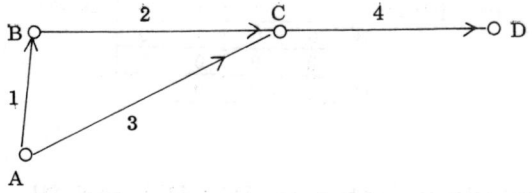

Fig. 1

3 Example. For the graph of Fig. 1 we have

$$P^{01} = \begin{array}{c} \\ A \\ B \\ C \\ D \end{array} \begin{array}{|cccc|} \hline 1 & 2 & 3 & 4 \\ \hline 1 & & 1 & \\ & 1 & & \\ & & & 1 \\ & & & \\ \hline \end{array}$$

4 *Definition of P^{10}, the matrix of incoming arcs.*

P^{10} has one column for each vertex, and one row for each arc. Every column in P^{10} selects the arcs which are precedents for its associated vertex.

Each column has value 1 in all rows that correspond to arcs which are precedents to the vertex of that column. Notice that P^{10}_T is a matrix which is similar to P^{01} and which indicates the terminal vertices of the arcs.

5 Example. For the graph of Fig. 1 we have

$$P^{10} = \begin{array}{c} \\ 1 \\ 2 \\ 3 \\ 4 \end{array} \begin{array}{|cccc|} \hline A & B & C & D \\ \hline & 1 & & \\ & & 1 & \\ & & 1 & \\ & & & 1 \\ \hline \end{array}$$

6 Example.

$$P^{10} \cdot P^{01} = \begin{array}{c} 1 \\ 2 \\ 3 \\ 4 \end{array} \begin{bmatrix} 1 & 2 & 3 & 4 \\ 0 & 1 & 0 & 0 \\ 0 & 0 & 0 & 1 \\ 0 & 0 & 0 & 1 \\ 0 & 0 & 0 & 0 \end{bmatrix} = P^{11}$$

7 **Example.**

	A	B	C	D	
$P^{01} \cdot P^{10} =$ A	0	1	1	0	$= P^{00}$
B	0	0	1	0	
C	0	0	0	1	
D	0	0	0	0	

12.16 Relations Between P^{01}, P^{10} and P^{11} and P^{00} Respectively.

In examples 12.15—6 and 12.15—7 we found that the products $P^{10} \cdot P^{01}$ and $P^{01} \cdot P^{10}$ respectively gave results which happened to satisfy

1
$$\begin{cases} P^{01} \cdot P^{10} = P^{00} \\ P^{10} \cdot P^{01} = P^{11} \end{cases} \quad {}^{1})$$

It is easy to see why this has to be so. If v is any selection vector for vertices then $P^{10} \cdot v$ gives the selection vector for the arcs preceding these vertices. Hereupon $P^{01} \cdot (P^{10} \cdot v)$ gives the vertices preceding these arcs and these are precisely the vertices preceding those selected by v that is $P^{00} \cdot v$ so that we shall have

2
$$P^{00} \cdot v = P^{01} \cdot P^{10} \cdot v$$

which can hold for arbitrary v only if $P^{00} = P^{01} \cdot P^{10}$.

We thus have obtained half of the theorem:

3 **Theorem.** For any pair P^{01}, P^{10} the relations in 1 above hold true. The other half of this theorem is proved in a similar way.

12.17 Definition of E^{10}, the Incidence Matrix.

We now define another matrix for the graph, which is often of great interest. We define the matrix E^{10}, which has one row for each arc of the graph (one dimensional elements) and one column for each of its vertices (zero dimensional elements).

---

[1]) An example is given in part 2, chapter 10.

1 Let $e_{ij} \in E^{10}$ then we define

$$e_{ij} = \begin{cases} -1, & \text{if } i \ll j \\ 1, & \text{if } j \ll i \\ 0 & \text{otherwise} \end{cases}$$

for the one dimensional object "i" and the zero dimensional object "j". e_{ij}[1]) are called incidence numbers, associated with the 1-cell "i" and the 0-cell "j".

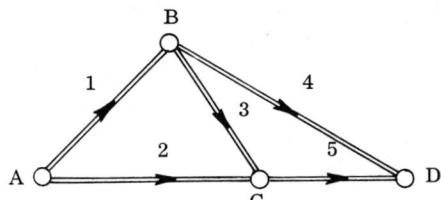

Fig. 1

	A	B	C	D
$E^{10} =$ 1	1	-1		
2	1		-1	
3		1	-1	
4		1		-1
5			1	-1

2 **Theorem.**
$$E^{10} = P^{01}_T - P^{10}$$

3 **Exercise.** Show that P^{00} can be obtained from E^{10}.

12.18 Boundary Operation on a System and the Incidence Matrix.

In our discussion of a very simple system, section 11.9, we mentioned that a common class of entities which exist in network-like systems, such as the one shown in Fig. 1, section 12.17, is the class of flows. A flow may be the flow of material through a production process, or, for instance the flow of electricity through a network.

---

[1]) The sign convention used here is opposite to the one most common in literature, see for instance 1Ax1957, 1El1966 and 1Ij1965. One is, of course, free to use any sign convention which appears most suitable. (Cf. section 27.7)

A typical property of many kinds of physical flows is the zero-sum property at each node of a network and over each branch of the network (cf. section 11.9). In mathematical systems theory one therefore often *defines* a flow to be an entity having the zero-sum property. The zero-sum property means that the sum of all flows meeting at a node will be zero, provided of course that flows directed towards the node are taken with a sign that is opposite to that taken for flows directed away from the node. Thus, if we assume, for instance, that in the system shown in Fig. 1, 12.17, there is a flow in branch 1 which has value 3 and is directed away from node A and if in branch 2 there is a flow of 2, likewise away from A, then the zero-sum property requires that there should be a flow from outside *into* node A which has the magnitude $3+2=5$. If we take flows away from a node to be negative we can write down our argument as

1 $\qquad$ (external flow at A) $- 3 - 2 = 0$

so that we must have

2 $\qquad$ (external flow at A) $= 3 + 2$

We see that when the flow is known (with respect to magnitude and direction) for all branches in a network-like system then one can easily compute the external flows that must be attached to the system at its nodes (in order for the zero-sum property to hold true at each node). We will often find it convenient to refer to the external flows at the nodes as the *boundary flows* (or "the *boundary flow*" of the system as a whole) and the nodes themselves will then appear as the boundary of the system.

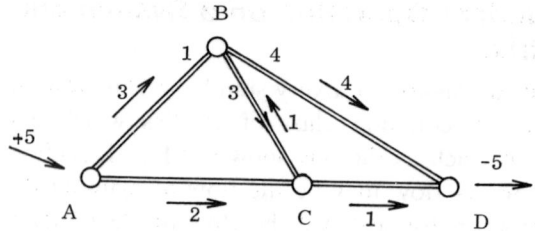

Fig. 1

In Fig. 1 we have indicated a hypothetical distribution of flows through the system of Fig. 1 in section 12.17.

The assumed flow is $(+3, +2, -1, +4, +1)$ where we have written the flow values for each of the branches in sequence of their numbering. The flow through branch no. 3 has been given a minus sign to indicate that it flows in a direction which is opposite to that shown by the arrowhead.

If we let q_A symbolize the boundary flow at node A (and so forth) we get

3
$$\begin{cases} q_A - 3 - 2 = 0 \\ q_B + 3 + 1 - 4 = 0 \\ q_C + 2 - 1 - 1 = 0 \\ q_D + 1 + 4 = 0 \end{cases} \qquad \begin{array}{l} q_A = 5 \\ q_B = 0 \\ q_C = 0 \\ q_D = -5 \end{array}$$

Thus all boundary flows are computed. This was done by a simple summing operation at each node. We now show that this boundary operation can be done for the whole system as one matrix operation involving the incidence matrix E^{10}. We multiply the transposal E_T^{10} of E^{10} by the vector p, where $p_T = [p_1, p_2, p_3, p_4]$ as given above: $p_T = [3, 2, -1, 4, 1]$. That is we compute $E_T^{10} \cdot p$. The vector p has 5 components, one component for each branch of the network and in $E_T^{10} \cdot p$ these components select one column each, from E_T^{10}. Now the columns of E_T^{10} correspond to the branches in the system so this is in order (it would not have been had we tried to multiply by E^{10}.) The result is

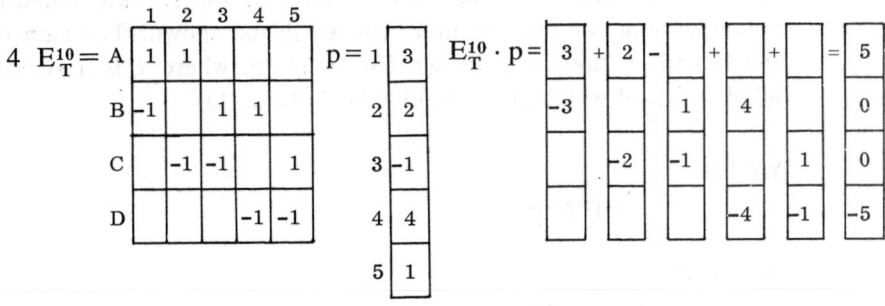

4

5 We get the vector $q =$ A: 5, B: 0, C: 0, D: -5

as the result. Thus in this case $E_T^{10} \cdot p$ resulted in a vector which associated with each node of the system exactly the value we found above (3) to be the value of the boundary flow which occurs at the nodes if the internal branch flows are as given by the vector p. It is not hard to see that this is not a coincidence but that we will quite generally have

6 $\qquad q = E_T^{10} \cdot p$

where q = vector of boundary flows
p = vector of internal branch flows.

7 We can express our result here by stating that E_T^{10} works as a *boundary operator* for flows p in the system. If we let ∂ symbolize the general concept of determining boundary flow values, i.e. ∂ is taken as a symbol for the concept of *boundary operation* so that $\partial(p) = (q)$, where we use (q) as a general symbol for boundary values, then we may say that we have found that matrix multiplication works as a boundary operation, where the incidence matrix after having been transposed, E_T^{10}, is a *matrix representation* for the operator ∂, when p and q are vector representations for internal flow and boundary flow, respectively.

8 We see in 5, and in Fig. 1, that the sum of all boundary flows equals 0. Thus the whole system has in common with each of its branch elements the zero-sum property for boundary flow. That this was not by coincidence, for instance because of the specific numeric values chosen for our example, can easily be shown. The sum of the boundary flows can be written as $1^T \cdot q$, where 1 is a vector, all elements of which are $=1$. $(1=(1, 1, 1, \ldots 1))$.

We have
$$q = E_T^{10} \cdot p$$

and hence
$$1^T \cdot q = 1^T \cdot E_T^{10} \cdot p$$

however $\qquad 1^T \cdot E_T^{10} = 0 \qquad = (0, 0 \ldots 0);$

which is easily seen as all columns of E_T^{10} have exactly two non-zero elements 1 and 1—1 respectively.

9 **Remark.** *"Boundary operation"* is defined in *algebraic topology* (homology theory, in a somewhat more narrow sense than ours[1]).

12.19 Co-boundary Operation and Incidence Matrix.

We found above (section 12.14) that by multiplying the internal flow vector p by E_T^{10} we obtained the boundary flow vector q. E_T^{10} thus defined the *transference* of flows from the interior to the boundary of the system. Obviously E^{10} would define a transference in the opposite direction (E^{10} is a reverse operator with respect to E_T^{10}.) If w is a vector which can be multiplied by E^{10} then w must have one component for each column of E^{10}, thus for each vertex of the system. Let us compute $E^{10} \cdot w$, using the matrix E^{10} of section 12.17.

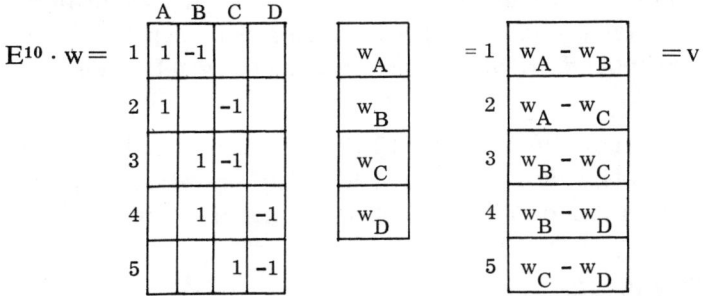

We see that the resulting vector v ($v = E^{10} \cdot w$) ascribes to each system branch the w-values of its end nodes (with minus sign associated with the node pointed to by the arrow indicating positive direction of each branch). If the w-components were to represent boundary flows in the nodes, the vector $v = E^{10} \cdot w$ would not make sense. If we assume instead that the w-values are representing potential values in the nodes, then we see that the vector v represents potential drops across the branches. Thus E^{10} performs a meaningful transference operation from the boundary to the interior, with regards to the interior, if associated with potentials and potential drops, respectively. This transference from boundary to interior is a *co-boundary operation* (δ). E^{10} is thus seen to work as a matrix representation for the co-boundary operator δ.

As we have discussed in section 11.9 each branch in a network may have associated with it a responsive property y, called for instance the *admittance* of the branch, and having the mathematical

---

[1] 1 Ax 1957, 1 HW 1960.

property that the product of the potential drop v (over the branch) times the admittancy equals the flow p. Thus for branch 1 we would have

$$y_1 (w_A - w_B) = p_1$$

and analogously for the other branches. We see now that if we form a matrix y that has the values y_1, y_2 etc along its main diagonal and zeros elsewhere then

so that
$$Y \cdot v = p$$
$$Y \cdot E^{10} \cdot w = p$$

with v as defined above ($v = E^{10} \cdot w$, $w =$ the vector of node potential values) and with $p =$ the vector of branch flows, the boundary potential *distribution* w generates an internal flow distribution p.

We know from section 12.18 that when p is determined then the boundary flow q, required to satisfy the zero-sum property at the nodes and over the branches, is determined by $q = E^{10}_T \cdot p$.

We thus find, using $Y \cdot E^{10} \cdot w = p$,

$$q = E^{10}_T \cdot Y \cdot E^{10} \cdot w$$

which is an equation by Gabriel Kron.

This equation has very interesting properties. It defines the boundary vector q which is the response by the system to an application of the potential distribution w. This is to say that the matrix

$$\overline{Y} = E^{10}_T \cdot Y \cdot E^{10}$$

is a response matrix ("admittance" matrix in this case) for the system as a whole, in the same sense that each Y_i is the responsive property ("admittance" — or "conductivity" for each branch i) and Y is the matrix of responsive properties of the set of branches of the system. Thus $\overline{Y}$ is an example of an important systems property which could be computed from the responsive properties of the system elements (branches) and from the topology of the system, as determined by E^{10}.

12.20 The Coincidence Matrix M^{10}.

We found above that the system response matrix Y could be computed from the matrix Y of branch response values y_i and from E^{10}, the incidence matrix. It should not go unnoticed that E^{10} also contains branch properties. It is often stated that E^{10} would just represent topological properties of the system. This was also stated above in section 12.15. For a full understanding of the system structure this misconception must be corrected. This may not be so important in the simplest applications (such as in electrical networks). Perhaps this is why the mistake is almost always unnoticed.

The branch property contained in the incidence matrix (when used as a boundary operator) is that flow through the branch obeys the zero-sum law. Thus in branch number i if the flow at one end is $=p_i$ then it is $=-p_i$ at the other end; that is the flow is the same but the signs are different because the branch flow is *away from* one end when it is towards the other end. We may express this by saying that if p_i is the flow in branch no i then $p_i^1 = \widetilde{p}_i$ and $p_i^2 = -\widetilde{p}_i$ are the *branch-end-flow values*. Thus if a single branch is studied alone it has two boundary points and if p_i is its boundary flow vector, $p_i^T = [p_i^1, p_i^2]$

We then have

1 $$p_i = \begin{bmatrix} 1 \\ -1 \end{bmatrix} \widetilde{p}_i$$

or

2 $$p_i = R^i_T \cdot \widetilde{p}_i$$

3 $$R^i = [1, -1]$$

4 We have assumed each branch element to have the property R_T, an *element boundary operator* such that $R = [1, -1]$.

Each branch element has ascribed to it two properties

$$z_i \text{ and } R^i.$$

5 In the example studied so far (as well as in the theory of electrical networks) only Y_i would vary from element to element whereas R^i was always $= [1, -1]$. In more general systems, however, also R^i will vary from element to element[1]).

---

[1]) See section 12.31.

6 Also in the general case a branch element may have a number of "boundary points" at each end and this number may vary from one end to the other. When we say that there is a number of boundary points at an end of a branch we mean that a number of distinct flow values is defined at that end of the branch.

7 In this general case we obtain

$$R^i = [(l_1^1, l_2^1, \ldots l_r^1), -(l_1^2, l_2^2, \ldots l_s^2)]$$

instead of $R^i = [1, -1]$. This indicates that if p_i is the internal flow p_i is obtained as the vector

8
$$p_i = \begin{bmatrix} l_1^1 \\ l_2^1 \\ \vdots \\ l_r^1 \\ -l_2^1 \\ -l_2^2 \\ \vdots \\ -l_s^2 \end{bmatrix}$$

(in the general case p_i is a vector and the l_j^i are matrices)

We found above that the transposed incidence matrix E_T^{10} worked as a boundary operator. (4 in section 12.8). It can easily be seen that in E_T^{10} each column i has strictly two non-zero elements, 1 and −1 respectively and that this corresponds precisely to the element boundary operator $R^i = [1, -1]$ for the branch associated with the column. This suggests that for a matrix to work as a boundary operator for a system of the more general kind where the element boundary operator for a branch is of the form 7 above, the incidence matrix E_T^{10} should be replaced by a matrix similar to E_T^{10} but modified in such a way that 1 has been replaced by the vector $(l_1^1, l_2^1, \ldots l_r^1)$ and −1 has been replaced by $(-l_1^2, -l_2^2, \ldots l_s^2)$. This can actually be shown to be the case. (See section 12.31 for a simple numerical illustration.) This means, however, that the definition of the new boundary operator matrix for a given system, the matrix of which we may again denote by E_T^{10} will be very complicated. Thus to set up E_T^{10} we no longer only have to determine the way each branch is connected to two system nodes but we must now define the incidence (or coupling) for each of the r+s boundary points of the branch. At the same time, we must also specify the elements $l_1^1, l_2^1 \ldots$ for each branch. In this situation it is of great importance to note that it is possible to factor the matrix. E_T^{10} into the form

$$E_T^{10} = M_T^{10} \cdot R_T$$

where, as we shall see, the matrix M_T^{10} defines only the system connections (i.e. how the branches are joined to the system nodes) and is independent of the branch boundary operators. R_T instead defines the set of branch operators. *This simple mathematical factoring has the important effect upon the systems analysis and systems description work, that one can separate the big task of defining the system connections from the likewise big task of defining all the branch boundary operators of the system. Yet one can, by means of a routine matrix multiplication, obtain the boundary operator for the whole system.* It is seen that the matrix M_T^{10} describes the system structure (or system topology) and nothing else. We call it the *"coincidence matrix"*. We have chosen this name because it reminds us of both the similarity and the distinction between the incidence matrix E^{10} and M^{10}. The incidence matrix defines for each branch its incidence with two of the system node points. "Incidence" in the mathematical discipline called algebraic topology (where the incidence matrix was defined) is used to denote the meeting of two "cells" of different dimensions such as lines (of 1 dimension) and points (of 0 dimensions). The coincidence matrix M^{10} introduced by us [1 La 1956] is defined similarly with the difference that for each boundary point of each branch we define which system point it coincidences with (i.e. which system node it is joined to). It follows from this description that the coincidence matrix M^{10} has one row for each boundary point of each branch and one column for each system node.

As a simple illustration let us establish the coincidence matrix M^{10} for the system Fig. 1 in section 12.17. We get

$$M^{10} =$$

	A	B	C	D
1_1^1	1			
1_2		1		
2_1^1	1			
2_2			1	
3_1^1		1		
3_2			1	
4_1^1		1		
4_2				1
5_1^1			1	
5_2				1

M^{10} has two rows for each branch. We have enclosed the pair of rows associated with one branch within double lines. We have chosen to denote that end of a branch from which the orienting arrow for the branch points away as the no. 1 end. Thus branch no. 1 of Fig. 1 in section 12.17 has its first end, 1:1 coincident with the system node A. This is indicated in M^{10} by putting a 1 in row 1:1, column A.

Theorem. Each row in M^{10} has exactly one element $=1$ and all others $=$ blank.

The proof is immediate. It follows from the fact that one end point of a branch can only coincide with one system node.

Of course, the natural way to store the coincidence matrix M^{10} (or its transpose M_T^{10}) on magnetic tape or other mass storages is to store one list for each branch which identifies the branch and for each of its boundary points the system node it is connected to.

When the author introduced the coincidence matrix[2] it was in connection with systems analysis of elastic structures and the development of automatic computation systems for elastic stress analysis, using programming systems capable of handling, automatically, large matrix operations. The coincidence matrices were of the order of several hundred columns and some thousand rows. In more recent computation systems of similar kind corresponding structures have been used. In the system Stress[3] it is also possible to simply list the elements and the system nodes they are joined to. They are using similar computational schemes but are missing the mathematical convenience of M^{10}.

To form the boundary operation matrix E_T^{10} we have to multiply M_T^{10} by R_T. How is R_T to be defined for this to hold true? It is simply formed as

$$R_T = \mathrm{diag}\ (R_T^i)$$

which means that R_T is formed as a matrix with the element boundary matrices R_T^i for each branch i placed along the main diagonal of R_T. It is easy to see that in this way R_T contains one

---

[2] 1 La 1956.
[3] Biggs. J. B., Logcher. R. D., "Stress: A problem oriented Language for Structural Engineering, The MIT press, Cambridge, Mass 1964.

row for each boundary point of each branch so that each row of R_T is corresponding to one column of M_T as it must in order for the matrix multiplication to be possible.

As a simple illustration let us form $M^{10} \cdot R_T$ for the system of Fig. 1 in section 12.17.

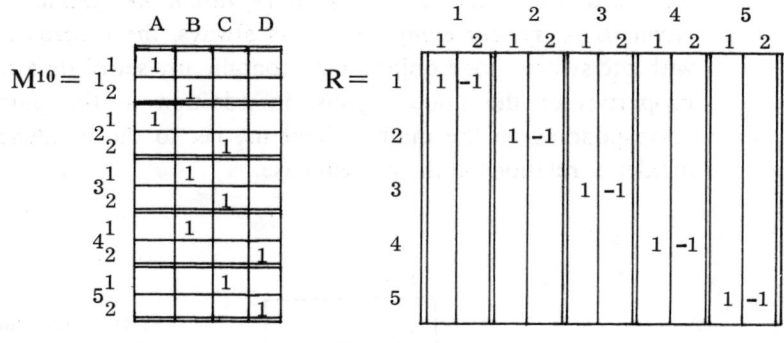

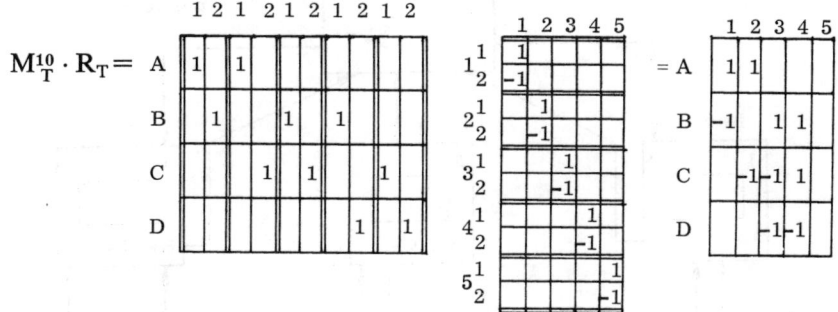

By comparison with E^{10} of section 12.17 we verify that the result is actually equal to E_T^{10}

For another illustration see section 12.31.

12.21 Data Structure Representation of Incidence and Co-incidence Matrices.

The incidence and coincidence matrices are data structures which contain representatives of two kinds of objects, referred to as system nodes (zerodimensional objects) and system branches (one-dimensional objects). As was shown to be the case with the system matrix P^{00} also the system matrices E^{10} and M^{10} normally will be represented by lists and linked chains of records. An algorithm for a matrix operation involving E^{10} or M^{10} will thus be an algorithm working upon this data structure. Contrary to the data structure for P^{00} we have for E^{10} and M^{10} to have two different kinds of records in the data structure, one, associated with systems nodes and another associated with branches. This way we also can illustrate *that it is always possible to add new record types to a data structure when necessary to represent new kinds of system elements or system components.* As always, the records associated with the system node objects may contain any set of data describing properties of the node objects, in addition to the pointer data corresponding to the matrix elements, i.e. to the incidence or co-incidence relations in the present case.

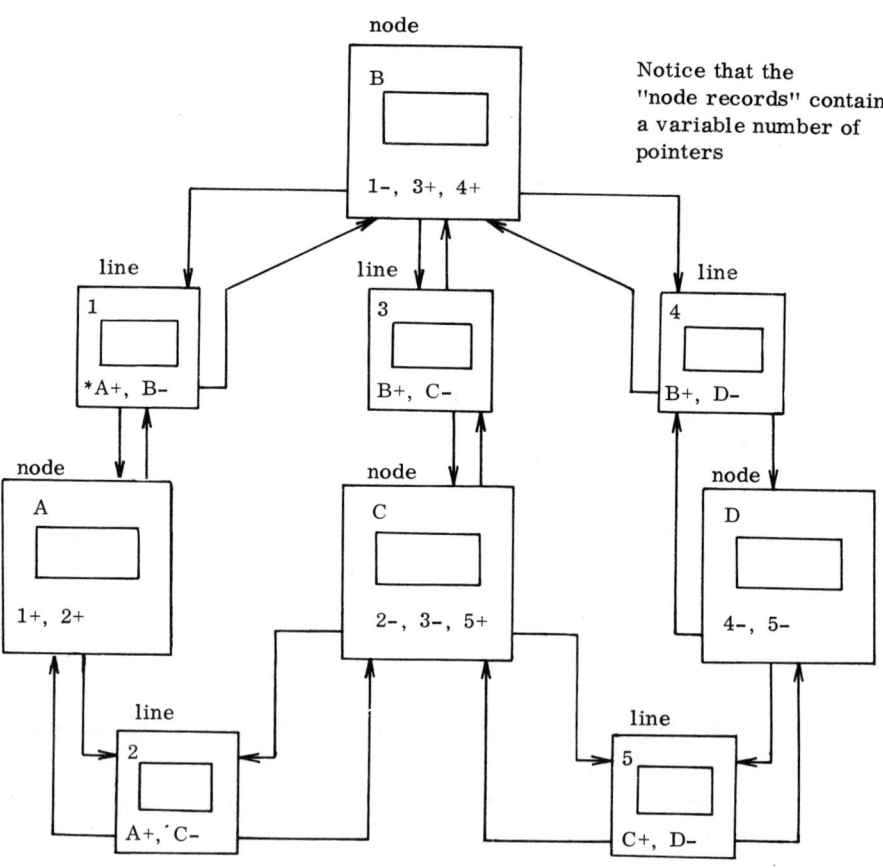

Fig. 1

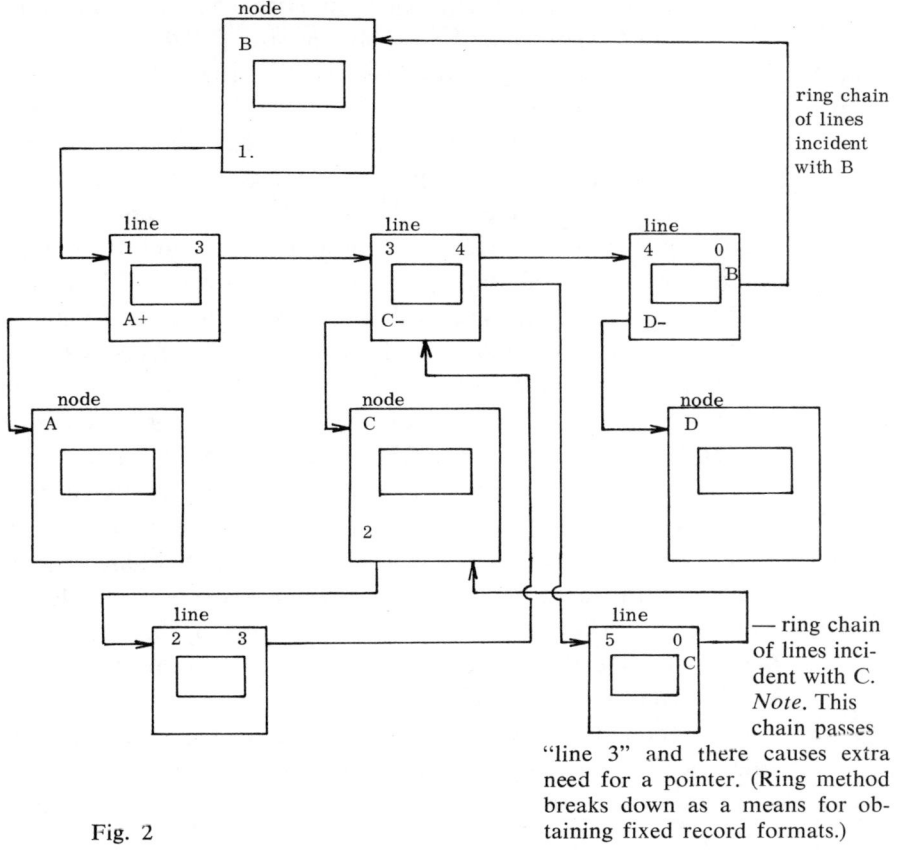

Fig. 2

In Fig. 1 we show a data structure for E^{10} of section 12.17. We have indicated two kinds of data records: records of type "node" and of type "line" respectively. A node record is assumed to have a set of pointers indicating all the lines which are incident with the corresponding node. In addition it is assumed that there is a subrecord containing data about the object associated with the node. This subrecord is indicated by the inner box. The set of pointers varies in length between the distinct node records. The line records instead always contain two pointers (to nodes).

In searching for a structure with fixed sizes of records of the same type (a property which is often desired when the data structure is on other storage media than tapes) in Fig 2, we have connected all line records associated with a node to a circular chain. The last line record in such a chain points back to the node. A problem here is that a line record may belong to more than one chain pointer. Thus the line record may be variable in size. On the other hand a line can be connected to two nodes only so it can only be contained in two chains. Therefore we may make the record have a fixed size by allocating two chain pointers to each line record, Fig. 3. In this design a record of type *line* has two pointers which point to the two nodes incident to the line. These pointers have been tagged by + sign or — sign, according to which end of the line is incident with the node pointed to. (For instance line 1 is assumed to have positive incidence with node A. Hence, the pointer is denoted in Fig. 3 by +A. Line 1 has negative incidence with node B, so it contains the pointer —B.) In addition each line record belongs to one circular chain of lines associated with each of the two nodes it is incident with. Therefore the line record type needs to have two more pointers, each of which points to its successor line in the circular line-chain, associated with each of the two nodes. There will be a problem for an algorithm working upon the data structure to recognize which of these two pointers belong to which chain. This can be solved, as in Fig. 3, by tagging the two pointers for the two line-chains with + and — respectively. As it can be seen in the record for line 1, it has negative incidence with node B (pointer is "B-"), then the pointer to the next line in the chain of lines of node B is the one with — sign. Thus "—3" indicates line 3 to be the next line in the chain of "B — incident lines".

The data structure for a system matrix (here E^{10}) is much more complicated in shape than the conventional matrix structure. It is clearly advantageous to have recourse to the matrices at least for the theoretical part of the systems design work. To apply the result of such work we then only recall that algorithms can always be designed perform all the matrix manipulations we may want on the data structure.

If the property data (indicated by the inner boxes in the boxes for the records, in our figures) are large, then the data structure in total may be much larger than the data structure for the matrix alone. Then it may be most efficient, from the data transport or retrieval point-of-view, to separate the matrix (i.e. the corresponding data structure) from the property data subrecords. By doing so we may make it possible to store the matrix in a faster storage during processing. This may lead to a large increase in speed of locating the record (or set of records) searched. For instance, if

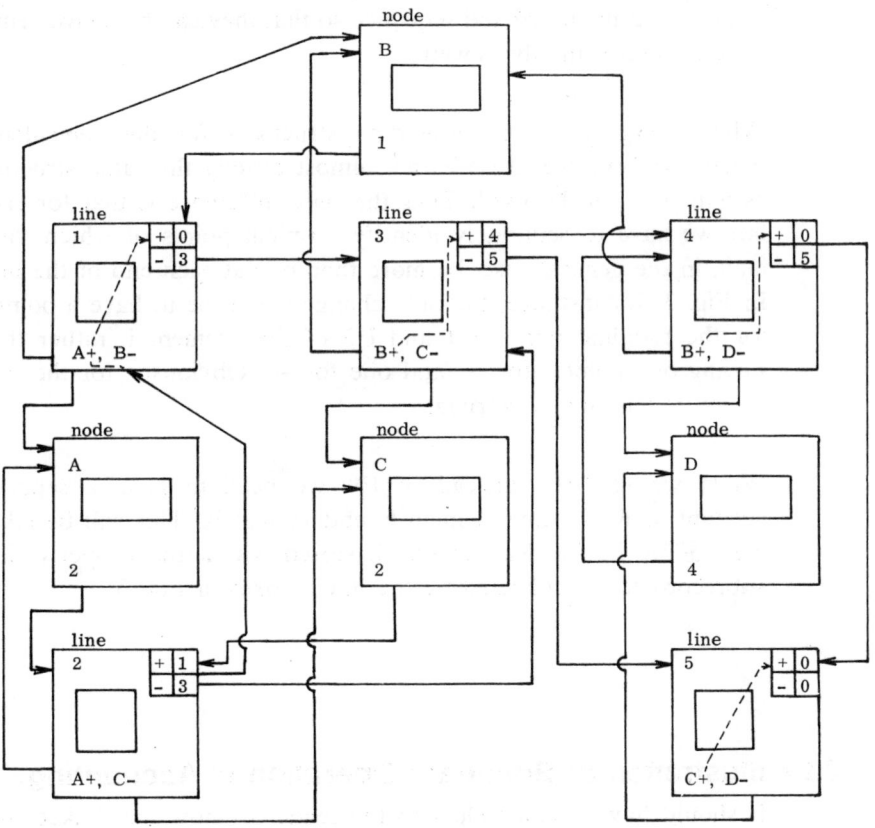

Fig. 3

the whole structure of Fig. 3 is stored on a disc storage it may take five (or more) accesses on the disc to reach the record "line 5", if we start at node B. If, on the other hand, the property data subrecords are stored separately in storage, with the records of Fig. 3 containing (in the inner boxes) only pointers to the property data subrecords then it may be possible to bring the incidence matrix data structure into the fast memory in its entirety (or in a sufficiently large portion) so that the retrieving of a single record may be done by one or very few access times for the slow data storage. This way of storing the references to the records separately (and not within the records) is usually (mostly in simpler cases) referred to as the use of "index tables" or "address tables". When the property data for the individual objects are stored in the "inner boxes" (cf. Fig. 3, for instance) then they may have variable length. They are often stored in an ordered sequence so that they can be conveniently processed sequentially as well.

When we go over to study data structures for the coincidence matrix M^{10} we see at once that almost exactly the same structure as with E^{10} can be used. Thus the only difference is that for each line we have to separately identify terminal points of which there may, in the general case, be more than one at each end of the line. In Fig. 3, for instance, the only change would be to have a pointer for the terminal points i 1 and i 2 of line element i, rather than having one pointer for + and one for —. Obviously, for the data structure this change is trivial.

When we use M^{10} instead of E^{10} we need to have a separate account of R, the line element boundary matrix. This will be taken care of by having R_i, for line i, stored within the property data subrecord for i, indicated by the inner boxes in Fig. 3.

12.22 Illustration of Boundary Operation in Accounting.

It should have become clear to the reader by now that linked data structures or system matrices are not merely theoretical, mathematical devices or computer methodology. Rather, they are models of existing real systems which are necessary aids for designing or controlling such systems. In order to illustrate this fact let us look at the accounting processes used in every business. It is immediately seen that double entry accounting is made up of operations on a data structure which describes the accounting system as designed by the business in question. We shall also see that this accounting system can be described by the incidence matrix E^{10}.

Remark. The use of incidence matrices in accounting was studied by Ijiri[1]).

---

[1]) 1 Ij 1965.

Code number of transaction	Type of transaction, assumed to be summed over one period
1	Purchase of material
2	Material used in production
3	Finished goods
4	Cost of finished goods sold
5	Revenue of sales

Assumed transaction vector for the period:

$$p = \begin{array}{c|c} 1 & 10 \\ 2 & 6 \\ 3 & 5 \\ 4 & 3 \\ 5 & 9 \end{array}$$

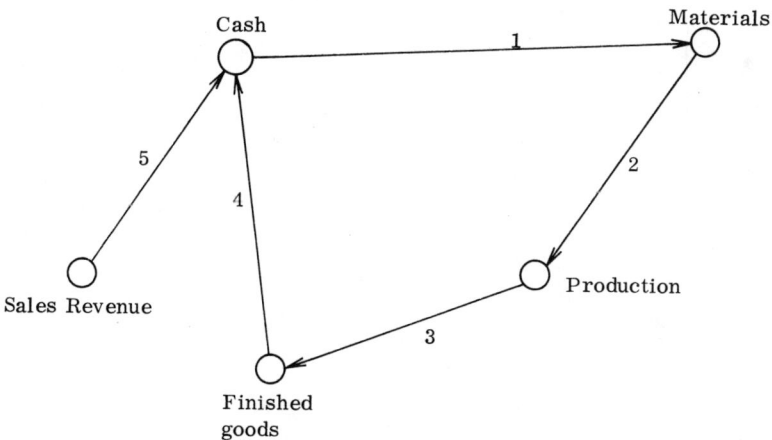

Fig. 1

If we compare Fig. 1 with Fig. 1 of section 12.18 we see that the boundary flow q obtained as $q = E_T^{10} \cdot p$ should compute the changes in the accounts associated with the nodes of Fig. 1.

On inspecting Fig. 1 we obtain E^{10} and then compute

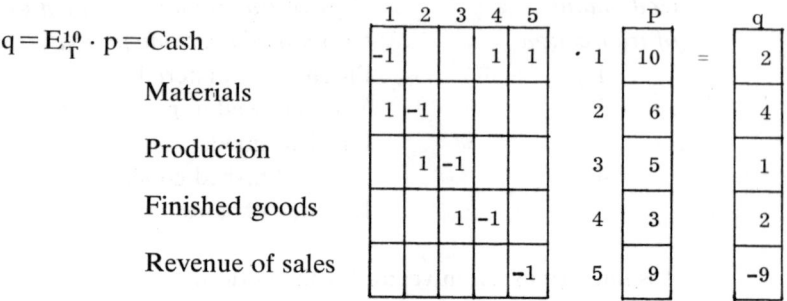

The result of our computation is thus that, during a given period Cash has been increased by 2 money units and Revenue has been credited by 9 (indicated by —9 in the last entry of q).

In Fig. 2 we have indicated roughly how the transaction system above would typically be reflected in the accounting system. It is seen that the traditional accounting system is in fact a system of data structures. We have emphasized this by drawing arrows in Fig. 2 corresponding to the pointers recorded in the accounts. These

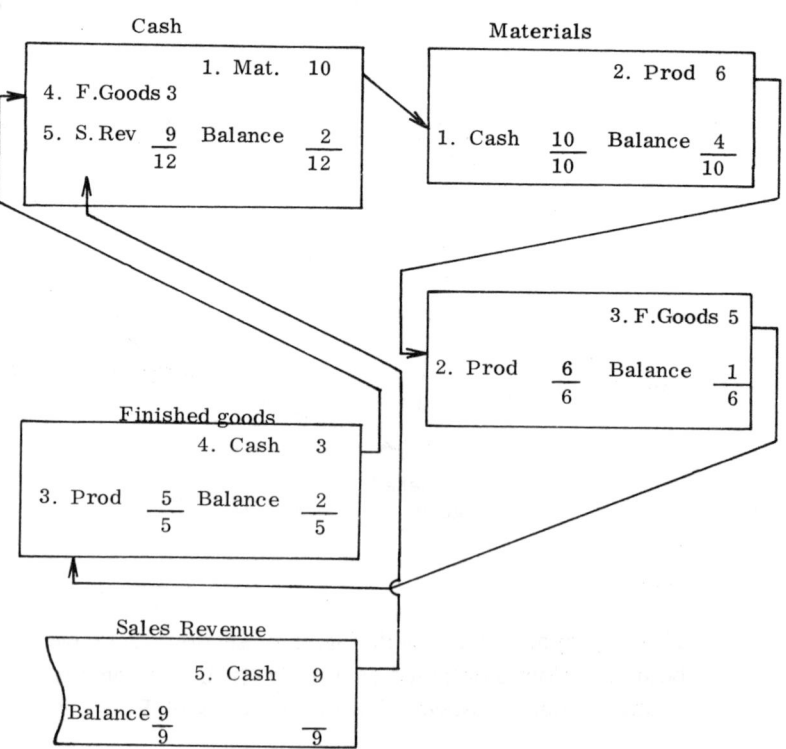

Fig. 2

pointers normally occur in accounting systems but the arrows do not (as they also do not in actual data structure of the types discussed before).

On comparing the system of accounts, as shown in Fig. 2, with the data structure of an incidence matrix as shown in Fig. 3 of section 12.17 we notice some differences. This is because the accounting system, as shown in Fig. 2, contains both the structural information, which is also contained in Fig. 3 of section 12.17, and the numerical data resulting from the transactions. These would go into the data subrecords (inner boxes in Fig. 3, section 12.17). This difference, of course, reflects the fact that Fig. 2 represents not E_T^{10} but $E_T^{10} \cdot p$ (with numeric values for the elements of p).

12.23 Built-up Systems and Gross Systems.

Important though it is to be able to study and design systems by defining them as built up from well defined parts by a well defined set of connections, that is as a "Built-up System" it will also often be the case, as we have already seen, that one will be interested only in some properties of the system as a whole, its external properties, without having to bother about how it is built up. For instance we shall see that a class of properties can be established in this way, for systems in general. This means that we save a lot of analysis to prove such properties for every new kind of structure that we may want to study. We see that thereby we obtain tools which may be used for workability tests, in some cases. We shall say that we then do "Gross Systems Analysis"[1]).

It also means that we can discuss a set of main properties of systems in general even before we have been very specific about details of the system structure. This will probably seem very abstract and diffuse to the reader at the first look. The reader should, in the first reading, try only to get a rough idea of the concepts of system problems and to become familiar with the definitions of such system properties as transference, response and boundary operation[2]).

Later in the book specific examples will show models where the concepts are represented in "concrete" form. After this the reader

---

[1]) The possibility of developing a general theory for gross systems analysis was presented and illustrated by the author in a guest lecture given at Chalmers Technical University in Gothenburg 1962 and in a guest lecture at Cornell University, 1963.
[2]) Cf. also section 11.17.

will be better prepared for a thorough understanding when re-reading this section.

It is also to be noted that when we talk of defining the properties of the elementary parts of the system then we treat these parts exactly as gross systems.

1 In gross system analysis we are interested in the relations between the system and different kinds of external entities which are impressed upon the system. These external entities we shall call *boundary variables*. It often will be convenient to regard the boundary variables to be active at a well defined set of points in the system. This set of points we shall call the *boundary* of the system.

2 The *properties* of the system will exhibit themselves by imposing *relations* between different sets of variables acting in the system. These relations may be between variables at one part of the system and variables of the same kind at another part.

3 Such relations we shall call *transference relations*, because they can be interpreted as a property of the system to transfer a certain set of values at one part to another set at another part.

4 As an example let q denote a set of boundary values of a certain kind, acting on the system S. Let the boundary of S be denoted by S_o and suppose S_o is partitioned into two parts S_o^1 and S_o^2.

5 Then suppose we have found that it is possible to compute the values q^2 of q at S_o^2 from q^1, that is the q-value of S_o^1. This may be symbolized as

6 $$q^2 = Lq^1$$

where L is a symbol for the "operator" which computes q^2 from q^1. L is an expression of a transference property of the system S with respect to the boundary variables q. (We may for instance look upon L as if it where a computer program, q^1 its input data and q^2 its output.) L will often be called a mapping from S_o^1 to S_o^2 and this will be denoted by

$$L: S_o^1 \longrightarrow S_o^2 \text{ or } S_o^1 \xrightarrow{L} S_o^2$$

As an illustration of transference properties we may take q_2 to represent the total cost for a product. q_1 may then stand for the costs of all parts and manufacturing operations. L will be a symbol for the procedure or operator computing total cost. L will obviously be a function of P^{00} for the product (or, rather, P_T^{00}). L expresses the transference of costs from input to output.

7 It will often be necessary to study values of variables acting at points of the system which are not regarded as boundary points, because there will never be an action from outside applied to these points. Such points will be called *internal*. They will be said to form the interior of S. If the system defines a transference from S_1, the interior of S, to S_o (its boundary) we shall say that the system defines a *boundary transference* or a *boundary mapping*. If p denotes the set of internal values of the variable of the kind denoted by q at the boundary, the boundary mapping can be symbolized as

$$\partial p = q \text{ and } \partial : S_1 \to S_o$$

Where ∂ denotes the *boundary operator*[3]).

8 Another important class of properties of systems are defined by relations between two sets of variables of different kinds but acting at the same part of the system boundary. Such properties we shall call *responsive properties*.

An example of a responsive property is the size "q" of the queue in front of a service station when the degree of utilization of the station is "p".
Another example is when q is the price and p the demand for a product. V is then the price elasticity and measures the responsive property of the market to a change in price. "Intangibles" result from responsive properties of the system.

9 *Note.* It follows from 6 and 8 that if $\partial^{(1)}$ denotes the part of ∂ which transfers from S_1 to S_o^1, then ∂ can be determined from $\partial^{(1)}$ and L.

10 It often occurs in a system that the boundary operator can be defined or computed in a simple and natural way while the converse transference from the boundary to the interior is not defined in the same simple fashion. Then it may be possible to compute the converse operator ∂^{-1}.

---

[3]) Cf. section 12.18-7.

11 $$p = \partial^{-1} q$$

by using ∂ as an auxiliary. ∂^{-1} is called an inverse *boundary operator*.

12 If in the system there exists some boundary variable, w for which the transference *inwards* — that is from boundary to interior — is defined in a natural way, then we call the inward mapping a *co-boundary mapping* and denote the corresponding operator by δ. Notice that δ and ∂^{-1} map in the same direction. The only reason for using the one or the other name and symbol is the existence or otherwise of a natural mapping in that direction.

13 We have made the supposition above that for some states in a system we shall find that the boundary operation is natural and that for some other kind of state a co-boundary operation is natural. When this is so we classify all states into three kinds: those which have natural boundary operation — which we shall call flows — those which have natural co-boundary — to be called, henceforth, *potentials* or *levels* — and those which are neither flows nor potentials.

14 A flow z may be such that the boundary operation ∂ maps it onto zero, that is

15 $$\partial z = 0$$

In that case we shall say that the flow state z is a *cycle*. Similarly if a boundary state r is such that its co-boundary disappears, that is

16 $$\delta r = 0$$

then r is said to be a co-cycle.

17 So long as we content ourselves with gross systems analysis only, we are not in a position to be able to deduce, or compute, the system properties such as the operators L, ∂, or δ. If they are given, however, we can use them for the mappings discussed. Only when we go to the detail of built-up systems analysis can we compute the system operators from properties of the system elements and the system connections.

18 As we have now supposed that in some way we have decided to subdivide the system into the *interior* and the boundary and also the kinds of system states into flows and potentials (if other states are neglected) we symbolically can consider the system as organized into four subsystems, i.e. internal flow, internal potential, boundary flow, boundary potential. This can be depicted as

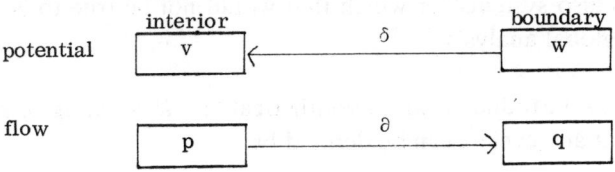

Fig. 1

19 However we have defined still more structure for the system states. Thus the internal flow can be partitioned into p_z and p_q, say, where p_z is a cycle flow, that is $\partial\, p_z = 0$. Likewise the boundary potential may have a component which is a co-cycle w^r. We thus have:

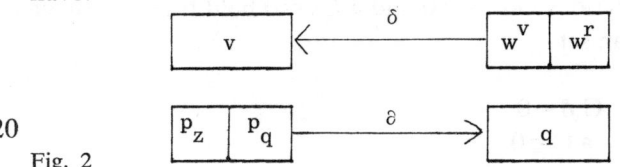

20

Fig. 2

21 We now notice that an arbitrary state may exist which is not of the type $\delta\, w$, that is a state which cannot be generated from any w, by δ. We can look upon δ as an operator which defines such internal states v as are compatible with the system connections. We therefore say that any v such that

22 $\qquad v \neq \delta\, w$ for any w (i.e. for any coboundary)

is an incompatible potential distribution and that it will generate "*gaps*" in the system connections. We introduce a (so far hypothetical) *gap-analyzing operator* G such that

23 $\qquad Gv = g =$ the state of gap caused by incompatibility of v.

We can now state:

$$G\,\delta\, w = 0$$

or: if the gap analyzer G is applied to a co-boundary (δ w) the result is zero or:

24 a co-boundary generates no gap. This is as it should be, for δ is defined by the compatibility conditions (or no-gap-conditions) set up by the system connections. Recall that "gap" so far has only been given the meaning of incompatibility. Only when we go down to specific structures shall we see how incompatibility will often manifest itself by gaps in the usual sense of that word. Our definition permits also systems for which that would not be true to be handled by our global analysis.

If we now introduce also a hypothetical "*cycle defining operator*" C such that any cycle z can be defined by

25 $\qquad$ z = Cx, x a cycle generating vector

then we shall also have

26 $\qquad$ ∂ Cx = 0

As the relations G δ w = 0 and ∂ Cx = 0 hold true for any value of w or x we can set

27 $\qquad$ G δ = 0
$\qquad$ ∂ C = 0

28 We can now extend the diagram Fig. 2 to obtain

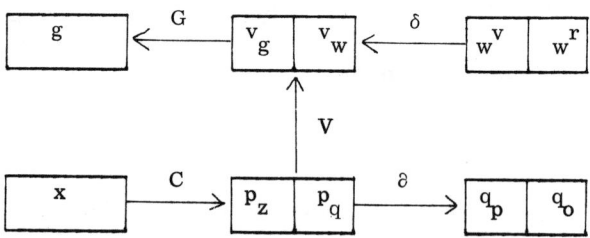

Fig. 3

We have added in Fig. 3 a mapping from p to v indicating a responsive property V of the system elements.

29 We can look upon the diagram of Fig. 3 in the way that an operator leaving a box (such as G and ∂) takes a survey of the status within the box it is leaving and determines if this status generates certain other status such as a gap distribution within v (found by G)

or a boundary value distribution generated by p (and found by ∂). Further any operator pointing into a box, like G points into g and δ into v_w, defines the status of that box or associated with that subbox. The lines subdividing boxes can be regarded as indicating that the mapping reaching one of them is annihilated by the mapping leaving the other (such as G δ = 0).

30 The diagram Fig. 3 illustrates, for instance, the fact that δ always "sends" a boundary potential state into a compatible internal potential state, that is a gap-free one. On the other hand, if we take any internal flow p, which may be such that it generates a prescribed boundary flow q:

31 $$\partial p = q$$

then it will also generate a potential state

32 $$v = Vp$$

33 This potential state will not necessarily be a compatible, that is a gap-free, state. We can test this by applying the gap analyser G:

34 $$GVp = g;$$

35 If g is not zero we test whether or not we can change p so that gaps are eliminated or at least reduced, in some sense, but without changing the boundary value ∂ p = q.

36 Obviously there is a possibility to do this change for if we add to p a cycle z

then $\partial (p+z) = \partial p = q$
or $\partial (p+Cx) = \partial p = q$

and this changes the gap distribution by the amount

37 $$\Delta g = GVz = GVCx$$

38 In such systems where it is possible to find a z such that Δ g of 37 (above) becomes equal to minus g of 34 (above) then our problem is solved.
Thus:

39 $$\left.\begin{array}{l} GVCx = -GVp \\ \text{and} \quad \partial\, p = q \end{array}\right\}$$

solves our problem. In many systems this equation system determines x in a unique way, for q given[4]).

40 One reason that it might be impossible to find a cycle, which eliminates the gaps and, hence, solves 39, would be that only positive flow is permitted, $p+z > 0$. Also limited flow capacity imposes a condition $p+z \leq m$. A cycle must contain both positive and negative component values or else it could not be different from zero and still generate zero boundary flow. Therefore if x_1 would reduce gaps and thus $\alpha\, x_1$ ($\alpha > 1$) would reduce gaps still more (or convert their sign), then $\alpha\, x_1$ would perhaps give negative flow in some components before α had been increased enough to eliminate $GV(p+\alpha\, x_1)$.

41 The best one could do if the condition $p+z \geq 0$ makes complete gap elimination impossible would be to try to minimize some weighted sum of all gap components. Alternatively there may be a cost "a" associated with every flow component $(p+z)_i$ so that the total cost would be

$$K = \Sigma a_i\,(p+z)_i = a\,(p+z)$$
$$\text{for } a = \text{the cost vector}$$

(Cf n-ary relations and their joins[5]).

42 Cost minimization now poses the problem: for given a and q find a cycle z and a flow p such that

$$\left.\begin{array}{l} \partial\, p = q \\ a\,(p+z) = \min \\ p+z \geq 0 \\ p+z \leq m \end{array}\right\}$$

We are thus led to the typical problem of "linear programming".

---

[4]) 1 La 1956, 1 La 1959. Notice that only if GVC has an inverse can 39 be uniquely solved for any q.
[5]) 2 Cd 1970.

12.24 System Connections, Boundary Operation and Cycles.

We have discussed above the *boundary operation*[1]) which for given internal state of a system determines an associated boundary state. We shall see that for a system state of a flow kind and for a system of a simple network character the transpose of the incidence matrix acts as a boundary operator. This interesting result leads us to ask whether or not some generalized sort of incidence matrix for more general systems could be defined that could be used as a boundary operator. The author has shown that this is actually possible[2]) and the tool used to achieve this is the coincidence matrix we are going to introduce below. At present we study the simple case for which E_T^{10}, as given above, is a boundary operator.

Let p_i be the state value of flow type, [3]) acting in the branch "i" of a network with incidence matrix E^{10}. Then $p_T = [p_1, p_2, \ldots]$ is the internal flow vector for the network. If we form the product

$$E_T^{10} p = q$$

we obtain

$$q = p_1(E_T^{10})^1 + p_2(E_T^{00})^2 + \ldots$$

Thus to a row "j" of q and of $(E_T^{10})^i$ there is a corresponding node "j" of the network and for each column of E_T^{10}, that is for each $(E_T^{10})^k$ which has $+1$ in row "j", there will be added p_k to the value of q_j.

Similarly if $(E_T^{10})^r$, has -1 in its j-th row there will be $-p_r$ added to q_j. It is seen that q_j will be obtained as the sum of all flow values in branches positively incident with "j" minus the sum of all flow values of branches with negative incidence in "j". q_j has the same value that the external flow into node "j" is to have in order to satisfy the node flow condition[4]) and q is seen to be the vector of node flows for the system. The operation $E_T^{10}p$ produces the boundary flow q from the internal flow p. E_T^{10} is thus a boundary operator for flows.

---

[1]) See sections 12.18 and 12.23.
[2]) 1 La 1956.
[3]) See section 12.23-13.
[4]) See section 11.9.

12.25 Positional Operator for the System Graph.

It was stated earlier that different kinds of descriptions of a system are needed in different situations, i.e. when they are to be used for different needs. We have shown how the description P could be used to point out the immediate precedents of any part in a system. We shall now introduce another description and operator τ, which will not only point out the immediate precedents but will also determine their geometric position on the graph[1]). τ will have as its elements non-negative numbers such that τ_{ij} tells the distance between the parts "i" and "j". We write τ as a matrix similar to P. Each column "j" of τ will have a non-blank number in each position corresponding to a precedent of "j".

In Fig. 1 the numbers written at the side of each arc measure the length of the vertical projection af that arc.

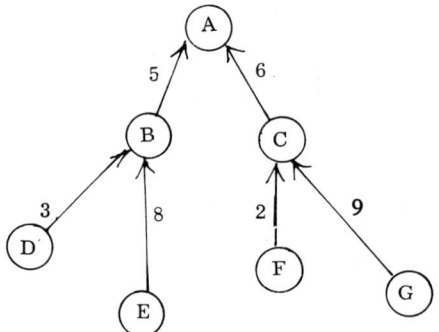

Fig. 1

The positional operator τ for the system

1    $\tau =$

	A	B	C
A			
B	5		
C	6		
D		3	
E		8	
F			2
G			9

shown in Fig. 1 will be seen to be as in 1.

---

[1]) The operator τ as defined and studied here was introduced in 1 La 1962-2. Natural applications of positioning as discussed here are for planning networks (Pert, CPM etc.) or production control. Note that position in the graph may represent the value of some state variable in the system.

We now define a new sort of matrix-by-vector composition where we use again the interpretation of the vector as a selection vector. We have now, however, a matrix and a vector which are no longer restricted to be of the logical type. We therefore define how the selection is to be performed numerically. This can be done in different ways as we shall see later. We choose for the present, however, a definition that will locate the parts in a natural, geometric way, in relation to a terminal part. Thus if for instance in Fig. 1 we locate A in 100 this is seen to call for a location for B which is $100 - 5 = 95$, if the arrows in the graph are supposed to be pointing in the direction of increasing location value. Thus, we see that when A selects its precedent B, it has to be subject to a subtraction by the value of its distance "above" B.

To indicate that the operation of τ upon a vector, t calls for a selection with a subtraction we use the symbol (—) for the composition.

Thus we define τ (—) t

to mean that every non-blank element t_i of t selects the corresponding column τ^i of τ.

The result column is then formed in the way that its r-th element is made equal to t_j minus the r-th element of the selected column τ^i. More precisely we define

2
$$\tau(-)t = t_1(-)\tau^1, t_2(-)\tau^2, \ldots$$

$$= t_1(-)\begin{bmatrix} \tau \cdot {}^1_1 \\ \tau {}^1_2 \\ \cdot \\ \cdot \\ \cdot \end{bmatrix}, t_2(-)\begin{bmatrix} \tau {}^2_1 \\ \tau {}^2_2 \\ \cdot \\ \cdot \\ \cdot \end{bmatrix}, \ldots$$

$$= \begin{bmatrix} t^1(-)\tau {}^1_1 \\ t^1(-)\tau {}^1_2 \\ \cdot \\ \cdot \\ t^1(-)\tau {}^1_n \end{bmatrix}, \begin{bmatrix} t_2(-)\tau {}^2_1 \\ t_2(-)\tau {}^2_2 \\ \cdot \\ \cdot \\ t_2(-)\tau {}^2_n \end{bmatrix}, \ldots$$

where as before an element of t which is blank will do no selection

3 Thus blank $(-) \tau^i = $ blank (or $\emptyset (-) \tau^i = \emptyset$)

Further if $t_j \neq $ blank, then

4 $\qquad t_j (-) \tau_k^j = t_j - \tau_k^j$ (conventional subtraction if $\tau_k^j \neq $ blank)

5 $\qquad t_j (-) \tau_k^j = $ blank if $\tau_k^j = $ blank)

6 Note that it follows from 4 that $0(-) \tau_k^i = -\tau_k^j$ if 0 is the value of t_j. Care must be taken to make a distinction between this result and 3.

7 In accordance with 6 we shall use the convention that when both empty ($\emptyset$) and zero (0) may occur then a blank box (empty box) shall always correspond to $\emptyset$.

8 **Example.** Assume in Fig. 1 that A has position 100. Thus $t(^1) = (100, \emptyset, \emptyset)$
Then

$\tau(-) t^{(1)} = $

	A	B	C
B	5		
C	6		
D		3	
E		8	
F			2
G			9

$(-)$

A = 100
100
$\emptyset$ B
$\emptyset$ C

$(-)$

A
5
6
$\emptyset$
$\emptyset$
$\emptyset$
$\emptyset$

$=$

95 B = $t^{(2)}$
94 C
$\emptyset$
$\emptyset$
$\emptyset$
$\emptyset$

Thus for position A = 100 we get
$\qquad$ position B = 95
$\qquad$ position C = 94

9 Now we get

$\tau(-) t^{(2)} = 95 (-)$

B
$\emptyset$
$\emptyset$
3
8 (E)
$\emptyset$ (F)
$\emptyset$ (G)

, 94 $(-)$

$\emptyset$
$\emptyset$
$\emptyset$
$\emptyset$
2
9

$=$

$\emptyset$
$\emptyset$
92
87
$\emptyset$
$\emptyset$

,

$\emptyset$
$\emptyset$
$\emptyset$
$\emptyset$
92
85

We have thus determined all positions of the parts in the system of Fig. 1.

10 **Exercise.** Interpret the distinction made in 6 in relation to a graph similar to that of Fig. 1.

12.26 Simple Paths and Closed Paths in a System Graph.

The system depicted in Fig. 1, section 12.25, has an especially simple structure. That is all paths that can be traced in the system are simple. By a *path* we mean a sequence of parts, each of which is an immediate succedent of one and only one of the other parts, in the sequence. Obviously, each path in Fig. 1, section 12.25, has an initial part, defined by being the only one in the path which has no precedent belonging to the path. Analogously each path has one and only one terminal part. We say that a path *joins* its terminal and initial parts.

1 **Example.**
In Fig. 1, section 12.25, (DBA) (EBA) (FCA) (GCA) are paths of length 2 and (DB) (EB) (FB) (GB) (BA) (CA) are paths of length 1. All paths in this system are simple.

In systems of more complicated structure *closed paths* occur. We have a closed path when two parts are joined by two different paths. The existence of closed paths in a system means a complication which brings up questions of compatibility in the analysis and design of systems. As a first example of this let us see what happens if we make the change in Fig. 1, section 12.25, that E and F are taken to be identical. The resulting graph is shown in Fig. 1.

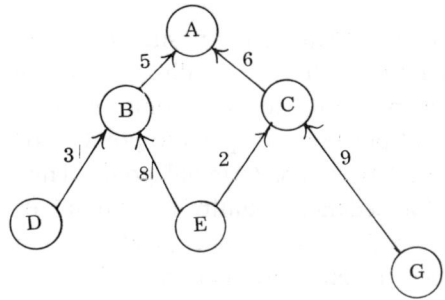

In Fig. 1 the path ECA corresponds to FCA in Fig. 1, section 12.25. We already know from 12.25—9 that the position given to E from this path is to be 92 (the position given to F in Fig. 1, section 12.25). On the other hand the path EBA gives the position 87 to E (same as for E in Fig. 1, section 12.25). Thus the fact that E is in a closed path brings the situation that two positions are assigned to E. This of course appears to be an impossible situation. Whether this is so in an actual system depends however on the interpretation of our word "position". It is certainly an impossible situation when "position" means the geometric position in the diagram.

This compatibility question arises in any closed path because the two simple paths in it may have different lengths. The difficulty may thus be omitted if we permit slacks in the shortest one of the two paths in the closed path.

To see how this problem comes out in the algebraic treatment of the problem we establish the τ matrix for the system of Fig. 1.

2 $t^{(2)} = \tau\ (\text{---})\ 100 =$
$\begin{array}{c|c} & A \\ B & 5 \\ C & 6 \\ D & \\ E & \\ G & \end{array}$
$\begin{array}{c|cc} B & C \\ \hline & \\ & \\ 3 & \\ 8 & 2 \\ & 9 \end{array}$
$(\text{-})\ \boxed{\begin{array}{c} 100 \\ \\ \end{array}} = 100\ (\text{---})\ \begin{array}{c|c} & A \\ \hline & 5 \\ & 6 \\ & \\ & \\ & \end{array} = \begin{array}{c|c} & \\ 95 & B \\ 94 & C \\ & D \\ & E \\ & G \end{array}$

3 $t^{(3)} = \tau\ (\text{---})\ t^{(2)} = 95\ (\text{---})\ \begin{array}{|c|} \hline B \\ \hline \\ \emptyset \\ 3 \\ 8 \\ \emptyset \\ \hline \end{array},\ 94\ (\text{---})\ \begin{array}{|c|} \hline C \\ \hline \emptyset \\ \emptyset \\ \emptyset \\ 2 \\ 9 \\ \hline \end{array} = \begin{array}{c|cc} & B & C \\ \hline & & \\ & & \\ & 92 & \\ & 87 & 92 \\ & & 85 \end{array} \begin{array}{c} B \\ C \\ D \\ E \\ G \end{array}$

The two values 87 and 92 come out for the position of E in $t^{(3)}_E$, as we found earlier. We also see that 87 belongs to the path over B and 92 belongs to the path over C.

4 *Remark.* The method for positioning, where one position vector is obtained for each path leading to the same point, thus assigning different positions to this point, is very space consuming. The number of positions assigned to points grows exponentially when we move away from the terminal point. This positioning is analogous to the "precedence quantity operation" $P^{00}\ (\cdot)\ d^i \rightarrow d^{i+1}$. In fact $\tau\ (\text{---})\ t^i \rightarrow t^{i+1}$ assigns one position to a point for each of the quantities assigned to that point by $P^{00}\ (\cdot)\ d^i$. This means in a scheduling operation that for a point x, corresponding to a part x to be manufactured $P^{00}\ (\cdot)\ d^i$ computes the number of x required by its different successors and $\tau\ (\text{---})\ t^i$ determines the points in time when the different requirements occur.

In many cases, or in many points of a graph for one case, it may not be necessary to consider these different requirement times and quantities. One may then be satisfied with getting the total quantity of x required and the *earliest requirement time*. In such cases the data volume is vastly reduced by computing $P^{00}d^i \rightarrow d^{i+1}$ (using common matrix multiplication). The corresponding positioning operation we denote by

5          $\min (\tau (-) t^i) \to t^{i+1}$

Only the lowest position value is retained for each point.

Example. *Incompatibility in information system design.* An incompatibility of data formats, rather than incompatibility of position may arise because of closed paths and is of special significance in the design of information systems. Data of the same kind may be produced by two different sequences of processes which thus form two different paths through the information system. Both these data may then have to be input to the same process. This process may require that the data from the two paths have exactly the same formats. Unless great care has been taken it may well happen that the designers of the two different paths of processes may come to specify formats which are not completely identical. The incompatibility thus arising will have to be eliminated by reprogramming (or by adding a corrective process).

12.27 Transposed Positional Operator, Forward Positioning.

We have seen in the study of P, the precedence operator, that when transposed it turned out to be a succedence operator. The same will be true for τ, that is while τ could be used to position the system parts backward, from the terminal part, τ_T can instead be used to position forward, from the initial parts. In so doing we have however to replace the operation symbol $(-)$ by $(+)$, whereby addition will replace subtraction.

As an illustration we take the example as in section 12.26, 1 *Example,* starting at the initial positions given by $t^{(3)}$ section 12.26, 1 *Example,* where we have taken the earliest position of E only.

We have

$$t^{(2)} = \tau_T (+) t^{(3)} = \begin{array}{c|ccccc} & B & C & D & E & G \\ \hline A & 5 & 6 & \emptyset & \emptyset & \emptyset \\ B & \emptyset & \emptyset & 3 & 8 & \emptyset \\ C & \emptyset & \emptyset & \emptyset & 2 & 9 \end{array} \quad (+) \quad \begin{array}{c|c} t^{(3)} & \\ \hline \emptyset & B \\ \emptyset & C \\ 92 & D \\ 87 & E \\ 85 & G \end{array}$$

$$t^{(2)} = 92 \, (+) \begin{array}{c} D \\ \hline \emptyset \\ 3 \\ \emptyset \end{array} \, , \, 87 \, (+) \begin{array}{c} E \\ \hline \emptyset \\ 8 \\ 2 \end{array} \, , \, 85 \, (+) \begin{array}{c} G \\ \hline \emptyset \\ \emptyset \\ 9 \end{array}$$

1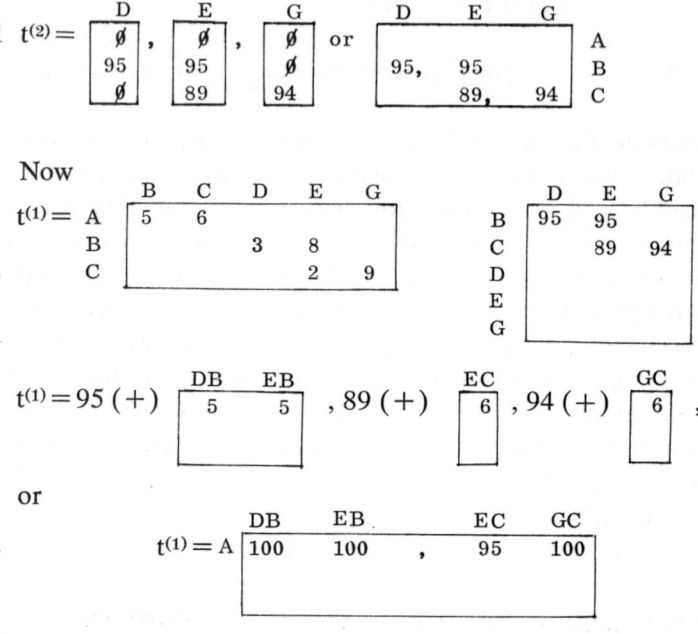

2   $$t^{(1)} = A \begin{array}{|cccc|} DB & EB & EC & GC \\ 100 & 100 & 95 & 100 \end{array}$$

Thus for C we get two positions, 89 and 94 and for A we also get two positions, 100 and 95[1]).

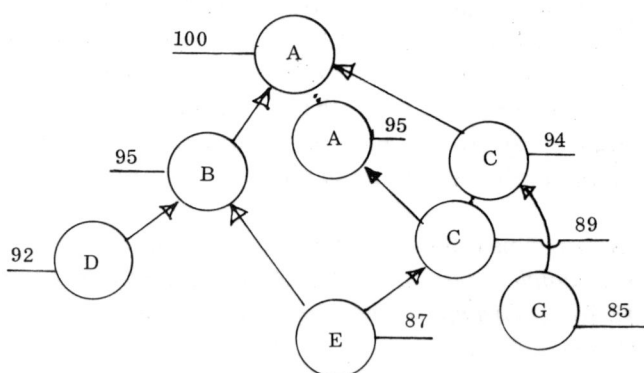

Fig. 1

If we assume that a positive slack (or a gap) can be tolerated in the system but not a negative slack (or an overlap), then we find that the earliest position possible for each part is the latest one obtained in this forward computation.

---

[1]) Notice that when storing the resulting positions we can save space by storing like A:DB, EB, GC; 100EC:95 rather than A:DB, 100GC, 100EC, 95 and still more, when sufficient, only A:100; using only the largest position value (thus discarding A:95) and not indicating paths.

Then for C we accept 94 and will find a slack of 94—89 = 5 in the line connecting E and C. As a result we find only the position 100 left for A.

12.28 General Positioning.

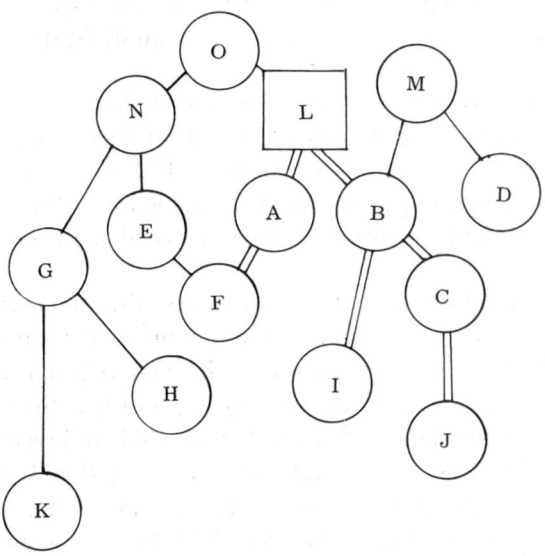

Fig. 1

We have assumed above that a backwards directed positioning would start out from one unique terminal point. In general, however, a system will have several terminal points. This problem can be overcome by introducing one additional point which is made a successor to all terminal points. A similar device can be used for the initial points in a forward positioning. We shall see now, however, that positioning can take any point as a fix-point. In Fig. 1 we choose L arbitrarily to be the fix-point. We position the precedents of L (which are A, F, B, I, C, and J) backwards, and O, which is a succedent of L, we position forwards.

Now we can position the precedents N, G, K, and E, of O backwards from O. Finally M is positioned forwards from B and then D is positioned backwards from M.

Other alternatives are obvious and the choice will depend on the objectives of the positioning operations.

12.29 Requirements Computation and Scheduling.

The author has shown[1]) that in a production scheduling process the required quantities and the associated time points can be computed by operations of the type $P \cdot d^i$ and $\tau (—) t^i$ respectively, where P is the "precedence matrix" giving the structural design information (or sub-assembly quantities), τ is the associated lead-time matrix, and d^i and t^i are required quantities and time vectors for the next higher level. The operations involved were shown to be a matrix-by-vector-multiplication or of a matrix-multiplication-like type[2]).

In the procedure indicated a "lower level part" may have one requirement computed by $P\, d^i$ and another requirement computed later by $P\, d^{i+1}$ and also perhaps by $P\, d^{i+2}$, ... In this way also the consequential requirements of the same lower level part are projected downwards at different computational steps, i.e. $P\, d^i$, $P\, d^{i+1}$, ...

1 When production policy influences the requirements projected downwards, this several-step requirement determination has some drawbacks. For example when the first requirement for a certain part "a", is obtained, as $[(P \cdot d^i)\, (\tau (—) t^i)]\, a$, then the requirement might be modified by the amount available in inventory at that time. When later the next requirement for a, $[(P\, d^{i+1})\, (\tau (—) t^{i+1})]_a$, is obtained, this may be associated with an earlier time. This might then mean that the deduction of $[P\, d^i]\, a$ from inventory, already made, should have to be cancelled or reversed.

In this section instead of applying the operation P on the whole of the preceding vector d^i, we only apply P to some elements of d^i and at the same time on some elements of all preceding d-vectors. (Such procedures are in use at different places but no detailed description or demonstration of feasibility has been published as far as the author knows). The rule for this procedure is simple. It means in effect that the total requirement for a part (or subassembly) "a" is computed during a series of P-operations. With the set of all requirement quantity-time data for part "a" available simultaneously it is possible to analyze the optimum scheduling of the production of part "a" according to some chosen policy[3]).

---

[1]) 1 La 1962-2.
[2]) Cf. sections 12.9, 12.25, 12.26 and 12.27.
[3]) Part of this analysis will be a taking together several requirements at different times to one batch. This is done for production reasons but it should be noted that it may also be necessary for data processing reasons as the number of requirements points multiplies level-by-level.

Any such policy can be programmed as a computer procedure and used after any (P,τ)-operation. Different policy procedures of this sort can be used at different assembly levels (that is after different P-operations) in one and the same production process.

Such policy procedures or basic scheduling operations are briefly discussed for "fixed batch production", "fixed period production" and "dynamic batch size determination". Any of these different procedures — or other ones still — may be inserted in the requirements computational process before projecting down to the subsequent generation. Thus a neat separation of the $(P—\tau)$-process from the basic scheduling process (although they are interleaved) is obtained, with the result that the total can be combined from a set of standard computer procedures.

It is also possible to let the basic scheduling operation be followed by any other operation which is desired for further modification of quantities or timing. This can still be done by simply inserting a procedure between the basic scheduling procedure and the P-operation to follow. For instance, a procedure, by which production start times are shifted because of machine over-loading, may be inserted here and its consequences for the production of precedent parts are automatically taken care of by the subsequent steps of the procedure. For this to be true the precedence relations must satisfy the condition of being "cycle-free".

It is also shown in this section (paragraph 13) that the timing data contained in the matrix τ may sometimes be simplified in a way which reduces τ to be a vector, τ say.

2 Computation of parts requirements.

For the scheduling of production the demand on different parts at different times has to be computed, given a master schedule for shipping. "Parts" is used here as a generic word for any item, whether assembly or simple part, bought or manufactured. It was shown above[4]) that the demand can be determined by the precedents matrix P (having the parts lists as columns) and the master demand vector d^0. Total demand is obtained as

$$d_{tot} = d^0 + P\,d^0 + P^2 d^0 + \ldots P^l d^0 \qquad \text{or}$$

---

[4]) See section 12.9.

$$d_{tot} = d^0 + d^1 + d^2 + \ldots d^l; \qquad \text{or similar expressions.}$$

Corresponding points in time are similarly obtained as

$$t_{tot} = t^0, \; \tau(-) t^0, \; \tau^2 (-) t^0, \ldots$$

τ is a matrix containing for each element p_{ij} of P an element τ_{ij} which gives the length of time associated with P_{ij}. Whenever $p_{ij} = 0$ we also have $\tau_{ij} = 0$[5]).

If P is written as $P = [P^{(1)}, P^{(2)}, \ldots]$ and $d = \{d_1, d_2 \ldots\}$ (a column) then $Pd = d_1 P^{(1)} + d_2 P^{(2)} + \ldots$

Instead analogous notations for τ and t are:
$$\tau(-) t = t_1 (-) \tau^{(1)}, \; t_2 (-) \tau^{(2)}, \ldots$$

where $t_i (-) \tau^{(i)} = \begin{bmatrix} t_i - \tau^{(i)}_1 \\ t_i - \tau^{(i)}_2 \\ \cdot \\ \cdot \\ \cdot \end{bmatrix}$ and $t_i - \tau^{(i)}_j = \emptyset$ if $\tau^{(i)}_j = \emptyset$

Because of the close analogy between computation of required quantities and required times it is sufficient to discuss only quantities.

For all practically encountered design the precedence operation P has the property that some elements of d^{i-1} are 0 for the current and all higher values of i although corresponding elements of d^{i-1} are $\neq 0$.

---

[5]) Notice that to determine all details of the process of computing requirements by analysing actual office procedures would have been much less practical and less reliable than this systematic analysis.

Thus, after suitable re-ordering of d^0, d^0 can be partitioned as

$$d^0 = \begin{bmatrix} d_0^0 \\ d_1^0 \\ d_2^0 \\ \cdot \\ \cdot \\ d_l^0 \end{bmatrix} \text{ in such a way that } d^1 = P\, d^0 = \begin{bmatrix} 0 \\ d_1^1 \\ p_2^1 \\ \cdot \\ \cdot \\ d_l^1 \end{bmatrix}$$

that is $d_0^1 = 0$ while $d_0^0 \neq 0$. Analogously it follows that $d_0^2 = d_1^2 = 0$, $d_0^3 = d_1^3 = d_2^3 = 0; \ldots d_0^i = d_j^i = \ldots d_i^i - 1 = 0$.

It is seen that the parts associated with d_0^0, d_0^1, ... (or d_0 for short) do only occur in d^0 and those associated with d_1 occur in d^0 and d^1 only. Generally d_i occurs in the first "n" d-vectors or *generations*. Thus we use subscripts 0, 1, ... l, to indicate for each part which is its lowest generation (that is the highest "i" for d^i in which it occurs).

We have $P\, d^0 = P_0 d_0^0 + P_1 d_1^0 + \ldots P_l d_l^0$ where $P = [P_0, P_1, \ldots P_l]$, partitioned according to the generation scheme. To simplify writing we use the notation $P_i d_i^0$ thus regarding P as an operator which is not necessarily a matrix.

$d^1 = P\, d^0 = P\, d_0^0 + P\, d_1^0 + P\, d_2^0 + \ldots + P\, d_l^0$

$$d^1 = \begin{bmatrix} 0 \\ d_1^1 \\ d_1^2 \\ d_3^1 \\ \cdot \\ \cdot \\ d_l^1 \end{bmatrix} = \begin{bmatrix} 0 \\ (Pd_0^0)_1 \\ (Pd_0^0)_2 \\ (Pd_0^0)_3 \\ \cdot \\ \cdot \\ (Pd_0^0)_l \end{bmatrix} + \begin{bmatrix} 0 \\ 0 \\ (Pd_1^0)_2 \\ (Pd_1^0)_3 \\ \cdot \\ \cdot \\ (Pd_1^0)_l \end{bmatrix} + \begin{bmatrix} 0 \\ 0 \\ 0 \\ (Pd_2^0)_3 \\ \cdot \\ \cdot \\ (Pd_2^0)_l \end{bmatrix} + \ldots + \begin{bmatrix} 0 \\ 0 \\ \cdot \\ \cdot \\ \cdot \\ 0 \\ (Pd_{l-1}^0)_l \end{bmatrix}$$

or

$$d^1 = \begin{bmatrix} 0 \\ (Pd_0^0)_1 \\ (Pd_0^0)_2 + (Pd_1^0)_2 \\ (Pd_0^0)_3 + (Pd_1^0)_3 + (Pd_2^0)_3 \\ \cdot \quad \cdot \quad \cdot \quad \cdot \quad \cdot \\ \cdot \quad \cdot \quad \cdot \quad \cdot \quad \cdot \\ \cdot \quad \cdot \quad \cdot \quad \cdot \quad \cdot \\ (Pd_0^0)_1 + (Pd_1^0)_1 + (Pd_2^0)_1 + \ldots (Pd_{i-1}^0)_1 \end{bmatrix}$$

$$d^2 = \begin{bmatrix} 0 & 0 & 0 & 0 & \mid 0 & \mid \\ 0 & 0 & 0 & 0 & \mid 0 & \mid \\ [P(Pd_0^0)_1]_2 & 0 & 0 & 0 & \mid 0 & \mid \\ [P(Pd_0^0)_1]_3 & [P(Pd_0^0)_2]_3 & 0 & 0 & \mid [P(Pd_1^0)_2]_3 & \mid \\ \cdot & \cdot & \cdot & \cdot & \mid \cdot & \mid \\ \cdot & \cdot & \cdot & \cdot & \mid \cdot & \mid \\ \cdot & \cdot & \cdot & 0 & \mid \cdot & \mid \\ [P(Pd_0^0)_1]_1 & [P(Pd_0^0)_2]_1 & [P(Pd_0^0)_3]_1 & \ldots [P(Pd_0^0)_{i-1}]_1 & \mid [P(Pd^0)_2]_1 & \ldots \mid \end{bmatrix}$$

3 $$d_{tot} = \begin{bmatrix} d_0^0 \\ d_1^0 + (Pd_0^0)_1 \\ d_2^0 + (Pd_0^0)_2 + (Pd_1^0)_2 + [P(Pd_0^0)_1]_2 \\ d_3^0 + (Pd_0^0)_3 + (Pd_3^0)_3 + (Pd_2^0)_3 + [P(Pd_0^0)_1]_3 + [P(Pd_0^0)_2]_3 + [P(Pd_1^0)_2]_3 \\ \cdot \quad \cdot \quad \cdot \\ \cdot \quad \cdot \quad \cdot \\ \cdot \quad \cdot \quad \cdot \\ d_i^0 + (Pd_0^0)_1 + (Pd_1^0)_1 + (Pd_2^0)_1 + \ldots (Pd_{i-1}^0)_1 + [P(Pd_0^0)_1]_1 + [P(Pd_0^0)]_1 + \ldots [] \end{bmatrix}$$

$$d_{tot} = d^0 + Pd_0^0 + P[d_1^0 + (Pd_0^0)_1] + P[d_2^0 + (Pd_0^0)_2 + (Pd_1^0)_2 + (P(P\ldots] + \ldots$$

Thus, whereas $d_{tot} = d^0 + Pd^0 + PPd^0 + \ldots$ corresponds to "P-operate" the whole of d_0 n the first operation and then the whole of Pd_0 in the second one and so forth, we may let the first P-operation see the 0-generation of d^0 only (as Pd_0^0) and then let the second operation see the 1-generation of d^0 (as Pd_1^0) together with the 1-generation only of Pd_0^0 only (instead of Pd^0) which now occurs as $P(Pd_0^0)_1$ or in total $P[d_1^0 + (Pd_0^0)_1]$ for the second operation.

It is also seen that 3 is equivalent to

4   $d_{tot} = d^0 + P(d_{tot})_1 + P(d_{tot})_2 + P(d_{tot})_3 + \ldots$

which defines d_{tot} recursively.

4 shows that the procedure followed from 3 computes the total requirement within each generation only after the total requirement for the earlier generation is completed. This means that all requirements for any part are computed before the requirements of its precedents are computed, rather than any requirement being projected for a part down to its precedents as soon as it is determined.

This is of the greatest importance for the scheduling because only when the total requirements for part "a" have been computed can production of "a" be scheduled efficiently. Production policy, such as batching prescriptions, will change the quantity to be produced. Hence the required numbers of presedents for "a" are to be changed and this can be computed in the correct way.

The process associated with 3 and 4 can conveniently be represented in a tabular form as in 5.

Lowest Generation	d^0	P^1	P^2	P^3
0	$d_0^0 \to P_0$			
1	$d_1^0 \to (Pd_0^0)_1 \to P_1$			
2	$d_2^0 \to (Pd_0^0)_2$	$(Pd_1^0)_2 + P(Pd_0^0)_{1\,2} \to P_2$		
3	d_3^0	$(Pd_0^0)_3$	$(Pd_1^0)_3 + P(Pd_0^0)_{1\,3}$	$(Pd_2^0)_3 + P(Pd_0^0)_{2\,3} + P(Pd_1^0)_{2\,3} + PP(P)$
.	.	.	.	.
l	d_l^0	$(Pd_0^0)_l$	$(Pd_1^0)_l + P(Pd_0^0)_{1\,l}$	$(Pd_2^0)_l + P(Pd_0^0)_{2\,l} + P(Pd_0^0)_{2\,l} + \ldots$

6 Example. Let the precedence relations among parts A, B, C, D, E, and F be determined as in Fig. 1. P then has the form:

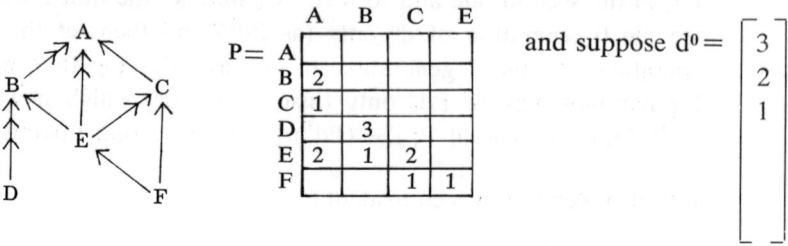

Fig. 1

$$P = \begin{array}{c} \\ A \\ B \\ C \\ D \\ E \\ F \end{array} \begin{array}{c} A \quad B \quad C \quad E \\ \left[\begin{array}{cccc} & & & \\ 2 & & & \\ 1 & & & \\ & 3 & & \\ 2 & 1 & 2 & \\ & & 1 & 1 \end{array} \right] \end{array} \quad \text{and suppose } d^0 = \left[\begin{array}{c} 3 \\ 2 \\ 1 \end{array} \right]$$

If we proceed in the natural way we get $d_1 = P(\cdot)d^0$

$$d^1 = \begin{array}{c} A \\ B \\ C \\ D \\ E \\ F \end{array} \begin{array}{c} A \quad B \quad C \\ \left[\begin{array}{ccc} 0 & 0 & 0 \\ 6 & 0 & 0 \\ 3 & 0 & 0 \\ 0 & 6 & 0 \\ 6 & 2 & 2 \\ 0 & 0 & 1 \end{array} \right] \end{array} \quad \text{and } d^2 = \begin{array}{c} A \\ B \\ C \\ D \\ E \\ F \end{array} \begin{array}{c} \text{BA} \quad \text{CA} \quad \quad \text{EA} \quad \text{EB} \quad \text{EC} \\ \left[\begin{array}{ccccc} & & & & \\ & & & & \\ & & & & \\ 18 & & & & \\ & & 6 & 6 & \\ & & 3 & 6 & 2 & 2 \end{array} \right] \end{array}$$

Notations such as BA heading a column indicate that the column gives precedence quantities required for A "via" B.

$$d^3 = \begin{array}{c} A \\ B \\ C \\ D \\ E \\ F \end{array} \left[\begin{array}{cc} & \\ & \\ & \\ & \\ & \\ 6 & 6 \end{array} \right]$$

$$d_{\text{tot}} = \begin{array}{c} A \\ B \\ C \\ D \\ E \\ F \end{array} \begin{array}{c} d \quad A \quad B \quad C \quad \text{BA} \quad \text{CA} \\ \left[\begin{array}{cccccccc} 3 & 0 & 0 & 0 & & & & \\ 2 & 6 & 0 & 0 & & & & \\ 1 & 3 & 0 & 0 & & & & \\ 0 & 0 & 6 & 0 & 18 & 0 & 0 & \\ 0 & 6 & 2 & 2 & 6 & 6 & 0 & 0 \\ 0 & 0 & 0 & 1 & 0 & 3 & 6 & 2 & 2 & 6 & 6 \end{array} \right] \end{array}$$

The generations are 0: A
                                1: B, C
                                2: D, E
                                3: F

If we use instead the procedure according to 3—5 we get:

Lowest Generation		d^0	P^1	P^2					P^3				
0	A	3 →P_1											
	B	2	6		→P_2								
1	C	1	3										
	D	0	0	6,	0,	18,	0		→P_3				
2	E	0	6	2,	2,	6,	6						
3	F	0,	0	0	1,	0,	3	6,	2,	2,	6,	6	

P-operation as a file processing.

P : : 0A(1B, 2; 1C, 1; 2E, 2) 1B(2D, 3; 2E, 1) 1C(2E, 2; 3F, 1) 2E(3F, 1);

d^0 : : A, 3; B, 2; C, 1;

$P^0 d^0 \to d^1$; $d^0 \smile d^1$: : A(3) B(2; A, 6) C(1; A, 3) E(A, 6);

Here for instance 0A indicates A and tells that A has lowest generation $=0$.

$P^1 d^1 \to d^2$; f ($d^0 \smile d^1 \smile d^2$) : : A (3) B (2; A, 6) D (B, 6; BA, 18) E (B, 2, BA6) C (1, A, 3) E (C, 2; CA, 6) F (C, 1; CA, 3);

sort $d^0 \smile d^1 \smile d^2$: : A (3) B (2; A, 6) C (1; A3) D (B, 6; BA, 18) E (B, 2; BA, 6, C, 2; CA, 6) F (C, 1; CA, 3);

$P^2 d^2 \to d^3$; f ($d^0 \smile d^1 \smile d^2 \smile d^3$) : : [$d^0 \smile d^1 \smile d^2$]; F (BE, 2; BAE, 6; CE, 2; CAE, 6);

sort $d^0 \smile d^1 \smile d^2 \smile d^3$: : [$d^0 \smile d^1$ d^2 d^3 F ( )]; F (BE, 2; BAE, 6; C, 1; CA, 3; CE, 2; CAE, 6);

7 The basic scheduling operation.

As we have seen the total "P-requirement" for any part, until 1, its lowest generation, is computed before it is P-projected down to lower generations.

In general the P-requirements will have to be modified in connection with the scheduling. Then, of course, it is the modified requirement that is P-projected. This modification must be determined before operating by P. Different principles for this modification are appropriate in different circumstances. We shall describe a few possibilities.

8 Use of fixed batch size production.

Let d_a be the vector of total P-requirements for part "a". It will be represented by a sequence $d_{a1}\ d_{a2}\ldots$ of quantity data, each tagged with information as to how it was generated.

Thus for instance the total requirement of E in Fig. 1 is seen to be represented by quantities tagged

$$A,\ BA,\ CA,\ B,\ C$$

indicating respectively demands from A directly, A via B, A via C, B directly, C directly.

Associated with each d_{ai} is also a time instant t_{ai} so that (d_a, t_a) represents the projected (via P, τ) requirements for "a" occurring as a pair of vectors d_a and t_a. The projection (P, τ) will not necessarily be such that $t_{ai} < t_{a(i+1)}$. However we assume it to be ordered in such a way before we proceed.

The inventory will contain part "a" in different quantities at different time intervals. Let (I_{aj}, T_j) be the quantity I_{aj} of "a" available from time T_j onwards.

Thus in addition to the requirements vector pair (d_a, t_a) we have an inventory vector pair (I_a, T_a).

For the earliest requirement (d_{a1}, t_{a1}) for "a", T_k may be the latest time such that $T_k \leq t_{a1}$. Then I_{ak} pieces of "a" are available for (d_{a1}, t_{a1}). In practical situations one may want to replace t_{a1} by $t_{a1} - s_{a1}$, where s_{a1} is a margin of safety permitting a pulling of the need for "a" to a date which is earlier by that amount.

If $I_{ak} \geq d_{a1}$ the modified $\tilde{d}_{a1}$ requirement will become 0. Otherwise if $d_{a1} - I_{ak} \leq \text{Batch (a)}$ then $\tilde{d}_{a1} \leftarrow B(a)$ and $I_{ak} \leftarrow B(a) + I_{ak} - d_{a1}$. Otherwise if $d_{a1} - I_{ak} > B(a)$ then $\tilde{d}_{a1} \leftarrow d_{a1} - I_{ak}$ and $I_{a1} \leftarrow 0$. (We have used B(a) to denote the batch size for "a").

9 **Example.** Batch $(a) = 30$

$$\left. \begin{array}{l} d_a \\ t_a \end{array} \right\} \quad \begin{array}{cccc} 3 & 18 & 33 & 60 \\ 81 & 89 & 94 & 98 \end{array}$$

$$\left. \begin{array}{l} I_a \\ T_a \end{array} \right\} \quad \begin{array}{ccc} 13 & 15 & 23 \\ 80 & 85 & 90 \end{array}$$

1. $\left. \begin{array}{l} d_{a1} \\ \\ t_{a1} \end{array} \right\}$ 3, for this 13 are available in inventory from time 80
    81

Thus of the 13 available after 80, 3 are reserved, leaving

$$\left. \begin{array}{l} I_a \\ T_a \end{array} \right\} \quad \begin{array}{ccc} 10 & 12 & 20 \\ 80 & 85 & 90 \end{array}$$

and no production is needed, so that $\tilde{d}_{a1} = 0$

2. $\left. \begin{array}{l} d_{a2} \\ t_{a2} \end{array} \right\}$ 18 available is $\left\{ \begin{array}{ccc} 10 & 12 & 20 \ldots \\ 80 & 85 & 90 \ldots \end{array} \right.$
    89

This time only 12 are available in time. A batch production has to be ordered.

$$\left. \begin{array}{l} d_{a2} \\ t_{a2} \end{array} \right\} \quad \begin{array}{l} 18 \\ 89 \end{array} \to \left. \begin{array}{l} d_{a2} \\ t_{a2} \end{array} \right\} \quad \begin{array}{l} 30 \\ 89 \end{array}$$

and

$$\left. \begin{array}{l} I_a \\ T_a \end{array} \right. \quad \begin{array}{cccc} 10 & 12 & (30+12-18) & 20+(30-18) \\ 80 & 85 & 89 & 90 \end{array}$$

or

$$\left. \begin{array}{l} I_a \\ T_a \end{array} \right. \quad \begin{array}{cccc} 10 & 12 & 24 & 32 \\ 80 & 85 & 89 & 90 \end{array}$$

3. $\left. \begin{array}{l} d_{a3} \\ t_{a3} \end{array} \right.$ $\begin{array}{l} 33 \\ 94 \end{array} \to \tilde{d}_{a3} = 30$
    $t_{a3} = 94$.

    $\left. \begin{array}{l} I_a \\ T_a \end{array} \right.$ $\begin{array}{l} 29 \\ 94 \end{array}$

4. $d_{a4} \begin{cases} 60 \to \widetilde{d}_{a4} = 31 \\ t_{a4} = 98 \end{cases}$

This time net requirement is 31 and is $>$ Batch (a) which is 30. Hence 31, rather than 30, is scheduled.

$\left.\begin{array}{c} T_a \\ I_a \end{array}\right\} 0$

Thus

$\left.\begin{array}{c} d_a \\ t_a \end{array}\right\} \begin{array}{ccc} 30 & 30 & 31 \\ 89 & 94 & 98 \end{array}$

is scheduled and used to compute requirement for the precedents of "a".

10 Use of fixed production period.

In this type of production different fixed production dates are used for different parts. Let these be

$T_{a1} \quad T_{a2} \quad T_{a3} \ldots$

Then $\left.\begin{array}{c} d_a \\ t_a \end{array}\right\} \begin{array}{ccc} d_{a1} & d_{a2} & d_{a3} \ldots \\ t_{a1} & t_{a2} & t_{a3} \ldots \end{array}$

If $\quad t_{a1} > T_{a1}$ and $t_{ak} > T_{a2}$ but $t_{a,k+1} > T_{a2}$

then $\left.\begin{array}{c} d_a \\ t_a \end{array}\right\} \begin{array}{c} \sum_{t=1}^{k} d_{ai} \\ T_{ai} \end{array}$ and so on.

No inventory vector need be computed for the sake of scheduling. It can of course (and should) be computed for the sake of economic analysis and statistics.

11 Dynamic batch determination.

Rather than using prefixed batch size or production cycle, one may determine for each (d_{ai}, t_{ai}) as it occurs (hence dynamically) the most economic batch size. This can be done by considering setup cost, unit cost and cost per time unit of keeping inventory. In that way cost per unit of part a for d_{a1} alone, for $d_{a1}+d_{a2}$, ... etc. can be computed and the batching, giving minimum per unit cost chosen.

12 Modification of timing.

It may be desired to modify time points for different part productions. If this is also done before projecting to lower generations it is appropriately taken care of by the process. Thus if the process finds that a job to be scheduled at a certain time t_a^i, say cannot be taken then, because the work station is overloaded, then it may apply some rule to replace t_a^i by some earlier time t_a^i, say. In this way a feasible solution is obtained but no optimization. To optimize one must at least choose which of the jobs scheduled for the station-period is to be moved. This is suboptimization for that station alone. Even this calls for a more complicated processing, e.g. a sorting has to be done. In addition — and before that — adjustment for random disturbances has to be made. Then in the modified requirement for precedent items (i.e. lower generation parts) this modified time is used as a basis for timing these precedents. These are thereby automatically moved to an earlier date.

A problem that arises in this connection is that it induces a set of set-backs on start times along a path in the timing graph. The sum of these is not known when the current modification is to be made. This problem may call for repetitions of the process with checking against present loadings.

13 Performing the basic scheduling operation.

We have seen that the different production policies are taken care of by applying one or another procedure to the total requirement-time vector for the part to be scheduled. This means that after the operation with P we input (part of) the data obtained into a "production policy process" or the basic scheduling operation. Thus we have a basic scheduling procedure for "fixed batch production" (FBS), another one for "fixed production period" (FPS) and one "for dynamic batch determination" (DBD).

FBS, for instance, takes (P, τ) (d, t) as input, together with (the inventory data for the part to be scheduled) and B (the batch size for the part).

Now the great advantage realized from working by generations is that it is now possible, to introduce all other of the basic scheduling procedures.

Such a procedure will be a modification of the demand computed. For instance, the modification may introduce an earlier time of requirement, perhaps because the planned operation station may be overloaded at the initially computed time. The modification can be introduced in two ways: before entering the operation P or after. We shall see that only the first one is practical. If d^i denotes the demand computed at the i-th P-operation and (d^i), denotes the same data after modification the alternatives may be symbolized as

and
$$d^i \xrightarrow{(FBS)} (d^i) \xrightarrow{P} (d_{i+1}),$$
$$d^i \xrightarrow{P} d^{i+1} \xrightarrow{(FBS)} (d_{i+1}),$$

It is important to note that although both alternatives give the same total results they differ vastly from an information processing point-of-view.

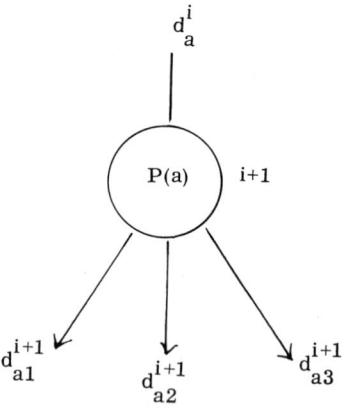

Fig. 2

This is easily seen from Fig. 2 where it is assumed that for one part "a" a requirement d_a^i is available and processed in the $i+1$—th application of P to give three requirements for the three precedents a1, a2, a3.

Thus if the modification process FBS is applied before P(a) it calls for only one set of additional data such as inventory on hand and batch size, i.e. those associated with "a", whereas if instead FBS is applied after P then FBS needs several (three in this case) sets of additional data, one for each of d_{a1}^{i+1}, d_{a2}^{i+1}, ... The latter alternative thus calls for larger files. This also can be seen by observing that the precedents a1, a2, ... of "a" will also occur as precedents for other parts so that they would call for the storage of their additional data several times. In the first alternative each such data set is needed only once for each part.

The two alternatives for introducing the modification of requirements are shown in Fig. 3a and b.

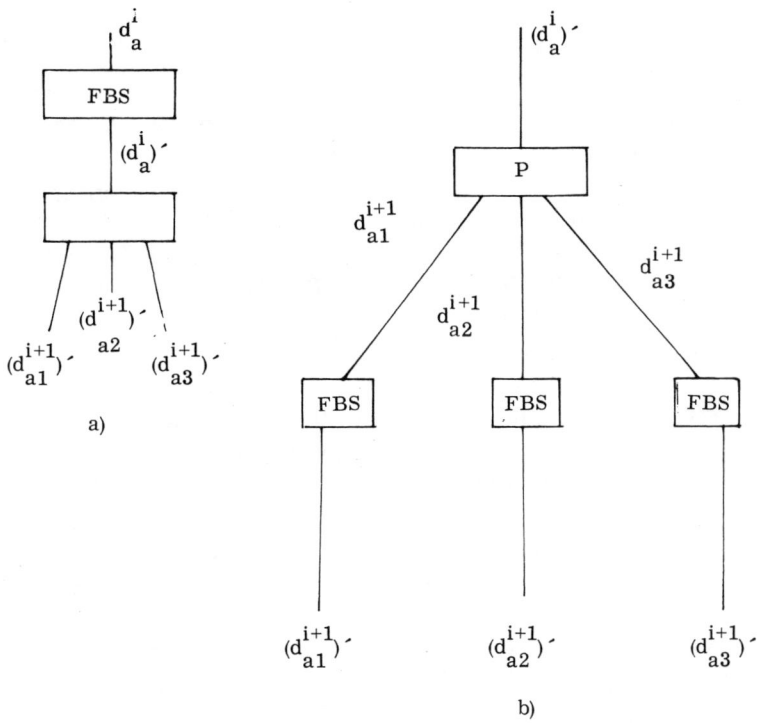

Fig. 3

To let process FBS go before P is best.

It is natural to expect different production policies to be used for parts in different generations. In fact it is entirely feasible to partition generations into "subgenerations" classified by the applicable policy. In the production of large constructions such as ships or buildings it is certainly not common to specify batch production for ends products or the higher level subassemblies, but for some lower-level subassemblies or parts this is quite feasible.

14 Simplification of time determination.

It was assumed in paragraph 1 of this section that with any requirement quantity (=element P_{ij} in P) will be associated a different time. When a part "c", goes into (i.e. is precedent of) two different parts, "a" and "b" then it takes different times τ_{ca} for "c" to go into "a" and τ_{cb} for "c" to go into "b". It may for instance be inserted at different stages of the process of making "a" and "b". In this case any arrow (in the precedence graph) leaving "c" is associated with the time it takes to build "c" into the part at which the arrow ends.

If instead we let any arrow leaving "c" be associated with the time for manufacturing "c" then the same time may in some cases be associated with all arrows leaving "c". In such a case we thus have $\tau_{ca} = \tau_{cb} = ---- = \tau_c$ so that the matrix τ degenerates to a vector $\vec{\tau}$ (say). This valuable simplification of timing is of course available only under certain conditions. It must then be assumed that the time for manufacturing a part is independent of the quantity or else that the quantity is independent of the successor part for which it is being produced.

The latter condition is always satisfied for those elements for which batch processing is always used (and this in the strong sense that the batch size is not only a lower boundary value). However, there is one more condition for the simplified timing procedure. All precedents of a part must be available at the start of its manufacturing. This is not always the case but is probably most often used.

When the vector $\vec{\tau}$ is permitted (rather than the matrix τ) then the timing can be introduced in a way that is similar to the quantity modification for production policy reasons (FBS in Fig. 3a).

15 Reduction of the P-operation.

The definition for each part of the lowest generation in which it occurs makes possible to use as the input for the P-operation — or as the source requirements — only those requirements which regard the latest generation computed. Instead the requirements used for this generation are those that were computed in all previous P-operations. While the source requirements are thus taken from one generation only, the "P-projected requirements" distribute through all lower generations. The use of one generation only for source requirements implies that only those columns of P which belong to that generation are selected. These columns, however, are taken as whole so that elements in any of the lower generations may be activated. (Those in higher generations are unaffected.) As a consequence the column selection procedure associated with the i-th P-operation needs only access to those columns of P which are associated with the i-th generation parts. Thus if $P^{(i)}$ denotes the part of P containing only the columns for items whose lowest generation is i then P can be partitioned into generations $P^{(i)}$, such that at the i-th P-operation $P^{(i)}$ rather than the whole of P can be used. This then means that in total after all P-operations, P has been scanned only once. This is not possible when the normal column selection procedure is used except for special cases[6]).

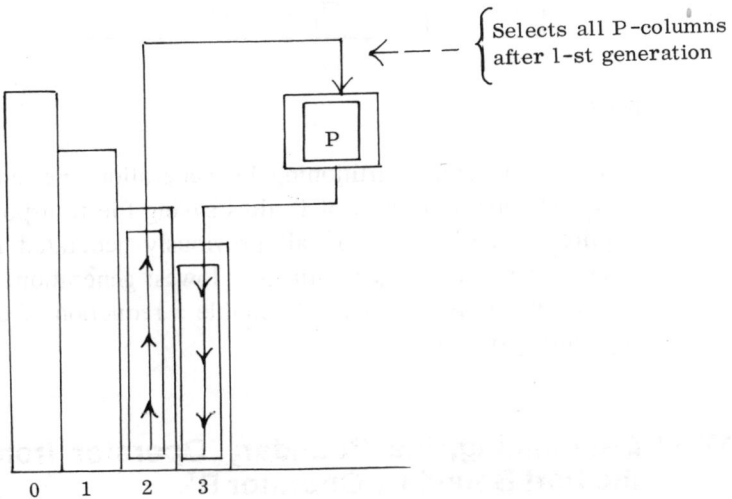

Fig. 4

Fig. 4 shows the situation for the P-operation producing the 3rd stage of requirements when the procedure with "total" column selection is used. Fig. 5 instead shows how the modified procedure appears where only one generation at a time is selected.

16 Problem. Compare the methods of Fig. s. 4 and 5 as regards data transport volume[7]).

---

[6]) 1 La 1962-2, pp. 91—111.
[7]) See part 2, chapter 7.

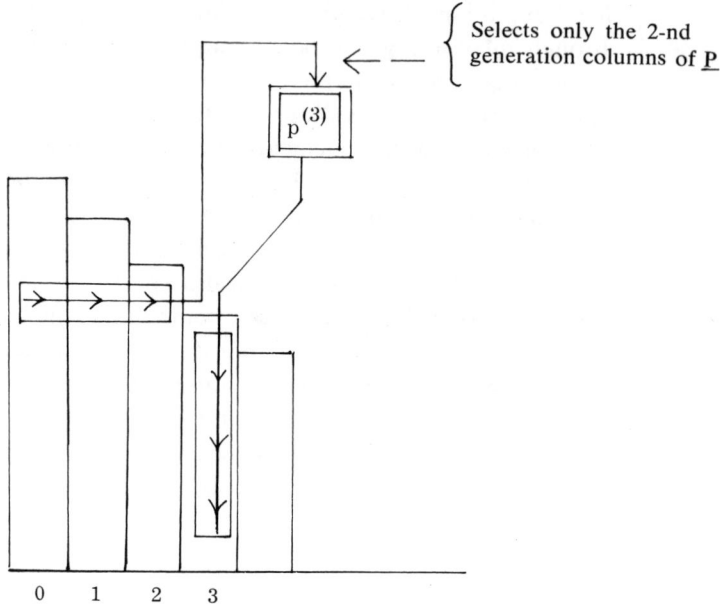

Fig. 5

Note that whereas partitioning by generations permits the use of only one generation part of P, thus saving file transport, the source requirements file relies on all previously generated requirements. These have to be tagged with their lowest generation. Only the use of several different files would enable a reduction of this file transport during processing.

12.30 Determining, the Boundary Operator from M^{10} and the Part Boundary Operator R^T.

It is easy to see that if we would try to use the transposed coincidence matrix M_T^{10} for the boundary operation we cannot let it operate on the internal flow vector p. We need a vector which has not one but two elements for each branch. This would be achieved in the appropriate way if we first operate each single part flow by the boundary operator for that part, for in that way we would obtain for each part the two end values corresponding to its internal flow.

The part boundary operator for a part in the simple network is $R_T^i = [1, -1]$ for each part "i", if we let the end number "2" be the negative end. If we form the matrix diag (R_T^i), i.e. the diagonal matrix having R_T^i as its diagonal elements, we obtain a matrix R_T ($=$ diag R_T^i) with $2\,l$ rows, if it has l columns and there are l parts in the system.

Now obviously the vector $R_T\,p$ has $2\,l$ elements and determines the end values for all parts, as induced by their internal flow value. We have thus obtained exactly the vector which, when multiplied by M_T^{10}, would give the system boundary flow vector q

$$M_T^{10} R_T p = q$$

It follows that we have

$$E_T^{10} = M_T^{10} R_T$$

and, hence

$$E^{10} = R M^{10}$$

It is not difficult to see that this is actually the case.

There is a great system technical advantage in the factoring of E^{10} into RM^{10}, in addition to its mathematical convenience. This is because it brings about a decomposition of the knowledge required to provide the input data for the analysis. While E^{10} would require combined knowledge the setting up of R can be left with each part to its own expert group, while the much simplified structure matrix M^{10} only need be designed by the system team.

12.31 Boundary Operator for Generalized Systems.

The factoring of E^{10} into RM^{10} opens up some interesting possibilities for defining boundary operators for more general systems. We are no longer limited to system parts which have constant flow values and hence the same value at the input end and the output end. If the values are different we just put different values in each of the two parts of R^i, that is we put $R^i = [l_1, -l_2]$. Further we need not have only one end value at each end for we may as well let l_1 and l_2 be matrices. Further, we need not even have equal numbers of end values at both ends of a part for l_1 and l_2 may have different sizes.

For this to be practical it is of course not enough that R permits a generalized form as M^{10} must be able to cooperate with R and this is possible for M^{10} also has flexibility. Thus we can have the number of rows in M^{10} which is required to each part end.

Also for the generalized case we could compute a generalized incidence matrix from RM^{10}. This would however no longer give all structural information required for the generalized system. It would act as boundary operator. The factored form however has its advantages as M^{10} is simple and has only unit element values and yet it completely describes the system topology.

1 **Example** (text below).

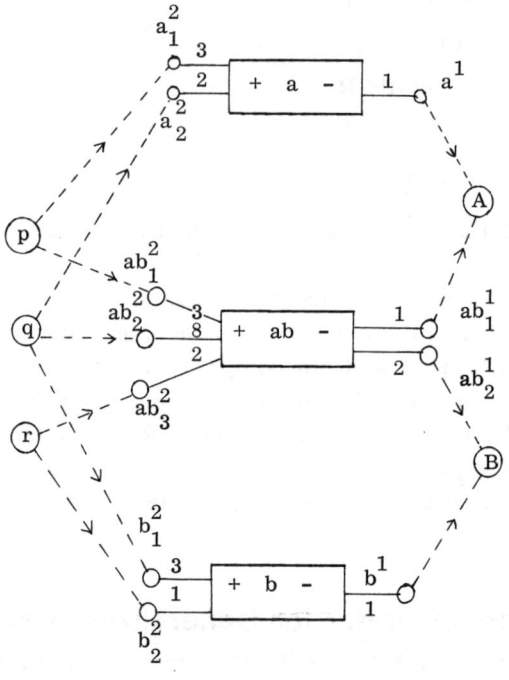

Fig. 1 a

produces no output. z is thus a cycle.

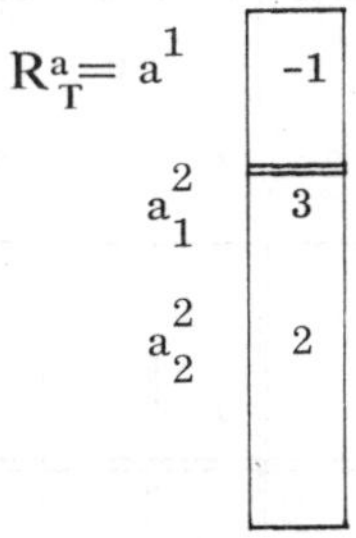

$R_T^a = a^1$
-1
a_1^2
3
a_2^2
2

Fig. 1 b

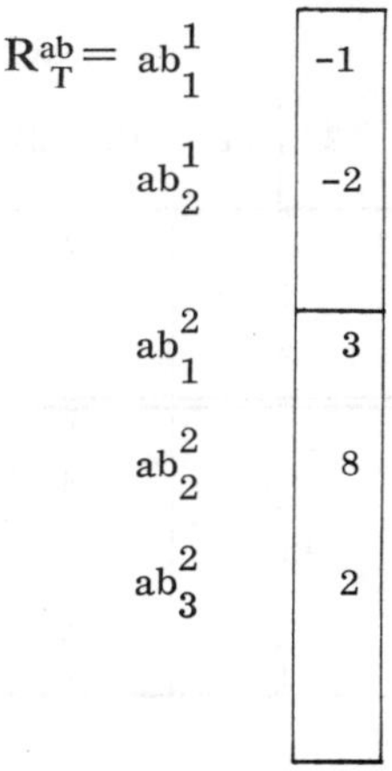

$R_T^{ab} = ab_1^1$
-1
ab_2^1
-2
ab_1^2
3
ab_2^2
8
ab_3^2
2

Fig. 1 c

$R_T^b = b^1$
-1
b_1^2
3
b_2^2
1

Fig. 1 d

a
ab
b
$R_T =$
a
-1
3
2
ab
-1
-2
3
8
2
b
-1
3
1

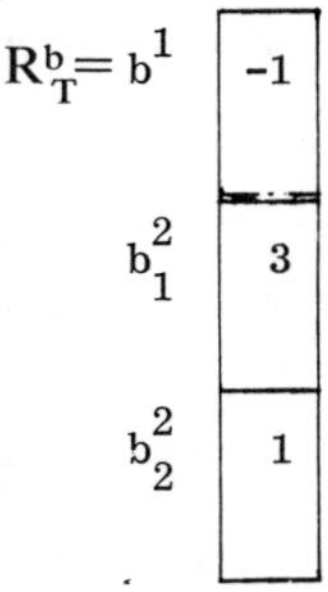

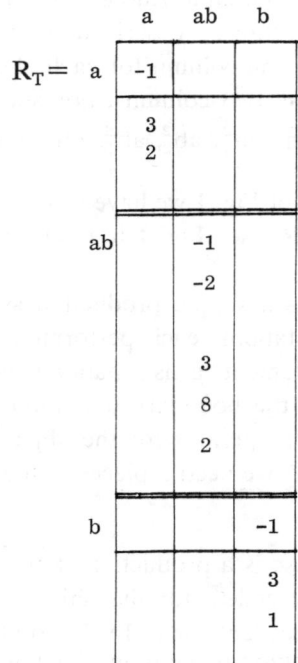

Fig. 2 a

	a			ab					b		
	1	21	22	11	12	21	22	23	1	21	22
A	1			1							
B					1				1		
p		1				1					
q			1				1			1	
r								1			1

Fig. 2 b

In Fig. 1 we have a simple system consisting of three different elements denoted by a, ab, and b. These elements are connected to the system nodes p, q, and r on the input side and A, and B, on the output side. The system of connections is described by the transposed coincidence matrix M_T^{10}. It has one column for each element terminal. For element ab it thus has two columns, ab_1^1 and ab_2^1 for its out-terminals and three columns ab_1^2, ab_2^2, ab_3^2, for its inputs.

For each element of the system of Fig. 1 we have given the boundary operator, in transposed form, R_T, see Fig. 1 b, c and d.

We can think of the system as a simple production system where the elements represent work stations, each performing a complete production cycle. The system element "a" is a station which produces objects likewise called a. R_T^a the boundary operation for "a" has as its input part the precedence operator for the object a. It states that to produce one piece of "a" we need 3 pieces of the part a_1^2 and 2 pieces of the part a_2^2.

The system element "b" likewise is a production station for objects "b". The part a_2^2 which is a precedent for the object a is identical with the part b_1^2 which is a precedent for b. In the total system this is made clear by using the common name q and having connections from q to a_2^2 and b_1^2. q may also be thought of as the store of parts q. Element ab produces a mixture of objects A and B[1]).

---

[1]) For instance the arrow drawn from terminal 2 of ab to B indicates that the output from ab_2 consists of objects of type B. Analogous remarks hold for the other outputs.

In Fig. 2 a we have shown the matrix R_T for the whole system.

$$2 \qquad R_T = \begin{bmatrix} R_T^a & & \\ & R_T^b & \\ & & R_T^c \end{bmatrix}$$

and in Fig. 2 b the coincidence matrix is shown.

If a given mixture of A and B is to be produced, it can be done by different distributions p of production intensities in ab and in a and b. It is easy to see from Fig. 1 that we can increase p_a and p_b (the production intensities or the flows) in "a" and "b" respectively and by simultaneous reduction of p_{ab} keep the total output constant. This is only possible as long as p_{ab} remains >0 if negative production is not feasible, which is of course normal. In fact we see that

$$z_T = [1, -1, 2]$$

produces no output. z is thus a cycle.

3 **Exercise.** Perform the multiplication $M_T^{10} R_T p$.

We shall have $M_T^{10} R_T z = 0$ and $M_T^{10} R_T p = q$. Rather than perform the multiplication $M_T R_T p$ we perform successively

$(R_T p)_T = \bar{p}_T$

	a			ab				b		
	$-p_a$	$3p_a$	$2p_a$	$-p_{ab}$	$-2p_{ab}$	$3p_{ab}$	$8p_{ab}$	$2p_{ab}$	$-p_b$	$3p_b$	p_b

$M_T^{10} \bar{p} = q$

q =		
A	$-p_a - p_{ab}$	
B	$-2p_{ab} - p_b$	
p	$3p_a + 3p_{ab}$	
q	$2p_a + 8p_{ab} + 3p_b$	
r	$2p_{ab} + p_b$	

4 **Exercise.** Compute $E_T^{10} = M_T^{10} R_T$
and then $E_T^{10} p$ and compare with result of 3 Exercise!

From this we see again that for $p=z$ we get $q=0$. $\quad p_a = 1$
$$p_{ab} = -1$$
$$p_b = 2$$

We obtain an optimizing problem of linear programming type if we put the cost =

$K = k \cdot p$:

$$\left.\begin{array}{l} K = k \cdot (p+z) = \min \\ M_T^{10} R_T(p+z) = q \\ p+z \geq 0 \end{array}\right\}$$

5 The reader should notice that the study in this section illustrates the concept of a *constructive subsystem structure* as well as that of *the (outer) properties of subsystems* which were basic to our theory of imperceivable systems (section 11.17). Of special interest is that the analysis could be done in two separate parts and then the combined result could be obtained by formal calculation. Thus, the analysis of the structure could be done as a separate analysis task and be strictly documented by means of the coincidence matrix. For this to be possible the *structural* properties of the boundaries of the subsystems had to be defined but not the quantitative properties. For instance, it was necessary to have decided that the subsystem ab was to have 3 input points and 2 output points. Then the task of defining the coincidence matrix could be done separately, while another research team would be doing analysis or experiments to determine the numeric values of the part boundary operators such as R_T^{ab}. For large, realistic, systems design tasks this is of the utmost importance for the organization and management of the system design project.

Part 2. Information Systems Theory

Chapter 1. Information Systems.

21.1 Information System Design.

By information system we mean here:

A system of information sets needed for decision and signalling in a larger system (of which it is a subsystem) containing subsystems for

>collecting
>storing
>processing
>distributing

information sets[1]).

Notice that decision processes are examples of information processes, whether performed by man or by machine. Also most information processes contain decision processes. Thus, *the set of decisions in an organization is a part of its information system*. To talk about information systems and decision systems as distinct, as is often done in the literature, is very misleading indeed. If one wants to talk about a "decision system" at all, one must remember that it is a *subsystem* of the information system. However, it is not advisable to do this either. For the set of decision processes to form a *system* they must be mutually interacting. However, the interaction between decisions is implemented by information sets, communicated among the decisions. Thus, decisions form a system only when considered together with the information system.

21.2 Formalization of Information System Design.

1 There is a need not only for a formal theory, giving procedures for analysis and design but also for a *systematic* analysis and presentation of the large volume of existing empirical evidence.

---

[1]) Regarding the meaning of the word "information". Cf. section 26.1.

2 System technique also is used in the design and implementation phases. Thus work is normally done on several subsystems in parallel. This is made possible by suitable partitioning into subsystems and formal definition of subsystem interfaces.

3 Further, emphasis is concentrated on one phase at a time, for each subsystem team. This is a consequence of formalizing the systems work.

4 In addition the different separate component problems are isolated and defined so they can be solved separately by different groups, mainly outside the central systems team.

5 The value-versus-cost of information approach means, that we could answer the question as to whether or not it would pay to collect and process data more often, as in real time. How much increased value would this imply for a certain kind of information? And how much additional cost would it take?

21.3 Component Problems of Information System.

The theory of information systems of course has to be concerned mainly with the problems associated with the genuine systems problems, that is, the problems arising from the interconnections of the different subsystems and components — and with the definition of the components and the components problems.

Many of the component problems are then of enough complexity and importance to make up objects for research of their own.

The special importance to be laid on the true systems problems is emphasized by the fact that while so much is talked today about information processing systems analysis, the talk always quickly deviates to a discussion of component problems — mostly those of an office rationalization character. Thus the need for treating the veritable total systems problem is a very marked one indeed.

Nevertheless the component problems are of course important parts of the total systems study. Some of these, because they are otherwise neglected, or because they are very closely related with the central systems theory, need to be treated in any ambitious systems theory.

These are for instance

1. Methods for storage and retrieval of information in fast memories, random access file memories, serial access memories, other types of memories (file handling or data base management).

2. languages or methods for description of systems and processes.

3. special processing or handling types, as suited to different storage principles.

4. error checking problems and reliability.

5. learning principles and heuristics.

6. man-machine processes.

7. the choice of direct processing or periodic processing. These are usually called on-line vs. batch processing. However the desirable time period may often be sufficiently longer than the time for processing a single transaction so that batch processing might have to be considered even in on-line processing.

   A problem here is whether or not advanced methods for decision analysis can actually be used together with direct processing. What kinds of changes in the mathematical methods in use so far would be necessary?

   This problem is more of a systems problem than a component one. However it has often to be solved separately, defining the bounds with which the systems solutions are then to be found.

8. the evalution of data processing environment (hardware — software system).

Different sorts of storage and retrieval problems are preferred for different types of memories. Thus in fast random access memories many access problems are eliminated. Instead the problems of dynamic storage allocation and of list structures describing complicated system interrelationships become of interest, for instance in compilation processes, network problems and learning systems.

For large random access file memories the problems of addressing file items which are numbered in a noncompact way cause problems of efficient space utilization which are solved partly by a "randomizing addresses" technique. The serial access memories, like magnetic tapes instead present problems of minimum-number-of-passes solutions and sorting and packing techniques. (As we shall see these problems remain when we change to random access technology, although they may have somewhat different solutions.)

The language and systems description questions are also component problems within the systems theory.

Much of what is called data processing systems analysis today is mainly concerned with the component problem of data collection or generation. As this is to be handled by local office bodies, one for each transaction type, this is rather a typical component problem which need not influence systems work greatly. The problems here may have become greater than earlier but are still of a conventional office rationalization type. Once information system analysis has specified what data shall be delivered and what formal requirements the system will establish it can best be handled locally by the office people concerned. The main interaction between this local problem and the systems problem is the possibility that the computer may be used in a way that will reduce the manual work necessary to present and verify the data needed.

Chapter 2. The Function of an Information System.

22.1 The Function of an Information System.

1 When an information system is needed it is as an auxiliary for another system, the *object system* or *managed system*. The information system has to provide the information needed at any point at any time, in an object system. The object system will often be an organization, i.e. a company or an administrative body.

2 It is usual to find that some information is needed often, but instead only in a limited part of the object system; while other information calls for data from many points in the object system, but can be sampled at more distant points in time.

3 It is of course important in information system design to be able to pin-point situations of this kind because by neglecting such special properties of the system one may either be doing too much data transport and processing, or less than necessary. Both extremes will cause a loss.

4 In order to be able to determine the right amount of information to provide we need to be able to find out why information is needed in a system. We shall find it practical to turn the question around and ask instead, "how we could make use of information?"

5 It is when a system changes its state within time that we need a continously working information system and, as a consequence, meet the problem of designing the information system for efficient information flows and information collection.

6 If the object system — served (or controlled) by the information system — is static, the information system becomes merely computational, for instance in the form of setting up a system of equations, finding its solution, and evaluating the solution.

7 A consequence of 5 is that information system design will most often be concerned with information for the control of a dynamic system. The information needs, timewise, will have to be determined by the rate with which they must be made available, and processed, to provide control stability of the (controlled) system.

8 The problems of how to control belong to control theory (or decision theory). The theory of information systems has to study the information needs, and processing needs, as established by control theory, and to find economic means for providing this information and processing.

It follows from what has been said that one basic problem for the information system design is to find different kinds of information which are of potential utility for the control to be effected by means of the information system. We thus have, as in any problem solving situation, a need for a search activity. Information system science can do a lot to aid in this search by establishing checklists of the information needs for the production of different kinds of information. For the development of such checklists both survey of information relations in existing object systems and study of theoretically established decision rules are useful.

22.2 Two Tasks of an Information System.

1 The different functions of an information system can be classified in two kinds of tasks (or "task-categories"). In one of these tasks information is necessary, in the other task information is more or less useful, while not being absolutely necessary. In order to determine whether or not to bring it in and use it in the system, one has to estimate both the utility and the information processing cost that would be the result of its introduction.

2 The kind of task for which information is necessary has to do with the *operative* functioning of the managed system. For this operative functioning any "administrative system" is dependent on information even if all questions of systems economy are disregarded. (For many technical (non-administrative) systems this is not the case.) Thus *operative* information is a necessity. *Each operation needs new operative information.*

3 When we also add to the requirement of operative functioning a requirement of total system economy, then new kinds of information are called for. We shall call this second category, *directive information*[1]). .We regard this second kind of tasks for information as not

---

[1]) Our dichotomy operative/directive and its implications for the analysis of the control and information system is almost exactly matched by that of John A. Beckett between "operations" and "nonoperations". 2 Be 1967. (Remark added in 1970 issue.)

necessary but only *useful* in that it appears that many, perhaps most, business systems today must (on closer analysis) be said to disregard total system economy and concentrate upon operative functioning, probably because before reasonably operative functioning has been achieved everything else is of secondary importance.

4 As we shall see the information needed for operative functioning at one system point can be delimited to a small, neighboring part of the system. Consequently this kind of information task puts limited requirements on the capacity for communication and information processing and also reduces the sophistication required. This may explain why manual systems have managed to handle these tasks fairly well and how practical experience has been a reasonably satisfactory background.

5 When interest is focused on total system economy, a completely different situation comes up before the information system designer (and its manager). Now the need arises of using information from all over the system and even from its environment, and this introduces both difficult communication problems and a need for sophisticated analysis. And now need arises to have clearly defined the goals of the total system management. Typically, a management which concentrates on the current operations can do without goals defined — and has done so forever.

6 Decision theory illustrates the point. If there is only one action to take when a certain signal or message is received then no decision is called for. The signal and other data which describe the action may be necessary (operative information) for the guidance regarding the detailed action steps involved.

If, as is more common, several *alternative courses of action* are available then *one of them has to be selected*. This is to say that then decision has to be made. Which of the alternatives to choose depends on which is *best with respect to the objectives of the decision-maker*. This depends on the *expected outcome of the action* taken which, in turn, will be dependent on the *state of nature* which can be expected to prevail at the time when the action is implemented. Decision theory studies how to design strategies, that is, rules for selecting courses of action depending on received messages (indicators) about observations of the state of nature or about outcomes of experiments. Thus the strategy descriptions are used as directive information which directs, or guides or influences upon, the processing of the incoming messages about the state of nature. (which messages thus appear as operative information).

22.3 Operative Information Requirements. An Example.

1 To see how information is a necessity for controlling a management system let us look at a very much simplified example of a firm. Thus we assume the firm has a store from which it ships goods to customers, Fig. 1. The system to be controlled is seen to consist of one *material subsystem*, i.e. the store and the inflow and outflow of goods.

Fig. 1 Vendors → Store → Customers

2 We study the requirements for keeping the material system running operatively. The basic operations of the store are 1: Shipping goods to customers; 2: Receiving goods from vendors. It is easy to see that each of these operations needs information to initiate them. To initiate a shipment to a customer a shipping order has to be sent to the store. (We shall express this by saying that the shipping order is an information precedent of the store function.) This order has to give information about the customer, the time the goods are required, the kind and quantity of goods, and other information as well. To initiate a refill order (or purchasing order) information about the status of the store is required, together with some *decision rule* which determines at what status a refill order is to be issued. (Again these are information precedents of the store function.) Also information about vendors is required. We thus obtain a system as in Fig. 2, where in addition to the material subsystem also a small *information system* has been introduced to handle the information requirements for the operative control. (Notice that information systems contain not only information but also decisions rules and processes for implementing the rules.)

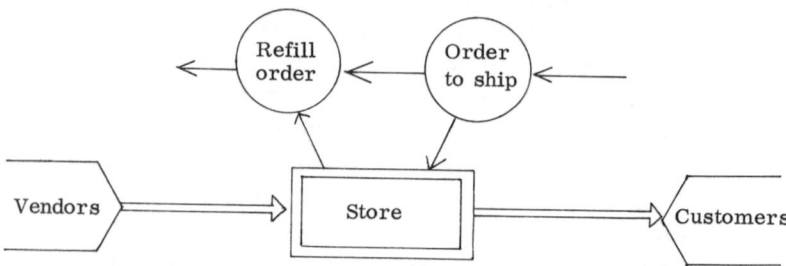

Fig. 2

3 In Fig. 2 we have added two circles to represent the "information" system. The arrow from the circle "order to ship" is directed toward the store to indicate that information is sent in that direction to initiate an operative action of the kind "shipping". There is also indicated in Fig. 2 an arrow directed toward the circle "order to ship". This indicates that information has to reach the system from outside to tell about a need of some customer. Finally an arrow is drawn from "order to ship" toward "refill order" to indicate that the function generating refill orders needs information that a shipping has been initiated, in order for it to know that it should check if a status calling for refilling has been reached. The "refill order" part of the information system needs information from the store about the status and this is indicated by an arrow. Also an arrow pointing away from "refill order" is introduced to indicate the need to send away a refill order, at the appropriate time, to a vendor.

4 The arrow from "store" to "refill order" corresponds to performing a physical inventory taking. This is an operation which is much more expensive than the decision process — a fact that is easily overlooked in a study which is predominantly concerned with the economic utilization of an electronic computer. It is therefore economic to reduce the frequency for physical inventory by introducing an *inventory status file* which stores information about the status of the store. By modifying this information each time a status change is initiated we make the inventory file a "mathematical model" of the store and the "refill order" function of the information system may fetch information about the store status from the inventory file, in a much less expensive way than by physical observation in the store. The need for physical inventory is not completely omitted by this trick for it is necessary to check, at appropriate intervals, that the inventory file satisfactorily represents actual status. This needs only be done relatively infrequently. We have indicated this by the corresponding dotted arrow in Fig. 3. Notice that this device introduces a new decision function into the system for it has to be decided when to initiate a physical inventation. This is also indicated in Fig. 3.

5 In Fig. 3 we have also drawn an arrow from the double-arrow representing delivery to the store and directed into "inventory status". This arrow represents messages about receipt of goods at the store.

6 We have seen now that the inormation system necessary for operative control needs to have units for fetching information, communication, making decisions, storing information, updating stored information and displaying information.

We observe now that two more subsystems, both of which are concerned mainly with processing information, have to be introduced: a *sales* function which fetches information from customers and supplies it to the function "order to ship" and *purchasing* which receives information from "refill order" and transmits it to vendors. "Sales" also performs some kind of operative control. It transmits information to customers which is supposed to "initiate an action to order goods from the firm", Fig. 4. We have in Fig. 4 also indicated the need for a second, "material", subsystem, *"personnel"*. The information needs of this subsystem will not be discussed here, however.

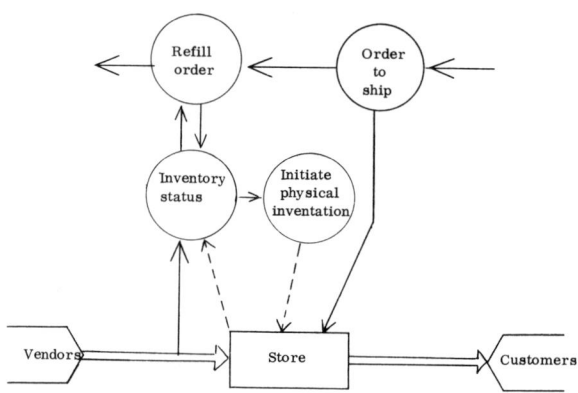

Fig. 3

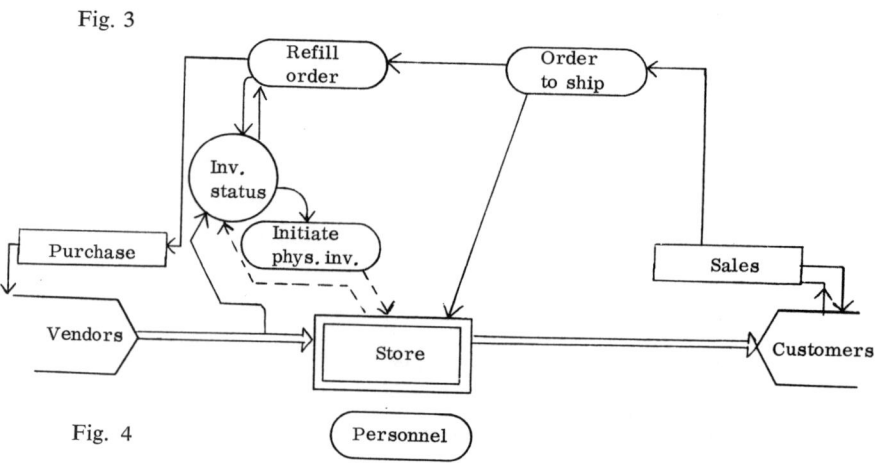

Fig. 4

22.4 The Value of Directive Information.

1 We have said previously that the operative information is necessary. If it is not provided the operative functioning of the managed system breaks down. Once operative functioning is achieved, however, the question arises whether economic improvements of the control are possible. We shall see that this question brings in new kinds of information needs. This new information (the *directive information*, as we shall call it) is no longer necessary in the sense that the system could not function without it. It is desirable however to the extent that it improves control. If so it should be used in the system if the cost associated is sufficiently small. It will become economically necessary when competitors use it to improve their efficiency.

2 *Two new and complicated problems* are raised by directive information which are not encountered in connection with mere operative control: *the problem of total system goals or criteria and that of total system overview information*. It is less difficult to determine whether or not a system is operationally functioning. In the simple system of the previous section, or instance, a failing of the refill function would quickly make itself noticed by the store becoming empty. Only local information is needed to make this fact obvious. When we come to the question whether or not we can improve the economy of the controlled system, things change radically. It is true that if the operative control is so bad that we may reduce the inventory level without causing any stock-outs then such a reduction is obviously an improvement. Likewise a speed-up of the information processing may save money by making it possible to keep a lower average inventory level. This has to be balanced against the increased information cost necessary to achieve it. To evaluate this balance may still be fairly simple because both factors have obvious monetary measures. Continuing our questions of economy we soon come to a situation where an improvement in one subsystem is bought by a cost in another subsystem and where different scales of measure are involved. In the illustrative example above we have the problem of whether or not it pays to reduce the inventory level even when this increases the number of times a year that we run out of stock. This brings up the question of how to compare inventory holding costs with costs of running out of stock. The crucial fact here is that such comparisons can only be made after it has been stated which goals are set for the system control and how the factors studied are influencing the goals.

3 The reason that this observation is important is that it shows that any length of experience in operative control may completely fail to be of guidance when we take up the question of total economy. Obviously, when this insight has not been acquired, much frustration is bound to be induced when executives are trying to base important decisions on experience which cannot possibly provide any knowledge of relevance to these decisions.

4 Let us study the problems of evaluating optional *directive* information for system control by looking again at a simplified model of a firm. We take a similar model as that used in the previous section but we add a manufacturing unit, a *shop*, and put the shop between two stores. From the foregoing figure, we see how the operative information system can be extended accordingly, as shown in Fig. 1, between the horizontal lines A—A and C—C. The operative information system is shown between lines A—A and B—B.

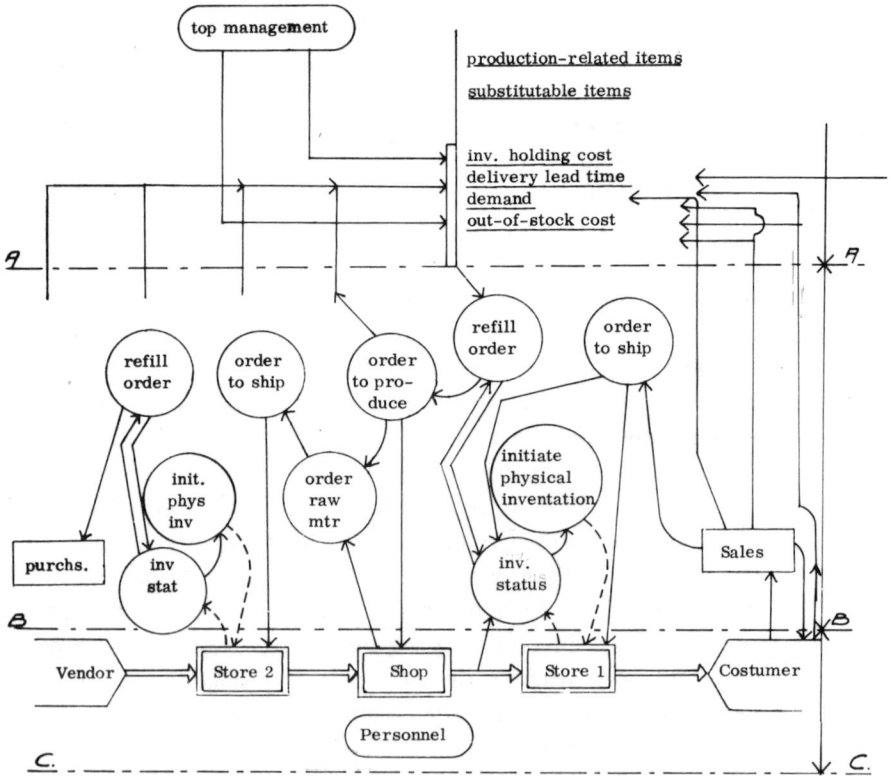

Fig. 1 Above A-A: directive information system
Between
A-A and B-B: operative information system
B-B and C-C: operative system

5 We can introduce the directive information system in the following way. We take any of the decision functions in the operative information system and ask which additional information would be relevant to it and might therefore be used to improve it. The improvement from any quantity of information will then have to be compared to the cost of bringing in and using that information.

6 Let us take the decision function "refill order" for "store 1" as an illustration. For operative functioning it may be designed so as to use a re-order point rule such that when the level of inventory on hand and on order falls below a certain value, the re-order point, then a certain quantity, the order quantity, is ordered. For operative functioning this decision will work for any pair of values of re-order point and order quantity which are high enough to ensure that the system will not run out of stock too often. When we add to the requirement of operative functioning a requirement of best overall economy this can be posed as a question of which is the optimum pair of re-order point and order quantity. These optimum magnitudes need information from different parts of the system as well as information about the goals set for the management of the system in order to be determined.

7 It is easy to see, intuitively, (and is well-known from inventroy theory) that information of relevance to the refill decision are out-of-stock costs and inventory holding costs and these have opposite effects so that they must be balanced against each other. As the risk of running out of stock is dependent on expected delivery time and expected demand, information about these is also of importance. Thus we have added four kinds of desirable information to the two kinds required already by the operative functioning, i.e. inventory level and order to ship. It is of interest to note that whereas the operative information needed for the refill order decision is locally available, i.e. is available at the store control subsystem itself, this is not the case for the added, directive, information. For instance, costs of running out-of-stock are certainly not determined by information that occurs at the store itself. Instead this cost depends on the situation at the market. It may also depend on the goals set for the firm. We have indicated these facts in Fig. 1 by drawing arrows from sales, customers and top management toward "out-of-stock cost".

8 It is typical that directive information not only has to be communicated from non-local sources but also that it is not directly

available at all but might have to be deduced, or computed, from other information, which, in its turn, has to be acquired or computed from other information. Eventually we need information from all over the system and its environment.

9 In Fig. 1 we have drawn one arrow originating above "purchasing" and another originating above "store 2" and both pointing toward "delivery lead-time" to indicate information of potential value.

10 The list of potentially relevant information for "refill order" for "store 1" also contains "substitutable items" and "production related items" to indicate that before deciding on refill ordering it may be valuable to inspect the store status of such items as may be shipped as substitutes or of such items which could use part of the production setup for the current item.

11 It is seen clearly from Fig. 1 that the system for directive information even for the single operative decision function of refill ordering has a very large number of potentially useful information sets. It should be obvious that the list given in the figure is by no means complete. It is also clear that a vast network covering the complete managed system and its environment as well has to be considered. As a compensation to the vast information need of directive decisions is that its value does not fall off as quickly with delayed processing as does the value of operative information.

12 If we would also show the directive information candidates for the other operative decision functions the diagram would obviously be too involved to be of any use as a guidance. We therefore do not show the rest of the system. Let us point out however, before we leave the subject that the out-of-stock cost of "store 2" will be the cost of idle capacity caused by it in the shop, and will therefore be well defined within the system.

13 We shall return to the information need and the relationship between the different information classes later[1]).

22.5 Effect of Time for Decisionmaking. Executive Decisions.

1 We have seen that, to make the ultimate out of control decisions, such as for instance a store refill order decision, one needs infor-

---

[1]) See part 2, chapter 5.

mation from all over the system. This then brings a need for enough time to acquire, communicate, and process all information. The more refined decision to be designed the more time it will take. Now it is typical of decisions for control of a system — *executive decisions* as we may call them — that there is a time interval within which they must be made in order not to lose all or part of their value although, typically, this is far less pronounced for directive information than for operative information. We may get a picture of this situation by studying the two diagrams in Fig. 1a and Fig. 1b.

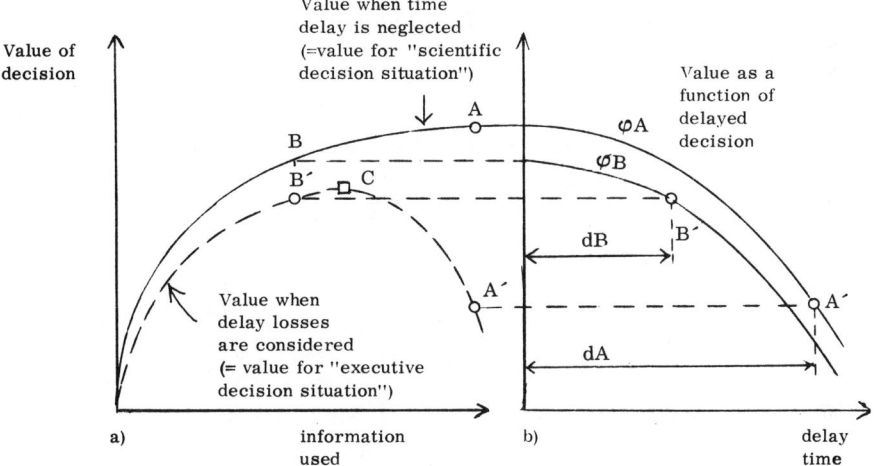

Fig. 1

2 Fig. 1a shows how the value of a decision may increase when an increasing amount of information is used. At point A we are approaching maximum value. Fig. 1b indicates how the value φ_A of the decision according to A is falling when an increasing delay of making decision occurs. Such would be the case with our refill order decision for instance. If it takes the time d_A to make the decision according to point A we find from Fig. 1b that the value, φ_A, will have been reduced by the delay d_A to the point A'.

3 If instead we make the decision by using only half the amount of information then we obtain the smaller value indicated by point B in Fig. 1a. We assume that the value of this decision falls with increasing delay as indicated by the curve φ_B of Fig. 1b. We now have a smaller delay, d_B, because we use less information to make the decision. We find the resulting value B' in Fig. 1b and mark

it out in Fig. 1a. In this way we may continue to find the value curve as dotted in Fig. 1a. It is seen that when the time effect is considered we no longer have an increase in value for every increase in information. Instead when we use an increasing amount of information we first get an increasing value but after a certain amount of information further increase will instead reduce the value. An optimum point, C, is thus found.

4 We learn from the discussion, and from Fig. 1, that the *optimum executive decision will always be a simplified one — and will therefore always look defective when compared with the idealized, non-executive (or "scientific") optimum decision as this is commonly defined in operations research.*

5 We have seen that the time delay imposed upon a decision by the work needed to acquire and process information reduces the degree of detail that is optimal to use in the analysis for decisions. We must also consider the cost of information processing used to make the decision. In Fig. 2 curve "d" shows a hypothetical function of the information cost. This cost typically increases progressively with the degree of detail in the analysis and, hence, with the used volume of information processing. If the curve "b" is the corresponding value curve for "cost-free" executive decision making we obtain the optimum "non-cost-free" executive decision at the volume "B". We see that the additional consideration of processing costs further reduces the volume of information processing corresponding to the "realistic optimum". It thus requires additional simplification of the model used for decision making. Curves "c" and "e" are hypothetical value and cost curves corresponding to an assumed increase in speed of communication and processing plus a reduction in unit processing cost as might be obtained from investment in more efficient equipment. The increased efficiency of equipment makes a finer analysis optimal, as shown by point "C". Thus we see that when computers become less expensive it is optimal to do more information processing.

6 Notice that the executive decision situation is such that if a too high ambition is taken the result will be much worse than with less ambitious, but perhaps more realistic goals. Thus in Fig. 1 if one aims at A then A' would result whereas aiming at the more modest goal B would give the result B' which is much better than A'.

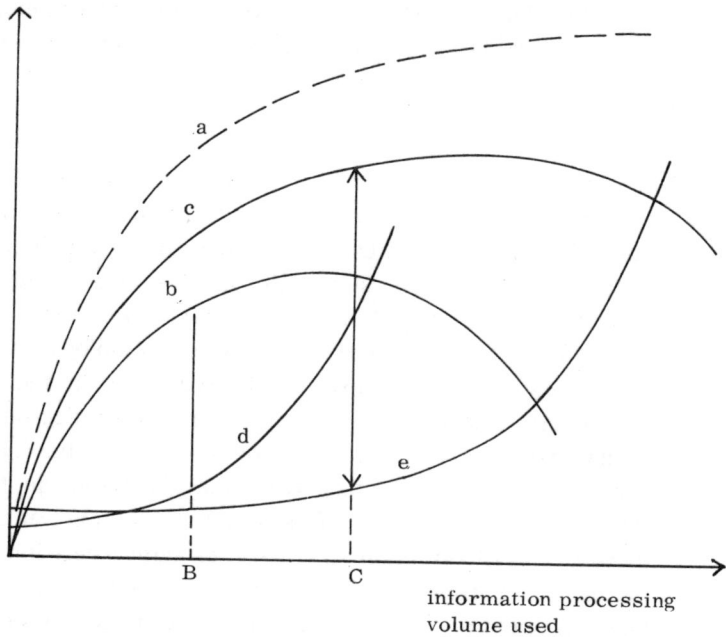

Fig. 2

22.6 Transient Decision Situation. Satisficing.

1 The points "B" and "C" in Fig. 2 of the previous section indicate the degree of simplification of the decision model that would be necessary to care for delay losses and processing costs which occur each time a decision of that kind is to be made. It remains, of course, to determine the actual decision process to be used as well as the frequency of using it. This decision making takes time and incurs costs. What do we do during this time? It is likely to be many times longer than the delay time of the executive decision itself. We may say that during this time we are in a *transient decision situation* whereas we are in a *stationary decision situation* once we have determined the process to use for the executive decision making. It is, of course, normal that the managed system must be operating also during a period of transient decision situation. (Note that this is distinct from "scientific decision making" where one may well await optimum design before letting operative actions be allowed to get initiated.) Thus the problem arises as to how to make executive decisions during a transient period. It is seen that this problem may well call for the using of a still simpler decision model for this may shorten the transient period. In this way we

may be led to a sequence of stages of using increasingly finer models until the one is reached which corresponds to optimum executive decision making in the stationary situation. This still does not solve the problem of how to make the executive decisions before the first of these simplified models have been obtained.

2 It is obvious that during the first part of a transient decision situation the executive decisions must be made on an intuitively defined basis. This will in most cases be most naturally obtained by intuitive setting of quantitative standards. In this way we obtain a basic understanding of why "*satisficing*" (that is "decided to be regarded as satisfactory") *decision making* (in the terminology of H.A. Simon) is so common in executive work. We have, in fact, found that satisficing is unavoidable in transient, executive, decision situations. It may even be said that in transient decision situations satisficing decision making is optimal. What may be wrong in the common satisficing attitude of executives is that one does not attempt to solve the problem of optimum stationary, executive decision processes in parallel with using satisficing. Thus one makes satisficing, (which may be optimal during a transient period) the stationary decision process.

3 It may happen that the circumstances of a system vary so often that a stationary optimum decision situation can never be reached. Then, of course, sotisficing decision making will always be optimal[1]).

22.7 Information Needed in a Simplified Model of a Manufacturing Shop.

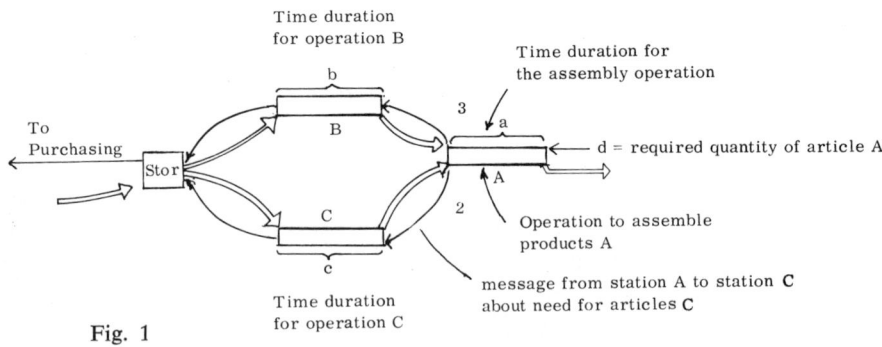

Fig. 1

---

[1]) The study of the illustration example is continued in section 25.1—8.

1 We assume the shop runs a production of objects A, each consisting of 3 subobjects B and 2 subobjects C and each made in one station. B and C made of parts stored in St and purchased when needed. (See Fig.1).

2 The following information is needed here: (a, b, and c are time durations for shop operations)

    A:d,   required quantity of objects. This information is to be sent to A.

    $P(A)$,   precedence information for obj. A. This information is to be available at A, or sent to A if new[1]).

    B:$P(A)_B \cdot$ d, a,   information sent from A to B, (quantity and time of demand).

    $P(B)$,   information available at B or sent to B from A.

    C:$P(A)_C \cdot$ d, a,   information sent from A to C.

    $P(C)$,   information available at C or sent to C from A.

ST: $P(B) \cdot P(A)_B \cdot$ d, a, b; $P(C) \cdot P(A)_C \cdot$ d, a, c; sent from B and C respectively.

Notice that the idea, sometimes advocated, that distributing information about sales (i.e. the information "d") to all parts of the system is of little help. The information to be distributed has to have meaning to a subsystem. (Such transformation is performed e.g. by the operation $P(A)_B \cdot$ d. This information rather than d is needed at B).

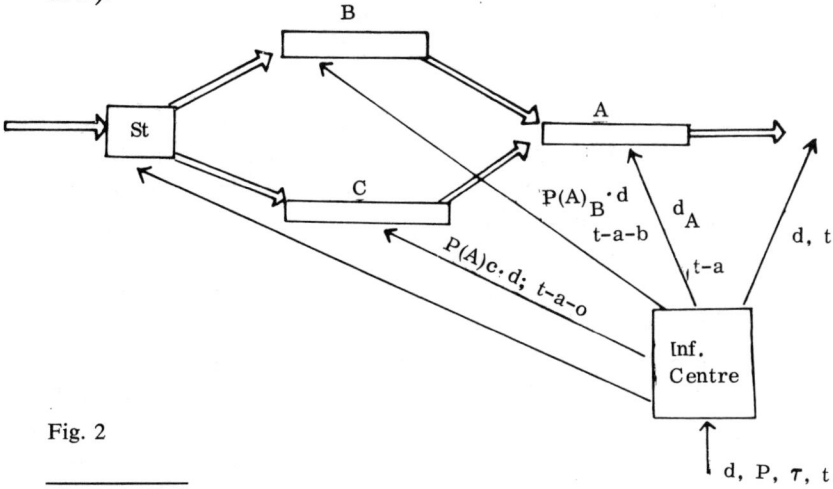

Fig. 2

---

[1]) See part 1, chapter 2.

3 Fig. 2 shows the same production system as Fig. 1, but here the information is sent from one center to all places in the shop. In both cases we have ignored the information necessary for the production activities at each station. In this case the information center also needs to have P, τ available and has to do the associated processing. (P = quantity precedence matrix, τ = the time positioning matrix).

All information moves simultaneously so that St knows what it has to do at the same time as A. In the present case this advantage should be negligible as information could go without delay also along the path A-B-St for instance.

4 Notice that a disturbance, for instance a fault made at B in Fig. 1 would call for a new message from B to St while in Fig. 2 it would call for one message B → Center plus one message Center → St. Fig. 2 thus is inferior in this particular situation.

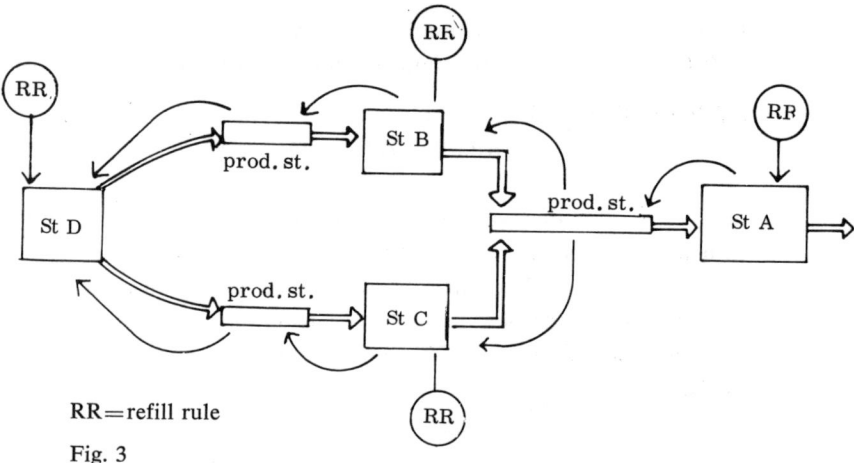

RR = refill rule

Fig. 3

In the model of Fig. 3 we have a simplified version of a "stock controlled production". Each production station (St X in Fig. 3, X = A, B, ...) produces only to orders from its succedent stock, that is the stock it is feeding.

It is possible to imagine this system as an "information free system". In order to do so we must assume that each stock (St X) is provided once and for all with a constant refill rule which tells when to order for refilling, from its preceding production station. We further have to make the assumption that each production station is in direct contact with its succedent stock so that it is always known when production of a specified amount is required.

We notice that even under these somewhat hard assumptions and definitions, which make our model an information free one, we have to require information from outside each time it would be necessary to change a refill rule.

5 We may express this by saying that in order to adapt to changing environment even our simple model of Fig. 3 needs at least *"directive information"* by which its way of acting is directed from some external, guiding authority. This authority in its turn may need quite a lot of information in order to establish the proper directive. That, however, is outside the area of our present, limited study[1]).

6 One thing which we observe regarding the need of our model for directive information is that the need is *infrequent* insofar as the refill rule directive, once given, is supposed to be valid for some time, that is for a number of stock output and refill periods.

7 A more natural view of the model of Fig. 3 is to regard each refill order from a stock station to its preceding production station to be an act of transmitting information. This means that we need a system of information channels connecting each pair of production station and succedent stock. These channels will be busy for an interval each time a refill (or production) order is issued.

All this communication, while busy, is limited to the very nearest "neighborhood".

8 We thus have found that even for our model, with the very simple structure of Fig. 3 and with the very simple operating rules we have discussed, needs a fairly extensive information system.

This information system we have found to be required to handle three different kinds of information:

1. *Operative information* of local character, frequently calling for a message, i.e. each time a refill is required at one of the four stock stations.
   The system for this operative information is shown by the diagram drawn in Fig. 3.

---

[1]) See sections 22.4 and 23.8.

2. *Directive information*, being transmitted from a central authority, outside the model system, but occuring at infrequent instants. This part of the information system is not shown in Fig. 3. We show in Fig. 4 a modified diagram indicating the full information system network for our model.

3. *Information* to the directive station *about the system state* at a set of system points (status information).

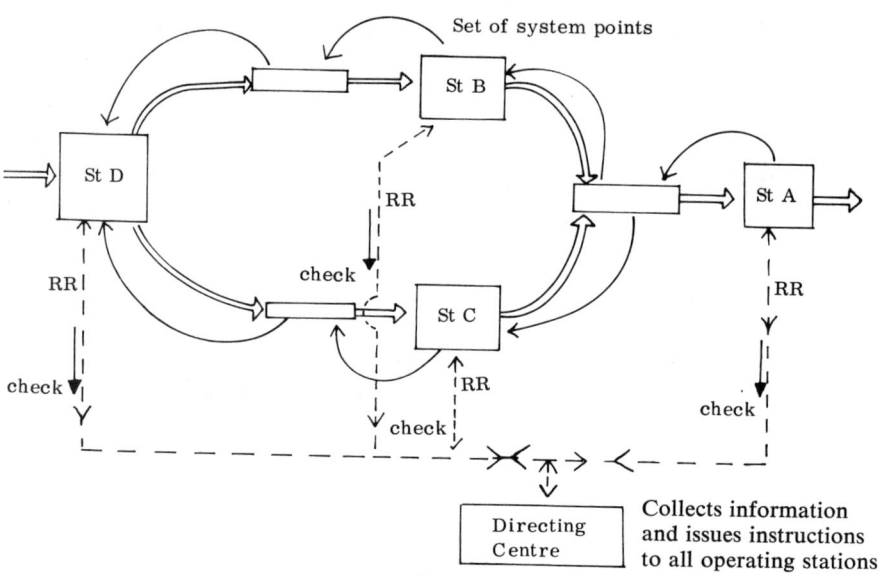

Fig. 4 A system where local operative information goes directly from station to station while directive information is distributed from a directing center and status reports are sent back to this center.

9 We notice in Fig. 4 that the information system (including the operating rules) is an economical one. It limits the busy communication actions to very local areas while putting small demand on the longer channels communicating between the system served and the directing centre. It also calls for infrequent computations within this center to provide the directive information needed. It is of course a very important question whether or not less simple rules and more communication with the center would bring such improvement of the system served that the more expensive information system, then needed, would pay. This is a question associated with the

value of information. Of course a design problem for the information system theory is to find means for making an efficient balance between increased information system cost and improved performance of the system served. We shall have occasion to return to this problem[3]).

10 A closer analysis may in some cases show it to be more economical, from a total systems point of view, to communicate more information with the center, than is done in Fig. 4 however, we want to point out already now that the principle exhibited in Fig. 4, of handling some information locally and some centrally, in a balanced proportion, is one of the most important ones in systems design. This is often forgotten and it is also often overlooked that the most efficient and economical processor for sub-problems of a truly local character, is often a human being. This may be the more so if a central computer can be used to reduce the local problem in a way that is tractable for a human being. It is quite probable that this may be an optimal solution if the human processor is the same man as the one who has to control the activity served by the information, such as is the case with a foreman at a production station in a workshop.

11 We observed above in paragraph 9 that decentralization of operative decisions to each separate station was economical from an information flow point-of-view. This is true when the directive from an overhead authority can be put in the form of a decision rule which can then be put to action for a sequence of successive operations. Thus the directive information flow can be kept at a minimum. It is not true however if directives would have to be distributed for each operation and would require the reporting back of each operation.

12 It is interesting to observe that the scheme with directives distributed only infrequently appears to be useful even in relatively difficult dynamic situations. Thus it is true that in a production system like the one depicted in Fig. 5 a significant change in the demand at A will become noticeable at B_1 only after a time delay during which that change has resulted in a change in the storage level at A and then at B_1. In addition it will take still more time before this is noted at B_2 and B_3. This delay might cause a gear-up of production before

---

[3]) See section 23.2.

B_3 long after an increased demand had converted to a decrease. This however will not happen if the directing center is informed immediately of all changes of demand. It will then send out new directives in due time to all stations.

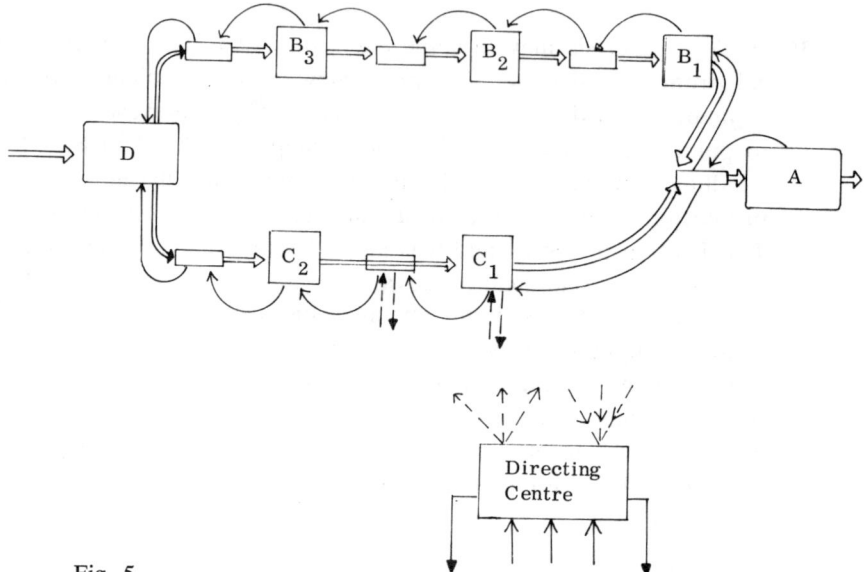

Fig. 5

13 It is obvious that in order to design the correct directives to all stations the directing center must be able to compute the optimum change in directives or decision rules for each station as a function of the demand.

14 It was mentioned in paragraph 9 that there is a possibility that a more direct guidance from the directing center could give so much better results that the increased costs for information flow to and from the center, for each single operation, would be paid. To see how this could be we notice that the possibility to send directives from the center at infrequent times is obtained only by using the inventory level at each store as an indicator to signal when a local decision for refill is needed. This can of course only be done at the price of some extra inventory fluctuation, for this very fluctuation is the information used. As a consequence the inventory levels could be reduced if a more direct control over the operations from the directing center were used.

15 It may be appropriate to point out at this time that the choice of a decentralized handling of operative data does not imply that a

central, automatic data processing unit could not be involved. It is not too difficult to see that to do so would not significantly modify what has been said about the advantages of decentralized decision making for operative decisions.

16 It is on the other hand not necessary that automatic data processing would be used to advantage for the operative information in Fig. 5. If some of the stores B_1, B_2, ..., C_1, C_2 would contain few different elements and still for some reason be watched by one man then he could easily check the occurrence of a re-order level for some element and he could easily give that order to the preceding work station. On the other hand all — or most — stores could be taken together and then manpower saved by using a computer also for the operative information.

Chapter 3. The Economic Quantity of Information and Processing.

23.1 The Economic Quantity of Information.

The question whether or not it would be of value to process — and to store — more information (or, perhaps, less) is of course important for the correct dimensioning of an information system. A cost-versus-value balance is needed. This involves the questions of the value of information and of the quantity of information. Note that these are different. The question may be whether more kinds of information should be introduced or whether shorter sampling intervals would be economic. One will also have to estimate the need or value of redundant data for reliability reasons.

The typical situation for considerations of this kind is when more information or more processing, or both, would reduce margins of indeterminateness. If so it would enable the reduction of safety measures such as safety stocks or safety margins of physical design. The gain obtained from such an analysis must then be compared with the cost increase caused by the additional work and equipment for gathering the information and for its processing. One must thereby also consider costs for increased precision which may become necessary in other parts of the system in order to make the improvement useful.

It is astonishing that this problem, which obviously is a central one in the design of an information system, is almost totally neglected, both in the literature and in the practical installations of data processing systems. When we say neglected we do not mean that system designers would not be aware of these questions, but the problem is not tackled with enough force or courage to find solutions. There have however been some cases where discussion at depth have been afforded to this question, e.g. in the literature on decision theory[1]). The author[2]) too has solved a problem of this sort which, although of a fairly specific kind, should be general enough to be useful as an indication of how solutions to this kind of problems can be obtained. We give below an account of this material.

---
[1]) 2 Ra 1961.
[2]) 2 La 1960.

It is easy to point at situations in almost any system where safety measures are used and cause significant costs. In all such cases it is of interest to consider the extent to which these safety measures — and hence their costs — could be reduced at the price of doing more information processing. This will not always be possible. This is easy to see. We can think for instance of a safety stock quantity which is dimensioned to guard against run out losses incurred by errors in sales forecast. These errors depend to a large extent on the random characters of changes influencing the development of sales. To that extent they cannot be reduced by carrying more data — the *information* that could be used for reduction is not available. If it were, there would not be randomness. However if the errors in forecasting are permitted to be larger than the minimum possible, because of the cost or labor involved in acquiring and processing sufficient amounts of information, then this means a possibility for reduction. In most actual safety stocks such reductions are probably available. The cost balance for this could be calculated if the cost of including additional information in the information system is determined. This is what should be done in information system design.

This is not to say that every possible bit of information, which could serve to reduce safety measures, has to be analyzed. The correct approach is to estimate the possible effect of different amendments to the information system and then to test them for economy of being included, starting with the most profitable ones and stopping when there ceases to be significant gains to be made by further inclusion.

23.2 Information Value as an Information System Design Parameter.

In the design of information processing systems the value of information does not seem to be given explicit consideration at present. This of course is a very serious neglect, for without consideration of the value of the information it is, of course, not possible to decide upon the right amount, the right kind, and the right time of the production of information. Also — as is only to be expected in view of this neglect — present systems are often designed only to do in a more automatic way what has been done in the past. This is to ignore the possible gain from more sophisticated design, but it is natural to make such a mistake when that gain cannot be evaluated. This is often claimed to be the careful way of introducing ADP, because it is not dependent on realizing new kinds of effiency increase which have not yet been proven in practice. However this conservative approach instead offers much smaller profit margins so that even moderate miscalculation may result in losses rather than profit. This also appears to have often been the case. At the other extreme there is presently much talk about the importance of introducing "on-line-real-time" systems, which then, sometimes, turn out to be overambitious. So far we have still to see satisfactory analyses of the economic factors involved to support the enthusiasm. If such processing is more expensive it is, of course, only to be used where it provides information of sufficiently greater value — by volume, kind or timeliness. In some applications this is obviously the case, in others only a detailed analysis can tell. While no literature treating the influence of information value on an information processing system design for business application[1]) has come to the knowledge of the author, he has himself done an analysis of this kind for an engineering design system[2]).

It was shown that because the design computations were done on the basis of simplified models a "finer" model would increase the quality of design and, of course, the amount of computation to be done. It was possible to obtain quantitative estimates of the "fine-ness" of the model and of the value of the product quality associated with it, and also of the associated computation cost. The analysis was capable of producing an economic optimum value of the amount of computation to be done on a project, given the cost per numeric operation. The kernel of the economic analysis for the engineering design problem was that a certain margin-of-safety (in the form of added material in a load-carrying structure) had to be added to the system being designed, because of the expected size of error in the analysis. A finer analysis, giving smaller expected error, calls for less safety margin. Thus increased production of information saved safety margin material. In that way the additional information brought additional value of saving, but each new unit of information provided less new value and required more processing work. In almost any system an analogous problem exist so that an analogous way of evaluating information seems feasible. In a manufacturing system, for instance, the time delay involved, not

---

[1]) Even in a recent symposium (1965) on the Economics of ADP, 2 Fr 1965, we still do not find a practical illustration.
[2]) 2 La 1959.

only in readjusting production levels but also in recognizing any change in demand, means that forecasting becomes important. Most often not all information of significance for the forecasting is acquired and used, for cost reasons. This means that one is satisfied with a greater forecast error. This has to be balanced by an increased safety margin in the form of safety stock. Optimization of the information processing in such a case calls for evaluation of the cost for using more information[2]), the reduction in forecast error it would bring (if any), the reduction in safety stock which can be done, and the amount of money this would save.

With any such *system* we associate an *information system* which has the objective of providing knowledge which can be used to improve the efficiency of functioning of the *system*. When it is necessary to be distinct we shall call the system served by the information system "*the managed system*" or the "*object system*".

We want to find out in which ways an information system can improve the efficiency of a managed system of the kind described. In this way the *value* of an information system is determined. From such insight we then want to find out how costs increase when we increase the quality of an information system and how then its value increases. This would give us the possibility of attempting to design information systems to economic optimum.

We shall see that while even a specific piece of information is associated by people with a vague and, in general, undefined meaning, it will have a definite value for *an object system* in a specified situation and it will have a meaning defined by the way it is treated by an *associated information system*.

We shall see, also, that a quantitative measure or "volume" can be given not to the information itself but to the data needed to communicate it. This data volume will be closely related to the measure used in "information theory"[3]) but this is not true for the value of the information.

---

[2]) "More information" is used here to imply increased number of kinds of information or more frequent gathering of information or application of more sophisticated and computation requiring methods, separately or in combination.

[3]) The restriction of the use of the name "Information Theory" to the narrow field it presently has is unfortunate and most probably cannot be adhered to in the future. Bar-Hillel proposes to use instead the name "Theory of Signal Transmission" which appears to be much more appropriate.

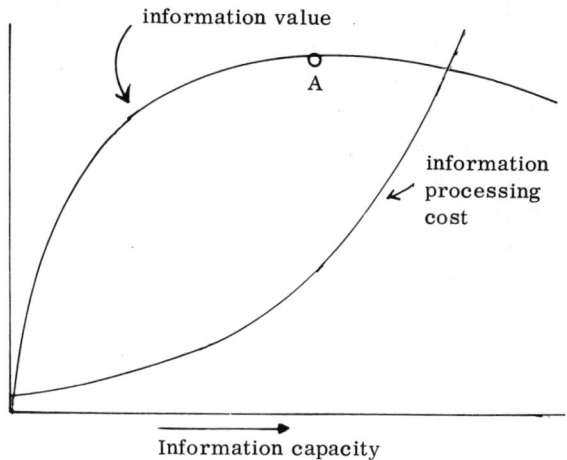

Fig. 1

Fig. 1 may help understanding the problem. We assume that information is gathered from the object system and is processed and used for its control. If we begin by using very little information the quality of control may be improved and we measure the value of information by the economic value of the improvement in efficiency of the managed system that it brings about. When more information is used the cost for acquiring and processing it will also increase. When more and more information is used the cost for its processing will typically grow progressively because more complicated relationships have to be evaluated. Instead the improvement of control will typically be smaller and smaller when the amount of information increases.

It may even change sign and fall again after a certain amount of information processing, point A, Fig. 1. This is to say that if the cost for the information (and its processing) were negligible then the point A would correspond to some kind of optimum design of the system management.

Such an optimum is often called a theoretical optimum. This, of course, is misleading for also in theory this is not an optimum as soon as processing cost has to be considered. Such is almost always the case as can be seen from the fact that one is almost always satisfied with some approximation to the "theoretical optimum". By bringing in the curve representing the information processing cost we are able to determine the true optimum, which is actually the one to be used[4]). This may be more easily seen if we replace the information value with a function which we may call the *simplification cost* function. This is to be defined as the opportunity cost incurred by using less information than necessary to obtain the optimum efficiency of the managed system. In other words: if we simplify the information processing, and thereby use less information, the loss of total information value that follows is defined as the simplification cost. "Simplification" is associated with how realistic is the chosen model as a basis for the information processing. A higher degree of model realism calls for more information and processing, and corresponds to less simplification.

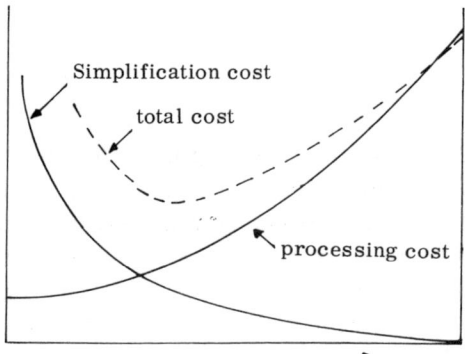

Degree of Realism of the model used.

Fig. 2

In Fig. 2 we have indicated the simplification cost curve together with the information processing cost. Summing these two costs we obtain the total cost whose minimum determines the amount of information for which the system is to be designed in order to be an optimum design.

In real situations the cost curves may not always be smooth as in Fig. 2. In Fig. 3 we have indicated a situation which may be encountered. In such systems we may have several minimum cost points. In Fig. 3 we have indicated two minimum points.

---

[4]) See however what we have said about *executive optimum*, section 22.5. The time used for information processing delays the use of the optimum decision results so that a simpler computation, less delayed, becomes *executively* optimal, in an executive situation, that is when time does matter.

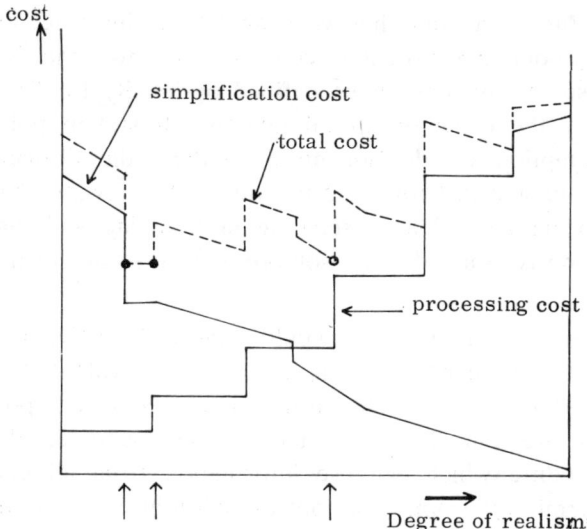

Fig. 3

23.3 Information and System Control.

We take up in general terms the function of an information system for the control of another system which we have studied earlier in connection with the special case of a system of two stores and a shop, sections 22.4.

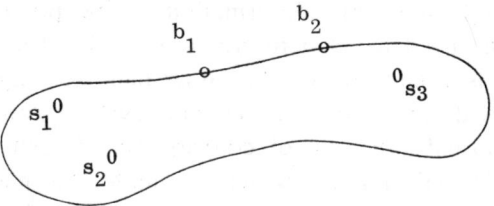

Fig. 1. System S with system points S_1, S_2, S_3.

We consider a system S, the behavior of which we observe by observation at a set of system points s_i ($s_i \in S$, $i = 1, 2, \ldots n$).

We assume that we are able to control the behavior by exercising influence upon it at its "boundary points" b_j ($b_j \in B$, $j = 1, \ldots k$)[1]).

---

[1]) Notice that in an administrative system we have several "physical subsystems" of the total system. For instance we have both the productive machinery system and the "system of workers" as subsystems. Therefore information about "state of the productive system" may contain messages about the worker situation of the day as well as (more rarely) about change of equipment. Also "state information" can be about action taken by people.

We further assume that we know how to influence upon any boundary point b_j (in order to control S, in a way that is optimal in the sense in which we have defined optimality for S) as soon as we know the behavior up till now of all system points s_i. By this assumption we do not mean to deny the difficulty in actually obtaining such knowledge but we want to assume that that problem is being tackled as a separate undertaking and that the best we can do is to use the best solution known so far for that problem.

When we said that we would "know the behavior" of a system point "up till now" this is intuitively equivalent to saying that we would have "complete information" about that point. Using this term we can then say that we have assumed that we have a procedure which can use information from all system points to determine the optimum control action at every boundary point.

There may well be analytic relations between different system points so that behavior at one point can be calculated from that at some other points. Then, of course, information from that point can be omitted if the control procedure also computes the corresponding values from the information from other points. Notice that whereas the analytical relation of one point to other points may eliminate the need for fetching information at that point, it does not follow that the need for that information in the decision for some other points is eliminated. On the other hand so long as the information is needed for control of the same system from which it is drawn (the normal situation, of course) then it seems probable that the same analytic relation which eliminates the need to observe some information also will eliminate the need of it for control. (This is, of course, a problem calling for special study.)

It is interesting to note that already the simple model we have established so far, is sufficient as a basis for determining

> the meaning of information
> the value of information
> the volume of the representation of information

with precision. All three concepts are usually treated only in a way that is vague in one sense or another. The possibility of this precision probably stems from our willingness to restrict these questions to the well defined system S. This restriction is in any case the natural one when we are interested in the problems of an information system which will only need to handle information given by or required by this single system S. (In making this statement we have taken S to include its relevant environment.)

23.4 The Meaning of Information within a System.

The meaning of a certain kind of information as defined above is well *defined with respect to the system*. It is knowledge of the status or behavior of one specified point within the system. This, of course, is subject to the condition that the identification of the system point has meaning with respect to the system. The system will have a well defined meaning if it is studied in the system-theoretical way so that all its parts are well defined. It also must define clearly how the parts are interlinked, and if the point is one of junction between parts. If the point is instead an internal point of a part then its meaning for the system is defined by the part it belongs to, if it has then a well defined meaning within that part.

The meaning of a point in the system has relevance for how information about it has to be used in the control of the system. We can therefore say that the meaning of a certain kind of information is determined with *respect to the information system* by the way it is being handled by it. As a consequence we may also say that a kind of information has meaning with respect to the system by the way it is processed by the information system plus the way the information system is related to the controlled system.

We have so far stressed that we have only been discussing meaning of a *kind* of information. When in everyday discourse we say that we obtain information we have something more precise in mind than just *kind* of information. We need, of course, also more precision to the concept of information in the analysis of information systems.

We have said that information about a system point is knowledge of the behavior of the system at that point. Behavior is naturally described by description of state and change of state at a given moment of time, or by description of state at a set of subsequent time intervals. One very natural way, therefore, to have complete information about a system point is to obtain a description of its state each time that the state has changed enough to be significant and then to store the descriptions for as many previous time intervals as are significant[1]).

We find that when we talk about getting information from a system point we will normally mean a new state description from that point, to be added to the total, stored, information about that point. Obviously we need to distinguish between "information" in the sense of kind of information and "information" as obtained from some system point. To this end we introduce the term "*message*" and use it to mean an addition to our stored information. We also define "*point message*" to mean a new description of state or of change of state from one point in the system. Thus a point message will occur each time any one of the state variables at a system point has changed enough to pass some predetermined significance threshold.

We have described that the meaning of a certain kind of information with respect to a system (and now also the meaning of a point message) is determined by identification of the point (in a way that has meaning to the system) and by the state or behavior at the point. We have to say a few more words about what is meant by state and behavior.

When we talk about controlling a system then one or more characteristics of the system change with time — thereby constituting a behavior of the system. The "characteristic" will typically consist of physical entities that exist in the system, flow through the system, or are handled by the system or, maybe, movements of the system and its parts. For each such physical entity we assume that a set of measures are defined[2]). Such a measure may be a magnitude such as length, weight, temperature, velocity, or it may be one characteristic out of a specified set such as a persons name or number or the indication of sex. The state of the system at a certain point will be described by the set of physical entities (or *state variables*) that exist in that system point, together with the values of these variables in that point-in-time (whereby, of course, also the value of the variable time is to be given). By *elementary state* we mean the measure of *one* of the state variables at a point in a time interval. An *elementary message* will consist of the identification of

---

[1]) When we use the word significant here we assume that the question of the different significance levels is settled as part of the total systems analysis.
[2]) We use the word "measure" here rather than "value" because we want to save the latter for the meaning "utility value".

the system point, the moment of time, and measure of one of the state variables of the system in the point as well as identification of the kind of this state variable.

Notice that while an elementary message has a certain information content, or semantic content, nothing smaller than an elementary message has. For instance, the value of a state variable alone does not bring any information at all, and neither does it when accompanied by an identification of its kind alone, or of the system point alone. An identification as to locality and kind without any accompanying measure is void of information, and a measure without an identification is without meaning. It is interesting to see how this fact has its counterpart in the broader question of semantic content in a linguistic message.

When Bar-Hillel[3]) states: "Nothing short of a statement conveys information, and this information is not built up piecemeal from an accumulation of the information carried by each signal..." he describes exactly the situation for the elementary messages as well[4]). On a closer analysis we even find that a message alone does not convey any information, it has to be combined with a "receiving structure"[5]).

It might be argued that if we take an elementary message minus one of its terms it then has no semantic content. Adding the missing term will add all its semantic content so that one might say that that term contains information. Notice however that it contains information about the message and not about the subject of the message. Note also that actually the missing term says nothing unless it is determined how to fit it with the message so that, in fact, this term *plus* the structural information about its place in the message is what is added.

---

[3]) 4 Ba 1964, 285—286.
[4]) This minimum condition is a syntactic one, meaning that a syntactically incomplete string of words (or measures) gives no information. Notice that it does not follow that the elementary message has minimum information (i.e. semantic content). This instead would be obtained from the denial of an elementary message for it excludes one of the "n" possible values at a point, of one kind of state variable whereas the elementary message excludes n-1 such values. Cf. Bar-Hillel, loc.cit, where "atomic sentence" is the linguistic counterpart of our elementary message and *content-element* is analogous to a denial of an elementary message.
[5]) Cf. section 23. 6—18.

Notice that we have said that an elementary message consists (at least) of a measure of a state variable plus identification of place, time and kind for that state variable. We have made a distinction between place and kind because such a distinction has an intuitive meaning to us. It does not follow however that this distinction has a meaning for the system to be controlled. Whether this is the case or not will depend entirely on whether it will be required to do some processing of information about place but not about kind. This we cannot decide before we have become more specific about the control of the system. It is therefore, so far, entirely possible that it may turn out that we may use one common identification for both place and kind. For instance if a system has five points and three kinds of state variables we might in some cases say that we have fifteen reference points (or "kind-points"). On the other hand it is very plausible already that the measure of a state variable at a point and the measure of time are regarded as distinct from the other parts of the message as they will, typically, change while place and kind remain unchanged. It is therefore plausible that the distinction between the "identifying parts" of a message and the "measure parts" has a meaning within every system and that this difference in meaning can be seen from a difference in processing. Likewise we expect that the measure of time will have a meaning distinct from measures of the state variables but that the state variables may or may not have any distinct meaning from the systems point-of-view. If they have not they may be regarded as a set of components of the same state vector. That the distinction would disappear so completely that they would be taken together into one single number is highly improbable in any normal system.

The clarifications made in this discussion have relevance from an economic point-of-view because to represent place and kind by separate variables may take more symbols than taking them together. For instance to represent ten system points we may need two decimal digits and to represent three kinds may take another digit making a total of three while representing the thirty possible combinations requires only two digits. We shall say more about representation below.

We must ask for the meaning of information which is not defined *within* the system and although intuitive to people, may be of no use in the information system. We must not forget that when people are accustomed to feeding information to the information system or accepting information from it, such a distinction may assist in the communication and therefore may be well motivated.

23.5 The Value of Information in a System.

The value of the information about a system point with respect to the system can be measured by the value it has for controlling the system. Specifically the value of the information carried by an elementary message is determined by the amount of value it adds to the information in total, i.e. by the increase in value for the whole system that corresponds to the economic gains that can be obtained by using (the information of) the message. When we define value of information in this way, using the concept of message and referring to a specific system and specific objectives for that system, then there is, fundamentally, no difficulty in obtaining precision. If we ask instead about the value of a message in an absolute sense, without relation to a specified system, then we do not find an answer. This is the way this kind of question is usually posed, however. It is then only to be expected that precision is not obtained.

We shall see that the value of a certain message does not only depend on the the system itself, it also depends on how much information has already been obtained (and stored).

Our solution of the problem of meaning was obtained at the price of restricting to points and state variables well defined. This means that we are not able to give information about changes of the system design and that even if we would be able to do that then the information system would not know the meaning. This is a case where we might instead well give the message in ordinary language and have a man understand it. The restriction here that the automatic information system (contrary to man) would not understand such a new kind of message is not very severe for we must in such situations provide the system with new algorithms for using the new kinds of information and therefore it would not be much trouble to give at the same time enough form specification for the new message to make it readable by the system. This is true provided we have designed the information system, from the beginning, in such a flexible way that it can be extended when need arises.

One requirement must be stated at this point. A system which is not completely formalized and for which one therefore will have to expect that new kinds of messages, with unforeseen kind of content, may become necessary occasionally — must, if it is to work in a fully integrated way, be able to accept such messages, although not understanding them, and without being able to use or process them, and have means for asking man for advice or asking man to take over control.

We see that the value (within the system) of a certain message is determined by the theory of control for that system and not by the theory of information systems. The value of the message is determined by the economic gains that can be achieved by using the message in all efficient operating doctrines for the controlled system which the theory for that system has been able to establish. That theory would also have to evaluate the gains. Information systems theory will have to explore the operating doctrines that are available and the accompanying gains. The needs for messages and their processing that are associated with each such doctrine must be established as well as the most efficient way of handling and processing this information. The most efficient handling will lead to the lowest information cost and this has to be compared to the information value, that is the economic gains it produces, in order to enable a decision as to whether to include that information in the information system or not.

Although in some cases the information value is mentioned in the literature [1], [2], [3] it is not usually shown how quantitative measures of information value could be obtained. We know only a few cases where means for quantitative evaluation have been discussed at some depth [4], [5], [6], [7] and only in two of these works are practical examples worked through [4], [5]. Se also 4 Fo 1968.

It is natural that the ignorance of the possibilities for quantitatively determining the value of information would lead to an underestimation of this value and, consequently too low a degree of ambition is chosen for the implementation of automatic management informa-

---

[1] 2 Gh 1963.
[2] 2 Md 1963.
[3] 3 Fr 1965.
[4] 2 Ms 1959.
[5] 2 La 1959.
[6] 2 Ra 1961.
[7] 4 Ac 1961.

tion systems. This has certainly been the case in the majority of ADP installations designed so far.

There is of course also the risk that information value within a system will be overestimated so that too expensive information processing systems will be installed. This appears to be the case in some presently planned systems where "on-line-real-time" is set as a goal without really assessing the gains and costs that are associated.

It is obvious that a rational design of an information processing system, including the decision as to the most economical degree of ambition, can only be obtained on the basis of a realistic evaluation of the value of different quantities of information (e.g. elementary messages) and of the associated handling and processing costs.

In order to show that our requirement for a quantitative determination of information value is not wholly unrealistic we give a simplified version of an example discussed by us in a previous work where we were able to determine the optimum quantity of information and its processing for an engineering design problem.

It is not uncommon that in engineering problems we have curves which have certain smoothness properties which imply that the curve

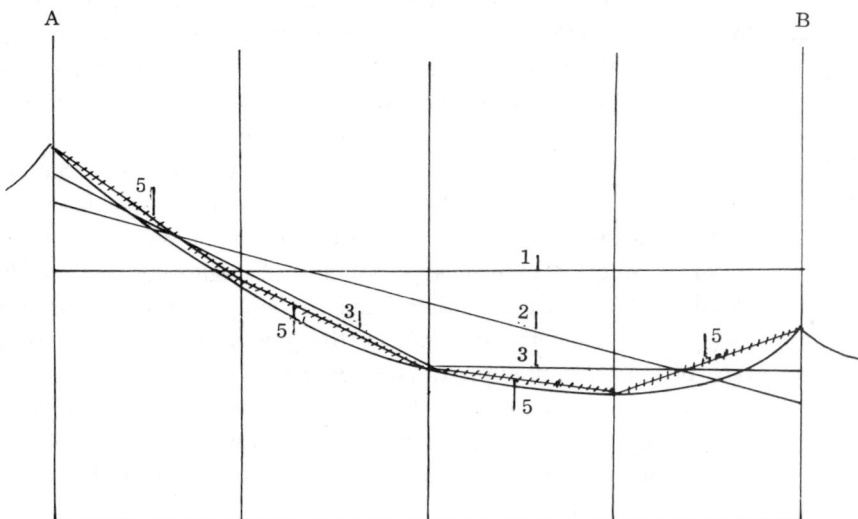

Fig. 1. Approximation of a curve segment, by polygons with 1 point (horizontal line), 2 points (sloping line), 3 points and 5 points, corresponds to halving the linear interval each time we go to the next higher number of points. The 5 point polygon has been shaded to make it visible.

can be subdivided into a small number of segments each of which, when approximated by a polygon, gives rise to an approximation error which is inversely proportional to the square (or some other power between 1 and 4, say), of the greatest linear interval of the approximating polygon. Thus, roughly speaking, if we double the number of linear intervals in the polygon we reduce the approximation error to one fourth of its previous value.

In Fig. 1 a curve is shown together with two vertical lines, A and B, which cut off one segment of the curve. This segment can be approximated with its mean value over the segment (or the horizontal line "1") or it can be approximated with a 2-point polygon "2", or 3-point polygon "3", or the 5-point polygon "5" etc. Each reduction to one half of the previous interval (or doubling the number of points) roughly cuts the error to one third of its previous value, indicating a power of slightly less than two for this curve.

It is normal that corresponding to an *expected* magnitude of the approximation errors in the model used for analysis, some safety measures are taken in the design or control of a system. It is also normal that a cost is associated with these safety measures and is proportional to the magnitude of the expected errors and that this cost (e) can be estimated fairly well for a specified safety measure. In this way we see that a certain fixed cost can be assigned to using the simple model of analysis corresponding to line "1" in Fig. 1. In refining the model by using "2" instead of "1" we cut the error cost to about one fourth, i.e. going from "1" to "2" is worth 0.75 e while going from "2" to "3" is worth only an additional $0.75 \times 0,25$ e and is leaving only the error cost 0.25×0.25 e $= 0.0625$ e. Each further doubling the number of intervals of the polygon brings an additional, fast diminishing, saving in error cost. We have, of course simplified the question of approximation by ignoring more sophisticated methods. On the other hand the simple approximation with polygons is often the best one in the general case when a specific type of curve to be approximated cannot be determined in advance. Likewise the estimation of the approximation error as a function of the number of polygon points could be determined in more detail only for specific cases where the mathematical characters of the curve were known.

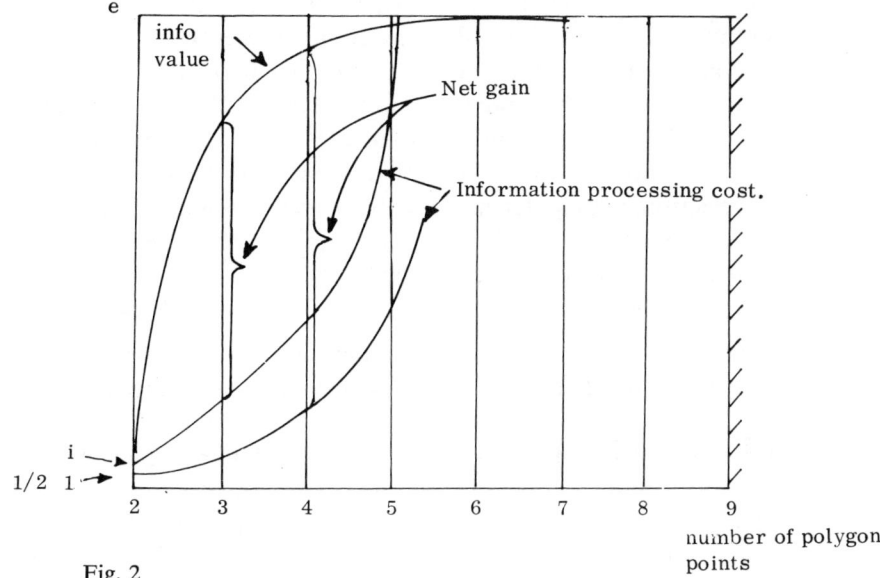

Fig. 2

Hypothetical value and cost for polygonal approximation of cost curve.

In Fig. 2 we have drawn a horizontal line corresponding to the assumed error cost e for using the simple model "1". The "value" curve indicates the value of refining the model, as a function of the number of polygon intervals for a segment of the problem curve. The vertical over the value 9 of the abscissa is shaded to show that in this case it is assumed that a further refinement beyond 8 polygon intervals (or 9 points) per curve segment would not be reasonable because of other limitations of accuracy.

The determination of the polygon "2" requires information about the two endpoints[8]). For "3" three endpoints and in general for "n" n endpoints are to be determined. The information and its processing to determine the endpoints may increase as the cube (or some other power > 2 say) of the number of endpoints. If the cost for information processing for the model "1" is i then for the model n it will be $((n)^3 i)$. In Fig. 2 we have drawn such cost curves for an assumed basic cost i and for the basic cost $= 1/2$ i. It can be seen that Fig. 2 determines the optimum model as the one for which the information value minus information and processing cost is

---

[8]) Fig. 1.

maximum. It is found that when the basic cost is i then the optimum model (with only one curve segment) is "3" (that is a polygon with 3 interpolation points) while if the basic cost is reduced to i/2 the optimum model is "4". When we are able to reduce the "cost per operation" of the information processing then a finer model is optimum. (Progressing from handcomputation to an electronic computer makes a finer analysis optimal.) For several curve segments and also for problems involving more than one dimension analogous results can be obtained.

It is worth noting that in common optimization work one often finds that the optimal strategy is too cumbersome and some less efficient but more convenient doctrine is adopted. In our model this will never happen because for a strategy to be cumbersome would mean that it would have a high information processing cost and this would be taken care of in our model. The optimum that we determine will therefore be a realizable optimum procedure. (In an executive decision situation we must consider not only processing costs but also delay losses, as shown earlier[9].)

We can illustrate this by a simple example from the theory of inventory control. In the (unrealistically) simple case of constant, deterministic rate of demand λ of one item at one stock point if A is the constant cost of placing an order, C is the constant unit cost of one item, I is the inventory carrying charge, the optimal order quantity is

$$1 \qquad Q^* = \sqrt{\frac{2 \lambda A}{IC}}$$

If we assume that the conditions are such that this simple formula can be used but that changes occur so that we do not know which values actually hold for the parameters λ, A, I, and C then we may use parameter values more or less in error and compute an order lot Q which differs more or less from the true Q^*. We will thus obtain a loss by running the inventory at the non-optimal level determined by Q. Something of this sort normally occurs because it appears too complicated to determine the exact parameter values. Fig. 3 shows[10] how the factor K/K^* varies with Q/Q^* where K

---

[9] All Section 22.5.
[10] Fig. 3 is based on a diagram that was given in Hadley and Whitin: Analysis of Inventory Systems.

and Q are the actually valid values of cost and order quantity and K* and Q* are optimal values.

In order to be able to compute the parameters for operating at the optimal point $Q/Q^* = 1$ we would have to acquire enough information from other parts of the system and process it. Using less than complete information will mean that rather than operate on $Q/Q^* = 1$ we would operate somewhere within an interval around this point. The less information (and its processing) that we pay the wider will be this interval. From Fig. 3 we can determine the loss factor K/K^* caused by this interval. The value of additional information is determined by the associated reduction of the loss factor. Alternatively we can say that the simplification of using less information causes the "simplification cost" determined by K/K^*,

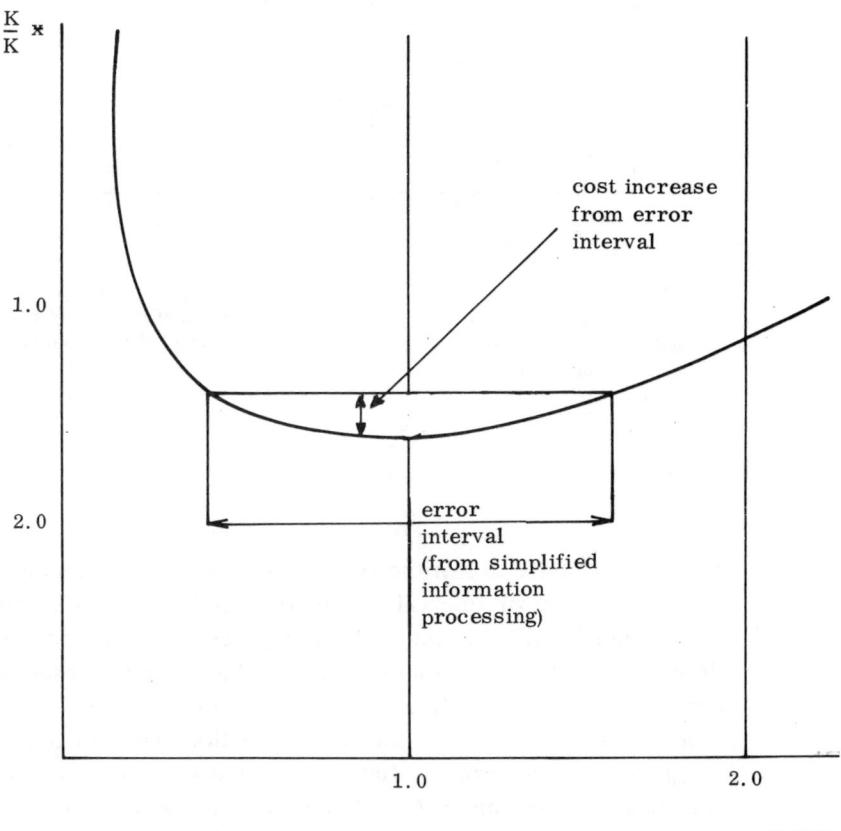

Fig. 3

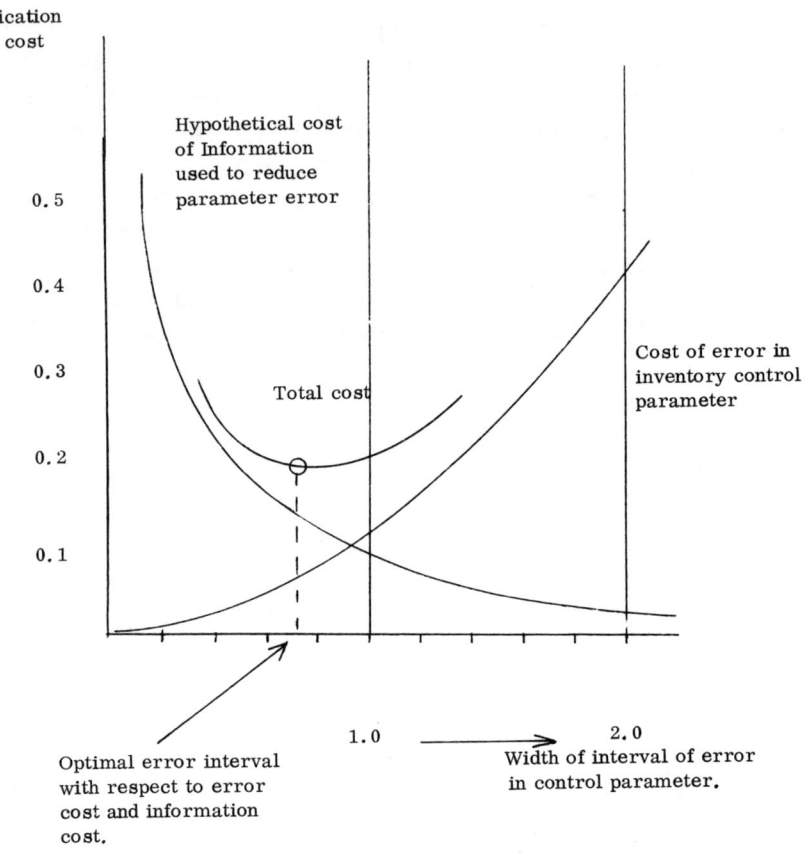

Fig. 4

In Fig. 4 we have drawn the simplification cost as a function of the width of the error interval as determined by the "effective" loss corresponding to the interval boundaries. This is obtained by drawing a set of horizontal lines in Fig. 3 and observing the corresponding values $(K/K^* - 1)$ and (Q/Q^*) max $- (Q/Q^*)$ min determined by each line in conjunction with an appropriate weighted average process. In such an analysis we would use the statistical distribution of Q/Q^* for any information cost level and determine an expected value of K/K^* but we do not show details of this as we only want to illustrate roughly the kind of thoughts that are relevant.

We have in Fig. 4 also drawn a hypothetical information cost and indicated how the truly operational optimum error interval is obtained. Of course in practice we cannot determine the lot size to use according to this optimum. We can however determine the operationally optimal effort of information processing which is then to be used in connection with computing the approximation to Q* which is to be used. (We have, in this very simplified example neglected the control delay caused by the time for making decisions. This being an executive decision the delay will cause losses which in a real situation must also be considered[11].)

When we have talked about information in our simple inventory model we have understood that by making use of a larger number of elementary messages we may improve the quality of control. We will be able to obtain more correct estimates of the parameters in the optimizing formula 1. We may take more messages either by using messages from more system points or from the same points but more often. Thus the value of λ that we use in the formula 1 is a forecast of the rate of demand for the item, to be expected for the time interval for which our control activity will be relevant. If the item is a part that is to be used in the assembly of some end products then the future demand of the item will be dependent on the future demand of end products and will thus be influenced by the state of other parts of the system (i.e. where end products are scheduled). Also if demand is changing rapidly it will be of value to obtain messages more often. The value of more messages depends on the properties of the system under control. The importance of a message from one system point depends on how "strongly connected" that point is in the system, to our control point. Similarly, the value of a new message from the same system point depends on how much the system has changed since latest message from that point arrived.

It can be seen from Fig. 2 that when successively more polygon points are made use of, i.e. when successively more messages are taken, the corresponding increase of value per message goes down. The reason for this is that we have assumed that the curve segment has certain smoothness characteristics. We may say that it is the information that smoothness can be expected that reduces the information of successive messages. This is equivalent to saying that messages from a certain number of points plus the knowledge

---

[11]) See section 22.5.

that smoothness is expected, is equivalent to messages from those same points plus a number of additional points. It is not to be taken as a general rule that availability of more information would always reduce the value of additional information. On the other hand this will often be so because it is often the case that we have information of a global character such as smoothness.

When value of information is at all mentioned in the literature it is in terms of distinct components such as: quality, quantity, relevance, reliability, and timeliness. We used instead as a measure of the value of information, the improvement in control effect that it makes possible. This can be measured whereas the components mentioned above cannot be separately mesured. Instead of talking about timeliness as if it had an inherent value we have stressed that distinct kinds of information may lose value in distinct proportion when they are delayed.

23.6 Data Representation of Information in a System. Volume of Data[1]).

1 "Data" is often used in everyday language as a synonym of "information". We have already pointed out that in a formal analysis we must be clear about the different meanings of different occurrences of "information" and we therefore need to use different words for different (even if closely related) concepts. We use "data" here to stand for "means for representing information"[2]). More specifically we shall define data to be plural of datum and "datum" to mean "a set of symbols to represent a part of a message". Thus data will often mean a digital or alphabetical representation of one or more parts of one or more messages. This definition still very much conforms to everyday usage, although more restricted. Our definition does not clearly include representation of information in socalled analog form. If we should need to use the word data at all in such connection we must, in our terminology, apply the prefix analog and say "analog data". We prefer to avoid this however and not use "data" in connection with analog representation. We shall call a data representation of a message *a record*.

---

[1]) See section 26.2 for further discussion of this topic.

[2]) We have seen that determining the value of a certain information we did not come to define "amount of information". We now come to see that "amount" or "volume" of the data representing information can be defined. We also shall see that data volume has no natural connection with the *value* of information but, of course, it has relevance for the *cost* of handling and processing.

An elementary record then will represent an elementary message. The singular form "datum" would correspond to the representation of one value such as the measure of a state variable or a name. Notice that whereas the data representing a message carry information a single datum will not carry any information whatsoever.

2 We will need to have a word for the part of a message that is represented by a datum and we shall call it a *term*. We have mentioned that an elementary message will typically consist of three term pairs identifying respectively a system point, a point in time, a kind of state variable and its measure. When all terms in a message are represented by data we have a data representation of the message.

3 For purpose of distinction we shall call a "physical record" a *block*. A block may thus represent one or more records. We can (within a specified system) regard each term as an operator which selects one element from a set. Thus the first term pair in a message may select one point out of a predefined set of system points. Likewise one term may be regarded as selecting one point in time. It may be objected here that as time is normally regarded as a continuous variable we do not have a well defined set of time points. This is not so, however, for as soon as we have decided to represent time by a datum (a finite string symbol) we have defined a smallest time interval in our information system. We then have actually defined time by a finite set of well specified intervals.

In a similar way we can see that any data representation of information is a selection of individual elements out of a certain set of sets.

4 As a consequence every term in a message can be represented by so many binary digits (or bits) as are required for selection out of all elements in the set from which the selection is made. In this way we come to a determination of the "size" of a message (i.e. the minimum size of a record representing the message). This however is not a determination of the amount of semantic information in the message (as understood by the system). If amount of information is to be proportional to value of information then the value of a message depends not on size, but on how many messages are used (among other things). The size of a message does have a direct relation to the cost of its communication (or transport) as well as on its storage and maybe also on its processing.

5 Because of this (often confused) distinction between data size and semantic content we cannot measure (semantic) information in bits and therefore need not distinguish between binary digits and "information bits". Therefore we use the more convenient word bit in place of the sometimes advocated "binit".

6 It is not without interest to observe that the size of the same kind of message, e.g. a point message, will be larger if the system grows larger (in the sense of having more system points) for then more bits will be needed for the datum representing (the term describing) identification of the point. Further increased demand for precision will lead to a twofold increase in the size of an elementary message, for to increase precision we may have to use more bits to represent a single measure of a state variable, and we may also have to define the state in more system points in order to reach a meaningful increase of precision. As the increase in the number of points used leads to an increased number of bits in the identifiers, both the identifier parts and the measure parts require more bits.

7 In the above discussion we have seen how the minimum number of bits required to carry the information in a message can be determined from the system characteristics. It is important to note that we do not have to make any decisions about the design of the information system in order to determine this minimum message size. Instead certain characteristics of the equipment for handling the data records representing the messages may lead to a larger size. Thus redundant data bits may be introduced for reasons of chosing a convenient code or for reliability purposes and extra space in the carrying media may have to be spent for instance in the form of block gaps or unused memory positions. This increase in size for ease of data handling will not be determined by the characteristics of the managed system but will be the result of design decisions during the design of the information system and this may have to be done in a complicated step-by-step procedure.

8 In the mathematical theory of communication which is, unfortunately, often called "theory of information" it is shown that some amount of communication effort may sometimes be saved if the signals most frequently transmitted are represented by fewer symbols than the minimum number of bits as determined analogously to our above discussion and if instead more rarely transmitted signals are permitted to be longer. In the general communication

situation the relative frequency of different signals has to be determined as properties of the language. In our case of a well defined system (served by the information system) one may instead ask if characteristics of this managed system will define different relative frequencies. One will also have to observe that for the economy of storing data, contrary to that of transmitting signals, other factors than relative frequency of transmission may guide the economy of representation.

9 To indicate how properties of the managed system might enable a reduction of both data communication and data storage (as central memory of the computer is concerned) let us assume that the system has a set of neighborhoods defined such that for any system point a set of other system points (called neighbors) is defined where the messages from the neighbors have much greater influence on the point in question than other system points. This then would mean that messages from the neighbors would be used (and therefore transmitted and stored) much more often in connection with control of this point than would messages from other parts of the system. One might then use one group of symbols in the point identifiers to identify the neighborhood to which the point belongs. This group of neigborhood symbols might then be omitted each time we use a message from the same neighborhood as the lack of this group would identify the neighborhood (provided some symbol in the record indicates where the neighborhood symbols end). In this way the average length of a record would be increased — because in general more symbols would be required to represent an identifier when it is structured to separate the neighborhood part, but the length of the messages most often transmitted and stored would be shorter, so in effect transmission and storage of data might be reduced in this way. Whether this could then actually be utilized for all control points requires a closer analysis and also special properties of the managed system.

10 For the subsequent analysis we shall assume that the size of a point message will be defined by the minimum number of bits required by the system characteristics as discussed above plus some assumed percentage of allowance for information processing equipment, which percentage can be taken as reasonable average for the kind of information system contemplated.

11 It must be observed that when we talk about the minimum size of the record of a message this is determined for the most general situation, for instance as when that message is the only one of its kind. If several messages of the same kind occur (as is, of course, the most common situation) then we may make use of the fact that we may store "global" information about the structure of the record and, therefore, need no longer carry all the "kind-indicators" with the message. Thus a measure of one state variable may stand alone in the record without being accompanied by the identifier of its kind. The kind of variable it refers to will then be identified by its *position* in the record *plus an identifier of the record type*. Notice that this kind of record would not conflict with our description of a message as always carrying information about kind of variable together with a measure for that kind. For the kind of the measure is identified by its position within the record and thus the other terms in the record, taken as a whole structure, do in fact give information about the kind of variable (that is, they do that in combination with a stored description for that type of record). On the other hand this way of identifying kind by position does eliminate the need for having a datum within the record for identifying kinds of variables and therefore the "identification-by-position" brings a saving in bits required and means that the record may in fact contain fewer than "the minimum number of bits" for the message in general.

12 It is of interest to note the possibility of saving bits by using "identification-by-position" has the same background as the possibility of saving point messages for a curve known to be "smooth". In both cases "global information", stored in the system and holding true for a number of occurrences, is the reason for the possibility of saving bits — or alternatively is a reason for reduction of new information carried by messages[3]). It is also important to note that identification-by-position in bringing savings in bit representation also reduces reliability, for the drop-out of one datum would falsify the meaning of all the subsequent data in the record. This is not the case where full identification by data is used.

---

[3]) Roughly the "smoother" we know a curve (function) to be the less points do we need to store for the representation of its form. Thus if we have information about its smoothness this can be used to save storage of point coordinates.

13 We have seen from the above discussion of the smooth curve that every additional information about a point position adds less to the quality of the curve description than earlier such messages. In that sense information from any additional point can be said to be smaller than that of previous ones. The sizes of the messages are all equal, however. Therefore no relation between information content (or value) and message size seems to exist. (This was also found when we discussed requirements associated with increasing precision of system observation[1].) It should be observed, however, that the reduced information value of an added point message stems from the fact that a prediction of the true message then can be made using information about the other points. This prediction becomes better as more points are known (given that the curve is smooth). We may conclude from this that it might, in theory at least, be possible to give information about a new point position in terms of its deviation from the predicted position. Then the better the prediction the smaller the expected deviation and, hence, the smaller the number of bits needed to represent it. If point messages, beyond a small basic set of them, would give deviation from prediction rather than absolute point position the successive messages would decrease in size respectively, just as their information content.

14 Notice however that only the state measure (point ordinate) is affected. The point identification (point abscissa) would not be influenced. We remark that this reduction in size of message is possible only at the expense of calculation work. In the extreme case when calculation costs nothing, for instance because it is done immediately by the observer himself ("perfect observer") and prediction can be made perfectly (point position analytically defined from other point positions already known) the new point message would contain no information at all. In this way we obtain a complete link to the theory of semantic (information) content by Bar-Hillel[4]). This is very interesting but we do not pursue the analysis further on this occasion.

15 *Remark.* We have seen how a point message, if taken alone, requires a well specified minimum number of bits for its data representation. We have also seen how both the required number of bits for representation and the amount of information in a message may be reduced if the message is regarded as existing or occurring together with other information. Although we found that no natural way for

---

[4]) 1 Ba-H 1964.

defining amount of information (in a message) could be seen we found the value of the information in a message could be determined as relative to other information and also the (minimum) size of the data representation could get such a relative specification. We now may well state that in spite of what has been said we still have well defined information about an elementary message i.e. defined by the minimum number of bits required by the elementary message if represented alone. This is so because even if we have any number of means available for reducing the size of the data representation of a message connected with other information — and even if we need no bits at all because we may compute it from other information — we will still require the defined minimum number of bits required for the message because we may be required to communicate this message alone.

16 If this philosophy is adhered to, we then will have to accept that the same kind of elementary message will have a greater amount of information if it refers to a larger system. While this is not obviously desirable, we may state that it is also not in conflict with intuition (because intuition appears to be fairly indifferent to this question). We leave this question of amount of information as we shall not need that concept in the present study (we do not know if it is needed at all).

17 All of our varied discussion regarding information is, of course, an indication that this subject is much more complicated than is generally realized and that, therefore, extensive research in this field is highly warranted.

18 *Remark*. We have talked as if a certain set of data would be able to contain or represent a unique quantity of information. This is also, quite obviously, generally believed. It is important to recognize that this is a mistake[5]). Instead the information "I" that is communicated by a set of data (symbols) is a function "i" of the data "D" the receiving structure "S", and of the time interval "t" during which the communication is allowed to take place:

19 $$I = i(D, S, t).$$

Notice also that for t given the amount of information at first increases when the amount of data is increased but it then reaches

---

[5]) This follows also from section 23.4.

a maximum after which further data reduce the information which is perceived.

The importance of 19 is to make it clear that the data "D" used to present a message to human beings must be designed with a view to suiting their semantic background "S".

23.7 The Information System for a Simple Inventory.

We define a *simple inventory* — or a *stock point* — as a set of one kind of goods, or other objects, from which shippings are to be made and into which deliveries arrive. Shippings and deliveries are assumed to be stochastical variables in time. The number of objects in the set will be called the *level* of the store. The level is, of course, also a stochastic variable.

We assume that a cost flow per unit of time is associated with the level, such that cost flow increases with level. It is seen that storage cost can also be regarded as store (with zero storage cost). If demand occurs when storage level is zero, we accumulate such demands as a negative store level, which is also assumed to have some positive cost flow associated with it.

The store would be unnecessary if either

      1a. delivery could be re-adjusted to demand of any intensity without any delay

or 1b. the delay of delivery were exactly predictable and demand were exatctly predictable at least as far in advance as needed to cover the delivery delay interval.

Notice the principal difference between those two conditions. The condition 1a places of course, completely unrealistic conditions on the *production system*, and also contradicts the assumption of stochastic delivery.

The condition 1b instead would be equivalent to requiring *complete information* about everything that is going to happen to production and transport involved in delivery as well as *complete information* about demand to occur in a certain future. Contrary to 1a it does not place the unrealistic demand of zero response time for the system managed.

While it is obviously realistic to postulate the impossibility of acquiring this complete information — and thus the impossibility of reducing storage cost to zero — we can already conclude from condition 1b that our possibility of reducing storage cost depends on our ability to acquire and utilize information.

We have here a very interesting property of information: it enables us to circumvent obstacles to our actions presented by physical systems — to the extent that we can acquire it. It is, of course, also true that, because of ordering costs and set-up costs, the inventory level corresponding to economic optimum is above zero.

We also see that the possibility of reducing the total costs of the system depend on whether the costs of acquiring and using the information is smaller than the reduction of storage costs obtained.

We have above obtained a basis of concepts and terms which enables us to discuss how an information system for the simple store should be designed. Also the meaning of "information system" will get precision during this discussion.

We start by assuming that we analyze the situation of the simple store to be studied in order to find out which different factors in its outside world could have an influence on its different functions for which we want to compute predictions or estimates. We mention some of the most important of these functions: demand on the goods stored, availability of goods as a function of lead time of orders, percentage of time that the store is empty, and cost flow of the storage level. Other functions will be used to estimate safety stock as a function of the quality of the predictions. We then define different possible algorithms which could use one or more of the kinds of information in our list, and process this information in different ways. We need not take up here the problem of how to define such algorithms but at this stage, merely refer to the fairly rich material which is already available in the literature of economics and operations research and the techniques developed within numerical mathematics[1]). The information processing is specified for any set of algorithms which can compute the functions: demand, availability (or delivery), cost of running out of stock, cost flow as a function of storage level and so on. Each of the algorithms

---

[1]) See for instance 1 Br 1962 or 1 Hd 1963.

specifies uniquely the amount of processing or computation it requires. This can be interpreted in terms of money for any specified computing system contemplated for performing it. Similarly each algorithm specifies the different elementary messages it requires as well as those it will produce. Assuming that we know the cost for providing the algorithm with each of the elementary records carrying these messages, we can sum to obtain the total cost for acquiring and transporting to the algorithm (or to the computer) all its input information. We now remark that the algorithms may use elementary messages acquired earlier, and hence the system for making the necessary information available will also have to contain stores for information. The amount and cost for these stores will also be fixed for any contemplated combination of algorithm, rate of information required and types of store.

We thus obtain a specified measure of the total cost for handling and processing information for any algorithm contemplated. Summing up for each feasible set of algorithms we obtain a total information processing cost for the management of the simple store according to the set of algorithms chosen. We have assumed here that when fixing on a certain set of algorithms we have also fixed the points in time when we want it to be applied, that is the *period of processing*. Basically it is applied each time a transaction occurs in the store, but it is important to find out to what extent a less frequent processing is economically superior.

(When we talk in the sequel of the cost of using more information it is in the sense of summing costs for data acquisition and for processing a larger algorithm.) If we then compare the total cost for two different sets of input messages required, the difference set of these messages can be assigned a value equal to the reduction in storage costs within the managed store brought about by the addition of the information to the input set.

It follows from this discussion that only if both the acquisition and storage of information and the processing of the algorithm have costs which are negligible as compared with the storage cost in the managed system will it be economically optimal to use the full set of all relevant data, at each occurrence of a transaction, and the associated set of algorithms. It is quite obvious that this is not the case today and it does not seem very probable that it will ever be.

In fact it will even be quite impossible for any computer to do such a processing fast enough to be able always to handle one transaction before the next one occurs. In a real system we will have to find an economical combination which can be assumed to be something like running some simple algorithm using few data each time a transaction occurs in the managed system (or periodically with a sufficiently short period) in combination with a larger algorithm using more data but being run less often. This, in turn, may be supported by a still larger algorithm using still more data and being run still more infrequently.

As the acquisition of external data and conversion of them to a "mechanized" form is expensive one will have to expect that choice of algorithms will be greatly influenced by the design of other parts of the information system. Some data may be already available within the system and therefore are less expensive to use than other data which have to be "purchased" from outside the system.

23.8 Operative versus Directive Information.

It would seem normal that use of "complete" information will be too expensive in relation to its value and too time consuming, we will have to find means for reducing the amount of data and thereby reduce the cost and delay for acquiring, handling and processing the data. A reduction can be obtained by using data less often or by using fewer elementary messages as input for the production of one output message or both.

We have also seen that for executive decisions the fact that a finer analysis takes more time means bigger losses of value by delayed decisions. This was another reason for requiring simplification of the analysis for decisions.

In order to make our discussions concrete, let us specify some assumptions about the detailed operations of the store (not all really necessary operations need be listed).

> accepting orders from customers
> shipping items to customers
> issuing re-orders
> accepting delivery
> providing information for accounting
> etc.

One important thing to have in mind, when we want to estimate the losses incurred in the managed system by processing data at a reduced rate, is that it is actually not the rate of arrival of transaction data which is of significance but the response time of the managed system. Thus for instance if the system permits shipping only twice a day while customer orders arrive at an average rate of 100 per day there is no reduction at all in the efficiency of the managed system if the order transactions are handled only twice a day, although this means that on the average the period of processing is fifty times that of transaction arrival.

If the processing period is made longer than the system response time one will expect increased cost by losses of system efficiency. In the case of shipping it may well be that customers would not accept a delay more than is unavoidable because of the response time. This corresponds to sharply rising system costs when the processing period is growing longer than the response time. In such cases it will be unneccessary to perform a finer economic analysis. It can be said at once that for such a system the processing period should be such as the response time determines.

Different transactions may well be associated with different response times. Thus the response time for issuing replenishment orders will probably be one day, even if shipping has half a day as its response time. Further it will be more normal for re-ordering periods to influence system costs only slightly when exceeding the response time slightly. Thus if response time is one day but lead time for delivery is 50 days then obviously an increase by a few days in the re-ordering period will only increase system costs by a slight amount.

While system response times may be long enough to enable the processing to be much less frequent than the operative transactions, the required processing rate may still be so high that all information of significance for the operative decisions cannot be taken in the process because this may be too costly or even require more time than available. A solution to this problem would be obtained if operative decisions could be made using a small amount of *operative information* while the *quality* of decisions could be improved by using more information, gathered and processed less often to form *directives* for the decision process. We shall then say that we use *directive information* in addition to the operative information.

If this directive information is processed less frequently this will then permit operative decisions to be made in time and will let a sequence of such decisions be made by an identical decision process. To the extent that the modification of the decision process brought about by the directive information changes slowly with time it will be true that processing directive information less frequently will correspond to an approximation to optimum decisions. Indeed it is most likely that the decision process corresponding to optimum executive decisionmaking is of this kind[1]).

We are not relying merely on hypothesis when we talk about the feasibility of partitioning the information and its utilization into operative and directive kinds. In fact the common use of the technique of re-order point is an example of this kind[2]). If anything is new here it is our interpretation of this technique and our taking it as an illustration of the very fundamental principle of separating the directive information and thereby reducing information communication and processing requirements. When re-order point techniques are used, the re-order level and the re-order quantities are regarded as fixed measures, fixed directives, over a set of subsequent operative instants and over a period of time. The operative information processing is using the directive information when, for instance, a shipping is ordered, the reduced inventory level is computed using this operative information. The result is then compared with the re-order point and if lower will cause the ordering of the re-order quantity. This system gives us the freedom to choose any frequency we find suitable for the up-dating of re-order point and re-order quantity, that is for utilizing the information determining the directives. It is seen that also our choice to use few or many kinds of information is focused on the determination of the directive information. Thus the directive information for operative decisions is obtained on the basis of different forecasting algorithms and it is these which may use more or less different information.

---

[1]) Cf. part 2, chapter 2.
[2]) Other examples of what we from now on call *directive information*, used to speed up production of efficient operative information, are given by precalculated smoothed machine loading in shop scheduling which helps producing the operative information or queue priorities at machine stations. On the next lower level then these same priorities are used as directive information for the operative decisions of picking the next job from queue.

We may conclude that the quality of the operative decisions may be improved by up-dating the directive information more often or by using more information for each up-dating or both.

We have been taking for granted, so far, that it is only for directive information that we have a choice as to the frequency of processing and that the frequency of operative information would be dictated by the managed system. This is not entirely true, however, for the operative frequency is controlled by system-economic considerations. For instance shipping of end products may be sent twice a day or once a day and the economic differences may not be so large as to balance against other factors. On the other hand shipping less often than once a day may be quite unacceptable, so no balance analysis is needed. This, on the other hand, can still be interpreted in terms of cost by stating that there is a sharp rise in cost if shipping frequency is reduced beyond a daily one. We thus encounter the question: how do we find an optimal (or efficient) combination of frequency of generation of operative information, frequencies of generation of the different directive information values, and the amounts of directive information to be used in the different analysis procedures?

We go on to analyze a simple example that will shed some light on the possibilities of such an approach.

The technique of using re-order point control illustrates the practical use of the principles of splitting out directive decision making. We can also give an example of where it might be used to advantage but does not appear to be used today. Cost analysis (for the pricing of products) is mostly done by burden cost methods although this is known in principle to be arbitrary and, hence will not do as a basis for efficient pricing decisions. To use specific cost ("out-of-pocket-costs") associated with the product alone is the only rational thing to do, from an efficiency point-of-view. The reasons why it is not much used apparently is that it is too difficult to determine the specific costs to be left over to the clerks doing routine costing (and errors on the low side may cause heavy losses). This is to say that the cost of appropriate information processing for rational cost analysis is too high. The splitting out of directive information in this case would correspond to making specific cost analysis infrequently and for a sample of products only. From that knowledge would be determined efficient factors to use as burden costs in the operative costing job done by clerks[3]).

23.9 An Example of Optimum Reduction.
Information Processing for a Simple Inventory.

In Fig. 1 we have indicated how the inventory carrying cost may be assumed to vary with the frequency used for updating the directive information. This frequency is measured as a percentage of operation frequency. For instance if the updating frequency is 0.5 % an updating is made for every 200 operations of the directive information. The index "1" used with the symbols on the different curves in Fig. 1 will indicate a system using one or a few different kinds of information (or "parameters") for producing updated directive information, S_1 represents the cost of holding inventory obtained if this information is used. P_1 represents the cost for acquiring and processing this information. T_1 is the total obtained as the sum of S_1 and P_1. We see that for this system the minimum total cost is about 5.5 and is obtained at a relative updating frequency of 0.3 %. If for instance 100 operations occur in the store each day this would correspond to updating about every three days and a total cost of about 5.5.

Similarly S_2, P_2, and T_2 are supposed to represent the use of a larger set of kinds of information. To this corresponds, of course a lower inventory carrying cost S_2 and a higher information processing cost P_2. The minimum of the total cost T_2 is seen to be obtained at an updating frequency of about 0.08 % (corresponding to updating every 2 weeks if we have 100 store operations per day) and has the amount = 4.8 cost units. S_3 corresponds to the inventory cost which would be obtained if we would decide to use the large information set for updating with a frequency of about 0.03 % and in between these updatings we would use a more frequent updating with the smaller set. If, in addition to making a "large updating" of the directives with the frequency 0.03, we also make a smaller updating at a higher frequency this will, of course, be expected to reduce inventory cost. This reduction will be less than if the large updating were used at the same frequency. Therefore the cost curve for this strategy, S_3 will leave the curve S_2 at the frequency 0.03 (that is at vertical A_3) and then it will run above S_2 when moving towards increasing relative updating frequency. Similarly the information

---

[3]) Bayesian decision theory illustrates our concepts "operative versus directive" information and volume of information 4 Fo 1968 and 2 EM 1969.

processing cost P_3 starts out from P_2 (at the vertical A_3). From then on its increase is to be same as that of P_1 so P_3 has to be parallel with P_1 to the right of frequency 0.03 (vertical A_3). With S_3 and P_3 thus drawn in Fig. 1 we obtain a total cost curve T_3 which has a minimum of 4.1 at a frequency of about 0.1.

As the mixed strategy has a lower total cost it is better than any of the pure strategies "1" or "2". Another "mix" may of course be still better so to find an optimum we would have to do a search. As we have used a wholly hypothetical set of cost functions this is not worth while for Fig. 1.

We have of course not proved that a mixed structure will always be better, by our study of a single, hypothetical case.

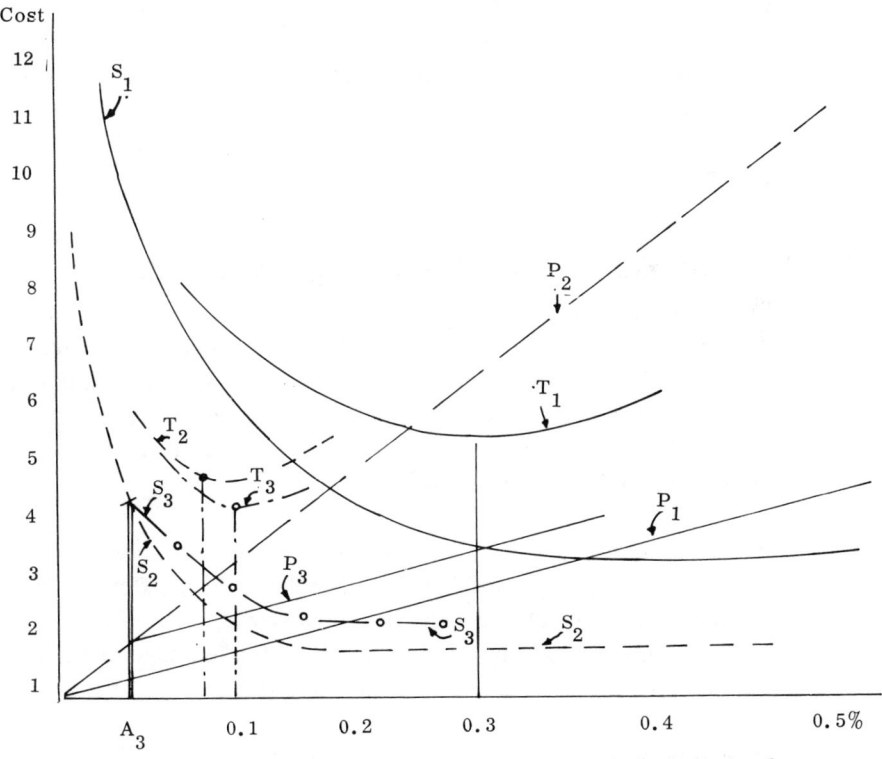

Fig. 1. S = Inventory Cost
P = Information Processing Cost
T = Total Cost
Index 1 = "few parameters used"
2 = "many parameters used"
3 = mixed strategy

We have not even proved that this would be typical. What we have proved is, however, that a situation *can* occur where a mixed strategy is the best. As the properties of the hypothetical curves which made the mixed strategy the best are very plausible properties we have shown, however, that it is quite necessary to try mixed strategic when one wants to find an efficient design for a system of this kind.

If on the other hand we would choose a still longer period for making the operative decision, it will influence the cost S. If the period is small in relation to the lead time for a refill order this influence will be small. On the other hand such a longer period may well reduce the cost of processing of the operative information significantly.

It is of interest to note that the principle of splitting up the information in a hierarchy of "directive" information sequences with a pair-wise relationship of directive/operative kind seems to give a new power of efficiency to delegation of authority in that it combines the best qualities of local and central knowledge, skill, and speed of action.

23.10 Information System for a Simple Work Station.

A second illustration can be given in another element which is also a very common one while not usually found in the literature. This is the work station. A work station will be defined as a unit which is able to produce a certain number of a specified object if provided with sufficient quantities of sub-objects and if run at a certain percentage of its maximum capacity.

We postulate that a work station has a certain fixed cost flow even when it is producing nothing. We thus have a cost flow when the station is idle which we call the *idleness cost flow*. For instance if the station is working 80 % of the time the idleness cost is 20 % of the maximum idleness cost per unit of time.

The supervisor (or the operator) of a work station will tend to see as his main duty to reduce, or eliminate, idleness cost by trying to run the station at full utilization. The information he would need to manage this is basically available at the station itself. However if the inflow of sub-objects to the work station has a random element then 100 % utilization of the station is only possible if there is a warehouse before the station which stores all needed sub-objects in such a way that the store is never emptied. This means that the station supervisor would order sub-objects from his suppliers in such a manner that a sufficient amount would always be available. This is only achievable if the store of sub-objects is permitted to grow indefinitely. In this way it is obvious that storage costs before a work station would far outweigh the saving by eliminating idleness cost completely.

It is seen that an economic running of the work station calls for knowledge of costs which may occur at other places in the system of which full information is not available at the station itself, for the store may, at least partly, be at another place, and in any case what cost factors are effective for the storage costs depend on many factors outside the local information range for the work station.

An optimization of the work station management which considers only such factors for which locally originating information gives measures is a sub-optimization which can be expected to be far from optimal for the system. On the other hand we may assume that a sub-optimization which is a good approximation to the total system optimization could be achieved if, as in the simple store system, directive information is given to the station, which takes account of the factors in other parts of the system, as well as from outside of the system. Inasmuch as such non-local information does not change significantly over a set of subsequent operations at the work station we would have a situation which, as was the case for the simple store, would give us freedom to choose the frequency of updating of the directive information according to different economic balances.

It is worth noting that it is not only storage costs for sub-objects input to a work station which calls for a less-than-full utilization of a work station. Thus if the station would run at a utilization which would be optimal from the input storage point-of-view it might well come to output too much as compared with the rate of demand at the output side of the system. This would cause an inventory to be built up at some point subsequent to the work station and the costs of such storage do, of course, also have to be taken into account. This may lead to requirements to let the load of the work station fluctuate as the demand on the output side fluctuates. Such fluctuation however will have costs associated with them and therefore a compromise will be called for, which balance fluctuation costs at the work station with increased storage costs after (and before) allowed in order to reduce the fluctuations. How this balance is to be made must, again, be calculated with use of information from other parts of the system, and is also to be given in the form of directive information to the station.

It is not only the relative loading of a work station and the fluctuation of this loading which affects the economy of the system. The *order* in which different jobs are done at the station may also be of importance. Like the other factors, this one has often significance for the station itself in some sense and for the rest of the system in some other. Thus for this one there may again be a temptation for the local bias.

Most of the information which is important for an efficient decision at a work station is of a kind which does not originate at the station. It may thus seem that all decisions for a work station would have to be made at a higher level within the system, where all information is available. This would seem to indicate a strong requirement for a direct control of the work station from a central point. For the work station the possibility to split up the decision information into local operative information and non-local directive information (which is needed at less frequent intervals) is the same as in the store case. The direct, centralized control is therefore not the only possibility and the choice has to be made on the basis of cost balancing, just as in the simple store case.

If we look at the different ways in which the management of a work station affects system economy we find that to a large extent this involves storage costs at associated stores. If we want to treat the work station as an element in a system of which the stores are elements then it is only the costs local to the work station itself that we want to determine when analyzing the work station as a system element[1]). These costs will be balanced against storage costs in the systems analysis phase when the interaction of work stations and stores is studied. For instance if we let the relative

---

[1]) Such costs proper to a work station are, for instance, idleness costs, and load fluctuation costs.

utilization of a work station be an independent variable, and if we know how station work costs are dependent on this variable, then to make a balance from the systems point-of-view we have to determine also the cost of the storage of input units for the work station as a function of this same independent variable, i.e. the relative utilization. This however is a problem that is quite familiar in the analysis of inventory economy; only average inventory level is determined as a function of the prescribed expected relative time for out-stock status. If the simple stores feeding the work station are refilled according to a re-order point or similar policy this problem has a known solution, the average level of storage is determined as a function of relative out-of-stock time (among other factors). If instead the store is being refilled by planned production, we have to plan such production to feed at an earlier time as corresponds to the average length of queue needed to give the expected service rate.

It is intresting to observe that while it is often thought to be impossible to estimate the cost of out-of-stock status because it depends on such things as lost customer good-will we have discussed above a model where this cost can be determined because it materializes as idleness cost in the work station into which the store is feeding.

The main operative decisions to be made at a work station are to be made each time one job has been finished and also at each start of a period for setting the activity level of the station. Thus the question as to which job to take next has to be answered each time a job is finished, whereas the decision on the level of activity (or the relative utilization) can only be made for an average over some reasonable length of time or a period. The latter is also true for the decision as to how fast a required change in activity level should be implemented. It is important that when less than 100 % station loading is planned; the loading has two components. The first is a consequence of a planned, reduced production of objects to ship which is reduced because of less favorable sales forecasts or too high stock levels. This may lead to a reduction of the work force at the station (by moving people to other stations for instance). One would then have to keep up a certain percentage of this reduced capacity which will require a certain storage level at stores feeding the station. (The second is because of random disturbances in the production system.) One may however instead keep up the capacity of the station at its top level and instead reduce the relative utilization of this capacity by keeping a lower level at the feeding stores. For instance if we want a reduced throughput corresponding, say, to 70 % and if we estimate 90 % utilization to be optimal one might have the alternative of reducing the capacity of the station down to about 80 % capacity which is then to be utilized at 90 %, giving about $0.80 \cdot 0.90 = 0.72$ of the top throughput. This would reduce cost flow of the station but would leave storage levels roughly constant. An alternative might be to keep capacity at the top but let utilization drop to 70 % by reducing storage levels. Which alternative is best will have to be found by a closer analysis. It may change from time to time which means that this will have to be produced as directive information at certain periods.

We have seen that the only operative decision to be made at the work station (or which requires information about the momentary status of the station) is the selection of the next job. This, on the other hand, could not be done over some period, including several transactions or operations, as was possible with the operative decisions in a simple store. The reason is that something may have happened or have become known at the last moment before the decision has to be made, which makes it impossible to take as the next job the one that we found at some earlier planning instant to be the most desirable (for some necessary input may have failed to become available) or which makes it less desirable (for an earlier change of plan may have made it desirable to take another job as the next because it might, for instance, be able to use a tool already set up). As a consequence it is often stated that only on-line-real-time data processing could handle the control of a work station in an efficient way. One must be clear, however, about the fact that even if it cannot be predicted in advance, with 100% reliability, in which sequence the alternative jobs are to be run at a work station, it may well be possible to determine in advance which order of priority is to be given to the alternatives available. If that has been done, and has been included in the directive information given to the station for the next period, then local information will be sufficient to handle the operative decision efficiently of each individual operation time[2]). Before one can justify the claim that on-line-real-time equipment is necessary

---

[2]) 2 Wi 1964.

one has then to prove that this would enable higher efficiency in the managed system and that the increase in information processing cost is not too high in relation to this efficiency increase.

Chapter 4. Some Problems of Information Systems Design.

24.1 Complexity of an Information System.

In a normal environment for an information system (a business organization, for instance) a large set of information classes are needed with widely different time-flow intensities (updating need) and large data volumes to be held in storage.

These many information sets are to be processed together in different combinations by different processes which are often complex in themselves and have complex interrelationships. The processes are defined in the form of instruction sets or computer programs, which are again sets of information.

Each program is in its turn a system of interconnected subprograms, many of which should be possible to be used for different processes.

1 All this is already seen to be complicated. In addition to this comes that, for reasons of hardware economy (among other things), the stored information sets are to be taken together into consolidated files from which the different items of information are retrieved most economically (time-wise) in an ordered sequence. This means that the data retrieval can become a time consuming transport operation.

2 The time to do all processing during each processing period will then be highly dependent on the time needed to sort data files and to transport data from the file storage to the processor and back (including set-up times). This time will depend on how the data sets are aggregated as files and on the limited number of file handling units that can be used simultaneously. This limitation then calls for a consideration of many, or all, the interrelationships between different information sets and the different processes. Further, to reduce data transport time, different processes need to be grouped together, which of course further emphasizes the importance of the existing interrelationships.

File input and output can run concurrently and simultaneously with processing if, among other things, memory can be allocated to alternative buffer areas. File data transfer can be speeded up by using longer records but this, again, requires more memory. Such speedup is more important for larger files than for smaller ones.

3 All this already makes the problem a very typical systems problem. This problem is emphasized by the fact that all the functions discussed and also the time consumed in the different *processes proper,* can all be done faster when having more "process memory' (computer central memory) available. Thus, for instance, information can be packed to take less space on file storage medium (tape or discs for instance) if more process memory can be used.

4 Likewise several (batch) processes using the same ordered data sets can be done in the same file scan, if their *programs* can be *in memory simultaneously*. Here again a complication is added for even if the programs cannot be in memory at the same time a one-run handling is still feasible if some programs are only seldom referred to. In such a case these programs can be stored in auxiliary store (tape or discs for instance) and be input each time the programs are called.

5 Further, the work to make the programs can be reduced if less care is needed to economize with memory space and time can be saved for the run operators if memory space permits more executive and monitoring programs to be stored during processing. Also *set-up time* can be saved by using larger files (which however causes duplicate transport) or by choosing another sequence between processes. Rewind time can be eliminated by using extra file stations. Simultaneous I/O can save transport time but consumes memory space.

6 As memory space is expensive its size has to be limited. This will mean that all the parts and functions mentioned are strongly interrelated over memory space and an optimum allocation of the latter to the different components will call for an overall systems analysis, considering all these factors.

7 As always in complicated systems we can see at once that it is wise to discard the call for an optimum. The objective of systems design is the finding of an *efficient* or a *better-than-present solution* or: best of a selected set of choices.

8 This may be stated more precisely as requiring one *feasible solution* and means for improving a feasible solution.

Heretofore even a technique for finding a feasible solution in a systematic way has not been available. If it were we would be able to reduce the time presently spent in ad hoc work on this step.

9 It is reasonable to expect that more formal methods for describing the information systems problem would pave the way for finding systematic procedures for establishing feasible solutions and steps to improve these.

10 It is also normal for complicated systems to have special properties which could be used to simplify the analysis. In fact this is often the only reason to use different methods for handling different systems. One example of such possibilities is that some interrelationships are relatively less significant than others, which may permit decomposing the systems analysis into that of analyzing subsystems separately at least as a first approximation, which can then be improved in later steps.

11 One such decomposition, which is natural in many information systems, considers the information storage and transport as separated from the processing proper. The latter then could be regarded as external to the information systems design, being a question of programming. This is of course only possible if the bounds of memory need for the programs involved in the system processes are specified and then taken as constants for the systems analysis. This can be made possible by specifying the way the program is to take care of the data transported to and from the process memory. This may have to be done for two or more alternative ways which will leave different amounts of memory space available for the data transport. This will enable a choice to be made afterwards between these alternatives.

12 When internal process time does influence total time, a minimum transport solution is not necessarily a minimum total time solution. Thus if one run is computer limited and a neighboring one is I/O or tape limited, a transfer of some processing from the computer limited run may reduce total time.

13 Set-up times too may call for modification of the system to be used (in specific cases when set-up time has not been fully included in the data transport).

14 It is easy to see however that in most practical cases the processing does not change the optimality of a system design which was obtained on the basis of data transport only. Thus in many cases, with very fast computers which have built-in functions for input-output editing, it may happen that the processing can run concurrently with input-output (through time sharing or buffering). In these cases the processing proper will have no influence whatsoever on the system design or on the total run time.

15 On the other hand it is very often the case that the computer is so slow that the processing proper will take so much central computer time that it will always at least partly exceed the time for input-output. In such cases the processing proper does have an influence on total run time but this is not influenced by changes in system design. Only if the system design is so heavily "skewed", that in some run the input-output time is not fully used up by processing, will a system modification be called for by consideration of the processing[1]). (Cf. part 1, chapter 2.)

16 It is thus seen that only for computers with medium speed — or fairly high speed but no special input-output editing facilities — will processing influence the system optimization. Even in such cases the best approach appears to be to design first with regard to data transport only and then, in a second phase, to see if processing calls for some modification. In such a case the modification will often be as simple as to move some elementary process from one run to another one, and to follow this up by some slight change in file composition.

Therefore it seems highly justified to concentrate much of the design of the information storing and processing system on transport minimization.

Obviously this problem needs much further study. Our statements refer to what is best to do in the present state of insufficient insight.

17 In systems using multi-programming other considerations are also required.

---

[1]) It is also important to remember that a process where total processing time is larger than total transport time may run with such an irregular distribution over time that part of the time transport dominates while in other time interval computation dominates.

18 Example.

In order to illustrate some of the points mentioned, we study here a simple but somewhat realistic example as shown in Fig. 1.

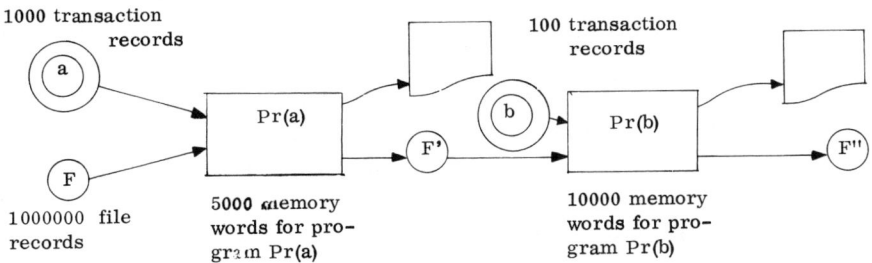

Fig. 1

F is supposed to be a (master) file which provides information to be used for the processing of batches of data "a" and "b" respectively. F is also "updated" during the process Pr(a) to become F' and during Pr(b) to F". We have assumed the batch of a (transactions file "a") to consist of 1000 records (or transactions). It is fairly common to have (or to want to have) a transaction frequency with respect to the master file of about 1 %, that is, to have about 100 master records per transaction. This would correspond to having 100000 records in F. However master records are often much larger then transaction records. We can choose to assume that the F-records might be 10 times larger than the a-records but to simplify we say instead that we have 10 times more records of the same size as "a", for this makes the same total file size which is sufficient for this example. Thus F has 1000000 (one million) records.

We assume all files to be stored on the same medium. The transaction files may have been stored separately on earlier runs during which they have also been corrected. If we assume that the scanning speed of the file storage medium is 100000 characters per second this may correspond to an effective speed of 20000 characters per second for the transaction files, taking into consideration time spent in set up and in scanning inter-record gaps. For the F file the effective speed will be larger for we have larger records and therefore fewer record gaps and we may increase effective speed further by having several records blocked together in each physical record. 50000 characters per second can be assumed for F.

If we now assume one record to contain 50 characters the time for transporting "a" will be $50 \cdot 1000/20000 = 2.5$ seconds. For "b" we then obtain 0.25 seconds. For F (or F' and F" respectively) we obtain $50 \cdot 10000000/50000$ or 1000 seconds for the transport to the process and the same for the transport from the process. The total transport time for the two processes will be about 4000 seconds, or roughly 1.2 hours, in addition to which must be added time for the processing proper and for printing the reports. It is common, however, that processing and also printing can be done simultaneously with data transport. In that case only the processing time would have to be counted if the processing is so large, or the computer speed so low in relation to transport speed, that processing takes more time than transport. Even then, however, processing will take place only in connection with the transaction records (and the associated master records). Even if processing would take 20 times the time for reading a transaction record, this would mean only $10 \cdot 5 = 50$ seconds for the "a" transactions, and 5 seconds for the "b" transactions.

It is also common that this processing is done while passing the master records not changed by transactions. Then this time for processing would again be absorbed by the transport time when the transaction frequency is as low as we have supposed here.

A large amount of time can be saved if transport out of the master file F' can be done simultaneously with in-transport of F, for then total time for process Pr(a) would go down from 2000 to 1000 seconds and total time would go down to about 2000 seconds or about 0.6 hours. For this to be possible (and also for processing to go on simultaneously with transport) we must however have alternate buffer areas of memory for both input and output of F (and F', F"). Thus normally four areas of the size of a physical record of F have to be set aside for this. Such a physical record must be fairly large in order to reduce wastage on record gaps. We assume them to be 1000 words. Thus 4000 words have to be spent on this. For the transaction records we need no alternate areas and also we do not need block records, for this transport time is negligible also without such arrangements. Their buffer area can be neglected therefore in this rough analysis.

We have now found that we may want to have 4000 words for buffer areas plus 10000 words for the program Pr(b). In addition to this we certainly need some memory space for different executive routines so that at least 16000 words seem to be required unless we split up Pr(b) or accept non-simultaneous in-transport and out-transport. This, on the other hand, could be completely reasonable if we can spend the time. Highest possible speed is not a goal in itself and we should use memory only if necessary from a total capacity requirements point of view.

If we now group together Pr(a) and Pr(b) into one composite, grouped, process Pr(a, b), Fig. 2,

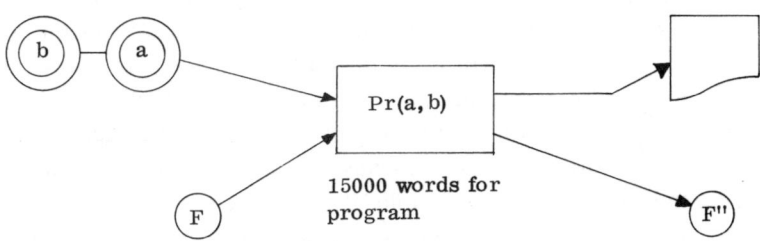

Fig. 2

we reduce total transport time to 1000 seconds, assuming also simultaneous in-transport, out-transport and processing if all programs can be in memory at the same time. We thus need 15000 words for program plus, perhaps, some additional program for co-ordination of Pr(a) and Pr(b) into Pr(a, b).

The total memory requirement then goes up to 21000 words or maybe 22000 words.

As an alternative we might consider having the program Pr(a) and Pr(b) on file storage. Then when a transaction of type "b" occurs after a transaction of type "a", we will have to transport out Pr(a) and in Pr(b), in all 15000 words which may be equivalent to 1500 records. Now by this program transport we save one transport time of F (two such times if we do not have simultaneous transports). Under the present assumptions we have 1000 records of F per a-record, so saving one transport F would be equivalent to saving a transport of 1000 records for each a-record. To achieve this saving by a program transport equivalent to 1500 records is, of course, no bargain. We would prefer not to group the processes unless we want to spend memory for this so programs would not have to be transported in and out. This would be still more so if the transaction frequency would be higher so that fewer master records would go per transaction record. We have been reasoning as if we would have to transport the programs in and out after each record a. That is we have disregarded the fact that the frequency of the transactions "b" is ten times smaller than that of "a".

Taking this into consideration we find that at most two program transports are required for each transaction "b" (Pr(a) out, Pr(b) in, and then Pr(b) out again after processing "b" and Pr(a) in again). (Actually it will be somewhat less than this because we have to expect that sometimes two or more transactions of type "b" follow each other directly.) This means that we have, on the average, at most $2 \cdot 15000$ words of program transport or, equivalently 3000 records of program transport per "b" transaction and, hence, per 10 a-transactions. Thus we have, on the average, a maximum of 300 records of program transport, per a-record. This means that, in the model of this example, it is in fact realistic to group Pr(a) and Pr(b) into Pr(a), b) even if we do not have memory space for both. This is thanks to the very low frequency of b-records (in relation to the size of the master file). Assuming the same effective transport speed for programs as for file F we have $50 \cdot 300 \cdot 1000/50000 = 300$ seconds to spend on program transport by not having both programs in memory. Thus for the grouped process Pr(a, b) total transport time is 1000 seconds if central memory is large enough and this goes up to about 1300 if memory is too small for the two process programs.

Remark. If we have a time-sharing (multi-access) or a real-time environment we may be swapping programs in and out all of the time. In that case there will be almost no penalty in grouping processes even when their programs are stored in backing store because one will be transporting programs in every "time slice" in any case.

19 **Example.**

In 18 Example we talked about "file storage" without specifying its character, but our reasoning followed the assumption of using "serial assess" storage, e.g. magnetic tape. Let us look at some changes which would occur if we would have instead a direct access storage, such as drum, discs or magnetic cards.

If we assume the same level of technology we may assume again a scanning speed of 100000 characters per second. Physical records have, typically, fixed size which may be of the order of the transaction records. Gaps between records may be smaller but the fixed physical record size leads to unused space on the average so we can assume, roughly, the same overall waste on gaps as in the transaction files above, but set-up time may be eliminated. The effective speed may therefore be somewhat higher, 30000 characters per second, for all files, now also for the master file. This size may be smaller, perhaps by a factor of 3, thus compensating for the lower effective speed. Now however we have also an access time caused by mechanical movements to access a record. The access time may vary with the circumstances[2]), in one and the same storage, but we assume here, simply, that every access takes 0.02 seconds (equivalent to the time for transporting about 200 records of F in example 18). For the 1000 a-records we obtain a transport time of $50 \cdot 1000/30000$ seconds plus 1000 access times[3]) or about $1.5 + 20 = 21.5$ seconds.

This time we only fetch those F-records which are called for by a transaction. Assuming, as we did, that now the F-records are only 3 times the size of an a-record we obtain $3 \cdot 1.5 + 20 = 25$ seconds (roughly) for in-transport and the same for out-transport if it is assumed that, in this system they are not done simultaneously, to avoid a more complicated operation. Total transport time for Pr(a) would now be about 70 seconds[4]).

Total transport time for Pr(b) would be about 10 times less because now also F-transport goes down as transactions transport does.

Total of F transport time for Pr(a) and Pr(b) is thus about 80 seconds[5]), against 2000 seconds for Pr(a, b) on tape storage. Notice however that if the transaction frequency were 100 %, rather than 1 %, so that F would be 100 times smaller, we would come down to about 20 seconds on tape system but no reduction would be obtained for the pseudo random access storage system. When we

---

[2]) Common access times are 30 to 600 milliseconds.
[3]) In actual cases we may arrange to have less accesses.
[4]) With an access time of 100 ms (or 0.1 sec.) which is more typical, we get 206 seconds.
[5]) With an access time = 0.1 sec. we get instead about 230 seconds for Pr(a) and Pr(b).

now come to the question of grouping the processes Pr(a) and Pr(b), we remark that this time one may save no F-transport at all by grouping, for all b-transactions may call other F-records than the a-transactions. It is the probability for a-transactions and b-transactions to coincide in their key identifiers that will determine this. This probability may be very small when the number of b-transactions is so much smaller than the case here, and also whenever the number of transactions is very much smaller than the number of master file records. One can also say that in this case, when the direct access property has been used to save master file transport by eliminating the transport of records not called by transactions, there is less opportunity for saving master-file transport by grouping.

When random access storage is used one is interested in the possible use of *direct processing*, which means that every transaction is processed as it arrives. This would then not hold only for the two transactions types "a" and "b" which are associated with F, but for many other transactions and files as well. This means that it is almost impossible to have a large enough (main) memory for holding all process programs involved. It also means that there is a high probability for any transaction to be followed by one of different type (except for a few especially frequent ones). As a consequence one will have to expect to transport one program out and one in for each transaction. In our example this means that for every transaction we have to transport 15000 words of program or the equivalent of 1500 records, that is $50 \cdot 1500/30000 = 2.5$ seconds. In addition to this comes 1500 access times but this time, considering the sequential arrangement of the program records one may have, perhaps, five times faster access, on the average or $1500 \cdot 0.02/5 = 6$ seconds, making in all, 8.5 seconds per transaction[6]). Under these circumstances the total transport time for Pr(a) and Pr(b) would be about $1100 \cdot 8.5 + 80$ or above 9000 seconds.

Thus while process grouping is of little use in some direct processing applications with direct access storage we find that program transport should be carefully studied and reduced when possible. One possibility here is that of the 1500 words of program space for Pr(a) and Pr(b) a large part may be in alternative program branches and therefore one might take advantage of the direct access property to bring in program parts only successively as they are called for.

---

[6]) The access time used is, as was also the case above, fairly optimistic. Today longer times would have to be expected.

It is worth noting that the direct processing of a transaction against all associated files is, in fact, a grouping of all processes associated with this transaction and this grouping does save repeated transport of this transaction record while also spending extra transport for files and programs.

Exercise. In which ways does the size of the main memory affect systems work, programming, data transport and process time?

Chapter 5. Precedence Relations between Information Sets in an Information System.

25.1 Data Structure of an Information System.

One problem of organizing data is concerned with the data transport needed to bring data from the storage place to the processor. Another is to organize data in a way that is meaningful for people[1]). In the context of the first of these problems it seems appropriate to consider such data as are stored in the main memory — or any memory in which they are available in one basic word-time — of the processor to be used for processing, as being available without transport work. The problem of data organization then is how to store data in mass storage so as to minimize the work needed to transport these data to the main store when needed or to make them available within the time required.

1 In business information systems it is common that data can be retrieved from files during a simple scanning of the file (and the batch of transactions) after sorting of transactions. When this is not possible, random access is often said to be required. Contrary to this, the situation in engineering data processing is often one where more complicated magnetic tape handling is required. This has also been found to be the case in many applications such as production scheduling.

The data transport minimization is not a problem only for so-called serial access memories. It is also true for those random access memories which require a general access time that is much longer than the word-time of the processor and have smaller access time to data which are placed in neighboring positions than to those in other positions. In fact these two classes of memories are merely different instances of one and the same kind of pseudo-random access systems (as was pointed out by the author)[2]). It will be shown later how many data handling routines which cannot be run as a simple scanning of the master file involved, can be classified as a more general handling type called rectangular handling[3]).

---

[1]) For instance: input has to be organized to system specification but also so that it is meaningful to the people gathering it before input.
[2]) 3 La 1961-1.
[3]) See section 31.4.

Obviously the type of handling of files required must be considered when searching for minimum transport system solutions. Likewise, it is obvious that the processing period, that is the time interval between two processing runs of the same file, is of importance for the transport work.

2 Analysis of the information needs of the firm.

We make the basic assumption about the firm that a set of "functions" can be defined which must be in action in order that the firm shall be able to fulfil its objectives. In fact it seems probable that the only way to define the objectives of a firm is to define its "functions".

Our approach to the system analysis will be to start by defining the basic functions of the firm and then proceed to find the relation of each function to the set of information classes available[4]).

3 The basic functions of the firm.

We take as the basic functions of the firm such operations as the firm has to perform in order to fulfil its objectives, and also such other operations which are not directly concerned with the objectives but are indirectly necessary in order for the firm to be able to perform the directly necessary operations.

Thus a firm which has as main objective to produce a set of objects has, of course, the directly necessary function of running the production. Another directly necessary function is buying the raw materials out of which the products are made. Indirect functions are for example the paying of salaries to the employees or the cost accounting needed to serve the directly necessary function of setting prices on products and controlling the efficiency of the firm.

In defining the functions it is important to isolate each single function on the basis of its proper reasons for existence if possible without being too much influenced by the present organization. To take a simple example: The function of paying salaries is concerned with the computation of the salary for each individual person at each salary period, that is to compute the amount payable after deductions, and to associate this amount with an identification of the person concerned[5]).

---

[4]) We refer to sections 22.3 and 22.4 for a simple illustration.
[5]) See also sections 25.4 and 25.5 for simple illustrations.

It is not within the scope of this function, however, to define which different products or customer orders are to be charged with the amount paid. The fact this is normally computed in connection with payroll processing corresponds to a common solution to the problem of economic data transport and is not to be mistaken for an indication that it belongs to the function of salary pay. The same is true for many other statistical data produced from payroll information.

4 **The information needs of firm functions.**

For every function of the firm a set of different *information classes* or *concepts* has to be provided by means of the proper data sets or files. This information will be needed either to monitor the performing of a function or as a basis for a decision which has to be made by a human being in order to control a function. An example of the first kind is the salary pay where the computed amount per person can directly be used to trigger a pay action. In contrast a function of sales forecasting will clearly be used as one basis for control of the production and sales functions.

5 The first step in the analysis of information need is to define the different classes of information needed for each function of the firm. Further for each such class we also have to determine the requirement of information as a function of time. The salary pay function calls for each person's identification and the amount to be paid to him. In addition it will also, in most cases, be required to list all deductions made for each person.

This information will be required at each pay period. In this way for each function a set of required information sets is defined and for each of these another set of information sets required for its production.

6 The definition of the basic functions does not seem to be computable by any routine procedure at present. Rather it has to be defined by careful analysis of the goals of the firm. This seems difficult and will certainly be so regarded by most firms. In fact it is believed in many cases to be an obstacle to taking an analysis of this kind as a first step to automatization of information processing. However, it should be obvious on a second thought that no firm can be assumed to work in a rational way, if it has not clearly defined its diffe-

rent functions and the information needed for each of them. This is not a problem that can be solved in one day or two. It is well worth much effort and even long research. A firm which really knows its objectives and how to fulfil them should find no difficulty in defining the basic functions and its information requirements. In fact one of the most important functions of management should be to work continuously on the problem of defining goals and functions for the firm.

Although no procedure for routine or automatic solution of this basic problem exists it is obvious that in principle this task can be made fairly easy by listing all the functions and their direct information needs of firms of different types. Thus to specify these entities for any firm would call for consulting such a list or set of lists for firms of the type in question and deciding which functions to accept and which to omit.

7 Such lists may not be available today. It will not be long after the introduction of an approach like ours, however, before they will become available and in a continuously improving set[6]).

8 In order to see how the information sets (or concepts) which are necessary or have potential value for the control of a managed system may be determined, together with their interrelations, we refer to Fig. 2 and an example used earlier[7]). We give in Fig. 2 in a modified way a part of the simple system, containing only "store 1", "shop", and "sales" as firm functions. Of the candidates for information to be used for "refill order" we have assumed, for simplicity, that it has already been decided that "substitutable items" and "production related items" are not to be considered in the study.

9 We may regard Fig. 2 as a precedence graph. We then say that information which is to be used for a business function is *precedent information* for that function. Likewise such information as is used to produce other information is said to be its precedents. Even our very simplified information system is seen to have a rather complicated structure. Precedence relations of fairly high order can be found in Fig. 2. Indeed the information set "8" (inventory status) is seen to be a virtually infinitely iterated precedent of

---

[6]) As is illustrated in sections 22.3 and 22.4 also an intuitive analysis is able to produce long lists of candidate information classes.
[7]) See section 22.4.

itself. The same is true for "13" (rate of demand) and "14" (delivery lead time) as these hold information which is predicted by means of earlier values of the same kind.

10 We may represent the information system with its precedence relations by the precedence matrix P ($= P^{00}$), se Fig. 3 below.
The fact that "8, 13 and 14" are precedents of themselves is indicated by a unit in the boxes (8,8) (13,13) (14,14) in P.
Notice that the precedence analysis emphasizes the fact that each elementary file is assumed to be a data base for all its succedents. In this lies the essence of the idea of data bases or integrated file systems[8]).

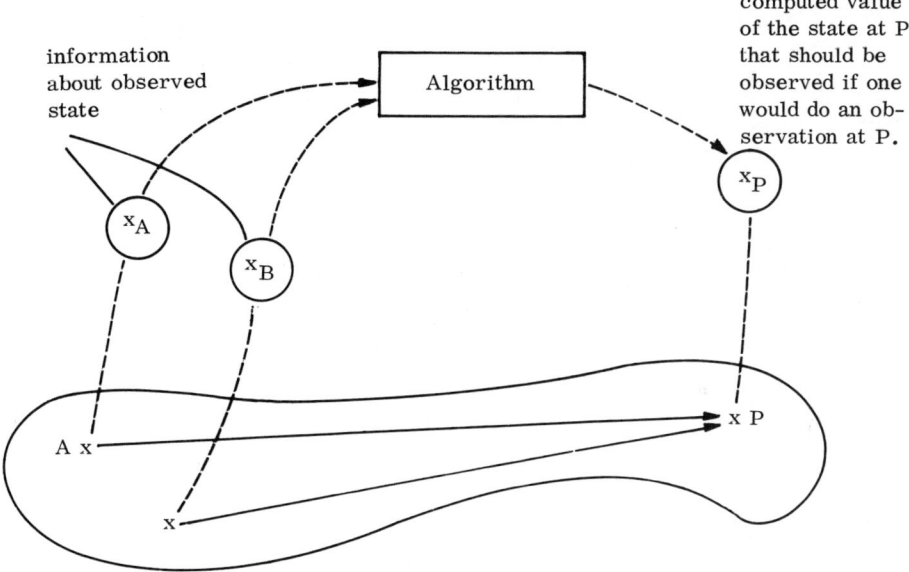

Fig. 1

If in the points P, A and B of a system S, Fig. 1, a state variable x can be measured or observed, then the properties of system S can be such that the value of x at P depends on the values x_A and x_B of x at A and B. It may be possible to work out a formula or an algorithm which takes the x-values in A and B as input and computes the x-values at P. x_A and x_B are thus *precedents* of x_P. *Notice that this follows from transference properties of system S and is not dependent on the algorithm.*

---

[8]) For "elementary" file see section 25.2.

281

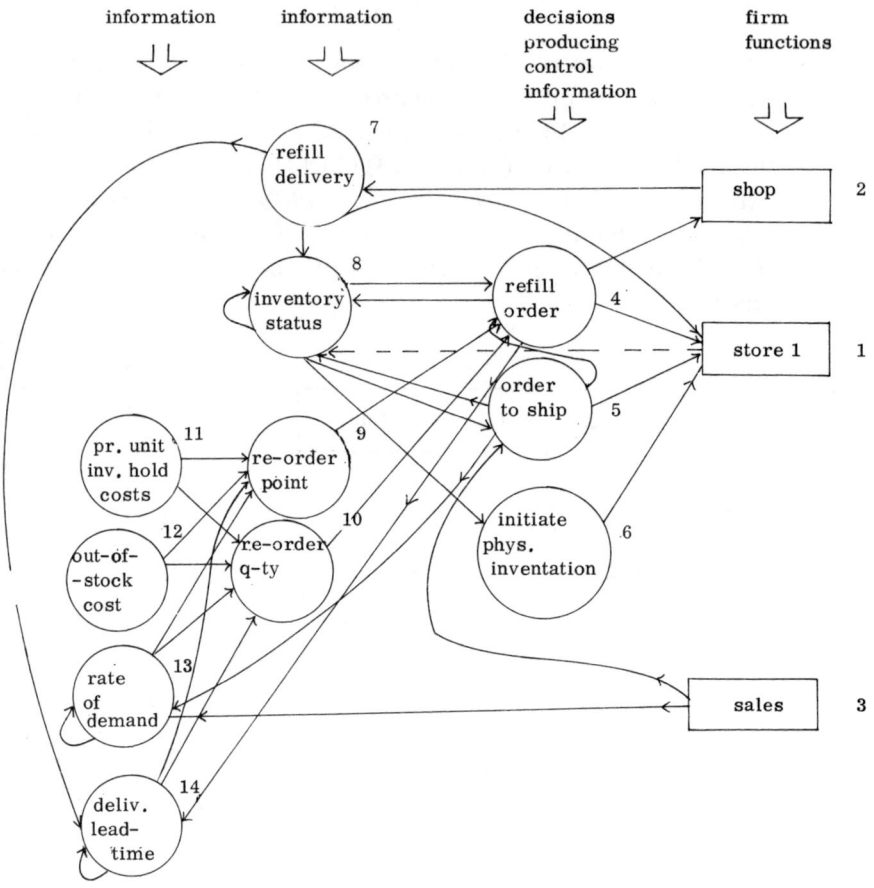

Fig. 2

assumptions: no substituable items
no production relation considered

only "sales" and historic data are considered in determining rate of demand

only historic data used to determine lead time

the introduction of new items or deletion is neglected

safety stock is neglected

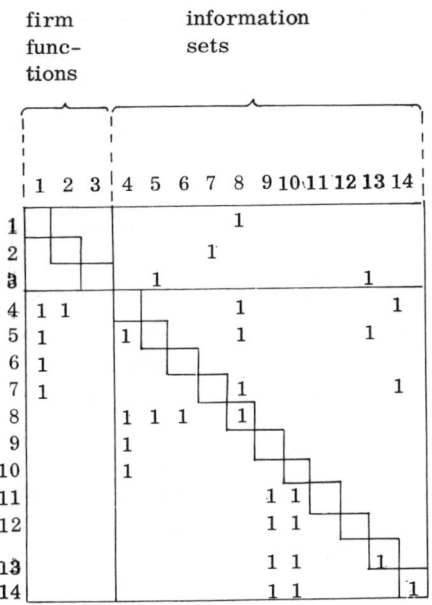

Fig. 3. Precedence matrix of the system in Fig. 2.

11 We may modify the information system in such a way that the apparently infinite iterations of "8, 13 and 14" are avoided. To do this we observe that the inventory status is changed during each of the *elementary processes* which take one of the information precedents of "8" as an input. These precedents therefore also have to be used in a certain logical order so that each of them feeds into an elementary process which has the best new version of "8" as another input and produces a still newer (*updated*) version of "8". We denote the starting inventory status file by "8" and "update" it with 7 (if any) to produce the new version to be denoted "8''''". This in its turn is updated in a second elementary process with "1" as another precedent to produce "8'''". Then "5" is used to produce "8''" and finally a process which uses "4" as a precedent produces the "fully updated version" "8'" (8 prime). "8'" is then used as the starting version for the next processing run. In this way we obtain the system of Fig. 3 (and the precedence matrix P of Fig. 5).

For "13" and "14" similar reasoning holds.

12 Each of the circles in Fig. 2 corresponds to a specific "kind-of-information", that is, to a specific concept. In the information

system to be constructed it will be represented by a part of the "information base". In some situations it will also be convenient to refer to each of them as an information base (of which there are then many in the system). This variability of naming the same concept is, of course, an illustration of the relativity principle for systems, mentioned in part 1, chapter 1.

The arrows in Fig. 4 correspond to precedence relations between the different kinds of information. In the implemented information system they are made operational by the transfer of some information message between information bases when information of the kind which is a succedent of it is to be produced. This transfer activity will be performed in different time periods for the different arrows in the figure. Therefore the information bases have an important function of storage of information so that it is available any time. The design of the information system is simplified because extensive syncronization problems which otherwise would have been tremendous are reduced.

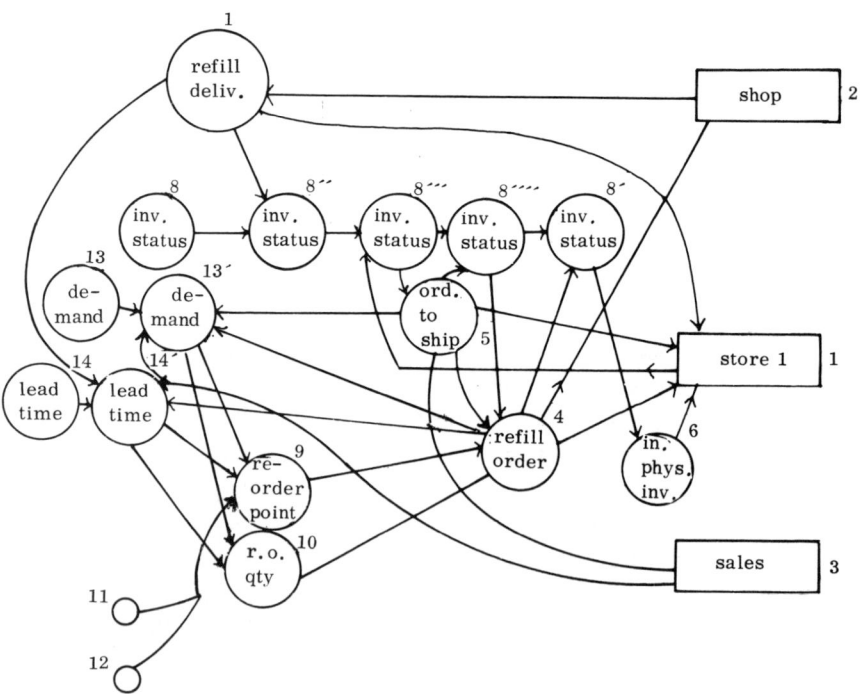

Fig. 4.

The associated precedence matrix P is

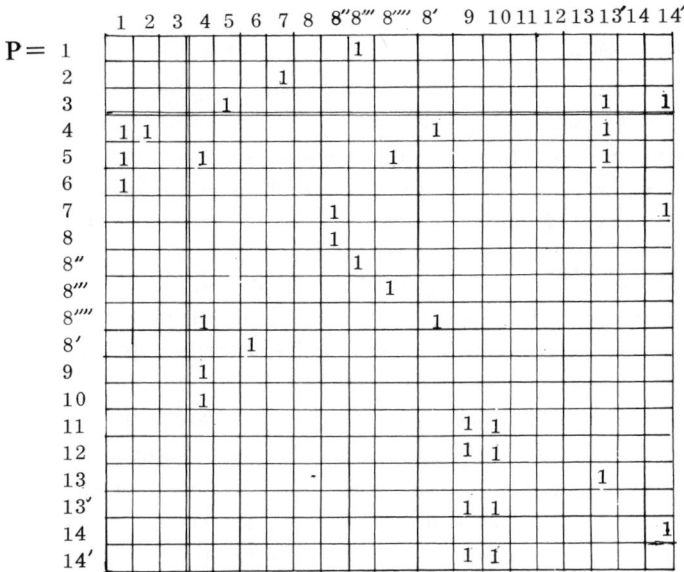

Fig. 5. Precedence matrix of the system of Fig. 3.

13 Every column in P corresponds to an elementary process which produces the information set whose name (or identifying number) is attached to the column. By inspecting a column of P we see which information sets are its precedents and, therefore, are inputs to the process producing the information set associated with the column. By inspecting a row P we find to which elementary processes its information set is an input (after having excluded "1", "2" and "3" which are firm functions and no outputs of processes). We find that, for instance, "8'''''" is an input to the processes producing respectively "4" and "8'" and "11" is an input to "9" and "10". We conclude that "8'''''" has to be input to two different elementary processes and, hence, that if these two processes could be grouped together into one composite process then "8'''''" would only need to be input once. Thus one input operation would be discarded. Further it is seen that if "9" and "10" could be grouped into one process one would save one input operation (out of two) for each of "11, 12, 13'" and "14'". It is seen that these possibilities for saving input operations can all be detected by inspecting the rows of P.

14 There is another possible saving of both input and output operations that is not so detected. It is instead detected still more easily. This is the fact all the intermediary versions of "8", that is "8'", "8''" and "8'''" might all be eliminated if the processes corresponding to them could all be grouped together. Thus in this way three output operations and three input operations would be saved. This is found simply by inspecting the identifying numbers of the information sets, provided the identifiers associated with different versions of the same set are equal save for a tag to identify the individual version[9]).

15 Although it might be easy to see from the matrix P how input or output operations would be saved if certain processes were grouped together, it is not so directly visible whether the grouping can actually be made. We find from Fig. 4, that for instance, the process producing "8'''" cannot be grouped with that producing "8'" for before "8'" can be produced we must produce "4" and "8'''" is a precedent of "4", that is $8'''' < $ "4". We shall se later how this kind of condition can be checked also on the precedence matrix using generalized matrix algebraic operations such as we have met in the system algebra.

16 In the precedence matrices we have marked off the rows and columns 1, 2 and 3 as these are associated with firm functions rather than with processes of the information system itself.

17 It is seen from P that "3, 8, 11, 12, 13 and 14" have empty columns and thus have no precedents and so are initial sets. Of these "8, 13 and 14" are special by having also an updated version "8', 13' and 14'" respectively. This indicates that the initial "8" is taken from the "8'" of the next preceding run and similarly for "13" and "14". The other sets, by not having updated versions, are found to be true initials which means, here, that they originate outside the information system described. This is important to see for it means that these sets have to be provided from outside and must therefore be designed for the double purpose of being conveniently and reliably handled both by the information system and by the outside originators, which are often human beings. We must observe that in this sense each time a firm function (i.e. "1, 2 and 3") occurs as a precedent it will be originating information from outside the information system described.

---

[9]) Note that this implies an important condition on the data-naming principle to be used.

18 We see that "1" as a precedent to "8''''" is to be regarded as an initial information set. We may denote it by "$1_8''''$". Likewise "2_7", "3_5" and "3_{13}" are initials.

19 In a similar way sets which are precedents to firm functions are to be regarded as terminal sets. In fact they are reported from the information system to the firm functions. We see from P that "4_1", "4_2", "5_1", "6_1" and "7_1" are terminal sets. We also see that there are no others, for P has no empty rows.

20 As we have seen the important function of defining the initial and the terminal information sets is well served by the precedence matrix[10]).

We now look back at the way we determined information needs of a firm (paragraphs 2 and 4). Let us now assume that the task of listing the functions and their information needs has been accomplished. Let us assume as a simple example, that the firm is so simple that only two functions are to be served. Let us call them A and B.

Further for these two functions we have found the information sets a, b, and c, d to be directly required.

21 We now have the problem to define for the information a, b, c and d which information is needed for its production. Again this might be done by means of lists if available. In any case it has to be done by considering the definition of the information a in terms of more elementary concepts. This kind of analysis will be referred to as *information analysis*. When it is done by use of precedence relations we also call it *precedence analysis*.

22 No programming or formula should be done to this end[11]). It may be necessary to make some calculations in order to determine whether or not some information which is logically motivated for a does actually play a significant numerical role[12]). See also examples

---

[10]) Continued in section 27.2—5.
[11]) We mean programs or formulas associated with the precedence relation itself, that is formulas which compute information from its precedents. We do not mean to object against a possible use of formal methods which could establish the precedence sets.
[12]) An example of this kind of analysis is shown in section 25.4. In fact it is one of the basic tasks of statistics to determine to what degree information precedence relations hold.

below. Precedence relations may be associated with causal relations (assumed to exist in the object system, e.g. for logical reasons) or empirical correlations. The latter constitute the main subject of some of the areas of statistics. These are thus seen to be of importance to information analysis.

Suppose we find in this way that to obtain a we need four information sets e, f, g, and h say. One of these may represent a set of computer programs.

23 Example.

To determine which information is needed to produce information about the best economical order quantity to use we do *not* have to work out the EOQ formula. To work out the formula we have *first* to decide which parameters to consider in the formula. Then, as a second step, we do an analysis in detail to work out the mathematical relationship among these parameters. Our technique is to postpone the second detailed mathematical step.

24 Example.

To compute the manufacturing requirements of parts at break-down level i of a product, we first decide that the production precedence matrix P^{00} and the demand on level i-1 is the information required. Only thereafter do we determine the formula saying that extended matrix algebra provides the detailed algorithm to be used. Again in the phase of analysis where information precedents are to be determined, only the first part of the problem is to be solved.

In information processing it is common to produce, from some precedents one of which is x, a new, updated version of x. We shall use the notation x' to denote the updated version of x. Obviously

$$x < x';$$

If we have the pair of precedence relations

25 $$\begin{cases} \mathscr{P}(a) = b, c, d; \\ \mathscr{P}(c') = c, d; \end{cases}$$

then we shall always suppose, unless otherwise stated, that c' is first produced and then a is produced after c has been replaced by c', whenever this is possible. More generally we shall use the rule (when no specific ordering is prescribed):

26 $\qquad$ whenever $x < y \wedge y \not< x'$ then $x' < y$

or in words: whenever x precedes y and y does not precede x' then we take x' to precede y, instead of x.

When a set a contains only elements which are also contained in another set q then we denote this fact by writing

27 $\qquad$ $q \supseteq a$ or $a \subseteq q$

and a is said to be a subset of q in case we do not know whether $q = a$ may be true or not. If $q \supset a$ and $q \neq a$ then we write

28 $\qquad$ $q \supset a$ or $a \subset q$

and call a a true subset of q. It is obvious that it is of interest to know which precedence sets are subsets of other precedence sets. Therefore when we list a set of precedence relations we shall try to group them by subset relations.

We shall have occasion to use the concept of set intersection $x = y \cap z$ which will be defined as the set x such that if $q \in x$ then $q \in y$ and $q \in z$ (or if q is a member of x then it is a member of both y and z).

For example let

$$y = a1, a2, a3, a4$$
$$z = a2, a4, a6, a8$$

then $x = y \cap z = a2, a4$.

Obviously, if $z \subset y$ then $y \cap z = z$.

Suppose we have a system as described by P⁰⁰:

29

	a	b	c	d	e'	i'	j'	l'
P⁰⁰ = a		1		1	1			1
c				1				1
e	1	1		1	1	1		1
f	1			1				
g	1		1	1				
h	1			1				
i		1	1			1	1	
j			1				1	
k			1				1	
l				1				1

The columns of P⁰⁰ correspond to the precedence relations
$\mathscr{P}$ (a) = e, f, g, h; $\mathscr{P}$ (b) = a, e, i; $\mathscr{P}$ (c) = g, i, j, k; $\mathscr{P}$ (d) = a, c, e, h, l; $\mathscr{P}$ (e') = e, f, g; $\mathscr{P}$ (i') = a, e, i; $\mathscr{P}$ (j') = i, j, k; $\mathscr{P}$ l') = a, c, e, l.

The precedents are listed to the left of the matrix, labelling the associated rows, whereas the succedents are listed above their associated columns. The rows of P⁰⁰ indicate the succedents of the set corresponding to the row. Thus g is seen to have the succedents a, c and e'. According to 26 we need not have e', i', j', l' among the rows. A set which is indicated to have i, for instance, as a precedent will in most cases use i' instead, following the rule in 26.

From inspection of P⁰⁰ (29) we find

30
$\mathscr{P}$ (e') $\subset$ $\mathscr{P}$ (a)
$\mathscr{P}$ (i') $\subset$ $\mathscr{P}$ (b)
$\mathscr{P}$ (j') $\subset$ $\mathscr{P}$ (c)
$\mathscr{P}$ (l') $\subset$ $\mathscr{P}$ (d)

Further we see that b and d have no succedents. In fact their rows are empty and have been deleted from P⁰⁰. They are terminal sets. Similarly e, f, g, h, i, j, k, and l have no precedents. They are thus initial sets.

The remainders have an intermediate position. They can be ordered by levels. These levels can be found by matrix multiplications involving P⁰⁰ [13]). In our example, however, we can obtain the

---

[13]) 1 La 1962-2.

ordering by inspection. We may want the ordering for instance in order to find out how to draw the precedence graph associated with P^{00} in a proper way. Thereby we want to draw sets, which are grouped by the subset relations, as neighbors. We therefore look for ordering relations for these groups[14]).

We want to place the terminal sets to the right. Both b and d are terminals. However b is grouped with i' and d with l'. Further

31 $\qquad a < i' < j' < c < l'$

Hence we obtain the order (cf. also 15)

32 $\qquad (a, e') < (b, i') < (c, j') < (d, l').$

We rewrite P^{00} in this order

33

$P^{00} =$	a	e'	b	i'	c	j'	d	l'
a			1	1			1	1
c							1	1
e	1	1	1	1			1	1
f	1	1						
g	1	1			1			
h	1						1	
i			1	1	1	1		
j					1	1		
k					1	1		
l							1	1

In Fig. 6 we have drawn the graph corresponding to P^{00}. If the reader will do this for himself he will find that it is much easier if he follows the order indicated by 33 than if he used 29.

---

[14]) Corresponding to such groupings we will group together the process associated with these sets, see section 27.6. Computer programs for automatic construction of the graphs from the precedence matrix or similar data structures have recently been implemented, see e.g. 2 Sc 1971.

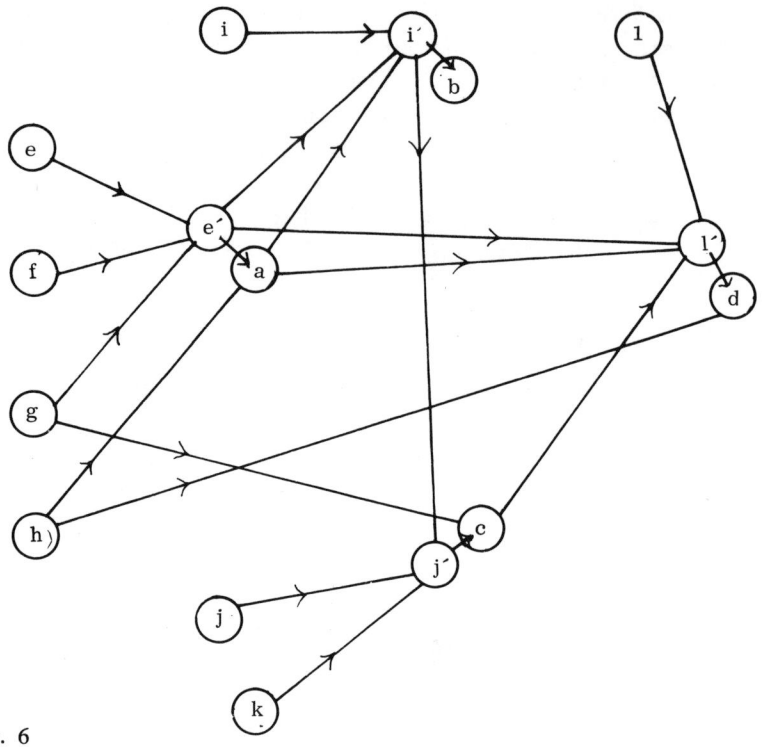

Fig. 6

In drawing Fig. 6 the rule in 26 has been followed. Further we have simplified the drawing by introducing the following device: if one information set has among its precedents all those of another set we symbolize this by drawing an arrow from the interior of the latter to the interior of the former. For instance the arrow from the interior of the circle around e' into the interior of the circle around a indicate that e, f and g are precedents not only of e' but also of a. (Thus $P(a) = $ e, f, g and h.)

34 In an information processing system a relation between an information set and its precedents will normally correspond to an elementary process that will take in a set of values of the precedence sets and produce a value of the set considered. The information sets will normally be represented in the system in the form of files. These we shall call *elementary files* and the symbols for information classes will be considered to represent elementary files.

The files commonly used in data processing systems are consolidated from a set of elementary files (although this way of looking at it may be new). One of the problems of designing an information processing system is to obtain an efficient set of file consolidations.

The concept of consolidated masterfiles is often a very basic one in existing data processing systems. The consolidation of the files i often advocated on very simple arguments such as that it is nice to have all data which are associated with one item (such as one person or one catalogue number) collected into one and the same record. This way of presenting the concept has many weak points. In the first place it does not explain why. Second (and this is a consequence of the first)it is often not efficient to use a masterfile concept such as the common one. *In a well designed information processing system all information associated with an item is safely available without having to be forced to belong to one and the same record of one and the same masterfile.* It is therefore more rational to take into consideration the different consequences to system efficiency of storing data for an item in different alternative ways before making the final design decision. It may, for instance, happen that some data for an item are needed in one processing run and other data for that item are not. They will then be subject to unnecessary handling if consolidated into the same file. This may be compensated by other advantages but we have to show that, in each case, before deciding.

Many of the information classes we are defining will have to be bundles of still more elementary information kinds. For instance infirmation about a "job" may well be considered an elementary information class or an elementary file. Yet we shall see[15]) that to define it we need its identifier, size, type and, perhaps, worker involved.

25.2 On the Definition of Elementary Files (e-files).

1 When we discuss which information is needed at any point in a system (whether it is the information needed for a decision in a main function within a firm or a precedent of such an information) we have to define the information needed as a set of more basic kinds of information which we shall call *elementary information sets*, or *elementary files*. Although this does not appear to be a significant problem we point to the fact that it is an instance of the general systems analysis problem called by us "the definition of inner boundary". It also conforms with our Fundamental Principle[1]).

---

[15]) See section 25.4—13.
[1]) See section 11.11.

293

We point out a problem that may arise here. It seems natural to consider a "conto number" as definitely a bottom level item, i.e. a term[2]). However in some processes (e.g. of a "data edition" kind) it might be necessary to handle only a portion of it separately. Having given this little warning we leave this subject and turn to the more difficult one of determining which group of terms we want to treat as records in *elementary files* or *e-files* for short[3]).

2 Let us first see what reason we have for introducing this concept. One reason is that we want to name and define such groups of terms — or groups of elementary information sets — as are natural entities for being handled in the most elementary processes we are thinking of.

3 What we have in mind here is to have names, and most desirably meaningful ones, which are associated with well known procedures within the actual field of application. This would mean that on encountering such names in a block diagram or flow chart for an information system we would know fairly well what kind of procedures are being used and what data terms are carried in the files. This is in extreme contrast to the present practice where diagrams and descriptive texts only use ad hoc names both for truncated files containing large numbers of different kinds of data and for processes consisting of large but vaguely defined elementary computation[4]).

As an example we may consider the precedence matrix P of a set of products. It is used in the "parts explosion" in production control. From our familiarity with it from the system algebra its naming immediately suggests its meaning. In data files for production control the "P-data" are usually hidden in large files called materials file or products file and these names have different meanings in different companies (because the files have different contents of other data

---

[2]) We use "term" instead of the common word "field" because "field" should be used exclusively to denote the area of storage (or input/output medium) where a term is stored (or where several terms are stored). "Term" as used here is equivalent to "elementary items" of COBOL.
[3]) Our insistence on breaking down to elementary files can be said to be based on working principles well known in engineering design. Counterparts are also the breakdown to basic activities in planning networks and to work elements in MTM methods of industrial engineering.
[4]) For further discussion on the e-files and related concepts, see 2 Sc 1971. Somewhat related concepts are also presented recently from other authors. see e.g. 2 Cd 1970.

than P which are also included in the file). Only when all data in such a file are named as members of such intuitive concepts files, hence elementary files, do we know what the file content is and what its use might be.

In American literature on production control the information corresponding to our precedence matrix P is normally called "bills of material". A bill of material is equivalent to a column in the matrix P.

4 The present practice makes it impossible to extract much useful information from available diagrams. When one tries to go below the surface of present systems one either is not able to get details or else only gets the detailed lists of all elementary terms in which case it is extremely difficult to find out what the meaning of each of the terms is.

5 If elementary files and computations[5]) are used in a reasonably standardized way, as in physics, then the descriptions could be much more intelligible. It is also much more feasible to standardize on elementary files than on the consolidated files of different structure in different firms.

6 Another advantage that will come out of an advance of the concept of elementary files and computations is that the possibilities of using standard programs or subroutines would be much improved.

7 To give some indication of the feasibility of a use of elementary files and computation in the way we propose, we may notice that the computation of parts requirements by means of the precedence matrix P (or combinatorial description) of the products and the demand vectors d^0, d^1 ... using computations of the form $P(\cdot) d^i = d^{i+1}$ is an example of using elementary files, e.g. P and d^i, as well as an elementary computation procedure, e.g. the quasi-matrix multiplication symbolized by $(\cdot)$[6])[7]).

8 **Problem.** In section 25.1, paragraph 14, it was mentioned that grouping of, or instance, 8'' and 8' "would save two passes of file

---

[5]) See section 27.1 for the definition of "computation".
[6]) See section 12.9.
[7]) For some illustrations to the concept of elementary files see sections 4 and subsequent ones.

8". While this was not directly visible from two 1-s in the row 8" of the matrix we pointed out that the use of identical parts of the file names, e.g. part "8", made it possible to detect this kind of potential saving by grouping. Show that this problem can be solved by a formal rule, applying on the matrix. Also show that this rule also works in similar situations where identical name parts are not appropriate.

9 The problem of 8 is solved by formal matrix operations, when the incidence matrix E^{10} is used rather than P^{00}. (cf. section 12.10).

10 **e-concepts.** As we have seen a set of e-records may be organized into one e-file (or set of e-files). Analogously the family of all e-messages of the *same kind* in the sense of having the same record type (or the same record description) may be regarded as belonging to the same *kind of information*. Often we need a shorter name for "kind of information" (as well as a precise definition, because "same kind" may be used with many different meanings). We therefore introduce "e-concept" (elementary concept) for the kind of information which is characterized by all e-messages of that kind having the same message type (giving rise to records having the same type). Thus any e-message will be regarded as an *instance of an e-concept*.

25.3 Inference Problems in Information Systems Design.

The problem of drawing inferences is a very central one in the design of information systems. It is one of the functions of an automatic information system to draw inferences from data available, in an automatic way. The most obvious example of this is when formulas are evaluated in regular numerical processes. The inference concept however, as we intend to use it, is more general and will be associated with any kind of process which makes use of some input information to produce output information and also will produce an estimate of the probability of the output being the "true" outcome of a situation defined by the input.

There are other ways in which inference can be an important function in information system design.

We have emphasized earlier that the precedence information associated with a certain output information should be determined in a way more direct than by working out formulas connecting the precedence information with its output. An inference should be made in the "backward" sense, i.e. the precedents would be the output of such an inference function when the desired output information is given as an input to the inference function.

We made the statement that probably no direct procedure or formula could be established that would determine the precedents for a given output information. It shall be defined on an "a priori basis"[1]. We also suggested however that by establishing lists of preestablished precedence relations these could be used as a guide for subsequent precedents determination work. (This of course will also require that a standardization of terminology and concepts definitions has been established.) In our present context (of inference) we can state our suggestion in the form: to define a relation

$$P(x) << x$$

is an inference problem using a priori reasons and possibly lists of earlier established precedence relations as its "basis".

If such an inference process should be automated it should be such as to accept precedence lists and a priori definitions. Some estimate of its degree of "incompleteness" should be made. The output of such a procedure would be a precedence list for the actual information together with probability values for its correctness and completeness. If the latter are low this will point to a need for more intuitive work.

In one obvious way can an inference problem like the one described, be improved during its use. Learning properties to some degree are exhibited by extending its set of lists of precedence relations for different classes of problems. To make this evolution automatic is not too difficult. There is however also another way in which it should be possible to use an automatic information system to improve continually the inference process. Thus the best possible way to find improvements to the methods of making inferences, and to define the information needed for this, should be obtained by having an information system collect and store information regarding the outcome of all trials of the kind. This would then be a basis for further research, which would also be more efficiently performed when it could have available ample information and automatic processing facilities for its use.

---

[1] See section 25.1—4.

25.4 A Further Illustration to Information Precedence and Elementary File Definition: Computation of Weekly Wage.

1. Let us assume that the wage will consist of components such as
   hourly pay

   piecewise incentive (swedish: styck-ackord)   or piecework rate
   group incentive (swedish: lag-ackord)   or gang rate

   The worker may have worked a certain number of hours on an hourly pay basis and also a specified numbers of hours on each of two assumed kinds of incentive. The system may well have to be able to cope with more types of pay but we disregard this at the moment.

2. We have so far established the precedence relations for information

   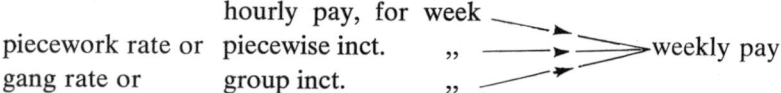

                     hourly pay, for week
   piecework rate or   piecewise inct.   „   weekly pay
   gang rate or   group inct.   „

3. To obtain the hourly pay for week for the worker, we need to know the number of hours in the week, worked under hourly pay. However there may be various types of work for hourly pay. Thus the day of the week as well as the hour of the day may determine the hourly pay rate. We need not at the moment specify all types that may occur but then it is necessary to provide for an unspecified number of "hourly pay work types".

4. We get the precedence relation

   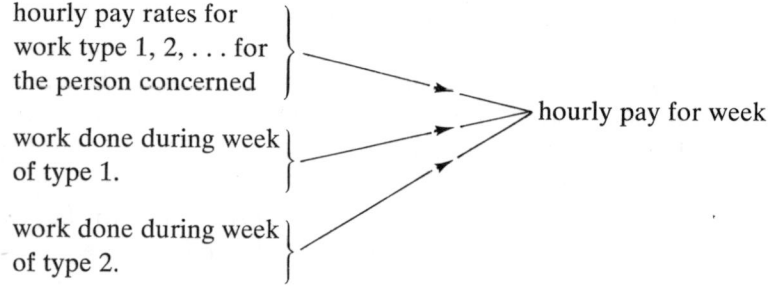

   hourly pay rates for
   work type 1, 2, ... for
   the person concerned

   work done during week
   of type 1.

   work done during week
   of type 2.

                                    hourly pay for week

   .
   .
   .

5 For these precedents we need again define their precedents. The first of them, the hourly pay rate, will as a rule be constant for a number of weeks and will therefore, in general, be taken from a standing file. This however does not eliminate the need for having a procedure for computing these values. Therefore precedents of the hourly pay rate need be defined. We leave this however and turn to the next item: work done during week, of type i; (where i stands for any of the values 1, 2, ...). Before we can proceed now, we have to be specific about the *flow* of information. To talk only of the *kind* of information, as we have done so far, is no longer sufficient. The reason for this is that the work to be paid is normally performed in a time sequence of well defined single jobs whereas the pay is to be computed per week, which normally implies summing the pay for different jobs or alternatively of summing the hours worked during the week on each of the different work types.

6 We see that we need to have some information for each job done, so that we know

> to which week does the job belong
> to which type „ „ „ „
> which number of hours have been used up

"type" here tells both if the job is on incentive (piecework) or on hourly pay and in the latter case which type of hourly pay.

7 In the case that the work type is determined by day of week and hour of day we have the alternative

> indication whether hourly pay or incentive (piecework)
> start of job, week, day, hour etc.
> finish of job, „   „   „   „

8 The fact that we have two alternatives here (i.e. 6 or 7) brings us into a decision situation. The decision can only be reached by considering questions which are for other people to decide — or for us to decide in another context.

Both these cases present an illustration of a point in the systems work *where documentation is necessary: which decision is taken, why, by whom?*

It is important for the systems work to handle thoroughly and carefully all such decision documentation.

9 **Remark.** The decision situation mentioned in 8 apparently most often is regarded as being rather a "knowledge situation" where knowledge of the situation presently in use in the system (the company) indicates the choice to be made. This is not a very fortunate way of handling the problem however for it is entirely possible that the present situation is not the best one. *Only the explicit presentation of each "point of choice" in the system design as a decision problem for the correct set of people to handle is therefore satisfactory. Thus rather than trying to find out what is in use today the problem is to find out what should be in use.* Systems analysis therefore is to be concerned about clear presentation of all decision points by careful analysis and documentation of what information is required for decision. This is an analysis of information precedence relations. This, then, should indicate which people or groups are involved. The present way of emphasizing the explorative part of the systems analysis work therefore seems to rather misinterprete the problem.

10 A consequence of the arguments of 9 is that "company knowledge" should not be given too much importance but be replaced by company-oriented decision operations. The man who "knows the company" may, more easily than other people, overlook the decision points. Company knowledge will of course, be made to enter when the decision question is made the subject of a discussion with the proper people.

11 **Remark.** The decision point may well have to be replaced by an explorative one if the problem is not to design one specific system but rather to design an information processing system which will have to serve several different systems. Thus if our problem is to serve different systems we cannot obtain decisions easily. This would involve standardizing conferences which, while well justified in themselves, may take too much time. We then may want to make an explorative study to define which different decisions have been made in the different systems concerned. Then the information processing system will have to be designed to cover all variants.

12 Let us assume that the second alternative (i.e. 7 rather than 6) has been chosen, for instance because an automatic registration of time points is available to the worker.

13 We have now come to find that one of the kinds of information needed, i.e. the information on an individual job, consists of a record giving one value for each of four different kinds of information[1]):

$$\text{job} \begin{cases} \text{employee number} \\ \text{main type (whether hourly pay, piecework rate} \\ \quad \text{/piece inct./ or gang rate /group inct./).} \\ \text{time for start, week, day, hour,} \ldots \\ \text{time for finish, week, day, hour,} \ldots \end{cases}$$

14 Thus this information comes in a bundle of different kinds of information, and in a sequence of groups of values, one for each kind, all values associated with the same physical item (the job).

15 The sequence of such value groups is a sequence of records and is thus, typically, a file. It is an *elementary file* in that it contains a group of different kinds of information which are required simultaneously to specify an elementary logical entity.

16 We have called this group of information, or this elementary file, a "job" value or a job file. We can look upon the elementary file "job" in different ways. Perhaps the most basic one would be to regard it as a set of different files "job i j", e.g.

job 01, job of piecework rate (piece incentive) type
job 02, job of gang rate (group incentive) type
job 11, job of hourly pay type 1,
job 12, job of hourly pay type 2,
.   .
 .   .
  .   .

17 Another way of looking at this is to regard "job" as one single elementary file, the elementary process of which will follow different lines depending on the value of "type".

---

[1]) Note that we are assuming the situation, mentioned in 7, that "type" is determined by the time information. Hence only "main type" needs be given in the record.

18 In the first case (16) we get the precedence relations

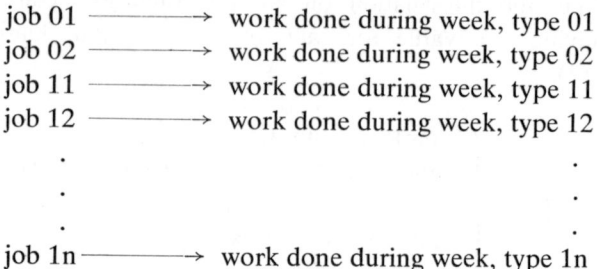

    job 01 ⟶ work done during week, type 01
    job 02 ⟶ work done during week, type 02
    job 11 ⟶ work done during week, type 11
    job 12 ⟶ work done during week, type 12

       ·   ·
       ·   ·
       ·   ·

    job 1n ⟶ work done during week, type 1n

19 In the second case (17) we get

    job ⟶ set of jobs done during week, tagged by type
                     (01 .... 1n)

20 **Remark.** In addition to the job specifications produced by each worker for each job, it would be wise to have something of a job type on which to report "complementary time" such that this will fill the standard number of regular hours for the week. This can be arranged in several different ways and, again, a decision problem therefore arises. This decision also requires some information (or directive) from "outside" the subsystem of payroll because the ease with which the worker can produce this will have to be considered.

21 On a closer inspection we find that it would be more natural to distinguish only between elementary files for the three different "main types": piecework rate (piece incentive), gang rate (group incentive) and hourly pay, because these call for differently structured processing. They may in fact call for significantly different information structure. The different types within the group "hourly pay" will all use the same kind of process only taking different values of pay-rate for the different "types". (Admittedly this is an assumption and is therefore to be made subject to an explicit decision procedure in any realization instance.)

22 The elementary file "job" contains information[2]) given by data reported by the worker or by some equipment. We have thus come to the bottom of our process of break-down of information into sequences of precedence sets.

---

[2]) E.g. start time and finish time.

23 In Fig. 1 we have compiled the precedence conditions so far discussed.

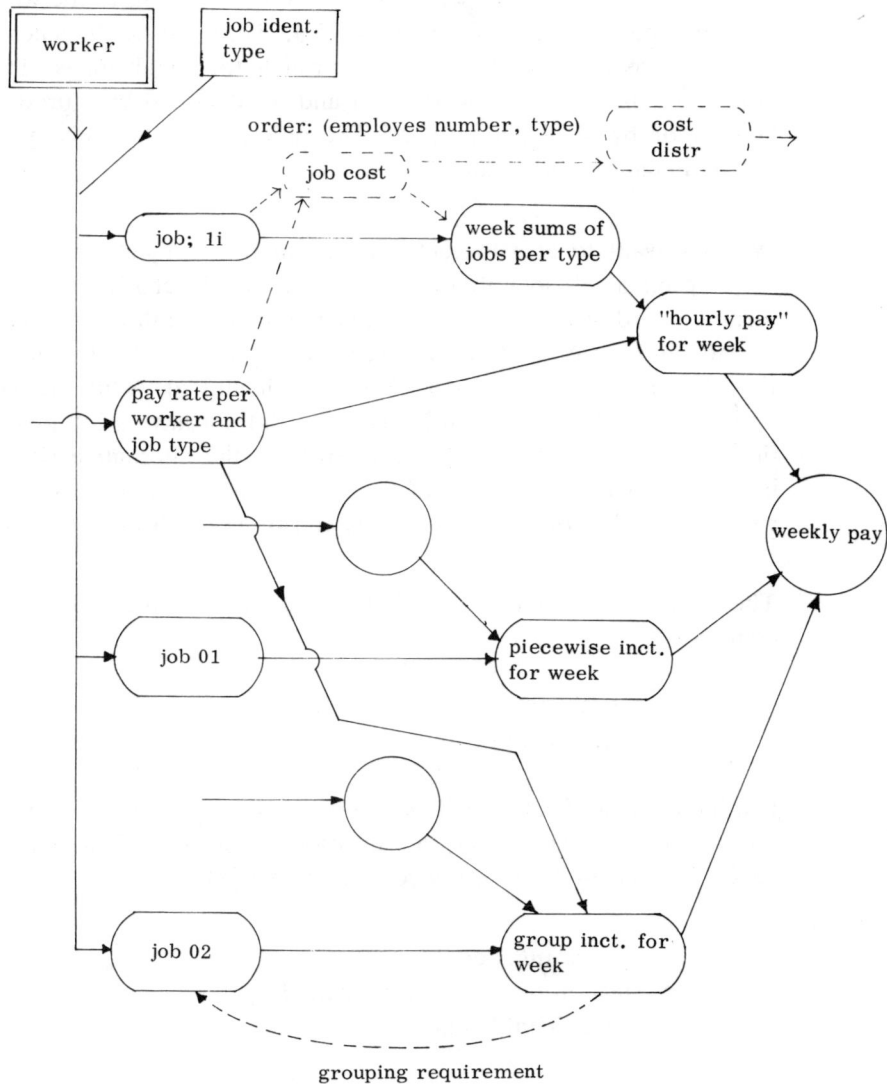

Fig. 1

24 Notice that in this analysis of information precedence we have followed the principle, advocated in the text, not to bother about details of computation processes but just to ask for "logical" and "natural" information need.

25.5 Cost Distribution of Job Costs as Another Illustration of Discussing Elementary Files.

1 The different jobs treated in the system discussed in section 25.4 each have a cost — or a set of costs — corresponding to the work pay computed for payroll. Section 25.4. These costs, in general, are to be assigned to the object to which the job belongs. This object may be a product worked on and be identified by a product number or by an order number. The object may alternatively be a department or work station.

2 We may want to give to each job one or more object identifiers. As a result a job identifier together with an object identifier will form a record of a natural *elementary file*. If several different object classifications are used we get several different such elementary files. It is not yet clear how a job is to be identified. A little reflection indicates that in section 25.4—6 we did not have a job identification (which must be added) whereas in the alternative shown in section 25.4—7 the "start of job, week, day, hour, etc." together with the number of the worker does constitute a job identification.

3 The elementary file for one kind of object assignment thus will contain

        job identification
        object identification

and the job identification will be composed of several terms (elementary items) depending on the decision taken regarding section 25.4—6 or 25.4—7. For instance we may thus get

4   worker number
        start of job, week, day, hour, etc.
        object identification.

5 It is clear that much of the data carried in the elementary file for job-object assignment is also contained in the elementary file "job". We waste some space if we do not at once decide to consolidate these two into one file: "job — object" identification. If we do not consolidate we could reduce the volume of the elementary file "job-object" by introducing a new term: "job number". This must then also be entered into "job" which is thus increased in volume.

6 In section 25.4 we used the elementary files "job" and "pay rate" to compute "hourly pay for week". This could be done in two ways. One could sum job times within each hourly-pay type over the week and then multiply by pay-rate for that type, to get the work pay for that type. Alternatively one could multiply each single job by the pay rate for its type (for that worker) and then accumulate to gain weekly totals. This calls for several multiplications whereas the first alternative requires only one. Thus for the pay computations alone the first alternative would probably be chosen.

7 The cost distribution requires the cost for each single job and therefore can only use the second of the alternatives. We see that if we want to do this job only once, we can only make the choice of method after all succedents have been defined and their specific requirements established.

8 The reason that we have two alternatives in 6 is that in fact we have not truly defined all elementary computations, for the second alternative is, in fact, more elementary. In this respect the first alternative can be regarded as a grouping of two computations — for arithmetic reasons and not for data transport reasons. This grouping then turns out to be inefficient because of the needs defined by "cost distribution".

9 Job identification must be initiated before the worker starts the job so that the documents needed by him for doing the job can be identified discretely.

10 We have seen in this section how we have been forced to change some decisions of design made in section 25.4. This change is often not detected until computer programming has been done, at which point change is extremely expensive. To establish P^{00}, the information precedence matrix, as completely as possible, before programming is started makes it possible to check with all precedents and all succedents before settling on all details of data formats and computations.

It was also found that a more complete breakdown to truly elementary files and computations could have eliminated the need for change.

25.6 Identification of Precedence Information.

1 It has been shown how the precedence matrix P^{00} is defined by all the direct precedence information lists for all information classes.

The definition of the precedents for an information class is primarily a "local" activity, to be performed by the group of people best familiar with the meaning of that information class.

2 Since several different groups may define the same information class — or the same elementary file — they may not all choose the same name for it. This would mean that in the resulting P^{00} matrix different rows would be associated with the same information class, while one and the same row should be used.

This problem is a central systems problem and it calls for an extensive job to establish a common terminology and to teach all groups in its use. Thorough documentation will also be necessary.

3 As this common terminology problem is bound to be a difficulty in any system except for the very simplest ones, it is also necessary to have a check on this procedure. To this end every time an information class — or an elementary file — is specified as a precedent it should be accompanied by a description of its meaning.

(It will then be a problem of the character of general information retrieval if one wants to let a computer check the naming used, on the basis of "key-words" in such descriptions.)

4 Every "user" of an information class as one of "his" precedents should be given the precedents list for that class as soon as it has been established. This gives him a possibility to check that it is going to contain exactly what he wants it to.

5 The documentation called for by these arguments is best obtained by having one document for every elementary file and one document for every single data term.

25.7 Use of the Information Precedence Matrix P^{00} for Compatibility Checking.

1 We have seen that in P^{00} we have recorded complete information about all precedents of an information set X and, therefore, of

comp (X^1). This is important for it becomes possible, when we design a procedure to realize comp (X), to go back to all precedents to check that the process for comp (X) takes care of the formats in which the precedents are presented. If this is not done an incompatibility situation may occur which calls for changes at several places in the system. Again in this way we detect this fact before programming has to be done[2]).

2 Still more important is, perhaps, that we can just as easily use P^{00} to identify all succedents of an information set X and thus obtain complete knowledge of all computations which are to use X as an input. This, of course, is necessary in order to be able to make sure that the format in which X is produced by the process for comp (X) will be such as to suit the computation of all succedents.

3 Note that while this possibility does exist in principle also in our information precedence graph it is not a realistic possibility. Note further that in the common flowcharts or block diagrams of data processing analysis the possibility does not exist even in principle.

4 The precedence graph is impractical for finding the totality of direct precedents or direct succedents because the practical systems are so large that the diagram cannot be put onto one piece of paper. It has to be partitioned on several sheets. The cross-references then necessary for complete checking cannot easily be put in the systematic way necessary. Note that this problem does not exist in using P^{00}, even if it is also partitioned on several sheets. Of course the best thing to do in this connection would be to store P^{00} on a file storage and let a computer do the scanning. Thus our analysis indicates a way of using computer-aided analysis and documentation.

This is however not a necessity. P^{00} lends itself well also to manual work.

5 The reason why the information precedence relations are not available from the common flowcharts is that these show only the way different consolidated data files are used as input or output to

---

[1] "Comp (X)" is used to denote the computation of X, see section 27.1.
[2] The importance of the incompatibility checking is high in any system design. It will become even more important in large "on-line-real-time" systems of the future. A central group of one or several people must be given responsibility for this checking and for the documentation and oral discussions necessary for efficient solution of this coordination problem.

complex processes consisting of several computations. It is not possible to see if an individual one of the elementary information sets contained in such a file is used or not in that process.

6 It is important to observe that the precedence and succedence relations between information sets are often much more involved, when real requirements are considered, than is recognized today. Present-day systems are oversimplified in this respect because information needs are seldom satisfied. One reason is that a systematic way of establishing all these needs has been lacking so far. P^{00} is such a means however. Another reason is a psychological one. Information is often used as a tool for requiring power within an organization. Then a desire for reserving access to it may be followed. Of course this is a tendency that has to be counteracted in any rational design of an information system. Top management must check that such desire is not permitted to act within the system design staff itself.

7 One minimum requirement for making the existing information known to everybody is to have an explicit documentation of every information item existing in the system with explanation of its source, meaning and use. Thus for each data term in every file there must be made a document giving all this information. It is the file of these documents which, together with P^{00}, gives all basic information about the information system in its "logical" existence. (The file will then of course also give reference to physical storage location.)

8 What has been stated in 7 does, of course, not mean that management may not have good reasons to classify some data and be able to make their availability restricted.

9 **Exercise.**

$P^{00} =$

	a	b	c	d	e
c	1				
d	1	1			
e		1			
f			1	1	
g					1
h			1		

Assume quantitative estimates have been made of the utility of the terminal information sets of this information system. (This may have been possible because the terminal sets control important functions of the controlled system.) Use notations such as u(x) for the utility of the information set x and u(x∪y) for the utility of the set of information sets x and y. What expressions can be given for the utility of the different initial information sets or of groups of such initial information sets? (assume, for instance, that if x and z suffice for producing the terminal information y, then u(x∪z=u(y)).

25.8 Some Other Uses of the Precedence Matrix P.

In the analysis of an information system it will be important to trace, for any information that is produced, all its precedences of all orders. This may be required in connection with auditing because in this way it is found at what places in the system there is a possibility to manipulate and falsify the information produced. It is obvious from the system algebra, part 1, Chapter 2, that matrix operations made on the precedence matrix of information sets in the system can be used to define all precedents of each information set in the system. (Often search algorithms which operate upon the data structure of P^{00} are more efficient.)

It is also important to be able to trace in the opposite direction, for instance, in order to point out where in the system errors may occur as a consequence of an error in an input record. This, from system algebra, can be computed by the transpose of the precedence matrix P, i.e. by the succedence matrix $S = P^T$.

The precedence matrix P is also a valuable tool in the planning of programming and testing the programs and subroutines of a large computer program system. A very successful application of this kind was made in the construction in Sweden of a powerful programming system for handling geometric information in connection with engineering design. This system is able to accept graphical information and to store on mass storage, such as magnetic tapes, the data of any geometric contour defined by graphical or numerical data together with a name given to it. This system is integrated with a system for mathematical design of engineering objects, such as ships, and contains an open set of subsystems for generating control data for numerically controlled machine tools. (It may be noted that this project was a very early and yet very advanced development of what is nowadays called *computer graphics*.)

The program system could be made in ALGOL, thanks to the very powerful procedure features of this language. Thus no new compiler had to be made and the system automatically got all the general properties of ALGOL in addition to its own special features. It was possible to make all subroutines for handling the geometric design as ALGOL procedures which could themselves be written in ALGOL. As the system had to be able to combine simple contours containing one or two curve segments with designs consisting of thousands of curves a dynamic memory allocation subsystem had to be developed. This could also be made as a set of ALGOL procedures which could be written mainly in ALGOL. For this to be possible a basic set of ALGOL procedures written in machine oriented code was designed and used by the other procedures.

To test run the complicated set of procedures it was important to start by testing those subroutines which were initial elements in the precedence system made up of all the routines and their mutual precedence relations. These initial routines were identified by the precedence matrix. Next all routines which had only the initial elements as precedents could be tested and then one could handle those routines which had all those mentioned as precedents and so on. It follows directly from the system algebra of part 1, Chapter 2, how this can all be planned by the aid of the precedence matrix P for the set of procedures.

In the construction of the compiler for the general purpose programming language ALGOL-GENIUS[1]), combining the COBOL data handling features with ALGOL similar technique for detailed planning was used and found to be very efficient.

(ALGOL-GENIUS was, perhaps, the first language implemented and used for general purpose applications. It is used for engineering calculations and business data processing. It contains many of the properties of later designs such as PL/I or SIMULA 67.)

The precedence matrix is also of value by identifying the succedents of each information kind. This is necessary for the estimation of the utility of each information kind to the system because it shows where in the system the information will be used.

---

[1]) 3 La 1964.

25.9 The Precedence Structure and the Dynamic Flow of Processing.

When the transaction messages, which are the precedents of a computation, arrive, they will either trigger a process or they will be put to a batch or queue, waiting for their proper time. In both cases the system must know which computations are succedents of a message, so that the latter can be brought to all the computations in due time. The system management program will look at the precedence matrix P^{00}. If a message of type E arrives, it will look at row E of matrix P. In our example matrix below, it will find the processes B' and K to be real-time (*direct processing* is a better term, although less common) succedents of E. (This is assumed to be indicated by putting "R" in the matrix elements in the corresponding columns, Fig. 1.) As row E has also a "1" in column S we see that message E will also have to be stored to wait for a monthly processing of the information S. In the column B' the R in row E indicates that each message of type E triggers the process producing B' upon the arrival of the message. X in other positions indicates that records from the files in the corresponding rows are to be input to process B' each time B' is triggered, i.e. each time an E-message arrives.

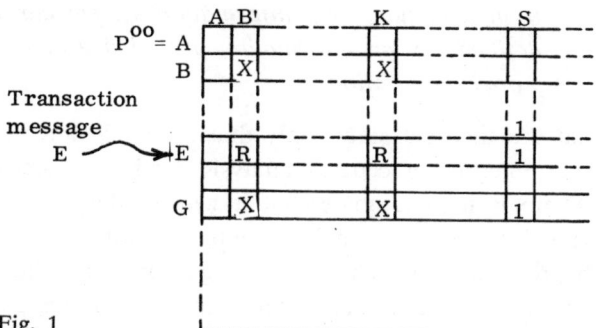

Fig. 1

The column in P^{00} for B', for instance, will then indicate that process B' will also have to take input from files B and G (as they are precedents of B'), see Fig. 2.

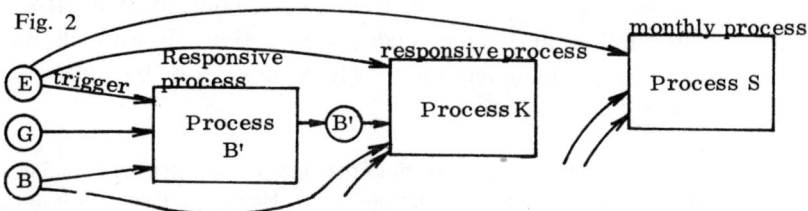

Fig. 2

311

25.10 Completeness Theorem of Information Precedence Analysis.

The method of information precedence analysis has a fundamental property which makes it a very efficient tool: it is *complete* in a certain sense. An information system for management control has the purpose of making integrated management possible.

PROPOSITION 1. Integrated management has as its purpose the obtaining of both "local efficiency" at each operating station in the organization and efficient coordination of the activites of all stations.

Corollary. Each management activity must have an influence, direct or indirect, upon at least one operating station.

PROPOSITION 2. A management activity excercises influence by means of information.

Theorem 1. Each information set in a management information system must be a precedent (of some order) of at least one operating station.[1]

Theorem 2. Completeness theorem. *Each and all relevant information sets in a management information system can be determined, and defined, by an information precedence analysis which starts at every operating station.*

Notice that the theorem states only that each relevant information *can* be determined by precedence analysis starting at some operating station. There is no guarantee that it *will* be determined because the individual precedence analysis steps are intuitive procedures, or search procedures, which cannot be guaranteed to be complete. In other words the method has been proved to be complete in the weak sense that any information that *can be found by some means can also be found by precedence analysis as described*. Whether it actually *will* be found depends on *how* the precedence analysis is performed. Nevertheless, the likelihood that an information which is relevant will actually be found seems higher when precedence analysis is used because it allows a concentrated effort on one information and its precedents at a time. It also allows a more systematic documentation, which can also be processed on a computer.

---

[1] We are talking here of *operations* management. Strategical planning systems, for instance, do not satisfy Proposition 1. Hence the theorems 1 and 2 do not hold for such systems.

25.11 Systematic Design of a Directive Information System.

It was shown in section 22.5 that executive optimum design (that is a design of decision making which takes into consideration the effect of time and cost for making the decision) of executive decision processes requires simplifications to be used. These simplifications are to be such that less time and cost has to be spent on collecting and processing information, when performing the decision processes. It follows that we want to know how to find ways of making systematic simplifications, such that reasonable approximation to executively optimum design of information systems is obtained. We may call such simplifications: *executively efficient simplifications*. In practical design situations one will normally start from the other end: extremely simplified designs. Then to approach executively optimum design one will introduce amplification of the system by using more information and more complicated decision processes. One is then interested in finding such ways of complementation which approach the executive optimum as much as possible. We may then talk about *executively efficient amplification* of the information processes.

Our studies, earlier, of operative information and directive information, give us quite a lot of guidance in searching for efficient simplifications or efficient amplifications. Thus we have learned that the most extreme simplifications which are feasible, are obtained when merely operative information is used for the operative control decisions. As the operative information is necessary for the performance of the operative actions it can certainly not be simplified. An example is the decision process for refill order decisions.

Operative information which is necessary for this kind of decision is information about products shipped and about inventory level. It is usual that some sort of re-order point is used for such decisions. As long as this re-order point information is not continually and systematically renewed, this could not be regarded as use of directive information. In fact there will then be no messages of this kind communicated in the system. This is also illustrated by the fact that the fixed re-order level may even be determined by physical construction as when the "two-bin" inventory control method is used. In such systems the products are stored in two bins and as soon as one of them is empty, re-order is initiated. Starting at such a simple decision procedure for re-order decisions, one may then search for executively efficient amplifications. One very natural amplification will suggest itself in this case: the introduction of a directive information process which will produce successively new values of the re-order point and re-order quantity. It is also obvious, in this case, that we have a fairly wide range of choices for the period with which this directive information will be produced or "up-dated". Thus if there had been no regular up-dating of re-order points and quantities, then semi-annual or monthly up-dating may introduce a significant improvement in inventory operations while not adding very much to information processing costs. This appears to be a step of executively efficient amplification of the information system. A further step of amplification may then be either by increasing the frequency of up-dating or by using more information or more sophistication in computing the re-order points and quantities.

Most data processing systems installed are simple and work mainly with operative information. The extensions mostly talked about now are concerned with improved and integrated management control. It will be common to find that the new design steps to be taken with information systems can be treated, suitably, as executively efficient amplifications. By "amplification" we mean the addition of more information or more processing. We say that the amplification is *executively efficient* if it brings the system closer to an executive optimum. An amplification is not executively efficient if, for instance, it requires more information to produce a more sophisticated decision and therefore is delayed so that the sum effect is negative, from the systems point-of-view (cf. section 22.5). To be executively efficient the amplification will probably leave the operative decision process much as simple as before — whereby it may be possible to run it in operative time (or "real time") — and amplify by introducing a direction of it by a less frequent process which produces directive information. Thus it makes use of more information but in a way which does not slow it down, waiting for that information.

The amplification of a decision process $D'(A)$ by superposing a directive process, $D''(A)$, run less frequently, is a quite general tool, basic to all information system design. It is illustrated, schematically, by Figs. 1 and 2. (It has been assumed, for simplicity, that about 100 operating actions occur per week, on the average, and that directive information will be produced weekly.) It is important

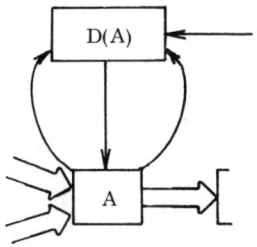

Fig. 1 Extremely simple decision process, D(A), for the operating station A.

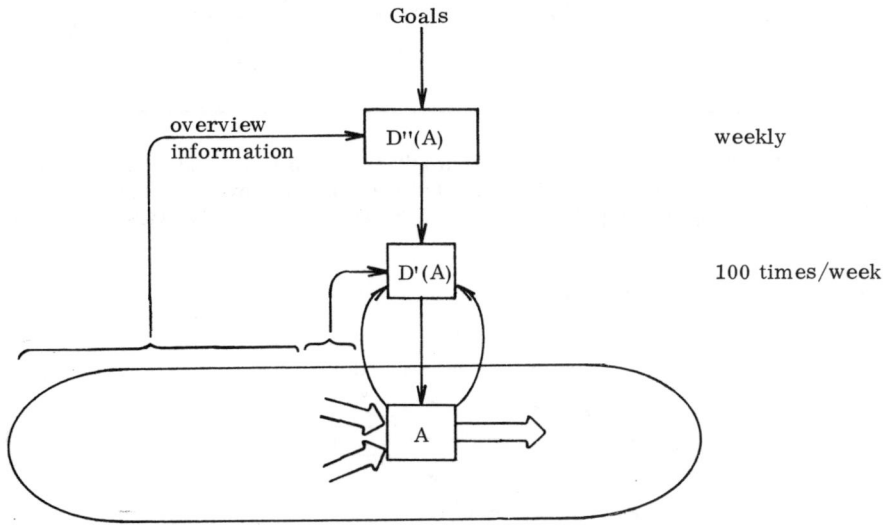

Fig. 2 Amplification of the decision process for the operating station A, by addition of a directive information process D''(A), run less frequently (e.g. weekly) to guide the operative decision process D'(A). Overview information collected and fed to D''(A) on a weekly basis.

to note that a directive process for one decision process may be approximately suitable for several decision processes. In such cases the economy of introducing the directive process is, of course, much improved, Fig. 3. Notice that a directive process such as D''(A), may appear to be not useful enough to pay the cost of introducing it, when regarded only for one decision process, e.g. D'(A1). One may therefore reject it, when determining the degree of ambition (i.e. the amplification) to be used in the design of the information system. It ,likewise, may be rejected when considered for use in the situation D'(A2) and D'(A3). However it may be strongly justified if evaluated with regard to all its uses taken together, i.e. for D'(A1), D'A2), and D'(A3), and, perhaps, several

315

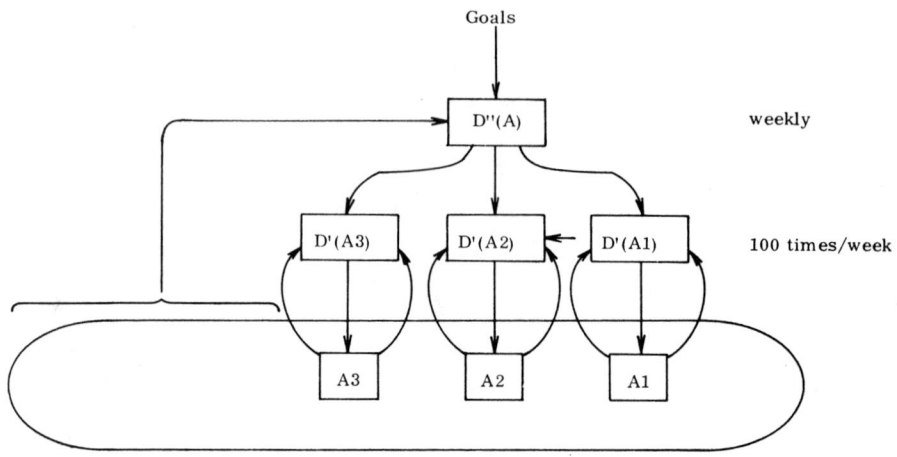

Fig. 3 Directive information from $D''(A)$ is used by several operative decision processes, $D'(A1)$, $D'(A2)$, and $D'(A3)$. This improves the economy of introducing the amplification brought by $D''(A)$ and the overview information.

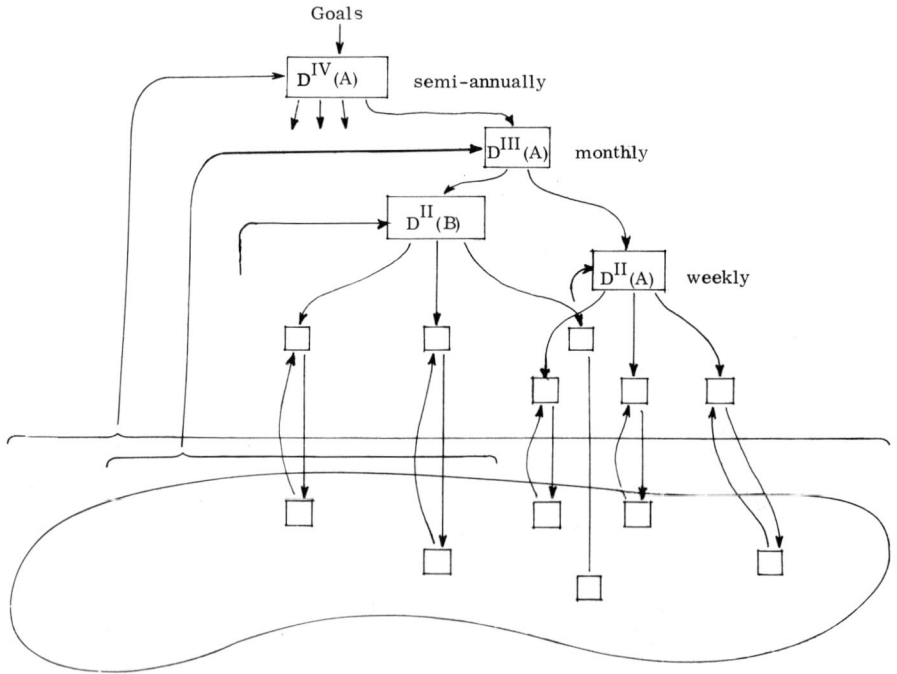

Fig. 4 Further amplification in information system by producing, through $D'''(A)$, directive information also for the directive process $D''(A)$- and, likewise, for e.g. the directive process $D''(B)$, and so forth.

other stations. This points to the importance of being able to determine, as early as possible, as many potential succedents as possible, of the information produced by D''(A). This is one situation where the precedence matrix (or any equivalent system documentation is extremely useful).

In Fig. 4 we have indicated that further amplification may be introduced by additional directive processes, with lower frequencies, e.g. monthly and semi-annually, respectively, and using overview information from larger and larger parts of the object system (e.g. the company).

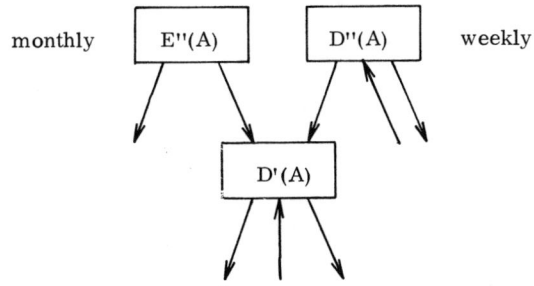

Fig. 5 An information process, D'(A), can be directed by more than one directive information process, for instance by D''(A), (run weekly) and by E''(A), (run monthly).

In Fig. 5 we point out that any process may be directed by any number of directive processes.

It may appear to be an extremely difficult task to determine which directive information to use, in different directive levels, and which updating period to use for each directive process. In practical cases one may well simplify this task by considering only a few different periods, e.g. weekly, bi-weekly, monthly, bi-monthly, semi-annually and annually. Also it should be noted that if one makes a mistake, it may be fairly easy to correct afterwards. For instance if one chooses to up-date re-order points monthly and then finds that the computer is not fully utilized one may, change to weekly up-dating, thereby utilizing the equipment better and producing better inventory economy.

Chapter 6. Data and Information Files.

26.1 Data and Information Files[1]).

There is a widespread confusion concerning the relation between the concept of information and that of data. Often "data" is taken as equivalent to "information" while in other cases the distinctions are that "data" would stand for process input and "information" would stand for output. We find the latter kind of distinction a very impractical one for any theory of information systems. The reason is simple: Most information produced by one process is taken as input to another one, and often to several. On the other hand any thorough analysis of a system handling data needs to make a distinction between the information and the data used to record or process this information. We therefore use the following.

1 *Definition of information.* Information is any kind of knowledge or message that can be used to improve, or make possible a decision or action[2]).

2 *Definition of data.* A datum is a representation of one term of a message, in a digital form. "Digital form" is used here to mean any representation by a finite set of different symbols, usually, but not necessarily, in the shape of decimal digits or alphabetical letters or binary electrical signals. Thus "data" denotes a set of terms.

The formal definition we have introduced for data seems to us to agree with most informal usage today. Notice that it means that an anolog computer is *not* a data processor and also that information representation by anolog signals like voltage is not a data representation.

An anolog computer is still an information processing machine and this broader scope of "information processing" as compared with "data processing" is one of the motivations for using the concept of "information processing". Notice, however, that the main

---

[1]) Cf. section 23.6.
[2]) It should be noted that to interpret a recorded message requires decisions. Also, the interpretation is dependent on knowledge and is thus not only determined by the current recorded message which is to be interpreted but *also on messages which have been received before.*

distinction is that between information itself (as associated with knowledge or messages) on the one hand and data or signals which are used to represent information or communicate information, on the other hand.

26.2 Size of Data Terms and Precision Required.[1])

Once we have agreed upon the definition of data as a general, digital representation of information, we encounter the question of determining how many digits, that is how many symbols out of a given set, are needed to representant a given term of information. To understand how this question may be answered, we observe that when we talk about individual "terms of information" these, in general, are associated with properties of an object. Both "property" and "object" may be associated with any measurable property, such as length, weight, cost, or a classification such as being a part of a certain kind being manufactured, or an identification as for instance "the 32nd individual part with part number 4387 manufactured today."

1 To give information about a property of an object we see that we need four terms of information,

    a *identity of object*
    b *kind of property* we want to specify for the object (or: an *attribute* of the object).
    c the *specification* of that property for that object. This is in information processing often referred to as the *value* of the property (or: the value associated with the attribute)
    d the point in time

These form an *elementary message*[2]) *or e-message*.

2 The first three terms of information can be seen to be associated with sets. Thus to give information about identity one gives in-

---

[1]) See also section 23.6.
[2]) Cf, section 25.1—34. e-records and e-files are closely related to recently published concepts such as "associative triples" and "tuples" (2 Cd 1970). See also 2 Sc 1970 and 2 Sy 1970.

formation which is equivalent to pointing at one element in a list of individuals. Similarly to indicate which kind of property we are going to talk about we name the kind of property from among a list of a set of properties. Finally to give the value for the kind of property we again have to identify within a list of admissible values the element to be associated with the actual object. This is obvious in the case that the property value is not a measurable magnitude. Thus if the kind of property we want to talk about is the profession, the object being an identified man, then the property value is the man's actual profession, as a physician, let us say. When stating this we identify the property value by identifying within a list of all professions that element which is called "physician".

If the property we talk about is a magnitude it may not be so obvious that the value is actually specified in a way that identifies a unique element in a finite, well defined list. To see that this is so we need only to recognize that even if the property value is a result of a measurement it is obtained by identification within a list. Thus for the kind of property we want to measure we can always give an upper limit for its possible magnitude even if giving the lowest upper limit may be difficult. It is equally wellknown that there is also some lower limit for the interval between values that can be indicated by the measuring instrument or rather the class of all instruments that may come to use for the evaluation in question.

These restrictions however mean that only a finite number of values can be regarded and appear as individual elements in a well-defined finite set.

3 We have to distinguish between the kind of a property and its *value*, which is defined by identification within the set of values of that property. Thus to each kind of property we associate a *value set*. We make this more clear by defining: property = attribute/value pair (or, alternatively, relation/2-nd object pair).

Note that property kind or attribute is in itself a value identifying the kind within a list of all (feasible) kinds of properties (or a list of all attributes or relations).

The information about an object is given by a set of values, one value identifying the object, another value identifying an attribute, a third value identifying within the value set for this attribute, a fourth value identifying a second attribute, and so on.

4 The object may be regarded as being simply the bundle of properties (or attribute/value pairs) associated with it.

5 We shall often call a single data representation of an attribute or a value a "*term*"; sometimes a *datum* or an *elementary item* (as in COBOL).

The storage space allocated for the storage of a term will be called a "*field*".

6 The length of a term will be determined by its actual value. It may thus be varying if the *alphabet* by which it is given digital representation contains a *trivial digit*, which may be omitted if it occurs in certain positions in the *word* giving the actual property value.

7 It is therefore possible to use varying field length for storing a term. There will have to be some kind of indicator of where a term starts or ends. This requires some kind of redundancy, either by permitting one digit within the alphabet to be reserved for this function, or by storing special data which hold information about term boundary positions.

It is possible instead to use a constant field length for a term. It must then be equal to the maximum term length and is thus determined by its maximum value or by the number of elements required in its property value set.

8 To be more precise we state that the minimum value possible for the maximum term length is the number of bits (or binary digits) needed to represent the number of elements contained in the property value set. This is true if the physical storage technique uses 2-valued signals as its basic operating elements. As this is practically always the case and as the binary representation has distinguished use in information theory we prefer to accept the statement as generally true.

9 It is important to note that when we have been talking about values of measuring, the precision needed for computation may be much higher than that provided by available physical measuring equipment.

10 This is because we will often have to compute values by taking differences between two of almost equal magnitude leaving a result with much fewer digits. The problems associated with such kinds of "ill-conditioned" computations are very important and must be carefully analyzed when an information system is to be designed, if not the accuracy of the results may become lost completely.

11 Also the "ill-conditioning" may well be the result of an inappropriate system design.

12 Very often the maximum term length used will be much longer than the minimum one of binary representation. Decimal representation already causes an increased length of about 20 % (the code allowance).

13 More significant allowance to term length is caused when the value (that is the association with the proper element in the value set) is not given by a number indicating the position in the value set, but rather a combination of groups of digits is used, for instance, for ease of memorizing or for giving some means for "understanding" the value. We may use this approach with person names.

14 When more of the information handling is being done automatically the advantages of structured numbers or alphabetical data is reduced. At the same time the cost for the extra space they need is more significant. Hence a reduction of this kind of representation is a natural consideration when automatic information systems are being designed. With increased use of automatic data processing one may expect to use numeric data in many cases where alphabetical data are presently used. On the other hand there is a marked trend of development toward more interactive use (or dialog mode use) of computers which instead will increase the use of alphabetical texts.

Chapter 7. Files, Computations and Processes.

It is often common, when doing systems work for data processing, to define one "run" which is supposed to handle, in one computer pass, all transaction data associated with a certain master file. Later on when a lot of computer programming has been done — and a computer ordered — it is then found that memory limitation or I/O-equipment consideration requires the run to be broken up into two or more smaller ones. This increases processing time, of course, and it may be discovered — too late — that the equipment cannot do the job as planned, or at least expensive reprogramming has to be done. This is common today. Efficient systems work requires that the systems analysts understand these problems clearly and have more rational ways of handling them. We are going to present here a method of analysis to achieve such efficiency.

Similarly largely consolidated masterfiles as a rule are designed from the beginning of a systems work. We here take up a more appropriate way of doing this with regard to the consequences of consolidating more and more data into one file.

27.1 Files and Processes.

We have seen that as a rule a certain kind a of information is obtained by some combination out of a set (P(a) (= the *precedence* set of a)) of other kinds of information. We shall use the word computation to denote the set of all procedures which take P(a) and produce a. In general it is wise to assume the possibility of producing different procedures. For instance one may know a procedure which will give an approximation to a, while one is still in search for another procedure which would produce "better values of a". We therefore use the word *computation* for a for the set of all feasible procedures for getting some approximation to a and write for short Comp(a). It is important to try to define P(a) with regard to the process for a, and not be satisfied with a subset of it which might be sufficient for one of the feasible procedures of Comp(a). We may also find it convenient to refer to the precedence set P(a) of a as the *precedence* set of Comp(a), denoted as P (Comp(a)) and also as a member of the succedence set S(P(a)) of the precedence set P(a) of "a".

The information in the succedence set "a" of a process as well as that in the precedence sets P(a)=b, c, d; will consist of a set of values of one information set, often called the *key* and for each value of the key there will be a group of corresponding values of the information classes contained in a set. One package consisting of one key value and the corresponding values within the set will be called a *record*. Thus for any value k of the key there may (or may not) be a record a_k of the output information set and a record, b_k, c_k, ... of each input set. A set of records for a set of k-values will be called a file and we shall in most cases consider a, b, c, ... to be the files of all a_k, b_k, c_k, ...[1]).

We define the set of data terms representing an elementary message to be an *elementary record*.

In some cases it will be important to make a distinction between "standing files" (or files proper) on one hand, and files consisting of temporary data such as input data, output data and intermediary results on the other hand. We shall then use the word *"transfile"* for the files of temporary data.

To each precedence relation there is associated a computation. The actual procedure may however be designed in a variety of ways. Thus whereas P^{00} or its graph is a unique representation of the system of computations, there may be different systems of actual procedures for the implementation.

Among the computations there will be "sort" operations and other data handling operations.

The number of entries $\neq 0$ in any row of P^{00} equals the number of computations for which the corresponding data set is an input. Thus for instance P^{00} of section 25.1—29[2]) shows that e or e') is used as input in six different computations. If the computations are all taken as separate computer runs we thus will have a multiplicity of data input transport for all files. This multiplicity may be even higher than that obtained by counting unit entries in P^{00},

---

[1]) Because "record" is used alternately to mean a set of data associated with an entity or a set of data stored in one area of storage it is now becoming increasingly common to use the word "entry" for a set of data associated with an entity when it is desirable to emphasize that they may not be stored in one single area. It would be justified to replace "record" in this page and those following with "entry". This has not been done here but we suggest that the reader will keep this in mind.

[2]) Recall that a number like this refers to item number 29 in section 1 of chapter 5 part 2.

section 25.1—29 because some computations may call for multiple scanning of several files. We can indicate this by replacing the units in P^{00} with those numbers giving the multiplicity of the corresponding input scan. Note that it is then not possible also to indicate in P^{00} a multiple scan of an output file. If however the precedence matrix P^{00} for the graph[3]) is replaced by the incidence matrix E^{10} then it is possible to indicate multiplicity of both input and output. We return to this point later.

It should be obvious by now that an elementary message together with the elementary messages which are its precedents and together with the "elementary computation" or elementary process (which produces the elementary message from its precedents) form a natural unit, when taken together. In fact one might say that just as the elementary messages form the smallest *information elements,* the set consisting of the e-message, its precedents and their associated computation form the smallest *information processing system element.* In the information analysis it is practical to forget almost completely the processes. Some time later ,however, one must take up the question about the processes and their relations to the data files. Actually when we talk about a computation we consider also its associated files so that in fact "computation" or "process" will often be understood to refer to both the files concerned and the algorithm. Recently Grindley[4)5)] defined what he called "element", a construct that is identical with our elementary process (including the elementary files associated with it). He then uses decision tables to describe (partly) the algorithm involved. Let us illustrate briefly how Grindley's "element" and our elementary process are related.

In an example from Grindley's paper we have the decision table.

| Sex | Male | Female |
Length of service	< 5 years	< 5 years
Pension contribution	2 s	1 s 6 d
Holiday entitlement	16 days	15 days

This table contains two elements, as it has two output entities, "Pension contribution" and "Holiday entitlement". Let us take one

---

[3]) As shown, e.g., in section 27.7
[4]) Grindley, C B B: The use of decision tables within Systematics, Computer Journal 1968.
[5]) This note added in the 1970 issue of this book.

of these "elements" and see how it relates to our elementary computation, Fig. 1 and Fig. 2.

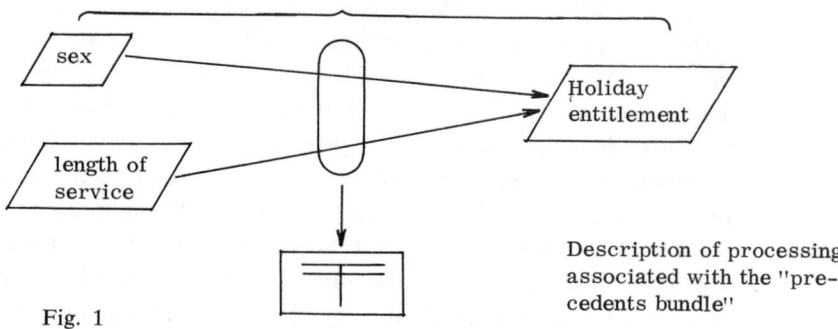

Fig. 1

Description of processing associated with the "precedents bundle"

In Fig. 2 the table describes the processing completely. In general the table will refer to other tables as well, for part of the processing, or to algorithms described in other ways. In Fig. 1 we have used the term "precedents bundle" (Swedish: "precedentknippe") to refer to a file together with its precedents.

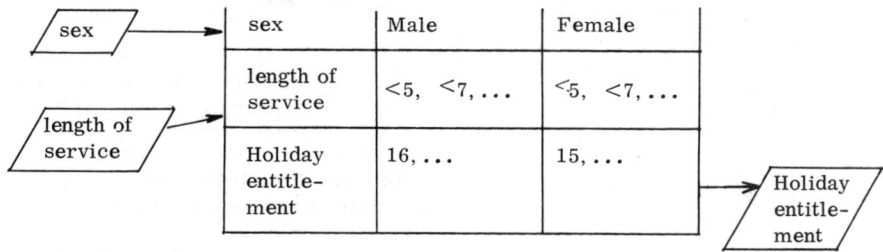

Fig. 2

Note that the first column identifies the attribute of the e-messages of an e-concept[6]) and the other columnes identify value intervals for the attribue associated with the respective rows of the table. Each e-message thus identifies a box in a table (identifies row and column).

Operative data processes.

In an information system for management or control the objects to be managed (co-ordinated or controlled) are the operating stations, i.e. the places where the results of the enterprise are produced. The

---

[6]) Cf. section 25.2—10 for a definition of "e-concept".

information system exerts control by having processes which produce operating control messages to the operating stations (operative information processes), thus initiating and guiding the activities at the stations. The system further exerts control by producing information which controls or guides the work of the operative information processes (directive information). There are some properties that are common to all operative information processes. Thus there must always be an initiating or *triggering* signal among the precedents of an operative process. (This can be, simply, the occurence of any precedent message record.) Further, the operative process must always be prepared to the possibility that the operative activity it is to control cannot be performed. Two reasons may always be indicated. The operative action may be physically impossible at the moment or the operative information process itself may be impossible to perform because all precedents may not be available. In both cases the process must issue messages about this. These messages will be sent to people or to other information processes for decision, Fig. 3.

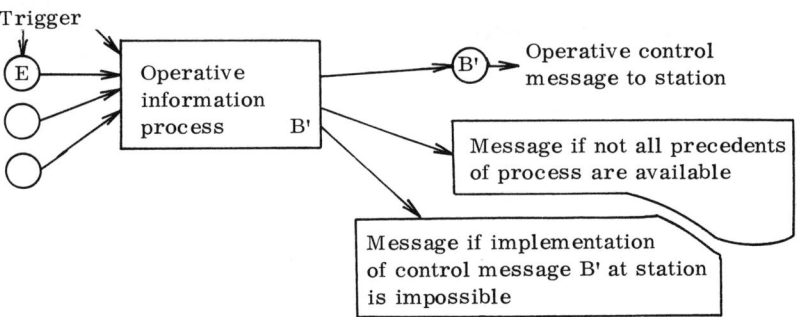

Fig. 3 Operative process B′, trigged by the arrival of a record of E.

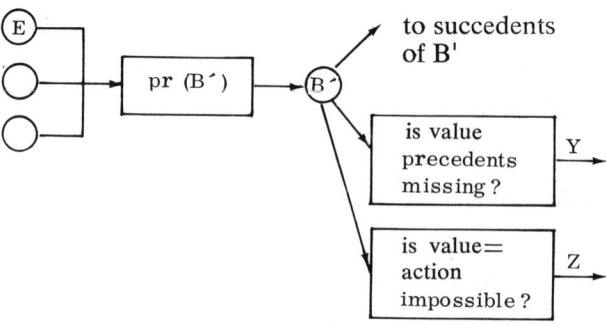

Fig. 4

It is seen that an e-process in real systems will need three information outputs rather than one. This is in contrast to our definition of an e-process. However one may instead regard the messages which signal missing precedents or impossibility of action as merely *special values* of the value term of the original single output message type (original output e-concept). Such special values will then be made to trigger appropriate procedures. Fig. 4 illustrates this. There is only one oooutput B' from pr(B') but this output is fed into two special procedures Y and Z in addition to being made available to the original succedents of B'.

27.2 The Size of a File.

When the file information is used in a process (whether or not it is changed by the process) typically it will have to be transported from its place in storage into the working memory of the processor. The design of the information system will then be concerned with organizing the file information for storing and processing in a way which minimizes the information transport required. The amount of transport of file information will depend on the number of times the file information is needed as an input for a process plus the number of times it is produced as an output (or even merely as a copy) from a process. It will also depend on the size of the file and on the performance of its store and transport equipment.

1 The size of a file, of course, will be a function of the information it contains. It might therefore seem feasible to define the size by means of an information quantity measure from the information theory. At least today it is not realistic to hope for a unique measure of this kind[1]). However any time when we have made a layout of the record formats of a file we can measure the record sizes in terms of the number of "characters" needed to store it. Now "characters" could be anything from a binary character (of one bit) to an alphanumeric character of six to eight bits. We need some definition which is reasonably convenient for all users and yet "reasonably unique". This can be done in different ways and to decide on this would need cooperation of many people. However, in order to have a precise understanding in our subsequent discussion we venture to propose a *"normal storage form"*, be it only used within this book. We propose to use decimal digits, coded in four bits, as our normal form for numeric data. We thereby assume that in defining the file data we specify the required precision for each number with the proviso that when floating point numbers of

---

[1]) Cf. however section 23.6

fixed size (for a specified computer) are to be used we give the number of decimal digits corresponding to the same number of bits.

For alphabetic or alphanumeric data we use the minimum number of bits per character; this permits the maximum number of symbols in the alphabet to be encoded.

Thus if we are satisfied with block letters and decimal digits plus a few other symbols, as is often the case in business data processing today, then we have to account for six bits per character whether six bits or more are actually used in this case. Instead if we use also minor letters then seven bits, at least, are to be accounted for.

Finally if some data in the file are merely associated with logical choice and need only one bit each, we use this number for accounting these data.

In this way a record size will be determined by several numbers, one for each type of character used. To make it one number we then count the number of bits corresponding to the different character quantities.

2 **Example.** A record containing 10 6-bit characters, 50 decimal digits and three logical terms has size: $60 + 50 \cdot 4 + 3 = 263$ bits.

When we have determined the size of the records and estimated the average number of records in the file we obtain a measure of the size of the file. If the storing in file storage requires a set of separators not needed in the memory of the computer these shall be included in the size of the file.

We do *not* include record gaps or unused physical block space in the measure of file size, however.

When we are interested in different hardware systems we also have to consider different transport speeds so that comparison can only be made on a time basis. This by the way is also true within the same system because its different file media will vary greatly in speed.

3 In order to cater for this, we consider in most cases a fixed period of time, preferably the shortest processing period (except perhaps

for very few exceptionally short ones). We then let the precedence numbers be multiplied by the number of times the associated process will be run during this *reference period*, thus mostly a number less than one.

The problem is that we need to do the same for the succedence information, that is for the output files. Both cannot be represented in the precedence matrix P^{00}, however, but we shall see later[2]) that by using an incidence matrix we can master this problem.

4 *Example*. Which will be the average size of a file record which consists of one alphanumeric term of a (dynamically) varying size between 3 and 30 characters, 10 decimal numbers of 7 digits with all values between 0 and 999 9999 equally probable, one code with only two values ("true" and "false"), and one number with a size varying between 1 and 2 digits with only one digit needed in 95 % of the occurrences?

The average number of characters in the alphanumeric term is estimated to 10 characters. A character based computer is assumed where a term separator (size one character) is required in the file storage, after each term for which we choose to use dynamically varying field length. For all fixed field terms no separator is required if only one record type is used in the file, while all terms must have separators if other record types are also in the file. An alternative for the latter case is to move the record to a specific work area of which one is then needed for each record type. In this way the need for separators of the fixed fields is eliminated.

Answer.

a. Only one record type is assumed.

The alphanumeric term will require on the average 11 characters if stored in varying fields (average size 10 plus 1 for term separator).

It would require a field of the size of maximum length, hence 30 characters if stored in fixed fields.

The 10 numbers of seven digits will have their maximum size in about 90 % of their occurrence for they will be shorter than seven

---

[2]) See section 27.7.

digits only when the first digit has value = 0. Hence nothing can be saved by storing these terms in varying fields. Thus 70 characters are required. The two-valued code will need one character.

The last term would be one character in 95 % of the cases which might indicate the use of varying field but as that would require one separator character we would still need two characters (and in 5 % af the occurrences we would need three). Hence a fixed field of two characters will be allocated.

Total average record size will thus be 84 characters.

b. Different record types are used in the file, and no separate work areas for each type of record is used.

In this case we will need a separator with all terms. This adds 12 more separator characters. However in that case the reason for using fixed field for the last term disappears. We use varying field which reduces its average size by about one character. Thus 12—1 = 11 characters are added under this condition, to give 95 characters as the answer.

c. Different record types are used and a record is moved to the specific area for its type before it is processed.

In this case the space required for the record in the file storage will be as in a, above.

Remark. One contribution to file size which is often forgotten in preliminary analysis is data terms needed for the administration and structuring of the data processing and the files themselves.

5 **Example.** File Sizes for the Simplified Firm Example[3]).
In order to determine the sizes of the files we list the input records (or initial records), the output or terminal records and the standing file records separately.

---

[3]) Continued from section 25.1—20.

"1_8" is an input file which is originated by physical inventory in the store. It may have the design:

1_8	size decimals	bits
1 Record label	3	12
2 Item no (with check digit)	5+1	24
3 Quantity in store	4	16
4 Date on which inventory was taken	6	24
5 Reason why inventory was taken	3	12
Total size	22	88

We have assumed that every record in the system has a distinct label and that there may be some hundreds of records. Therefore three decimal digits are required, that is 12 bits. We have further assumed that the number of distinct items may run into tens of thousands and that for satisfactory reliability a check digit will be used. The fifth term, reason for inventory taking may contain a number running over the set of orders for doing physical inventory issued that day, plus one decimal digit for indicating any special reason that might have initiated the inventory taking.

"3_5" is a file consisting of messages about sales and may be regarded as the central information for keeping the system studied in operation. A sales order may have a varying number of "lines", each specifying a request for one kind of item. We may regard it as consisting of two (or more) different elementary records, "3_5a" and "3_5b".

3_5a	size decimals	bits
1 Record label	3	12
2 Order number	5	20
3 Customer number (with check digit)	5	20
4 Date of order	6	24
total	19	76

Note. We have left out name, address, credit conditions and other information about customers because we have estimated it to be most economical to let the information system supply that information itself. This calls for a "customer file" which must then be added to our system. We add it below to the set of standing files.

We give it number "15". "15" will be needed as an input to process "5" but as it cannot be stored in the order used for "5" we shall need a special process for making records of "15" available to "5"[4]).

$3_5 b$		size decimals	bits
1 Record label		3	12
2 Line no within order		2	8
3 Item no (with check digit)		6	24
4 Quantity ordered		4	16
5 Delivery date		6	24
6 Delivery conditions		1	4
7 Pay conditions		1	4
	total	23	92

Every record of type $3_5 b$ is taken to be associated with the $3_5 a$ record immediately preceding it (possibly separated from it by some other $3_5 b$ records). We do not show, in this example, any more designs for input records. As an illustration of an output record we take "5_1", the "order to ship" sent to "store 1". Again two records are used, one specifying the customer and the addressee and another specifying items and quantities.

$5_1 a$		AN-characters	size decimals	bits
1 Customer no			5	20
2 Customer name		15		90
3 Customer address		15		90
4 Ship to		15		90
5 Address for shipping		15		90
6 Order no			5	20
7 Date of delivery			6	24
8 Delivery condition			1	4
	total	60	17	428

$5_1 b$		size decimals	bits
1 Item no		6	24
2 Quantity to ship		4	16
	total	10	40

---

[4]) We have to observe later that file 15 is not represented in the matrix P given earlier.

We do not discuss the other output record designs but go over to the standing file record "8".

We see from P[5]) that "8" or any of its versions is input to "4, 5 and 6". We therefore inspect all these to find out what information must be stored in "8" in order to serve them: "4, 5, 6" will need
    "quantity on hand"
and "quantity on order" from "8".

8		size decimals	bits
1 Record label		3	12
2 Item number (with check digit)		6	24
3 Item class		1	4
4 Quantity on hand		4	16
5 Quantity on order		4	16
	total	18	72

In the record we have added a term "Item class". This we have done in anticipation of a need to handle different items in a different way.

The standing file "13", through its version "13'", is input to "9 and 10". "13" is also input to "13'". "13'" will need information from "13" about past demand. We will assume here that this will be taken from sales orders. The forecast of demand may use a set of past sales orders and this set would then have to be stored in "13". An alternative which is usually preferable is to use exponential smoothing for prediction. This eliminates the need to store several past sales orders.

One will then have to store only the smoothing parameter α, the last smoothed value of demand (predicted value), and the current actual demand[6]).

If one considers it desirable to use also double and triple smoothing this defines a need for some more data. We assume for simplicity, in this example, that these can be neglected.

"14" will need data about past delivery lead times in complete analogy with the need for demand data for "13".

---

[5]) See section 25.1—11.
[6]) 1 Br 1962.

13		size decimals	bits
1	Item no	6	24
2	Current demand	4	16
3	α-demand	3	12
4	Last smoothed (predicted) value	4	16
5	New smoothed demand	4	16
6	Forecast from Sales	4	16
7	Predicted demand	4	16
	total	29	116

The term "6" (Forecast from Sales) indicates that we have planned to compute demand prediction not only by numerical extrapolation of demand history but also let estimates from "Sales" have an influence. The predicted demand, term "7", is composed from "5" and "6". We do not need to work out the exact formula or algorithm aleady now. The term "6" must not necessarily be filed as it is used just for the computation of term "7". We have decided to introduce it into the record, however, in order to have it available for possible statistical analysis.

For the file "14" a completely similar record will be obtained, where delivery lead time takes the place of demand and terms "6 and 7" are deleted.

It would be possible to replace files "13 and 14" by a single file, giving "demand during lead time". This is the common way. We do not go into details of that analysis here, however.

Again we skip the analysis of the file "15" (customer file). We have made only a simplified and brief analysis, so that further analysis might well have indicated the need to have more data in the file. In comparing with existing systems we must remember, however, the we have defined *elementary* files whereas common files are to de considered as aggregates of several elementary fils, at least this is true for the standing files.

We can now insert our record sizes in tables 1, 2 and 3. For those records which we have not analyzed we put the size equal to 100, for simplicity, except for output records which we have, equally arbitrarily, set to 300 bits.

Table 1.
Input records

Numbers within parentheses are "numbers of characters"

	size of records a	b	number per day a	b	Filesize in 1000 bits (characters) (per day)	
1_8	88 (22)	—	200	—	8.8 (2.2)	Physical inventory reports
2_7	100 (25)		5		0.5 (0.1)	Delivery documents, from shop
3_5	76 (19)	92 (23)	100	600	70.4 (17.6)	Sales orders
3_{13}	100 (25)		1		0.1 (0.03)	Forecasts made by Sales
11	100 (25)		0.1		0.01 (0)	Specifications of inv. holding costs
12	100 (25)		0.1		0.01 (0)	Specification of out-of-stock costs

Table 2.
Output records

	size of records a	b	number per day a	b	Filesize in 1000 bits (per day)	
4_1	300 (50)		5		1.5 (0.25)	Refill order (copy)
4_2	300 (50)		5		1.5 (0.25)	Refill order
5_1	428 (77)	40 (10)	200	600	109.6 (21.4)	Order to ship
6_1	300 (50)		100		30 (5)	Initiate phys. inventory
7_1	300 (50)		5		1.5 (0.25)	Refill delivery

Table 3.
Standing file records

	size of records a	b	number in file	Filesize in 100 000 bits	
8	72	—	40000	28.80	Inventory status
13	116	—	40000	46.40	Rate of demand
14	84	—	40000	33.60	Delivery lead time
15	100	—	1000	1.00	Customers

In making up the Tables 1, 2, and 3 we have made reasonable assumptions about the numbers of the different input and output messages a day as well as about the number of items in store and the number of customers. (These later assumptions were made to determine the number of digits necessary for item number and customer number respectively.) We have also assumed that in files where there are two different records, "a" and "b", then there are on the average three "b" records for each "a" record. This would mean, for instance, that the average number of lines on a sales order would be three[7]).

27.3 File Volume and Transport Volume, Processing Period.

1 We have defined the size of a file in terms of the number of its records and the number of bits required by one record[1]). There are several reasons why the space taken up in file storage by the file will be larger than its size measure. If the file storage has fixed block size (physical record size) there will normally be unused block space. If instead the file storage is using variable block size, as is normal for tapes, then there will be inter-record gaps which consume space — the more, the shorter block we use. Also additional data may have to be inserted in a file for the mere data handling itself. We need a new name for the measuring of the file in the actual storing situation and we shall use the word *file volume*. Thus the *file volume* is equal to the number of bit positions actually used up by the file when stored in file storage.

---

[7]) Example continued in section 27.3—16.
[1]) See section 27.2.

The file volume will often be equal to the sum of its size plus the number of bits wasted in block gaps or unused block space. This will however not always be the case for we may modify this number by using a different form of code than the "normal form" used to define the size of the file. For instance we may store a decimal integer in binary form which will reduce the volume.

While the file size will be a fixed quantity — or at least will be so regarded during certain phases of system design — the file volume will be changed by design decisions. We may increase it in order to save memory space or we may spend memory space to reduce it. This will depend on what memory space will be available and what alternative uses we have for it. For instance during the design work one may want to study small block sizes, to reduce memory space need for buffering. This leads to more space in file storage being used for inter-block gaps. It thus leads to a larger file volume for the same file (having the same file size). Alternatively the designer may try larger blocks in order to reduce the file volume, at the price of more memory space used for block buffer storing.

2 More precisely it will not be the volume of a file that we will try to reduce in the design work but rather the transport time that will result from its volume. Therefore we shall often talk about this time and, in fact, use it as a measure of the volume of the file. We shall define the *file transport volume* to be the time (in some suitable units, hours in some cases) taken to transport the file volume to and from the computer memory during the run of a process reading or writing in the file[2]).

A file of a certain fixed size will have its transport volume vastly reduced when it is copied from a punched form (punched tape or punched cards) onto magnetic tape or into some other common type of file storage.

3 Analogously we define the *file transport size* to be the transport time corresponding to the file size and the nominal transport speed.

---

[2]) It is important to remember that if the file storage used necessitates set-up time and dismount time (as for instance magnetic-tape reel set-up, rewind, and reel dismount) this is also included in the transport.

4 The total amount of transport for a file, over a certain *reference period* of time, will depend on the number of times it has to be transported during that period, and on its transport volume.

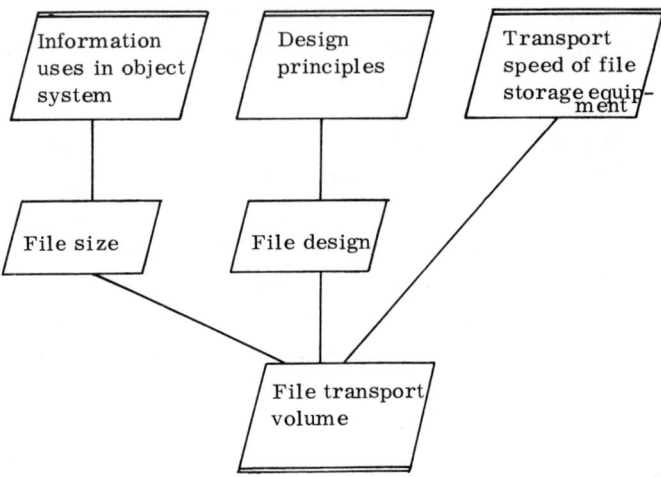

Fig. 1 Factors which determine the transport volume of the files, i.e. factors which are precedents of the information about file transport volume.

5 The number of times a file needs be transported depends on the relations between all information sets and processes in the information system — or on the *topology of the information precedence system*. It will also depend on the number of times the different processes will be run during the reference period.

6 Example.

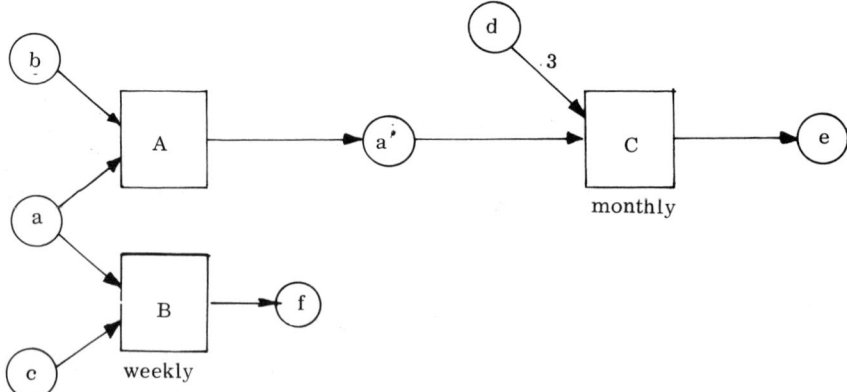

Suppose we have a data processing system as shown in the diagram above. Reference period 1 week. (1 month ~ 4 weeks). Number of file scans in reference period (*reference system*).

a	b	c	d	e	f	a¹
2	1	1	$\frac{3}{4}$	$\frac{1}{4}$	1	$1+\frac{1}{4}$

7 We now define
file transport of one file to be the amount of transport or the time for transport required from the file in the reference system, that is the number of file scans during the reference period multiplied by the file transport volume.

8 We define *system transport* (trp) or information transport for the system to be *the sum of the products of file transport volumes and number of file passes in the reference system*. Thus if μ is a vector of file scan multiplicity in the reference system, that is μ is a vector with one element for each file in the system, and such an element has its value equal to the number of scans of that file in the reference system, and if v is the vector with elements giving the respective file transport volumes, then

9 $$\text{trp} = \mu^T \cdot v$$

computes the trp in the system (for a reference period).

10 **Example.**

In the example above, 5, we had:

$$\mu_T = \begin{array}{|ccccccc|} a & b & c & d & e & f & a^1 \\ 2 & 1 & 1 & \frac{3}{4} & \frac{1}{4} & 1 & 1\frac{1}{4} \end{array}$$

Suppose the file transport volumes are

$$v_T = \begin{array}{ccccccc} a & b & c & d & e & f & a^1 \\ 10 & 1 & 1 & 1 & 1 & \frac{3}{2} & 10 \end{array}$$

The system transport becomes

$$\mu_T \cdot v = \overset{a}{2 \cdot 10} + \overset{b}{1} + \overset{c}{1} + \overset{d}{\frac{3}{4}} + \overset{e}{\frac{1}{4}} + \overset{f}{\frac{3}{2}} + \overset{a_1}{\frac{50}{4}}$$

or

$$\text{trp} = 37.$$

In order to make it convenient for the designer to take advantage of the fact that file size is constant during a stage when he studies different designs that lead to different transport volumes we can introduce some "design factors". These design factors change with changes in design and can be used for simple calculation of the corresponding changes in file transport volume.

First we notice that the advantage of using the transport size and transport volume is that it leads to a more realistic view of the relations between files which are on file media with vastly different characteristics. The designer may take this into consideration in early design stages, before equipment has been ordered, by using in his calculations only *nominal* performance figures which are *typical* for the *classes* of file transport units he is considering. We thus will have a

11 trps = nominal file transport size = $\dfrac{\text{file size}}{\text{nominal transport speed, for the file unit type considered}}$

We then introduce a *speed factor* η_s such that we can easily go from the *nominal* file transport size (for a chosen *type* of equipment) to the *actual* file transport size (for the specific equipment chosen — when that choice has been made). We obtain simply: actual file transport size $= \eta_s \cdot$ nominal file transport size if we define the *speed factor* η_s

12 $\qquad \eta_s = \dfrac{\text{actual transport speed (for the specific equipment)}}{\text{nominal transport speed (for the } type \text{ of equipment considered in early design stages)}}$

Further, we introduce the *volume factor* η_v for a file:

13 $\qquad \eta_v = \dfrac{\text{file volume}}{\text{file size}}$

We obtain
nominal file transport volume $= \eta_v \cdot$ nominal file transport size
$\qquad\qquad\qquad\qquad\qquad\quad = \eta_v \cdot$ trps
and

14 trpv = file transport volume $= \dfrac{\eta_v \cdot \text{file size}}{\eta_s \cdot \text{nominal transport speed}}$

It is important to observe that we use here the term transport speed as a measure of the *total time* it takes, on the average, to transport a file during its processing. This means, of course, that we must take into consideration the effect of any auxiliary operation that must be involved. For instance if the file is on a magnetic tape unit the time for mounting the tape reel (and for tape rewind after the processing) is to be included, unless it is *assumed by the designer* that extra tape units are to be used so that these auxiliary operations can go on in parallel with processing. Thus, in choosing the figures for nominal transport speed and actual transport speed the designer must specify which arrangement he has in mind in each case. For example if tape scan for the type of unit considered is 100 000 characters/second then rewind time and tape reel exchange time may reduce the "nominal transport speed" to 60 000 ch/sec. If then the equipment actually chosen (at a later design stage) has a 20 % lower scanning speed (transfer rate) the speed factor η_s would seem to be 80 %. In reality it is likely to be somewhat higher because reel exchange time may not be 20 % longer when transfer speed is made 20 % lower.

It should also be noted that the way we take together the different time elements involved (such as transfer speed, reel exchange, rewind etc) into one single speed factor is only to be used in early stages of design calculations. These, however, are the only ones we consider here.

We may write

15 $$\text{trpv} = \frac{\eta_v}{\eta_s} \qquad \text{trps} = \eta_{tv} \cdot \text{trps}$$

where $\eta_{tv} = \frac{\eta_v}{\eta_s}$ can be called the *transport volume factor*

η_{tv} tells how many times larger than the transport size the transport volume is.

16 **Example, transport size.**
continuation of 5 Example, section 27.2.)

In computing file transport sizes for input files on punched tape or punched cards the analysis into bits will often be unnecessarily fine. Also, while it may make quite a difference in punching operations whether numeric characters only or alphanumeric characters are to be used, the input speed will, as a rule, be independent of this. It will therefore often be sufficient, as far as input of punched data is concerned, to measure file sizes in characters and measure speed in characters per second. As the table of input files (Table 1, section 27.2) was made in terms of four bits per character we can most easily proceed by computing the nominal input speed for the assumed medium in characters per second and then multiply by four to obtain an equivalent number of bits per second. In this way we obtain too low ideal speeds as the actual number of bits that could be carried by a card columns is much larger than four. On the other hand, if we do not expect to have to compare with alternative types of recording, this effect can be neglected without any drawback. Let us assume that input files are on punched cards and that 600 cards per minute is the nominal reading speed. This amount to 10 cards per second or 800 characters per second or the equivalent of 3200 bits per second.

Output files can be treated similarly.
We assume 1000 lines/minute printing speed, 120 char/line which amounts to 200 char/second output speed. We assume 400 000 bits/second to or from mass memory.

Table 1.

input files

	transport size (per day) seconds
1_8	2.8
2_7	0.13
3_5	22.0
3_{13}	0.03
11	0
12	0
$\Sigma = 26$	

800 char/second

Table 2.

output files

	transport size (per day) seconds
4_1	0.13
4_2	0.13
5_1	10.7
6_1	2.5
7_1	0.13
$\Sigma = 13.59$	

2000 char/second

Table 3.

standing files

	transport size seconds	and one output transport size for one input
8	7	14
13	11.5	23
14	8.4	17
15	0.25	0.5
	$\Sigma = 27$	$\Sigma = 55$

400 000 bits/second

If the mass storage is magnetic tape then the whole files have to be scanned and the sizes are as in Table 3. If instead direct access store is being used the total file size is still as in Table 3 but only part of it will be activated however. Instead there will be an extra access time for each access to a file record. This problem is more suitably taken up when discussing transport volumes in the following paragraph.

17 Example, transport volumes.

We have assumed input records to be on punched cards, thus to have the volume of 80 characters. For file 1_8 we had a record size of 22 characters and therefore, if we take one record per card, we have a volume factor $= 80/22 = 3.65$. (If we had assumed punched tape a much better volume factor, close to 1, would have been obtained.)

The speed factor would be about $\eta_s = 0.8$, taking account of some idle time mainly caused by the interaction between the machine and the operator. The transport volume factor η_{tv} is thus (for file 1_8) $= 3.65/0.8 = 4.6$.

In the case of card files it is, however, simpler not to use the factor η_{tv} but rather to compute the transport volume directly from the number of cards involved and the "card speed" modified with the speed factor. Thus in our example we use the modified card speed $10 \cdot 0.8 = 8$ cards per second. From our earlier data 3) we obtain for file $1_8 \cdot 100$ cards per day, hence $100/8 = 12.5$ seconds. For the other input files we proceed in similar fashion. The result is recorded in Table 4. If we apply the same procedure for the printed output and also the same speed factor, $\eta_s = 0.8$, we obtain 13 lines per second. We thus obtain the results shown in Table 5.

Table 4.

	Card input files Transport volumes in a reference period (one day (one day) (seconds)
1_8	12.5
2_7	0.6
3_5	100.0
3_{13}	0.1
11	0.0
12	0.0

Table 5.

	Printer output Transport volumes in a reference period (one day (one day) (seconds)
4_1	0.4
4_2	0.4
5_1	61.5
6_1	7.7
7_1	0.4

---

[3]) Table 1 of Section 27.2

We see, on comparing with Tables 1 and 2, that the transport volumes are (in this case) considerably larger than the transport sizes thus indicating a large effect of the hardware properties.

To determine the file transport volumes for the standing files on magnetic tapes or direct stores is much more complicated and requires a set of choices to be made first.

The file volume will depend on the recording form. If binary coding is used for instance, we need no "code allowance" but may have a word allowance of 30 % if data are not packed to words and if data are packed we may still have about 10 % of allowances when subrecords terminate within a word and any new subrecord starts in a new word. If instead data are stored as 7-bit (or 8-bit) characters, which is by far the most common today, then we use twice as many bits for numeric data as are necessary. As most data are numerical we find that in character based coding we obtain about 100 % code allowance, corresponding to a volume factor of two. As recent equipment is less wasteful with mass storage space we can assume a factor of 1.5 as typical and use this in our example. This is still not the whole waste of space, however, and we will have to add at least space for inter-record gaps and, most likely, for unused block space (when fixed record length is used).

We now make the assumption that magnetic tapes will be the mass storage medium used. To determine the effect of inter-record gaps we assume 4000 bits per gap which is about typical. As we found our (elementary) standing files to have a record size of about 100 bits we see that if we would store each elementary record separately we would obtain a volume factor of 41 already because of gaps. This is of course quite unacceptable. In practice the consolidation of elementary files to more complex files with much larger records and the blocking together of several records into one block[4]) means that we will have sizes of physical records between 1 000 and 20 000 bits, corresponding to a volume factor of 5 to 1.2.

The degree to which records should be blocked to reduce the volume factor depends on the memory space available and this can not yet be decided. As a first trial it is practical to use short blocks, say 1 000 bits, for files with small size and, say, 10 000 bits for

---

⁴) We use the term *"block"* in place of the clumsy and ill-defined "physical record".

large files. We would thus obtain the volume factors 5 and 1.4 respectively.

Table 6.

		100 000 bits	
	η_{v1} · file size	file volume = η_{v1} · η_{v2} · file size	
		block size	
8	43.2	10 000 bits	60.5
13	69.6	"	97.4
14	50.4	"	70.6
15	1.5	1 000	7.5

$\eta_{v1} = 1,5 =$ effect of code allowance, word allowance etc.

$\eta_{v2} =$ effect of record gaps

$\eta_{v2} = 5$ for record size 1 000

$\eta_{v2} = 1.4$ for record size 10 000

Before we can determine the file transport sizes we must also determine the speed factor. This is dependent on rewind time and reel replace time and the latter has a relative effect which is larger the smaller the file is, in case the file volume makes up less than a full reel. Also the effect of simultaneous read and write on tapes has a significant effect on the speed factor. The possible use of "flip-flop" arrangement of tape handlers eliminates the effect of reel replacement and rewind. A read backward feature also eliminates some rewind time. The rewind effect is easy to determine as one part of the speed factor. Thus if there is no flip-flop arrangement and if rewind is "r" times faster than nominal transport speed then this generates a speed reduction factor
$= \eta_{s1} = 1/(1+1/r)$. Let us assume for this illustration that $r = 3$ which is common, then we get $\eta_{s1} = 1/1.33 = 0.75$.

To determine the effect of reel replacement we assume that this takes 100 seconds. We further assume a tape length 29 000 inches and a recording density of 7 000 bits per inch. Thus the gross storage volume of a tape is 200 million bits. Now for instance file 13, the largest, has a volume of about 10 million bits (Table 6). This is only 1/20th of a reel which appears to indicate a very high effect of replacement time. Recall however that the files we have described are elementary files which, when stored on tapes, are likely to be aggregated to other files. Again how this consolidation of elementary files will be done is one of the things we have to decide upon during design and therefore is unknown to us at the moment. However as mentioned above the records of our elementary files appear to be at least ten times smaller than common consolidated files. As a first approximation to the computation of the effect of reel replacement time we may therefore make the assumption that one tenth of a reel replacement time has to be charged to one of our elementary files — if it has to undergo a replacement, which is not always the case.

We have come to the conclusion that to determine the file transport volume, when there is no flip-flop arrangement and when the file goes on one single tape reel, we use η_{s1} · speed or 0.75 · 400 000 bits/second = 300 000 bits/second and then add 10 seconds. (With modern software the change between using flip-flop and not using it is easy. However the decision whether to use it or not has an effect on memory space required and number of file units and therefore still need the concern of the designer.)

Table 7.

	file volume 300 000	file trp volume	file trp volume with flip-flop
8	20.2	30.2	15.1
13	32.5	42.5	24.4
14	23.5	33.5	17.5
15	2.5	12.5	1.9

We have entered the results in table 7. When there is flip-flop on files 8, 13, 14 then the 10 seconds are not to be added and $\eta_s \cdot = 1$ rather than $= 0.75$). This is also shown in table 7.

The transport volumes of table 7 are very small. If we recall again that the elementary files are likely to be consolidated with other files so that ten times larger volumes occur and that files are likely to be transported several times we may expect realistic times to be about 40 times larger. For instance for file "8" we would then come up to 1 200 seconds if we use no flip-flop and no simultaneous read-write[5]).

Direct-access storage.

When we are using direct-access storage for the files additional considerations are needed. Thus while we still may be using "batch processing" in a way that may be regarded as processing a batch of transactions (i.e. a "transaction file") against a number of standing files, we may or may not scan the whole files. If the batch is fairly large in a way which means that a high percentage of the file records become involved, then a strict sequential processing — which scans the whole file — may be used. Then the situation will be very similar to tape file processing. However rewind and reel exchange times will then not be involved (although disc pack exchange may be). If, on the other hand, the batch is small, then one may only access and transport those file blocks which contain file records which match the transaction records. In this case we may still use the theory model outlined above but then it will be necessary to observe that the file *transport volume will be a function of the batch size*. In this situation it is often more convenient to replace "file transport" with "record transport", and analogously for the other concepts.

---

[5]) Example continued in section 27.4—4.

With direct-access storage it becomes possible to use *direct processing* (often called real-time processing, sometimes incorrectly). Then one may still regard the set of transactions occurring over the reference period as a transaction file. However in this case one must also consider the repeated transport of the processing program for each occurrence of a transaction. Alternatively one may go over to using "record transport" instead of file transport.

One additional change, when going over to direct access storage, is that the effect of block size becomes more pronounced as it now also determines the number of access operations involved in batch processing.

27.4 Transport Factor.

When we do design work with an information system we try to reduce total system transport by reducing file volumes and the number of file scans in the reference period. These different factors will compete for memory space and we try to find an optimum (or, rather, satisfactory) balance. We will try different system modifications (as we shall see) and compare their relative merits by comparing the resulting transport. We may however also want to be able to compare the successive results with those obtained at other places. Before that can be done we must, of course, compensate for differences in file sizes. Thus, if we compare with another system that has twice the transport size on all files, (assuming for instance double file sizes and the same transport speeds) then we must multiply by two before we can reasonably do a comparison. However in most cases we will find that the situation is more complicated. We may for instance find that some files have greater transport size in our system while certain files have greater transport sizes in the other. How then do we normalize the results of the different systems to make comparison reasonably meaningful? And what do we do in order to be able to compare an alternative solution for our own system with different hardware leading to a different measure of file volumes?

We want a measure which gives the same value if all files are increased in the same proportion and the same structure of design is used. But we also want this measure to grow if, without changing the total file transport volume, we increase such files which in the design are transported several times; if file transports are changed while retaining the total file transport volume, the measure shall reflect the influence of this change of system transport. We obtain such a measure if we take the system transport. $\mu_T v$, and divide it by the total file transport volume, i.e. $1_T v$.

We want however the measure to be increased if we increase the volume (eg by using shorter blocks). This is because one important design question is whether to use memory space eg to reduce volume or to reduce eg transport multiplicity. We see that if we define

1 *the transport factor* η by

$$\eta = \frac{\text{system transport}}{\text{total file trp size}} = \frac{\mu^T \cdot v}{1^T \cdot s}$$

where 1 is a vector having all element values = 1 so that the product $1_T s$ equals the sum of all values of s.

2 **Example.**

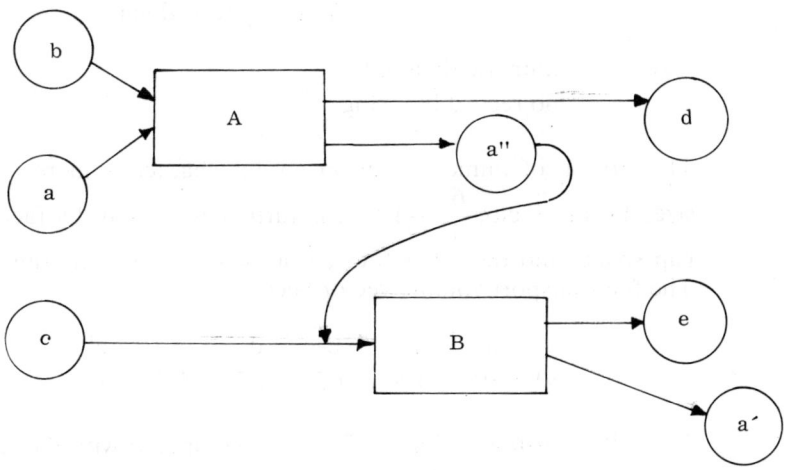

Let the file transport size vector be

	a	b	c	d	e	a'	
	10	1	1	1	1	10	Total transport size = 24

This includes time for setup, dismount and rewind. We have recorded both the file "a" and its updated version "a'". This we can do at the outset because we know that "a" is a file of the standing file type, and is updated once per reference period.

We may well come to make a design wherein a will be updated several times, passing intermediate stages such as a'', a''' ... This we do not know at the outset and we do not yet ask for this kind of information. It will be taken care of by the file scan multiplicity vector. Therefore a'', a''' etc. are *not* counted in the "size"[1]).

To determine the transport volumes we make the following assumptions for this example:

> mode of storage[2]): 6-bit characters
> record lengths : (file a, a') = one record gap, the other files = $\frac{1}{2}$ record gap.
>
> numeric data only
> no record blocking

The storing of numeric data in six bit characters increases all file sizes by the factor $\frac{6}{4} = 1.5$; a is further increased, by factor 2, for gap space, and the other files get a factor "3" for the same reason. The file transport volume vector becomes:

	a	b	c	d	e	e'
$v^T =$	30	4.5	4.5	4.5	4.5	30

Total file transport volume = 78 (to be compared with the size = 24). Now that we have a layout of the information processing network we can define the file scan multiplicity vector.

---

[1]) Note that in ADP systems where files are not copied during updating then also the updated version a' of a, should not be counted in the total size. Also, if direct access is available to files then at most part of unused (unchanged) file data are affected by the data transport. In such cases one may come to find that only input and output data should contribute to the total size.

[2]) Concerning the normal storage form see section 27.2.

We count all intermediate transport for a (i.e. a'') under a:

$$\mu^T = 3 \quad 1 \quad 1 \quad 1 \quad 1 \quad 1$$

The resulting system transport becomes

$$trp = \mu^T \cdot v = 3 \cdot 30 + 4 \cdot 4.5 + 1 \cdot 30 = 138$$

and the transport factor $\eta = \dfrac{trp}{trps} = \dfrac{138}{24} = 5.6$

3 Example.

What will the transport factor be if in the example above choose
a. the processing period twice as long
b. another application where all files have double size
c. another solution where numeric information in standing files are stored packed in 24 bit binary words, averaging four bits per decimal digits (rather than six bits) and all standing file data are numeric (assuming same number of bits per second transport speed). Which is the percentage of change in total transport volume and in η?

a. If we double the processing period but keep the same reference period, the only change in file transport sizes will be that standing file multiplying figures are cut to half their original values.

The number of transactions (which form the records of the files b, c, d, and e) per reference period does not change when processing period is changed.

$$\begin{array}{ccccccc} & a & b & c & d & e & a' \\ \mu^T = & 1.5 & 1 & 1 & 1 & 1 & 0.5 \end{array}$$

Hence $trp = \mu^T \cdot v = 1.5 \cdot 30 + 4 \cdot 4.5 + 0.5 \cdot 30 = 45 + 18 + 15 = 78$

$$\eta = \frac{trp}{trps} = \frac{78}{24} = 3.4$$

Relative difference in μ : $(5.6 - 3.4)/5.6 = 39\%$
,, ,, ,, trp: $(138 - 78)/138 = 44\%$

b. When file size is doubled and nothing else is changed we would obtain the double of system transport and the same transport factor.

However when the file sizes are increased the relative influence of set-up and take-down time may be reduced. This would then make the file transport volume less than twice the other one when file size is twice the other.

c. When the file data are packed so that four bits, on the average, are used per digit, rather than six bits, then the record sizes go down by the factor 4/6.

The files "a" and "a'" had a record length equal to g (g = length of record gap). This amount now goes down to $2/3 \cdot g$. As we have now 4 bits per digit this amount equals the size of the record. One record plus one gap thus gets the volume $5/3 \cdot g$.

Thus the file transport volume of "a" (and a') is larger than the file transport size by the factor $5/2 = 2.5$ (volume factor = 2.5).

The other files had a record length of $1/2 \cdot g$. This now goes down to 1/3 (which again is the record size). One record plus one gap becomes 4/3. The volume factor is seen to be four in this case.

Using these volume factors we obtain

	a	b	c	d	e	a'
$v^T =$	25	4	4	4	4	25; thus system transport = 66

Thus, while file sizes where reduced by $2/6 = 33\%$ the system transport was reduced by $(78-66)/78 = 16\%$ only.

As before

$\mu^T =$	3	1	1	1	1	1

so that we get

$$\text{trp} = \mu^T \cdot v = 75 + 16 + 25 = 116$$

$$\eta = \frac{\text{trp}}{\text{trps}} = \frac{116}{24} = 4.8$$

Thus η is reduced in the proportion $(5.6-4.8)/5.6 = 14\%$

4 **Example.** (Continued from 27.3-17).

Transport factor for the simplified information system.

The transport factor measures such effects as volume increase and speed reduction for hardware reasons as well as multiple file transports.

The latter will be highly dependent on the way we decide to group processes and consolidate files. In fact these decisions have as one of their main purposes to minimize system transport and, hence, the transport factor. As such decisions have not yet been drafted we determine the transport factor for the system as defined so far. We have to introduce one system modification, however, before we proceed. We have assumed all input files to be in punched form and all outputs to be printed. Often however input files will have to be sorted before they are processed. It is most reasonable to assume that this will be arranged in such a way that a special process is added to the system for each input file, which will convert it to an auxiliary mass storage file (magnetic tape file in our case). In this process a lot of editing and control is normally done as well. Of course several such processes may be grouped, as other processes may. Then we also have to add sorting processes for the input files. (If direct access storage and direct processing is used there will, of course, be no sorting. Instead there will then have to be added processes for retrieving the required file records. Auxiliary files occur in this case in the form of "file directories".)

It is of course possible that in some cases some of these processes and auxiliary files may be avoided, but one should only base the analysis on such as assumption after it has been shown that this is actually feasible and efficient. Many system designers — and much of the literature — underestimate the total time and equipment requirement by making too optimistic assumptions in this connection. The auxiliary mass storage input files will be of increased advantage when input files are precedents to several distinct processes as they have much smaller transport volumes than the corresponding punched files.

All of the above is true for the output files as well.

As a consequence we should now modify the precedence matrix P by adding the auxiliary files *as well as their sorted versions*. To produce a sorted version, the file has to be transported a number of times which we may represent by indicating a corresponding precedence magnitude in the matrix P. This number will depend on the file size, the memory size and the sorting procedure and we must then, of course, also adjust for the number of sorting operations that will be done in a reference period. If a longer processing (or updating) period is used, a smaller number of sorting operations will come during the reference period, but the file to be sorted has then been collected from transactions during a longer period. Hence it will be larger and the sorting process will require more transports. As this number is proportional to $\log_2$ (file size) we find that, roughly speaking, each time we double the processing period we only add one file pass in the sorting process[3]). As a consequence we may neglect this variation in a preliminary analysis. Therefore we assume in this example that average file transport for sorting during a reference period varies in inverse proportion to the updating period (as is also the case for updating of files).

To simplify we make the assumption that every sorting operation is done in 20 file passes. If, for instance, $1_8'$ is the tape version of the input file $1_8''$ is the sorted version of $1_8'$ then $1_8'$ is output once from the conversion process creating it, and then has to be input 20 times to the sorting. This being a crude analysis we simplify to record $1_8'$ only and assume it to have 20 transports during a processing period.

To compute the transport volume of the auxiliary files we make use of the sizes (in bits) of these files as given in Tables 1 and 2 of section 27.2. We thereby assume that although these files are small, they are to be transported 20 times, so we use long blocks, corresponding to a volume factor of $1.5 \cdot 1.4 = 2$ (as in 27.3, Table 6). The calculation of the effect of sorting is done in a crude way here. We can simplify further by reducing the transport speed by not only multiplying the nominal speed (of 400 000 bits per

---

[3]) in general $\log_2$ is to be replaced by $\log_{n/2}$, n being the number of sequence files (e.g. nr of tape handlers) used in the sorting run. Our argument thus applies for n=4 (which is most common) but is only slightly modified for other values of n.

second) by the speed factor (0.75), as in 27.3—17, but then also dividing it by the volume factor. The resulting effective speed to use in the analysis will thus be 150 000 bits per second. Using this figure and the file sizes of Tables 1 and 2 of section 27.2 we get the transport volumes for the auxiliary files as represented in Table 1.

It should be noted that sorting on tapes usually requires setting up of four or more tapes and therefore our neglecting this time here may introduce a significant error and in an analysis for an actual system one should be more careful on this point.

Table 1.

	Proc. period = ref. period μ	Proc. period = 5 ref. periods μ_5	v	$\mu \cdot v$	$\mu_5 \cdot v$
1_8	1	1	12.5	12.5	12.5
$1_8''$	20	4	0.05	1	0.2
2_7	1	1	0.6	0.6	0.6
$2_7'$	20	4	0.003	0.1	0
3_5	1	1	100	100	100
$3_5'$	20	4	0.47	9.4	1.8
3_{13}	1	1	0.1	0.1	0.1
$3_{13}'$	20	4	0.007	0	0
4_1	1	1	0.4	0.4	0.4
$4_1'$	20	4	0.01	0.2	0
4_2	1	1	0.4	0.4	0.4
$4_2'$	20	4	0.01	0.2	0
5_1	1	1	61.5	61.5	61.5
$5_1'$	20	4	0.72	14.4	2.8
6_1	1	1	77	77	77
$6_1'$	20	4	0.2	4	0.8
7_1	1	1	0.4	0.4	0.4
$7_1'$	20	4	0.01	0.2	0
8	7	1.4	30	210	42
13	4	0.8	42	168	33
14	4	0.8	34	136	27
15[1])	1	0.2	12	12	2.4
Total system transport (for this subsystem)				808	363

---

[1]) File 15 is not represented in P. It was introduced in 27.2.—5. We assume it to be transported once only, in our small subsystem.

Hence:
Total file transport size for this subsystem = 95.
We obtain the transport factor η_{trp}:

$$\eta_{trp} = \frac{808}{95} = 8.5 \quad \text{for daily processing}$$

$$\eta_{trp} = \frac{363}{95} = 3.8 \quad \text{for weekly processing}$$

5 **Exercise.** What is the value for η_{trp} if
   a) we use flip-flop
   b) we use simultaneous input-output

6 **Remark.** There are some obvious reasons why the value of the transport factor η_{trp} as calculated in the 4 Example is lower than could be expected to be normal in actual systems and why especially for future systems higher values are probable. First, the transport factor reflects system integration and may therefore be significantly incorrect when measured over a subsystem only. One should therefore supplement the determination of η_{trp} over a subsystem with an estimate of the number of time its files are transported "across the intermediate boundary circumscribing the subsystem", i.e. are transported to processes in other parts of the total system. For instance the inventory status file "8" was found to have a multiplicity of transport equal to 7[4]), and this was established for the system of Fig. 3, section 25.1 which is only a subsystem of the system shown in Fig 1, Section 22.4. This system, in its turn, is only a small subsystem of a real system. Already in this subsystem, however, is it obvious that the inventory status file (8) will have to be fed into more processes for it will, at least, be required for the scheduling of the shop. This file is also most likely to have uses outside this subsystem for it will be used in some financial analysis.

Second, more ambitious information system designs of the future will require more multiple transports. Thus, for instance, the inventory control principle assumed above handles each inventory item as an independent one. Now, theoretical studies have revealed that an inventory control system which also takes interactions between the various items into consideration is able to lead to significantly improved economy. Such procedures, in fact any

---

[4]) See Table 1, 4 Example.

procedure which considers interactions between system parts, will need more complex handling of file data and, therefore, will imply a higher degree of multiplicity of file transport. (This will be true whether files are on sequential type or on direct-access type storage. To the extent that batch processing is used. With direct processing this will make itself felt by a larger number of file records accesses in one reference period.)

27.5 Topological Transport Factor.

1 While the transport factor as defined above[1]), was useful as a general measure, it takes in not only the topological properties of the information system but also other factors affecting the system transport.

It will be of value to have even a rough measure of the influence of the topology of the information system as it depends on the basic precedence relations for the elementary files of the system. One would then for instance be able to classify different information systems by their topological complexity.

The influence that the topology has on the system transport is that it shows up relations which indicate a potential need for multiple file scans. A simple measure of this topological property might be simply to determine the total number of file scans and normalize it by means of dividing by the number of files. We could call such a measure *"the topological multiplicity m"*.

2 The total number of input file scans called for by the basic topology is obtained by $1^T P^{00} \cdot 1$, for $P^{00} 1$ computes the row sums of the matrix P^{00} and puts them in a vector which, when multiplied by 1^T, has its elements summed up.

The number of files is obtained by $1^T 1$, assuming in both cases that 1 has one element for each of the files to be counted.
Thus

$$m = \frac{1^T P^{00} 1}{1^T 1}$$

3 However "m" does not consider the fact that the effect of a multiplicity of a file scan is to be greater, the greater the file size is.

---

[1]) See section 27.4.

We take care of this also by using the file trp size vector s and form the *topological transport factor* η_{top}:

$$\eta_{top} = \frac{1^T (P^{00})^T \cdot s}{1^T \cdot s} \qquad ^2)$$

4 Thus the topological transport factor considers the information need of the system, through "s", and the multiple transport need called for by the topology of the precedence relations between different parts of the information need and forms a (very rough) total average measure for the system. This measure is unaffected by the design factors which are instead reflected in the system transport factor η_{trp}, as defined earlier[3]).

Use of transport factor statistics.

If we have statistical data for transport factors these can be expected to be a function of memory size and the number of I/0 units for each value of the topological transport factor. As the topological transport factor would be the same for the same kind of system we may have statistics for its value for different classes of systems.

Then knowing the file volume (which may also be a function of the file size which is statistically evaluated), we would directly obtain the total transport time for an application when the processing period and memory size are determined. This would permit us to find the optimum by varying design factors.

27.6 Grouping of Computations into one Process.

We have seen that the basic topology of the system may call for multiple inputs or outputs of an elementary file because it is a precedent of more than one computation. It follows that file transport could be saved by grouping a set of computations together in such a way that in connection with one and the same process of reading an elementary file we use the file data for more than one computation. We shall then say that we have *grouped* compu-

---

[2]) Notice that η_{top} as computed by 4 is only the topological factor for input. While this is often the most interesting quantity it is worth noting that to obtain the full η_{top} we have simply to add $\Sigma\, s_{output}$ by which we denote the sum of all output file sizes each multiplied by its proper multiplicity factor (thus $\eta_{top} = \dfrac{1^T \cdot P^{(00)T} \cdot s + \Sigma\, s_{outp.}}{1^T \cdot s}$). The incidence matrix (introduced below) takes care of both input and output, contrary to P^{00}, cf. section 27.7.

[3]) Cf. 27.4—1.

tations into one *process* (or, in a multiprogramming system, possibly into a group of simultaneously operating computing processes).

We study now how grouping computations can be used to save file transport in the system having a basic topology defined by a precedence matrix P^{00}.

It is worth noting that file transport is saved by grouping of processes for every kind of mass memory used. If we use batch processing with magnetic tapes or direct access storage we might save one or more runs and if we use direct processing (on-line real time) we still save some access operations for file records (see examples given earlier)[1]).

If we indicate also assumed file transport volumes for a reference period for each file, along with P^{00}, it will be possible to see how much transport is saved by combining two or more computations into the same process (or group of simultaneous processes). (A practical instance of such a grouping is when we take two different transaction types as input to the same run.)

We introduce also a multiplicity of five input scans in our example (just to illustrate the possibility) for the file "c" when used as input to the computation for "d". For simplicity we also assume all processing to be done once in the reference period.

1 File transport volumes

a	b	c	d	e	f	g	h	i	j	k	l
1	1	2	1	10	2	1	1	10	20	2	10

Total = 61 for the input transport volume.

Considering also the outputs e', i', j' and l' we get 111 as the total file transport volume.

The system as described by the matrix in 2 may be called the *basic topological system*. It should be defined for a chosen reference period. For simplification we have taken most entries in P^{00} to be = 1. Notice that they will change when we change the updating frequencies.

---

[1]) See section 24.1—18 and 24.1—19.

	a	e´	b	i´	c	j´	d	l´	V	input
2 $P^{00}=$ a			1	1			1	1	1	
c							5	1	2	
e	1	1	1	1			1	1	10	
f	1	1							2	
g	1	1			1				1	
h	1					1			1	
i			1	1	1	1			10	
j					1	1			20	
k					1	1			2	
l							1	1	10	

3 We obtain from 2 the file transport of each input file in the topological system. For instance for c we get $(5+1)2=12$.

For the input multiplicity we obtain from $1^T \cdot P^{00}_T \cdot V_{input}) = (P^{00} \cdot 1)^T V_{input}$

4 File   a   c   e   f   g   h   i   j   k   l

Input file transport   } 4   12   60   4   3   2   40   40   4   20   input system-transport = 189

5 Output system transport = 55 for (a, b, c, d, e', i', j', l'), thus total system transport = 244. (189 for input + 55 for output if all output is single.)

6 We see that the topology of the system of precedence relations requires an increase of the system transport as compared with the total transport volume of the files. We measure this by the *topological transport factor*[2]).

---

[2]) See section 27.5.

Hence we find that in our example the computations system implies a system transport for input of 189 against the transport volume 59 (=61-b-d) for single input. We here make the simplifying but unrealistic assumption that the file transport sizes equal the file transport volumes. This gives a topological transport factor of about 3.2, considering only inputs.

7 The multiple transport can be reduced by taking some computations into the same computer process. For this to be possible the computer memory must be sufficient to store the programs for these computations and for their control within one process, or else there will be data transport for shuffling programs to and from the memory when different records call for one, the other or both computations.

8 Grouping computations corresponds to grouping columns of P^{00}. It is easy to see from P^{00} how much transport is saved by grouping any computation with any one else. Thus from 2 we find that grouping "a" and "e'" saves one scan of e, f and g, i.e. it saves a transport volume = 13.

9 No other computation saves as much when grouped with "a"[3]). We list all the pairs which save most by being grouped.

        a, e' saves 13
        b, i'   ,,   21
        c, j'   ,,   32
        d, l'   ,,   23
Total input transport saved by the groupings = 89.

10 The other possible combinations, such as "e" and "b" do not have to be considered since whenever $P(e) \subset P(a)$ $P(a)$, then $Vol(P(e) \cap P(b)) < Vol(P(a) \cap P(b))$. (Vol(x) is used to denote the transport volume of x).

This follows from

11 $P(e) \subset P(a)$ is equivalent to $P(a) = P(e) \cup s$ (s = some set ≠ ø)

hence

---

[3]) It is important to note that it does not follow, in general, that the best solution is obtained by grouping "e'" with a. Cf. example in paragraph 22.

12 $P(a) \cap P(b) = (P(e) \cup s) \cap P(b) = P(e) \cap P(b) \cup s \cap P(b)$

and therefore

13 Vol $(P(a) \cap P(b)) =$ Vol $(P(e) \cap P(b)) +$ Vol $(s \cap P(b))$

As Vol $(s \cap P(b))$ cannot be negative, the truth of the statement follows.

However we have found earlier[4]) that we have the order relations

14 $(a, e') < (b, i') < (c, j') < (d, l')$

It follows that $(a, e') < (d, l')$ and $(a, e') \not\ll (d, l')$ or in words: (a, e') is a precedent but *not* an immediate precedent of (d, l'). This means that among the inputs to (d, l') are some information sets which are produced by means of output from a process *following* the process (a, e'). This, in turn, means that before (d, l') can operate it must have available results from a process which in its turn can only run after $pr(a, e')$ has produced its results.

We can state this result by the

15 **Restriction rule for Grouping:** *Processes cannot be grouped together if they have precedence relations of more than 1st order.*

As processes which are not neighbors[5]) generally cannot profit from being grouped we find that candidates for grouping are mostly such processes which are "strict" neighbours. This reduces the grouping problem very much. However a process which is not a "strict" neighbor may become so during the process of grouping.

Instead $(a, e') \ll (b, i')$ because it follows from 14 that there is no precedent of $pr(b, i')$ which succeeds $pr(a, e')$. The fact that $(a, e') \ll (b, i')$ or that (a, e') is an immediate precedent of (b, i') means that these processes can be grouped because in this case the output from $pr(a, e')$ is available to $pr(b, i')$ when they are in the same group.

Thus feasible solutions of the problem how further to group the pairs studied are in this case (provided there is enough memory space)

16 *either*

$$\text{pr}(a, e') \cup \text{pr}(b, i'), \text{ saving } 10$$
$$\text{pr}(s, j') \cup \text{pr}(d, l'), \text{ „ } 0$$

17 *or*

$$\text{pr}(a, e'), \text{ saving } 0$$
$$\text{pr}(b, i') \cup \text{pr}(c, j'), \text{ „ } 10$$
$$\text{pr}(a, l'), \text{ „ } 0$$

18 Thus we can only come down, by grouping by pairs of the earlier pairs, to an input system transport = 90.

19 Thus with the grouping by pairs of processes only (which happens to correspond to grouping by the subsets defined earlier, 14) the input system transport is reduced to 100 corresponding to the much improved transport factor of $100/59 = 1.7$ (as compared with the topological transport factor of 3.2). Grouping by pairs of pairs (as in 17 or 18) reduces system transport to 90 corresponding to the factor $90/59 = 1.5$.

[5]) Cf. chapter 2, part 1 for the definition of these concepts.

20 The grouping of computations may call for shorter data blocks in the files in order to leave memory space for the group programs. This will then lead to an increase of transport volume which will also have to be considered[7]).

21 In the general case of practical systems one will also have to test for different combinations of computations whereby the memory space and the space requirements for the different programs have to be considered.

We have seen that the subset relations (such as $P(e) \subset P(a)$ give valuable aid in suggesting efficient computation grouping and reducing the number of possible combinations and that the order relations simplify matters by limiting the possibilities.

---

[4]) See section 25.1—32.

22 **Example.** Let 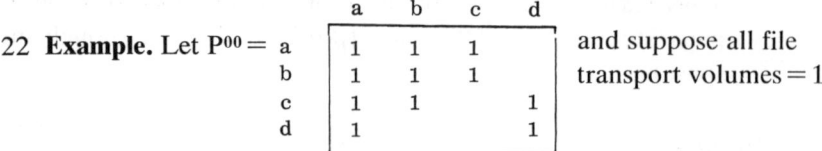 and suppose all file transport volumes $=1$

The transport saving that can be obtained through grouping some process with a is greatest for the pair a ∪ b for which it is 3. The total saving possible is then

$$3 \text{ for } a \cup b \text{ plus } 0 \text{ for } c \cup d, \text{ total saving} = 3$$
while $\quad$ 2 for a ∪ d plus 2 for b ∪ c, gives a saving $= 4$
and is thus better.

We have disussed in a superficial way the possible methods for efficient process grouping. The mathematical formulation of these problems is sketched in Capter 14 of this volume, i.e. Section 214.1 but no numerical procedures for solution are given so far[8]).

23 **Remark.** It is necessary to remember that when information is represented by files then the sequence in which the records come in the file is of importance for the information that can be extracted from the file. The sequence — or the *ordering* — of a file may have to depend on the process or on the other files involved in the process. Two processes which require the file to be in a different order may therefore not be grouped (unless if some special conditions apply).

As a consequence, when a file changes its ordering it shall also have its name changed. Thus if the system contains versions of a file which have different sorting sequences they must be given different identifiers in the system documentation.

27.7 Incidence Matrix of Processes and Files.

We have seen that the precedence relations and the precedence matrix P^{00} are suitable to describe some of the relations of our study. However, some facts could not be described in that way. Thus the number of file passes in a process could not be specified in P^{00} for both input and output files. Further P^{00} does not offer a convenient description of how computations are grouped into

---

[7]) Cf. section 28.3.
[8]) After the first issue of this book a mathematical optimum solution for this problem has been obtained by J. F. Nunamaker, cf. 2 Nu 1971.

composite processes. Both these deficiencies are remedied if we introduce the concept of incidence between process and input and output. In this way the precedence matrix is replaced by the incidence matrix E^{10}. The incidence concept considers not only precedence relations among data sets but also shows how any process takes some data sets as precedents (or input) and other data sets as succedents (or output). In the incidence matrix E^{10} one row is taken for each process (or computation)[2]) and one column for each data set. The number of times that a file is treated by a process is used as the incidence number between the file and the process. Incidence numbers are given different signs for input and output. Here we use the minus sign (-) to indicate output[3]).

1 To start with a simple illustration let us take the computations
        comp (a): $P(a) = e, f, g, h$;
        comp (e): $P(e') = e, f, g$;
illustrated by the first two columns in P^{00} [1]) and write the corresponding incidence matrix E^{10}

2

	a	b	c	d	e	e'	f	g	h	i	i'	j	j'	k	l	l'
$E^{10} =$ comp(a)	-1						1	1	1							
comp(e')					1	-1	1	1								

3 Note that we have now written numbers for both input and output so that by replacing the units by any appropriate number we are able to indicate any number of input and output scans as shown in E^{10}.

4 Note further that in E^{10}, as well as in P^{00}, we can easily see the fact that $P(e') = P(a)$ and also that consolidation for instance of g and h would cause a deadweight transport of h in comp(e').

---

[1]) See section 25.1—33.
[2]) In this way we also introduce identifiers for the processes. As a consequence we thereby also provide for establishing entries in the data base for the system description which entries contain description for the processes (e.g. programs). (Cf. section 12.21.)
[3]) Notice that this sign convention is opposite to the one more commonly used in mathematical literature. We make this change here simply because outputs are usually fewer than inputs and thus we minimize the number of minus signs (—) to write in the matrices (cf. Section 12.17).

5 Also, a row in E^{10} indicates cleary the number of input and output sets for the associated process.

6 Now suppose that we decide to group comp(a) and comp(e') into one process pr(a, e'). This decision could have been made on inspection of P^{00} or E^{10}. It can be performed by replacing the rows comp(a) and comp(e') by one single row "pr(a, e')":

	a	b	c	d	e	e'	f	g	h	i	i'	j	j'	k	l	l'
E^{10} = pr(a, e')	-1				1	-1	1	1	1							

7 We may also introduce a change in the graphical representation which is analogous to the change in passing from P^{00} to E^{01}. We introduce also in the graph a representation of the process (or computation):

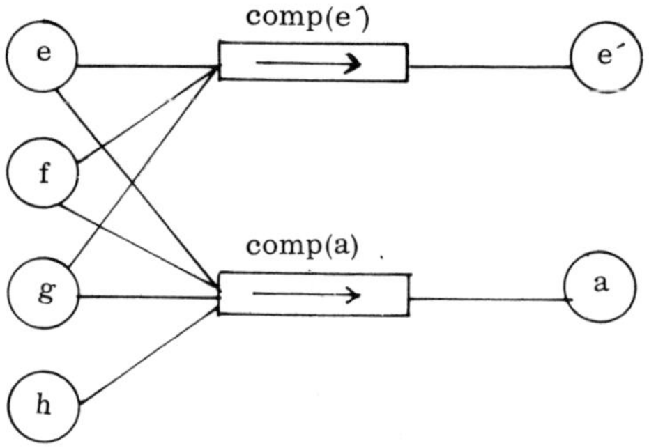

Fig. 1

We have used a rectangular element (or a line element) to represent the computations or processes, whereas the data sets are represented as points. This is because processes have two ends, the input and the output end, like a line has. Thus data sets are represented as 0-dimensional entities and processes as 1-dimensional ones. It was therefore that P^{00}, being a relation between zerodimensional entities, has got two superscripts of 0 whereas in E^{10} the first superscript (the one associated with the rows of the matrix) is 1 to indicate that the matrix rows are associated with the onedimensional objects called processes.

When the two computations are grouped into pr(a, e') this is illustrated by Fig. 2.

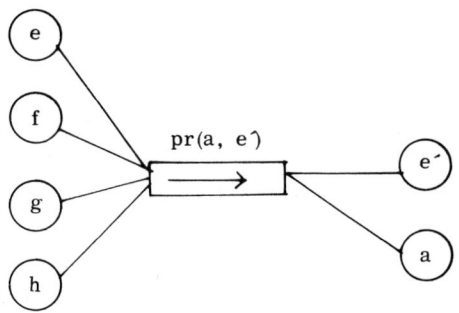

Fig. 2

Now we can write down the incidence matrix E^{10} corresponding to P^{00} of 25.1—33. Thereby we assume that the output set d in pr(d, l') has to be scanned the same number of times as its input c, i.e. five times. This fact could not have been indicated in P^{00}. We make the assumption in writing E^{10}, that we have decided to group all computations, which have input sets being subsets of input sets of other computations, with these latter computations. Thus pr(e') is grouped to pr(a), giving pr(a, e') and similarly we obtain pr(b, i'), pr(c, j') and pr(d, l').

	a	e´	b	i´	c	j´	d	l´	e	f	g	h	i	j	k	l
8 E^{10} = pr(a, e')	-1	-1							1	1	1	1				
pr(b, i')	1	1	-1	-1								1				
pr(c, j')				1	-1	-1					1			1	1	
pr(d, l')	1	1			5		-5	-1				1				1
File transport volume	1	10	1	10	2	20	1	10	10	2	1	1	10	20	2	10

Total file transport volume = 111 and system transport = 159.

Note. In 8 we have indicated e' as input instead of e in all processes except pr (a, e'), as it should be, (likewise for i', j', l').

In 8 we have also added a row (the last one) to indicate the assumed file transport volumes.

369

In Fig. 3 we have drawn the graph corresponding to E^{10} of 8.

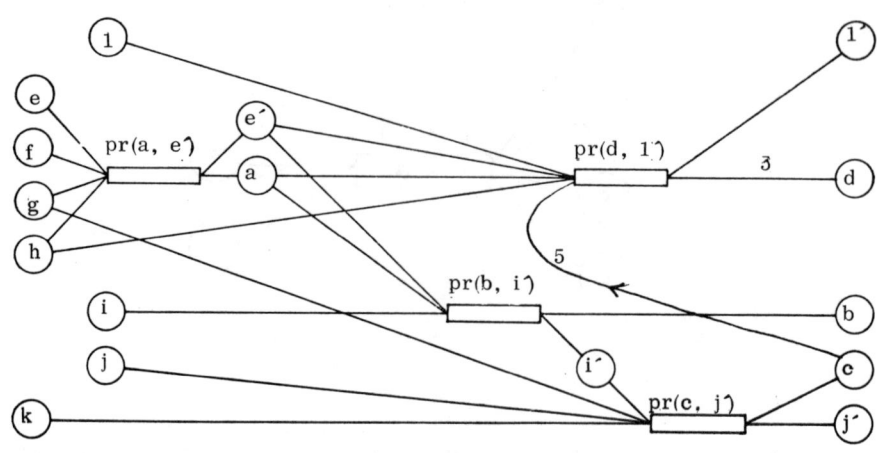

Fig. 3

Exercise.

Show that the transport factors η and η_{top}[4]) can be computed by

$$\eta = \frac{1^T \cdot /E^{10}/ \cdot v}{1^T \cdot s}; \quad \text{(v=file transport volume vector}$$
$$\text{s=file transport size vector)}$$

and

$$\eta_{top} = \frac{1^T \cdot /E^{10}/ \cdot s}{1^T \cdot s}; \quad (/E^{10}/ = \text{matrix obtained from } E^{10}$$
$$\text{by replacing all minus signs by plus signs.)}$$

---

[4]) Cf. sections 27.4—1 and 27.5—3.

Chapter 8. Effect of Process Grouping.

28.1 Effect of Process Grouping on the Transport Factor.

Grouping of two processes will reduce the transport volume if the two processes have some data files in common, as input or output.

By scanning the incidence matrix E^{10} for the file system one can find which files are used in the different processes for a column in E^{10} which will contain nonzero entries in the row positions corresponding to each process which handles the file associated with the column.

When some files are associated with several processes then of course more than two processes will be considered within the same grouping. This will generally make a large number of combinations possible and the scanning of all of them may be too much even for a computer. In practical cases it is expected however that different kinds of restrictions will reduce this complication considerably. One typical restriction is memory space.

One may often be interested in estimating the effect of marginal increases of memory size. In the first steps of such a procedure only a few combinations will be possible so that then a complete analysis seems quite feasible.

One might for instance determine the smallest marginal memory increase which will enable any process grouping. For this one may then compute the best total set of groupings in the system which it will enable. From this a change in transport volume will be computed. As a second step one may then compute the possible reduction of transport volume which would instead be obtained if the increased memory were used to reduce file volume through using longer tape blocks (or through more data packing). There is of course also the alternative of using memory space to speed up internal processing. This might of course save more time. We disregard this possibility here because we have chosen to study the data transport only. In a realistic situation some consideration must be given to this, of course. This procedure may then be repeated for a second step of marginal memory incrementing.

It is of course possible that, in a given file processing system design, an improvement of the transport factor can be obtained without incrementing memory. If this is so, it is however because earlier steps in determining optimum process grouping have not been completed or were not correctly performed.

Just to make life more complicated we have also to remember that there is one more possibility for exchanging memory space for time. This is when the computer permits simultaneous writing and reading on tapes. To make use of this we need double memory areas for both reading and writing (if we want to avoid complications). To see when this possibility should not be used let us assume the record length is $x \cdot g$, $g =$ the record gap. If simultaneous read/write is not used, space is saved which would permit using double record length. (This again could well be impossible because of the extra program space called for by blocking records. But for the moment this is disregarded.)

The length of tape allocated to one record is

$$g + x \cdot g = (1+x) g$$

If instead we use double length records we get (for the length of one physical block)

$$g + 2x \cdot g = (1+2x)g$$

Which means that a single (logical) record takes $(\frac{1}{2} + x)$ g of tape length in total. We see that only for $x = 0$, i.e. for zero record length the tape length per record is reduced to one half, thus doubling effective tape speed. Whenever x is greater than zero then simultaneous read-write is better than blocking of records (as it will always lead to roughly doubled effective tape speed, regardless of the value of x).

On the other hand omitting simultaneous read/write may in some cases save more than two file passages by leaving space for process grouping, in which case no simultaneous read/write should be used.

Obviously grouping must be by more than two, i.e. by three least, in order to be better than simultaneous I/O.

Simultaneous I/O requires two (at least) extra record areas for each file pair. Grouping by three requires three program spaces, that is two spaces extra. It is seen that if n I/O file pairs are involved, and the average record area is r and the average program area is p, then only when $p < n \cdot r$ will grouping be possible with less space than is called for by simultaneity of I/O (and be saving as much time).

28.2 Memory Requirement Associated with Process Grouping.

We have seen above that in order to group several processes associated with the same file, to save file scans, we need memory space. Each process needs a program and a work area for the transaction item calling the process.

If several processes are grouped into one it is necessary to have program space for each of the processes. This is because otherwise each time a transaction item calls a process the corresponding program would have to be transported to memory. Note however that the data areas could be shared by all the different transaction items for these only have to be in one at a time (otherwise we would not have the choice of not grouping which, exactly, is the main point of our problem). It may not be the case, however, that the programming system used takes advantage of this fact. It is seen that to save one file scan by grouping a process "a" with another "b" one would call for a transport of "program a" into memory for each occurrence of an item "a" and then a transport of "program b" to restore the memory after "a" has been handled.

Thus if i(a) is the number of "groups of transaction" items, i.e. transactions of type "a" which follow each other densely so that no item of other type comes between them, and if prog (a) and prog (b) are the transport volumes for transporting the program for "a" into memory (before a group "a") and the program for "b" (after the group "a"), we have the transport volume for program $a = i(a)$ (prog (a) + prog (b)). If this transport is less than that of a file scan then grouping process "a" into the larger process will save transport volume even if the program for "a" cannot be kept continuously in memory during the whole run[1]).

---

[1]) See example in section 24.1—18.

If trpv$_f$ is the transport volume of file f then the condition is

1 $$i(a) \{ prog(a) + prog(b) \} < trpv_f$$

or

2 $$i(a) < \frac{trpv_f - \text{a practical margin}}{prog(a) + prog(b)}$$

Example. A fairly normal size of a program for an elementary process is 4000 bits and for a file record 1000 bits. In that case the condition would be

$$i(a) < i(f) \frac{1000}{8000} - \text{margin or } i(a) < \frac{i(f)}{8} - \text{margin.}$$

In that case it would be of advantage to "group in" "a" if the "transaction frequency" for "a" would be less than 12 % — margin — for instance it may be $< 8 \%$ required. This is not uncommon. One might therefore estimate that *grouping will often pay even when all programs cannot be held simultaneously in memory.*

We may need to have space available in file storage for storing programs of a group of processes, if the memory cannot hold them all. One must make sure that the gain is worth the cost. If in any case an auxiliary unit is used to hold the program library, there may be no cost. Then one may still find that if 2 is satisfied, but only with a small margin, the realistic options still will be only either to require enough memory or not to use grouping of "a" into the other process.

It is common to have the total transaction frequency even for heavily grouped processes well below 100 %. It is realistic to expect something like the well-known 80—20 per cent rule to hold often and therefore one will have to expect that about 80 % of the transactions are of a kind which occurs only about 20 % of the time. This suggests that some of the transactions comprise less than 10 % of the total transaction frequency. If total transaction frequency is less than 30 % (a common situation) this means that sóme transactions should be expected to have a proper frequency of only about 3 %.

The conclusion is that when accounting for memory requirements for possible grouping of processes one should always also list expected transaction frequencies, for one has to expect that in many cases this will indicate the requirement to be less severe than might otherwise be expected.

These observations also indicate that auxiliary memories like magnetic drums, and even tapes, may be of great interest in connection with process grouping so long as they are significantly less expensive than the central memory. This, on the other hand, is not always the case, for we may then have to add an extra cost for attaching another type of equipment to a system.

The grouping together of two or more processes naturally has some effects on the computer programs. If a set of different transactions are entered into the grouped processes working on one master file (or several files), then each time a transaction is entered, the program has to analyze the type of the transaction. One of the transaction types may be associated with only one of the processes and the analyzing program on recognizing this transaction record type will set up a "program switch" to the process in question. Another transaction type will need a switch to another process program while a third type may switch in both programs, one after the other.

28.3 Computer Programs and Memory Space for a Process.

The possibility of saving file transport by grouping processes depends on whether memory space is sufficient for the need of all processes in the group, The question is how to determine the memory space needed by a process. This memory need is made up of several distinct components:[1])

1 Space for operative program system.

2 Buffer areas for the data needed by the process. Some of these are in common with other processes in the group for otherwise there would be no reason for grouping. They do not then have to be counted when we test for possible inclusion into a group. Simultaneous I/O and processing calls for duplicated buffer areas.

---

[1]) It is worth noting that the optimum problem is simpler for very small or very large memories. In small memories alternatives are few, and in large ones we can do anything of advantage.

3 If the process uses I/O equipment not used by other members in the group this may require the addition of some I/O-routines to the executive program subroutines.

4 Memory space for the programs for the procedures realizing each of the processes which check data and results.

5 Space for programs that move such data to the updated files, which are not processed by the procedure.

6 Work areas for the procedure. These will often be shared by other procedures in the group. To the extent they are not or exceed the maximum need of the rest of the group they are to be accounted for.

7 The most difficult memory need to determine is that for the procedure proper. This problem has in fact plagued the programmers and computer users for more than a decade, with no general solution being produced.

8 The proper thing to do to solve this problem, or at least to reduce it, seems to be to try to collect statistics. If the reader feels this could hardly lead to sufficient accuracy in estimating actual need he should recall that the only possibility he has today is much worse — he can only guess. Today people do not tackle the problem at all and are deeply disappointed when they find their integrated system cannot be implemented because of memory limitation. Thus today even a systematic guessing, in combination with the grouping space analysis we propose here, is a real improvement. If statistical data could be used to even slightly improve our guess it is very desirable.

9 Two things serve to make the use of statistical data for process space estimation seem promising today. One is that our technique of analyzing the information need down to elementary files and elementary processes, or computations, makes it much more feasible to find similarities with already implemented systems. Hence the statistical data will be more relevant.

10 The other reason is that the increasing use of problem-oriented programming languages such as COBOL and ALGOL makes it possible to obtain computer independent statistical data. If we hawe an estimate as to how many ALGOL statements, for instance, that

are included in some implemented procedures corresponding to an elementary process then we may be able to make a good estimate of how many ALGOL statements we are going to have. We will then, as a rule, have usable estimates of how many machine instructions our specific compiler will produce from these ALGOL statements.

In fact the availability of modern efficient procedure languages also help in another way to solve our problem. Thus we will be able to write down a whole first draft of an ALGOL procedure for the process we want to estimate, as this can often be done in fairly short time which is not the case with machine-oriented programs.

11 Also the space according to 5 is not so simple to determine. It depends on how many elementary files are consolidated into the master files[2]). The program for moving any specific elementary file (or data group) can, in principle at least, be used by any process which does not do computation work on that specific elementary file. Such programs therefore are common (or should be) to many of the elementary processes.

12 If for instance the master file contains the files A_i ($i = 1, 2, 3, \ldots k$) and process p_1 uses A_1 and A_5 while process p_2 uses A_3, A_4 and A_5 we need programs like:

13 pr(p_1);   move A_2 to new master; move A_3 to new master; move A_4 to new master; move A_6 ...; move A_k ..;

and
14 pr(p_2);   move A_1 to new master; move A_2 to new master; move A_6 to new master; move A_k to ....;

We see how several move programs are common to both processes.

15 When different computations are grouped into one process then there will also have to be an administrative program which coordinates the working of the different computations. In general the situation is that when one input transaction record is entered it will be of a type which calls for a specific computation, and that one alone. The

---

[2]) See chapter 9 part 2.

coordinating program will sense the type and switch in the appropriate program which then performs the computation and the corresponding move operations. It is natural to expect that the coordinating administrative program will have one part which is common for the group (we can call it "adm(group)") and in addition one part for each of the computations (such as "adm(1)" for the computation p1 and "adm(2)" for p2).

We can set up this (for the example above) in a tabular form, using one selection row vector for p1 and one for p2.

	pr(p1)	pr(p2)	adm(group)	adm(1)	adm(2)
p1	1		1	1	
p2		1	1		1

	m(v1)	mv(2)	mv(3)	mv(4)	mv(5)
p1		1	1	1	
p2	1	1			

Tableau showing different programs involved in p1 and p2 respectively.

Thus if p2 is already in a grouped process the addition of p1 into the group adds a memory requirement:

$$\text{adm}(p1) + \text{pr}(p1) + \text{mv}(3) + \text{mv}(4)$$

instead of only pr(p1)
pr(p1) may already be known. (It may for instance exist as an ALGOL procedure.)

28.4 Example of Process Grouping with Memory Limitation.

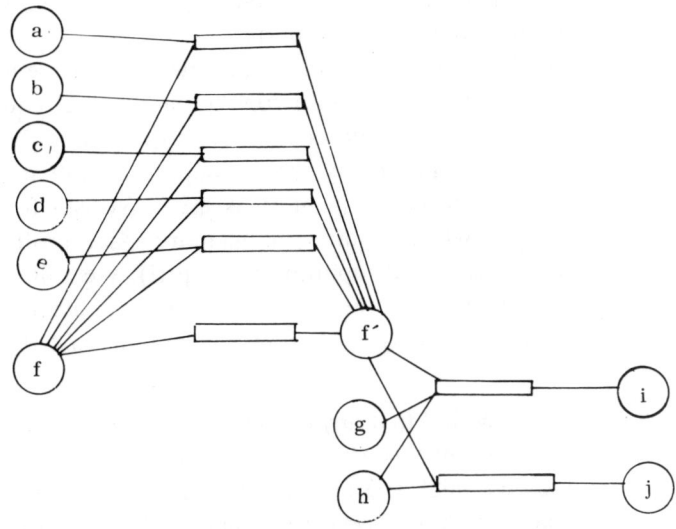

1 record size	100	100	100									Progr. space
	a	b	c	d	e	f	f´	g	h	i	j	
pr a	1					1	-1					500
b		1				1	-1					1300
c			1			1	-1					800
d				1		1	-1					600
e					1	1	-1					1500
f							1	-1				800
i								1	1	1	-1	1000
j									1	1	-1	2000
File trp vol	1	1	1	1	1	10	10	20	35	10	10	100
syst.transp	1	1	1	1	1	60	80	20	70	10	10	255

Fig. 1

$$\text{trp factor} = \frac{255}{100} = 2{,}55\text{[1]}$$

---

[1]) Comparing with section 27.4—1 and section 27.3—15 we find that our result for "trp factor" should have been multiplied by η_{tv} (the transport volume factor) which tells how much larger is the file volume than the file size. We ignore this refinement in this example as it is of no significance for the operations we want to illustrate here.

We make the simplifying assumption that all record sizes are 100 memory positions. We also assume that a buffer area for one record is included in the "program space" given in the right hand column of 1. Thus, as long as the blocking factor is = 1 we need not allocate additional memory for buffers.

We find from the table 1 that we need a memory size of 2000 at least, for this is seen in row "j" of 1 to be required for process "j" alone. Now it follows that as process "i" only requires 1000 it is possible to group any process requiring 1000 at most with pr(i) when 2000 positions of memory is used. We can for instance group "f" with "i" which requires the memory space 1800. If we do so we save the operation of inputting f' for pr(i). We still need to input "f" for pr(f) and to output "f'". We have thus saved on scan of f' which, from 1 is seen to save a transport volume of 10^2).

We now find that any of the processes pr(a) through pr(e) if grouped in pairs will save one scan of both "f" and "f'". or 20. It is possible that we might be able to form two such pairs within the memory space of 2000. We try this and find in fact that pr(a $\cup$ e) requires 2000 and pr(b $\cup$ d) requires 1900 so both are feasible.

Step 1.

Assuming 2000 positions of memory available we find the following design feasible:

	a	b	c	d	e	f	f'	g	h	i	j	m
pr (a $\cup$ b)	1	1				1	—1					1800
pr (c $\cup$ d)			1	1		1	—1					1400
pr (e)					1	1	—1					1500
pr (f)						1	—1					800
pr (i)								1	1	1	—1	1000
pr (j)								1		1	—1	2000
File transport						40	60					

---

[2]) Notice that if we group "f" and "i" we must assume that all processes a to e have been finished before processes "f" and "i" get started. Note also that the process "f" (updating file f by itself) is empty in most practical applications. We have added it here for theoretical completeness.

We see that our reasoning in words is very difficult to follow up or review. Therefore while we are not able to present an algorithm for the analysis we show that it is very advantageous nevertheless to attempt a concise presentation which gives us a chance to see in total what we are doing.

We see that the only changes in transport which resulted from the process groupings are those associated with the files f and f'. We therefore only need to record the column sums for these. This transport is found to be $40+60=100$ against 140 in the primary scheme 1. The system transport is thus seen to have been reduced by 40 resulting in a total of $255—40=215$ and a transport factor of 2.15.

Step 2.

We may try another solution which still uses the minimum 2000 of memory space. This time we see if we can use the facility of simultaneous I/O, which we assume is available on the computer we plan to use. The reason we tried without using this facility was, of course, that we wanted to use the very minimum of memory space which does not permit simultaneous I/O for pr(j). While we are thus still not able to use simultaneous I/O for pr(j) we now see if it can be used to advantage in the other processes. We cannot be sure, for the space required for alternate buffer areas by simultaneity may prevent us from using some grouping of processes.

Step 3.

In order to make possible the use of simultaneous input of file f and output of file f' we allocate two additional file record areas in the main memory. This requires 200 positions. We see from the incidence matrix under 2, right-hand column, that this is possible in all processes except "pr(j)" and therefore we can introduce this modification without structural change. The only thing we need to do (if we assume that simultaneous 1/0 eliminates virtually all output of f' when f is simultaneously fed in), is to ignore the "—1" in the matrix rows corresponding to pr $(a \cup b)$, pr $(c \cup d)$ and pr(e). This reduces the transport of file f' by another 30 thus giving a total reduction of 70 as compared with the initial system 1. We show in Fig. 2 the structure of the last design.

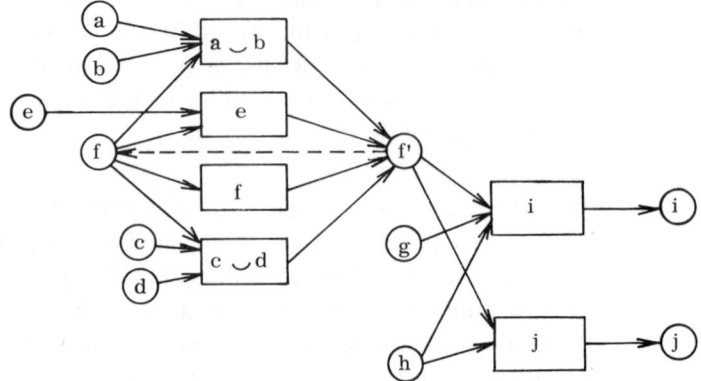

Fig. 2

Notice that we have only used two symbolic names f, and f', for the sequence of updated files of type f. We thus assume that process (a ∪ b) is run first, giving f'. Then f' is taken as the new f (i.e. f:=f') in the subsequent process (c ∪ d) which outputs a new f' which, again, is substituted for f. In practice it is recommended that new names (i.e. identifiers) are given to each new version of a file, although this leads to larger matrices or diagrams.

One consequence of our use of only two identifiers for the f file (i.e. f and f') is that we cannot identify some of the processes by their output (i.e. f') because this is not unique in this sort of representation. Notice that normally the process is best identified by its output, as for instance process (i). This means that in many analysis situations it is waste of time and space (for documentation) to explicitly mention the processes. They are identified anyway by the identification of the information which is their output.

We can check in Fig. 2 that the number of passes of f and f' given in the incidence matrix is correct. Thus according to Fig. 2 f is transported four times and f' 6 times giving the transport volumes 40 and 60 respectively.

We now go on to see what design is feasible if we assume the memory size available to be 2500. As we found in 3 that using 200 memory positions for alternate buffer areas to make simultaneous I/O possible was advantageous in the kind of system structure we have in this example, we set aside 200 positions and have 2300 available for process grouping. Process j can still not be grouped. We start by looking at the process with the second largest space i.e. process (e).

$m = 25000 \cdot m_{alt} = 200 =$ buffer area size

$\bar{m} = m - m_{alt} = 2300$

e: $\quad m(e) = 1500 \ (=$ memory size of proc (e))

$\bar{m} - m(e) = 800$. Processes ≤ 800 are:

$\quad\quad$ pr(t) : m(a) = 500
$\quad\quad$ pr(c) : m(c) = 800
$\quad\quad$ pr(d) : m(d) = 600
$\quad\quad$ pr(f) : m(f) = 800

It is seen that we are best off if we choose pr (c) or pr (f) for grouping with pr (e). Let us choose f [e $\cup$ f].
The largest remaining process is pr (b)

b: $\quad m(b) = 1300$

$\bar{m} - m(b) = 1000$. Largest remaining processes ≤ 1000 is pr(i). [b $\cup$ i].

Continuing similarly we get:

c: $\quad m(c) = 800$

$\bar{m} - m(c) = 1500$. Remaining processes are:

$\quad\quad$ pr(a) : m(a) = 500 $\bigg\}$ $m(a) + m(d) = 1100$
$\quad\quad$ pr(d) : m(d) = 600

[c $\cup$ a $\cup$ d]

Remark. The fact that pr(i) and pr(j) do not change f' means that if pr(b $\cup$ i) and pr(j) are run after the others then pr(b $\cup$ i) needs not output f' and one transport of this is thus saved. One might however want to update f' in the run pr(b $\cup$ i) and thus output f' for other possible use. This is outside our exercise, however.

		a	b	c	d	e	f	f'	g	h	i	j	Progr space	
m = 2500	a∪c∪d	1		1	1		1 (-1)						1700	(—1) indicates that f' is
m_{alt}=200	e∪f					1	1 (-1)						2300	transported simultaneous
m̄ = 2300	b∪i		1						1	1	1	-1	2300	with f.
	j								1	1		-1	2000	
	file transp						30	10						Saving: 140—40 = 100
m = 3000	a∪c∪d∪f	1		1	1		1 (-1)						2700	No alternative buffer areas
m_{alt}=200	b∪e	1					1	1 (-1)					2800	Change in f, f', h;
m̄ = 2800	i∪j								1	1	-1	-1	3000	
	file transp						20	10		35				Saving: 210—65 = 145

We have recorded the analysis for m = 2500 in the matrix above. As each new analysis takes a new matrix with the same columns it is practical to record into a sequence of rows using the same set of columns. This is shown above in that also a design for m = 3000 is recorded. The corresponding flow diagrams are shown in Figs. 3 and 4.

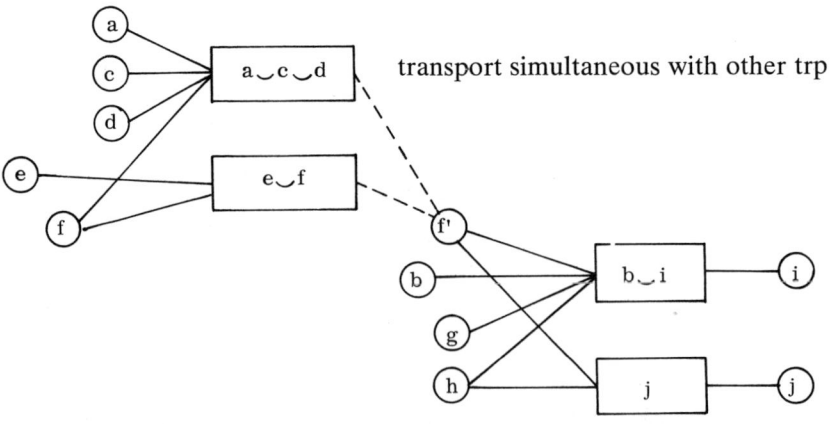

Fig. 3

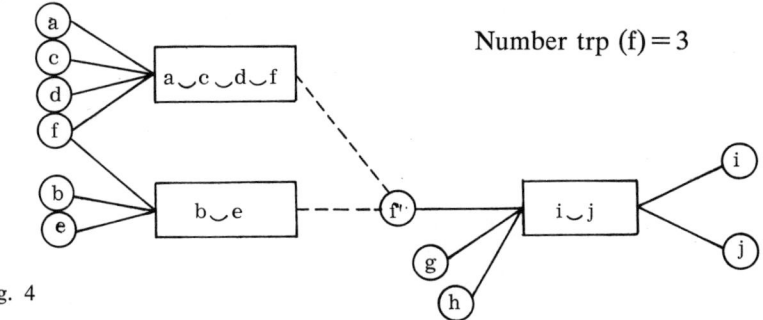

Fig. 4

4 **Problem.** Discuss the consequence in the problem of Fig. 1 of adding a requirement of common space $= 600$ for a, b, c (meaning that grouping "b" to "a" does not call for an addition of 600 (i.e. $\text{vol}(a \cup b) = \text{vol}(a) + \text{vol}(b) + 600$). Discuss for memory $= 2000$ and 2500 only.

5 **Problem.** Discuss what modification to the problem of Fig. 1 would be feasible if "e" occurs with only 1/20 of the frequency of the other items.

6 **Remark.** In a practical system the number of elementary input files will be much greater than in this example. A fairly realistic number would be about ten times as many. On the other hand it is also normal for the program space requirement for each elementary process to be ten times smaller. Hence our example is fairly similar to a real situation where we have already done consolidations so that a, b, c, ... can be considered as being consolidated from ten elementary files on the average. This first stage of consolidation may well have been done as guided by a set of commonly used subprocesses and thus commonly used memory areas[3]). This first stage could also be done without regard for memory as it was to lead to program sizes still well below the planned minimum memory (or 2000 positions).

---

[3]) Cf. section 28.3.

Chapter 9. File Consolidation.

29.1 Reducing the Number of Transport Equipment Units.

The precedence matrix P^{00} or the incidence matrix E^{10} also gives information about the input and output (or transput for short) requirements[1]. Thus the column for a shows in P^{00} that in addition to an output unit for a there are needed input units for e, f, g, and h. Five units in all would be needed for this computation. If it is grouped with that for e', there will have to be a unit for e' as well thus increasing the number to six units altogether.

The group a, e', d, and l' similarly is seen to call for twelve transput units.

In general the amount of transput equipment with a computer has to be small for cost reasons. One then will have to take together (or consolidate) several of the *elementary files* we have considered so far, to larger files. A consolidation of files corresponds to grouping of rows of P^{00} or columns of E^{10}[2]).

Consolidation of files may cause excessive data transport by causing data to be input to a process where they are not used. It may, to some extent, reduce transport by eliminating the need for duplicating storage of record identifiers. Grouping of computations on the other hand may eliminate such excessive transport. Hence grouping of computation in general should have a still greater beneficient effect than we have seen above.

The actual consolidation of files can be done by storing records from both or all of the basic files in the same file medium or by combining the basic records to composite records[3]).

1 As a simple illustration we may consider what happens if the files g and h in the system with the P^{00} matrix, section 27.6—2 are consolidated. We write the corresponding rows of P^{00}.

---

[1]) E^{10} as given in section 27.7—8 and P^{00} paragraph 27.6—2.
[2]) Another frequent reason for consolidation of files and hence reducing the number of transput units is the saving of set up time that will result if the files are sufficiently small.
[3]) See paragraph 2 of this section.

P^{00}:

	a	e'	b	i'	c	j'	d	l'
g:	1	1	0	0	1	0	0	0
h:	1	0	0	0	0	0	1	0

We see that in two of the three inputs of g we will have to transport h as a deadweight. Similarly during one of the two transports of h we will have g as a deadweight. Thus a deadweight transport of $2h + 1g = 3$ is induced. Grouping of "a" and "e'" will eliminate one of these "h" transports and grouping a, e' with d, l' eliminate also the excessive g transport, reducing the total deadweight transport caused by consolidating g and h to g.

As further examples we note that consolidation of k and j would imply no deadweight transport, whereas consolidation of i with j causes one excess scan of j and one of j', so that in that case the

resulting deadweight transport would be 40. Grouping of b, i, c, and j on the other hand would enable i, j, and k to be consolidated without any deadweight transport at all. This is easily seen from P^{00}.

When we consider consolidation of files, the picture of excessive data transport becomes somewhat complicated. The transport is composed of duplicate input from some files to several processes, and of deadweight transport of some data in these files which are not utilized as input in some of the processes to which they are transported together with the true input data for those processes.

However, the total number of excessive transports is very easily detected, being simply the number of passes of that file minus one. Thus we need not keep record of the different kinds of excessive transport.

Likewise if two files are small enough to be carried on one tape reel, to consolidate them — but also to put them after each other — may save transport by eliminating a need for tape reel set-up.

2 Consolidation of files.

We talk of *consolidation* of files when we take two or more files together on the same file medium, e.g. mass memory, and thereby arrange the individual records in the sorting sequence specified for the file. We notice that we can put several files on the same magnetic tape reel without having a consolidated file, for if one complete file is followed by another file then these files are not considered consolidated according to our definition. We shall then say that such files are *concatenated*.

In consolidating files we may retain the records of the individual files as separate records of different types. In this case we must add to each record a data term carrying the *type code*. We call this arrangement: *consolidation by record collection*. This is the way punched card files of transactions are commonly consolidated. Alternatively we may consolidate files by taking their individual records together to form *consolidated records*. This is the common way to consolidate standing files.

3   To illustrate the different ways of consolidating files let us suppose that we have a file "a" such that each record of "a" contains a *name* "i" (or *key*) and a set of other *terms* (*properties*) "a_i". The record number i thus is (i, a_i) with a comma used to separate the name. Let the file "a" be:

$a = $(a) (1, a_1) (2, a_2) (7, a_7) (8, a_8) (13, a_{13})

where (a) is indicating a *file* label identifying the file to be of "the kind a". Notice that a_1 etc. does not contain the label "a".

4   Let another file "b" be:

$b = $(b) (1, b_1) (2, b_2) (3, b_3) (8, b_8) (9, b_9)

5   Let *a b* denote the file obtained through consolidation by *record collection*. Then:

a b = (a b) (a, 1, a_1) (b, 1, b_1) (a, 2, a_2) (b, 2, b_2) (b, 3, b_3) (a, 7, a_7) (a, 8, a_8) (b, 8, b_8) (b, 9, b_9) (a, 13, a_{13})

Notice that we had to insert the "type codes" "a" or "b" respectively into each individual record. Thus the data size of *a b* is greater than the sum of the sizes of a and b.

6   Now, let instead "$a \cup b$" denote the file obtained by consolidation by *record consolidation*:

$a \cup b = (a \cup b)$ (1, a_1, b_1) (2, a_2, b_2) (3, —, b_3) (7, a_7, —) (8, a_8, b_8) (9, —, b_9) (13, a_{13}, —)

The hyphen between 3 and b_3, for instance, denotes an empty space corresponding to the size of a_3 (which is missing).

We see that this time we save one occurrence of the record name, in each pair a, b, of records. For instance in *a b* we had the name "1" with both a_1 and b_1. In $a \cup b$ it is occuring only once with a_1 and b_1 together. We also save the type code because in $a \cup b$ we know where the a terms and the b terms are placed. Instead we see that file storage space is wasted on the missing subrecords (such as a_3 or b_7) indicated by the hyphens. Instead of leaving empty space for missing subrecords we may use a type code to indicate what is missing. For instance we could have

t_0 to indicate that no subrecord is missing
t_1 to indicate that the a-subrecord is missing
t_2 to indicate that the b-subrecord is missing

We would then have

7 $a \cup b = (a \cup b)$ (1, t_0, a_1, b_1) (2, t_0, a_2, b_2) (3, t_1, b_3) (7, t_2, a_7) etc.

With this arrangement the size of $a \cup b$ will be smaller than the sum of the sizes of "a" and "b" to the extent that the type code "is smaller" than the name. The size of $a \cup b$ in this arrangement will always be smaller than the size of *a b* (to the extent that the type code in $a \cup b$ is smaller than a name plus two type codes in *a b*). We see that in $a \cup b$ we have records of varying lengths.

The way the file will be treated by a problem-oriented language such as COBOL or ALGOL-GENIUS will be different for the two kinds of file consolidation. Thus a "read" verb will make one record at a time available for processing so that if the file is consolidated by consolidation of records then all data associated with the same identifier value will be made accessible in one call. Instead if consolidation is by record collection a program will have to issue a "read" for each elementary record with the same identifier value.

On the other hand, if only one of the elementary records has to be available at a time then the file having collected records, rather than consolidated records, will require less working space in memory.

8 The data files which are used in typical data processing systems and using magnetic tapes are usually many times larger than the elementary files we have been talking about. They can therefore be regarded as being built up (*consolidated* is the word commonly used in this connection) from several elementary files. Normally the systems are designed so that as many data as can possibly be collected under the same object terms (or *keys*). For instance, in a "person file" people usually try to collect all data about each person in a single record which thas the identification number of the person as its key term. The number of tapes to be handled in the system may be reduced as a result. File space and file transport may be saved by only having to record the key once. One sometimes finds it necessary at a later design stage to split a file into smaller files. The use of largely consolidated files will always cause an excessive (or dead-weight) file transport, in the case of serial access file systems, e.g. magnetic tapes and often also with direct-access storage. This, of course, is not desirable and may in many cases lead to serious inefficiency in the system. It is therefore important to strive for a more systematic approach to file design. This makes it natural to regard the files as being consolidated from a number of "elementary" files and to regard the effect of this consolidation of the performance of the system as a relevant design consideration.

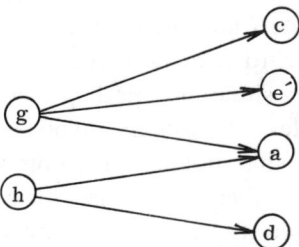

Fig. 1

If the files, in Fig. 1, are on a serial access storage, e.g. magnetic tapes, then consolidation of files g and h into one file (g, h) allows all the data of file h to be transported into the two processes producing c and e', respectively, without being used in these processes. Similarly, the data of file g would be transported as a deadweight into the process for d. (If, instead, we consolidate file (g, h) and examine the effect of splitting it into separate files g and h, we find that this will reduce file transports correspondingly to the quantities mentioned.)

If, instead, the files are on a pseudo-direct-access storage, e.g. discs, the consolidation of "g" and "h" into one file will not cause the whole of file g to be transported as a deadweight into the process for "d". Only those records of the file g, which are consolidated with such records of file h which are called by transactions during the run of the process, will be transported into the process for d. Whether this will cause excessive transport or not will then depend on details of the system design.

(It is seen that in direct-access files it might sometimes be better to think in terms of consolidation of records rather than of files.)

Thus, when the computer takes in data from the direct-access storage, it takes a block (or "physical record" or "bucket"). The size of this block may have been determined by other factors so that it may be regarded as being fixed in the present decision situation, where we are to decide whether or not to consolidate g and h. The record from "g" and the record from "h" (if both exist for the same value of the record number, i.e. if both have the same value of the "key") both might be able to be stored within one block. The fact that for instance, "g" is input to the process for "d" without being used in this process, does not cause any excess transport because the whole block would be transported in any case. On the other hand, in this situation the input to process "a" will require the transport of one block only, as this would contain both the g record and the h record. In this case, thus, transport is saved. In real situations, perhaps, 20 or 40 rather than only two elementary files, are usually involved as input to a process. Then it is possible that not all of them will find room in one block. To consolidate them into one "logical record" would then mean that one would transport as many blocks as necessary to carry the whole consolidated record and thus the consolidation would cause deadweight transport similar to the case when we assume that (g, h) cannot be stored in one single record in the example above. (It is now justified to ask whether one could say that records are in fact consolidated when not stored in the same block.) In summary, we find that with direct-access storage one may sometimes save transport (and access time) by consolidation of files. More often one will cause excess transport by consolidation, just as was the case with tape storage — although the effect will be milder. However, the argument for consolidating magnetic tape files — in spite of the fact that this causes extra file transport — is the necessity to minimize the number of tape handlers and to reduce manual tape handling. This argument ceases to be valid when we pass on to direct-access storage, as in such a system several files can be stored in one unit. It is obvious that the conclusion will be that much smaller and less consolidated records may be appropriate in a direct-access file store than in tape storage.

29.2 The Effect of File Consolidation in Direct-access Stores.

An illustration is given in Fig. 1. There it is assumed that the auxiliary store has a block size (physical record) equal to 2 and that the records of the files p, q, and r all are equal to 1.

For instance, when a transaction calls process a it is shown in Fig. 1 that process a will retrieve one record from the files p and q. This will require two access times for the auxiliary store operation. (We have, for the sake of simplicity, assumed that the "file directory decoding", needed to locate a file record in the store, is done completely in core storage thus causing no access operation. In real systems a number of access operations may be required already for this localization of the record. In our simple example this could be taken care of by using a correspondingly longer access time.) Because the records (of size one) are stored in blocks of size two the transport of the two records for input to process a will cause a transport of four. Thus, for process a there will be two accesses and a transport of 4. In total we obtain six accesses and a transport of 12.

In Fig. 2 we see what happens if the records of the files p and q are consolidated (denoted in the figure by the symbol p ∪ q). The consolidation of the files p and q to form the file p ∪ q does not cause any unnecessary transport in the system under study because p and q are precedents to the same processes, a and b. The number of access operations is reduced because one access is sufficient to retrieve one p and one q record, as they are contained in a p ∪ q record. The transport is reduced because we have assumed a block size of two and the record sizes are all assumed to be one. Thus when, for instance, one record of the (unconsolidated) file p is retrieved, a block of size two is transported. The same is true of q. Therefore to retrieve one p and one q record a transport of four is necessary. On the other hand, when one p and one q record are consolidated, they can be stored in one block and therefore only a transport of two is required. In total, for the system of Fig. 2 we obtain four accesses and a transport equal to eight. Thus, the consolidation p ∪ q led to improvements in both factors, access and transport.

In Fig. 3 we have shown what happens if the files q and r are consolidated instead. The total results are in this case five accesses and a transport of 10. Fig. 4 shows the results when p and r are consolidated.

Exercise. Repeat the study for block sizes of one and three.

Exercise. Do the analysis under the assumption that the consolidation is replaced by linking the records together by pointers.

When all three files are consolidated (into p ∪ q ∪ r) as shown in Fig. 5, we must specify our assumption about how to store and retrieve the records of p ∪ q ∪ r. These are of the size three while block size was assumed to be two. As one record now needs more than one block for its storage a simple assumption is that two blocks need to be retrieved and transported when one record is to be retrieved. Thus, such an operation will take two accesses and a transport of four. (In real systems the access time for the

(blocksize = 2)

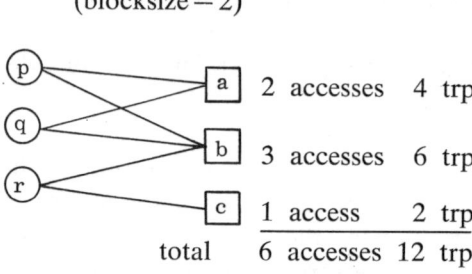

Remark. The effect of blocking two records into each block does not save any transport in random processing, as assumed. It will save in batch runs, however, which will probably also occur in the system.

Fig. 1

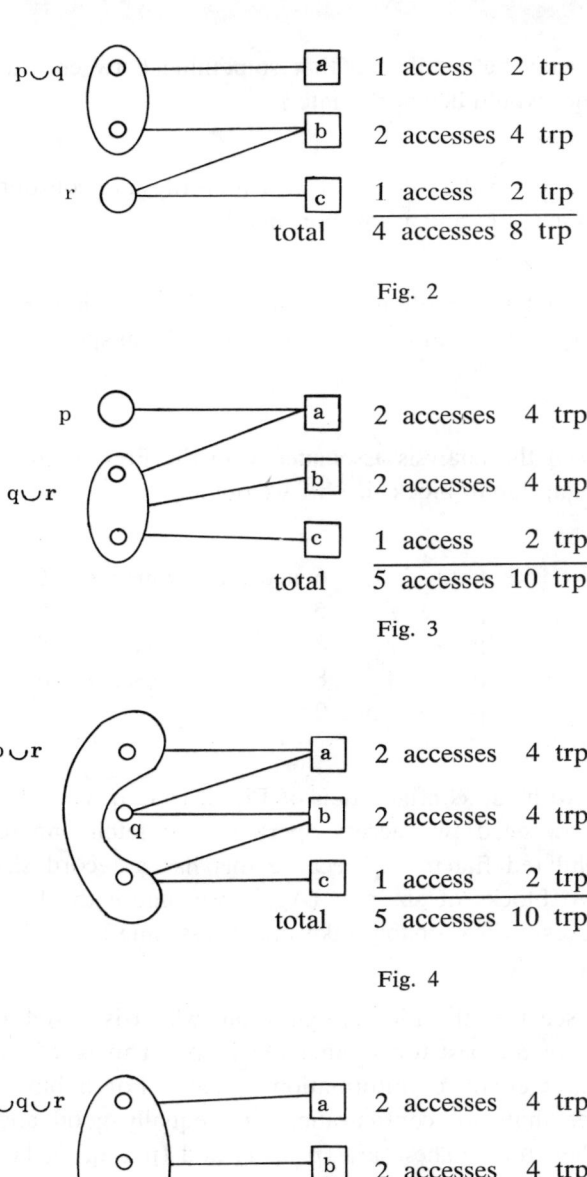

Fig. 5. We assume one record goes into two blocks. We assume also that this means that reading one record (the size of which is three) will take two access times. (In real systems the second access time may, or may not be shorter.)

second block may be smaller so that something between one and two access times would be appropriate.)

As indicated in Fig. 5 the total result, when all files are consolidated into one, is six accesses and a transport of 12.

It is obvious that the configuration of Fig. 2, i.e. using the files $p \cup q$ and r, is best (when only access time and transport time are considered).

When we repeat the analysis associated with the Figs. 1 through 5 under the assumption of block size = 1 we obtain

block size = 1	files p,q,r	6 accesses,	transport	= 6
	$p \cup q$, r	6 ,,	,,	= 6
	p, $q \cup r$	8 ,,	,,	= 8
	$p \cup r$, q	8 ,,	,,	= 8
	$p \cup q \cup r$	9 ,,	,,	= 9

For instance, with the configuration of Fig. 2 ($p \cup q$, r) and block size = 1 we now need two access operations to fetch one record of the consolidated file $p \cup q$ because this has a record size = 2 and needs two blocks of size = 1. (Again we ignore the fact that the second access will probably take much less time.)

We can now see that the file configuration, which is best for one block size, is not the best for another block size. This is, of course, a general characteristic of information systems. For a block size of one we see that two configurations are equally good and are better than the others. These are (p, q, r) and ($p \cup q$, r), both of which have 6 accesses and a transport = 6. For the block size = 2 we find the configuration ($p \cup q$, r) to be the best one. Its values are four accesses and a transport = eight.

One may now ask which block size is the best one (of size 1 or 2). If we let

a = "access work" (with some suitable definition)
t = "transport work" (suitably defined)

then we find the "total work" to be:

block size	total work
1	6a + 6t
2	4a + 8t

It is obvious that if our objective would be to find the configuration for which the total work is minimum we cannot decide which of the two is best unless we determine the relation between a and t. This is the situation which is typical when one tries to minimize two factors or two objectives. Notice however that even if the decisionmaker cannot specify the relation between "a" and "t", the formal analysis was still not useless. True, it was not possible to determine formally which is the best configuration but it was possible to eliminate several configurations from consideration. This, of course, is an important result, especially when the relation a/t cannot be quantified. In that situation the decisionmaker will have to make his final choice himself, based on intuitive judgment. Then he is in a much better situation when he has only two (or a few) alternatives which are worth considering.

Often when one is required to determine or estimate the relation between two factors one is ready to refuse doing so, on the argument that the factors cannot be measured. However, it should be observed that it may turn out that a very crude estimate will be totally sufficient for the determination of which alternative is the better one. In our problem we shall see that this happens to be the case.

Suppose $t = \theta \cdot a$ (and that then total time can be used as measure, for instance as waiting time)

Then block = 1, time : $(6 + 6\theta)a$
block = 2, time : $(4 + 8\theta)a$

Times are equal if $6 + 6\theta = 4 + 8\theta$
Hence $2\theta = 2; \theta = 1$

If $\theta < 1$ then block size = 2 is best
If $\theta > 1$,, ,, ,, = 1 ,, ,,
If $\theta = 1$ then secondary effects (assumed negligible so far) should be studied more carefully (actually, a careful study might prove some of them to be too important to be ignored in any case!)

For a specified block size we then know which file consolidation is optimum.

There was also, however, a question of optimal block size. This depends on the relation of acess time to transport speed and to record sizes as related to speed.

29.3 Effects of the Size of File Blocks (Physical Records).

To get a feeling for the effect of varying the block size we also study the different file configuration of Figs. 1 through 5 for the block size = 3.

Block size = 3

(Figure numbers refer to section 29.2)

Fig. 1	2 acc	5 trp		*Fig. 2*	1 acc	3 trp		*Fig. 3*	2 acc	6 trp
	3 ,,	9 ,,			2 ,,	6 ,,			2 ,,	6 ,,
	1 ,,	3 ,,			1 ,,	3 ,,			1 ,,	3 ,,
total	6 acc	18 trp		total	4 acc	12 trp		total	5 acc	15 trp

Fig. 4	2 acc	6 trp		*Fig. 5*	1 acc	3 trp
	2 ,,	6 ,,			1 ,,	3 ,,
	1 ,,	3 ,,			1 ,,	3 ,,
total	5 acc	15 trp		total	3 acc	9 trp

Thus:

Block size = 3 : optimum consolidation (Fig. 5) = 3 accesses, transp. = 9

Thus we obtain
optimum block size (of 1, 2 or 3):
Total time (for access plus transfer), block size = 1 : $(6+6\theta)a$
$\phantom{\text{Total time (for access plus transfer), block size =}}$ 2 : $(4+8\theta)a$
$\phantom{\text{Total time (for access plus transfer), block size =}}$ 3 : $(3+9\theta)a$

We know before that if $\theta < 1$ then block size 2 is better than 1.
We see at once that if $\theta = 0$ then block size 3 is better than 2.
At what θ-value are block sizes 2 and 3 equally good?

$$4+8\theta = 3+9\theta; \qquad \theta = 1$$

Thus, in this example, when $\theta = 1$, all three blocks give equal times, and at $\theta < 1$ block sizes 2 and 3 are better than block size 1. In other words: If $\theta < 1$ then the smallest block size is inferior. This suggests that if $\theta < 1$ the largest block size would be better. Can this suggestion be verified? At $\theta = 1$ all block sizes have equal time. If we reduce θ by some amount ε ($\varepsilon < \theta$) then θ is replaced by $\theta - \varepsilon$ and the time is reduced by 8ε for block size $= 2$ and by 9ε for block size $= 3$. Thus, block size $= 3$ is optimum if $\theta < 1$ and block size $= 1$ if $\theta > 1$.

Our study so far indicates that the smaller the transport time is in relation to access time, the larger the block size should be (if waiting time is used as the only criterion). Other criteria will then have to be considered such as that more memory space is consumed when larger file storage block sizes are used and CPU time (central processing unit) will be greater with larger block transfers. Much CPU time may also be required for each access operation (for file directory decoding). How does the optimum consolidation vary with block size?

In our example:

Block size	1	2	3
Optimum consolidation =	Fig 1 or 2	Fig. 2	Fig. 5

(figure numbers refer to section 29.2)

There is a slight hint here that larger block sizes lead to more consolidation as the optimum design. In general there still may be a choice between distinct configurations with, roughly, the same degree of consolidation.

At this stage of our broad study the question naturally arises as to whether or not in actual systems the value of θ will fall within an interval where it is useful to continue this kind of analysis. We know that if θ is near to 1 then further analysis may be useful whereas, for instance, if θ would be close to zero then one might, perhaps, just choose to use large blocks and far-reaching consolidation (if memory space and CPU-time for transfer can be disregarded). We have to add the remark here that rather than comparing *times* for access or transport respectively one would be interested in the associated *costs*.

For a first analysis we set the cost aspect aside and we look at the time effects only.

On the one extreme we have the case when the file is stored on equipment (e.g. core storage) which has the same access time as the memory of the computer. In this case access time tends towards zero and there is only transport time. This corresponds to $\theta \to \infty$ (θ tends to infinitely large values). This suggests, in combination with the results above, that for minimum total time one should have smallest possible block size and this then implies "no consolidation". This is in agreement with the fact that we only consider consolidating data terms into records when we are using file stores which, normally, have longer access times than the main memory.

Typical "direct access" file storages of today are magnetic discs or magnetic drums. Typical access time for discs is about 100 ms (milliseconds) and for drums about 20 ms. Typical transport speed is around 1.000 bits/ms. Thus, about 100.000 bits are transported in one disc access time and 10.000 in one drum access time. These large numbers would appear to indicate that records can be consolidated into size of 10.000 bits or more before concern about possible further consolidation is ever called for. One may ask: Will such large records ever occur, however deliberate we may be about consolidation? This possibility cannot be ruled out in advance. For instance personel records may run into that size, if totally consolidated.

In our example above we quite simply assumed the unit of transport time t to be chosen in such a way that $t=1$ for the transport of one "non-consolidated" record. It appears, so far as we know at present, that an elementary record will, typically, have a size of 100—1.000 bits. Of these, however, 50 or 100 bits are likely to belong to the "object identification terms" which are common to all elementary records that could normally be consolidated. Thus, it appears that, when files are on disc or drum, 20 or more elementary records may well be consolidated together before we need to be seriously concerned whether or no to consolidate further.

This somewhat surprising result suggests that one should look closer at some of the factors involved in the analysis which were estimated very roughly by us.

These are

1 the system studied had a special structure

2 the costs of memory space were neglected

3 the costs of access, versus that of transport, were ignored for instance access time versus CPU-loading

4 the advantage of the "best" design over the second best one may be so small that it is wise to disregard the difference, in view of the fact that many aspects are neglected in the analysis

5 the block size may have been decided upon other arguments or such arguments have to be balanced against those studied here.

If we look first at the system structure we see that always when a record has a succedent (i.e. procedure for which it is an input) in common with another file then an access time is saved if they are consolidated and then stored in one and the same block of file storage. On the other hand, as soon as there is a record which has a succedent which is not also a succedent of another record then the consolidation of them will cause a deadweight transport. If we have consolidated a larger number of records into A, Fig. 1, and if A and B have a process "a" as a common succedent and B has another succedent b which is not shared by A, then the consolidation $A \cup B$ saves one access time in the system but adds the dead-weight transport of A into "b". Our result above corresponds to the statement that if this transport is faster than one

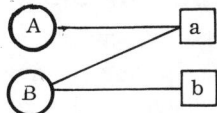

Fig. 1

access time, the consolidation is advantageous from a total access-time point-of-view. Obviously, the advantage of the consolidation becomes steadily smaller the more records we go on and consolidate into A.

We have learned from the last discussion that our tentative conclusion — from our calculations in connection with the simple case above, that as long as $\theta < 1$ one should go on and increase block sizes and consolidate records — was caused by the fact that all records in the system studied were linked together by having at least one succedent in common with another record. The conclusion that one shuld go on and consolidate up to 20 or more elementary records — if so many actually exist that are associated with the same object or key — is thus valid only to the extent that records — not yet consolidated with record A, for instance, (in the design process) — have at least one process as a succedent in common with the record A. It seems unlikely, however, that so many elementary records as 20 or more should be logically related in this way. It seems indeed more likely that the elementary records have distinct succedents, at least when these are elementary processes and this, in turn, is more likely when we design systems for direct-access processing, as process grouping is much less advantageous in such systems than in connection with serial access stores (e.g. tapes). Perhaps the records will be consolidated in groups of two to five elementary records, the groups being largely separated from each other. (This is one of the many subjects in data processing which still are in lack of empirical study.) We may conclude (although tentatively) that, when direct-access stores are used, file records will best be small, consisting of a few elementary records only. While it seems possible to reach some general arguments about how to design direct-access file systems, it has also become clear from our study that it may be necessary to study the consequences of the system structure in a systematic way in order to reach an efficient design. Thus, the structure matrices, P^{00} or E^{10}, for instance will be important design tools.

29.4 The Effect upon CPU-time.

The data transport from file store to memory takes time from CPU. In a time sharing or multiprogramming environment one, simply, cannot disregard this time even if the access-time would be longer than CPU time. CPU time used up in data transport has a cost. For each word of a file block transferred, one cycle time is taken away from CPU ("cycle stealing"). In addition there will be an overhead of CPU time for the administration of the interrupted signals associated with data transfer as well as with initialization and administration of block transfers. This is time spent by CPU in the executive program software. In addition the application program has to spend time in handling the file data and this, of course, comes as another overhead of CPU time spent on file transport handling. These often disregarded effects are strong enough to have caused many disappointments in connection with using "third-generation computers" for multi-programming or time sharing. In fact this time might well become the dominating factor.

Perhaps still more important may be that larger blocks occupy communication channels to file storage for longer time intervals thereby creating waiting queues before the channels and reducing the number of access operations that can be made to a storage unit in a unit of time.

29.5 Conclusion about File Consolidation and Choice of Block Sizes.

In addition to the discussion about choice of block size in connection with direct-access file storage system we also point to the well-known fact that in sequential file storage, e.g. magnetic tapes (as well as in direct-access storage) larger blocks mean fewer block gaps and, thus, reduced file volume.

We may conclude our discussion on this subject by presenting a few propositions. They are to be regarded as hypotheses which have support in the examples we have studied and also in some basic, theoretical facts. More study is needed to validate them more thoroughly as well as to develop more precise rules. They can be regarded as guiding rules for the designer of information systems. He should, however, validate for himself each application he makes of them.

PROPOSITION 1. Increasing the block size reduces the file volume and, thereby, tends to reduce file transport in sequential processes of sequentially organized files. (This holds for all types of file storage but may be most noticeable in tape storage.) Increasing block size on non-sequential files tends to reduce access work.

PROPOSITION 2. Consolidation of files tends to reduce access work or set-up work in all types of file storage. It tends to increase transport but in direct-access storage it may lead to reduced transport, to the extent that consolidation does not generate file records larger than the chosen block size.

PROPOSITION 3. The larger block size that is chosen, the greater impact will good file structuring have on file transport. In general larger block sizes tend to favor "larger consolidation".

29.6 Adaptation to Hardware System.

In designing the information system we have to consider limitations imposed by hardware design or hardware cost.

Thus for all practical considerations we can take as an axiom that standing files and transput files are stored in a type of storage which is much slower than the main memory of the computer. Therefore we say that the file data are transported to and from the main memory. In addition to this general property of auxiliary file storage we have to consider mainly two hardware limitations. The first is that limited memory space may make it uneconomic to group too many computations together, because all necessary programs cannot be kept in the main memory simultaneously. Therefore programs may have to be repeatedly transported to the memory. This may be a larger transport volume than the data transport it saves[1]). The second limitation is that the number of file storage (or data transport) units cannot be chosen large enough to transport all data sets separately. (This is predominantly a problem with magnetic tape files.) This limitation may again be a reason for not grouping some computations although this might have saved data transport. As an example note that comp (b) needs three input data sets and one output, i.e. it would need four transput units[2]). Instead it is seen from E^{10} [3]) that pr (b, i') needs three inputs and two outputs or five transput units in total. Alternatively the number of transput units needed may be reduced by consolidating several files into one file[4]), giving rise to deadweight data transport and extra runs for merging files.

Finally, it must be born in mind that using memory space to group computations and thereby reducing the number of file scans may necessitate shorter data blocks which will increase data transport by increasing the number of interrecord gaps which are also a source of deadweight transport.

---

[1]) See section 28.2.
[2]) See section 27.6—2.
[3]) See section 27.7—8.
[4]) See section 28.2.

The optimum design of the data structure for a system will have to consider all the above-mentioned effects upon data transport and try to minimize resulting total transport.

This problem is to establish different feasible solutions, by which will here be meant system layouts which are compatible with memory and transput equipment limitations, and to find one among these which corresponds to minimum transport, in other words to find an optimum solution. This is easily seen to be a complicated problem. The possibility that the computation program complications associated with grouping of computations may add one further difficulty makes the problem a very difficult one, indeed[5]).

We do not take up here the problem of constructing an efficient algorithm for finding an optimum solution. Instead we give some brief study to the much more modest problem of finding a feasible solution.

For purposes of simplification, we assume that first a system of grouping of computations has been selected. Thereafter we look for a way to define a consolidation of the files which will reduce the number of transport units to a prescribed value.

We now study the problem of finding a feasible solution by assuming that we have already decided on the grouping of computations of our previous example as given by E^{10} above[6]). We assume that we have to comply with the limitation of having only four transport units (in this specific example).

In trying to find a suitable file consolidation (or a feasible solution) we might start at the initial end (that process which involves files which have no precedents), that is with pr $(a, e')^2$. We may illustrate the consolidation construction by listing the input-output relations and then use parentheses to enclose consolidated sets.

Note that the consolidation will often itself require a separate process. Thus the transport increase caused by file consolidation will be greater than indicated by P^{00} or E^{10} only.

---

[5]) It is however, in general, easy to see ways for simplifying this problem in practical situations as the system naturally splits into subsystems such that only with a subsystem is file consolidation and process grouping relevant — at least as an approximation.

[6]) See section 27.7—8.

1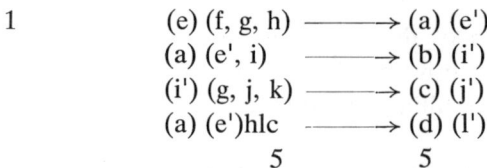

2 When considering which consolidation to choose for the first row in 1 (that is 1_1), we notice that a is much smaller than e'. Hence, since a is an output that may have to be printed in a separate process, it may be wise to keep a and e' separate. Similarly it may seem wise to keep "e" separate from f, g, h. This leaves the consolidation of (1_1) as shown[8]).

3 For (1_2) separation of b is natural for the same reason as given for a in (1_1).

4 Obvious arguments now lead to (1_3). When we come to (1_4) we see that no solution can be obtained in a straightforward way. We will be forced to go back and start all over again. It is obvious that we may have to iterate this scheme some times. In the vastly more complicated cases of real applications this may be a rather complex operation. In the normal way of handling this problem one will most often have done a lot of programming for the earlier procedures before one reaches a stage where it becomes clear that one will have to do the design job all over again.

5 Therefore in actual practice the manner of analyzing for feasible solutions using E^{10} or the graph may save man years of programming.

6 In most cases a more straightforward solution procedure may result if we start at the terminal sets rather than at the initial sets.

7 We therefore now try to start at the terminal end, i.e. at the process giving d.

8 First we do some simple calculations. We observe that "c" and "d" are passed five times in pr (d, l'). Hence it is reasonable to try to keep them separate from other files. This forces consolidation

---

[7]) Cf. section 25.1—32.
[8]) The assumptions we make here are somewhat typical but not generally justified. They could best be regarded as assumptions specified for the illustrating example being studied.

of input data such as "h" with standing files such as l and e (we assume all files to be updated in some process, that is e, i, j and l, and only those, are standing files). This means that for instance the operation pr (h) where copies of h from punched tape to h on magnetic tape (pr (h) : h → h) will have to be performed as pr (h) : h, l e → h, l, e thus causing two extra passes of l and e. h is used to denote the h-data when in punched form). This extra transport has a volume of 2(vol(l)+vol(e))=40. Instead if we would have to consolidate as much as a, f, g, h with e it means an extra transport of 5 (vol(a, f, g, h)=25 which is far better. On the other hand when punched data are read in, the accompanying file storage transports may be read without an effect on time. This is mostly true when data transport is either buffered or handled by time sharing. Therefore it may often be sufficient to consider the transports studied here. Data transport buffering or time sharing may often permit us to count only input transport. In the example below we have written the produced results above the arrows. Thus in (2_1) d, l' over the arrow indicate that in the output set d, a', e'', l' only d and l' are produced, a' and e'' being only copied, from a and e'.

9
$$(h, c) (a, e', l) \xrightarrow{d, l'} (d) (a', e'', l')$$
$$(i, g) (j, k) \xrightarrow{c, j'} (c) (j', k)$$
$$(a, e', l) (i', g) \xrightarrow{b, i'} (b) (i', g)^9$$
$$(a, e, l) i, g, h, f \xrightarrow{a, e'} (a, e', l)^{10}$$

10 Now we rearrange to original sequence and at the same time introduce the modifications made in files in later stages in all stages thus for instance f is to go with i, g, h in a, e', therefore also in b, i').

11
$$(e, l) (i, g, h, f) \xrightarrow{a, e'} (a, e', l'')$$
$$(a, e', l'') (i, g, h, f) \xrightarrow{b, i'} (i', g', h') (b)$$

---

[9]) g is introduced into both sides of 9_3 because it is required in pr (c, j) and we have already (in 9_2) consolidated it with i.
[10]) l is introduced into 9_4 in order to define at once the file (a, e', l) used in other processes.

$$(i', g', h') (j, k) \xrightarrow{c, j'} (h'', c) (j', k')$$
$$(h'', c) (a, e', l'') \xrightarrow{d, l'} (d) (e'', l')$$
$$5 \phantom{\xrightarrow{d, l'}} 5$$

In Fig. 1 the graph of the feasible solution 11 is shown.

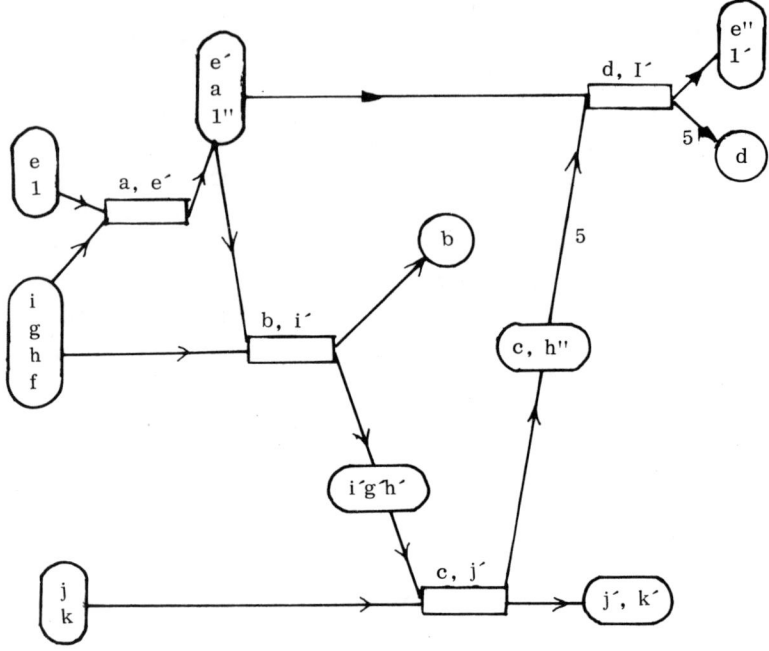

Fig. 1

12 During updating of a file we have now also cancelled such data which are not used any more. For instance "f" is not used after pr (a, e'), which can easily be seen in 9 because we underlined those data which are used in the process. Therefore when (i, g, h, f) is updated during pr (b, i') we leave f out. Here for instance the notation h' is used instead of h although h'=h here. This is necessary since h and h' occur in different files in the same program, and similarly for g', k', e'' and l'' in other files.

13 In order to estimate the quality of our solution we compare the resulting data transport volume with that of the system, section 27.7—8, without transport limitation and with the basic topological one as well as with the theoretical minimum.

408

	a	b	c	d	e	f	g	h	i	j	k	l
14 (from 27.7—8)	3	1	6	5	4	1	2	2	3	2	1	2
15 (from 11)	3	1	6	5	5	2	4	10	4	2	2	5
File transport volumes	1	1	2	1	10	2	1	1	10	20	2	10

16 System transport   (14) = 159 (processes grouped in pairs)
                              (15) = 223 (processes grouped in pairs and files consolidated)

17 Total file transport volume, counting old and updated files, is 111 which constitutes the theoretical minimum transport.

18 Thus in our example the excess transport because of limited process grouping is 48 or about 43 % of total file transport volume. The additional transport caused by limitation to four transport units is 64 or about 64 %.

19 We also compare our total transport volume with that associated with the basic topological scheme of section 27.6—2. Thereby we have to add four times vol (d) because in 27.6—2 we did not consider five scans of d at the output as we have done here. We therefore obtain the system transport = 249 for the basic system.

20 We have mentioned that whereas the grouping of some processes or computations into a larger process may reduce the volume of data input transport, this saving may be partly lost by the necessity of using shorter blocks. This may be necessary for storing all programs needed in the grouped computations.

21 In order to show that this is actually a problem worth considering when small memories are used, let us take up an example which, although much simplified, uses fairly realistic file volumes. In the above studies topological structures rather than numerical relations were of primary importance. Our following problem depends largely on size relations between input data, programs and memory space. In order to be of interest the example has to use fairly realistic values or relations.

22 **Example.**

We assume that we have two processes, pr(b, i') and pr(c, j'), and we want to see what can be saved by grouping them to one single process, pr(b, i', c, j'). Let us assume that the number of elementary input files is 10 for each of the processes, pr(b, i') and pr(c, j'). Further assume that the number of inputs to pr(b, i', c, j') is 15 rather than 20 so that grouping the two processes together saves a transport volume corresponding to scanning five elementary input files once.

23 We further assume that each record in an elementary file contains 30 characters (or an equivalent amount of information). This would mean that the total input set for one processing would be $10 \times 30 = 300$ characters for pr(b, i') or pr(c, j') and $15 \times 30 = 450$ caracters for pr(b, i', c, j'). This is seen to be fairly normal sizes. For each of the four computations (for b, i', c and j' respectively) there will be one program and in addition one program is needed for the overall organization. Let us assume 2000 characters for each program which means $5 \times 2000 = 10\,000$ for the grouped process, a normal figure.

24 We now assume that the elementary files are consolidated into three tape files with fiwe elementary files in each. We thus obtain three tape files, 1, 2 and 3, say. For pr(b, i') we read in 1 and 2, for pr(c, j') 2 and 3 and for pr(b, i', c, j') assuming three input units) 1, 2 and 3. Each consolidated file record will then contain 150 characters.

25 We also have to consider the inter-record gaps on the tapes and the memory size. We assume the inter-record gap to correspond to 150 characters and we assume the memory to be just sufficient to accept the grouped process pr(b, i', c, j').

26 Under these assumptions we must use tape blocks with only one record. Thus the block length will be 150 characters and the input size for each process step will be $3 \times 150 = 450$ characters for the three file records and in addition the same amount in record gaps will be transported. The resulting volume[11] is seen to correspond to 900 characters.

27 Now if we use the separate processes pr(b, i') and pr(c, j') each run has the extra available memory space of the programs for the two computations left out. Thus in addition to the earlier input data space

---

[11] Volume is here taken as the total number of characters, including gap space, that are needed for inputting one set of records (one record from each file) associated with the same value of the key.

of 450 characters we now get $2 \times 2000 = 4000$ characters. This leaves 4450 characters for two input blocks in each run. Hence we can use blocks of 2200 characters, say. In this case the interrecord gaps represent only about 7 % of the blocks. The volume of the input transport in this case will be 2 times that of the 300 characters for each run of pr(b, i') and pr(c, j') or 600 characters for computing one set of b, i', c and j', that is about 640 with allowance for gaps. Thus in our example the grouped process will lead to an increase in input volume from 640 to 900 rather than the saving which might have been expected.

28 It is also of interest to note that we have assumed three input tape units in the grouped process but only two in the separate processes. If we make the more "fair" assumption of permitting only two input tapes for the grouped process as well we may assume 225 characters per record in each file to obtain the same total of 450. Rather than increasing the volume this will reduce the volume because there will now be only two inter-record gaps (of 150 characters) against three gaps above. In this way the volume is reduced from 900 to 750. This is still a larger volume than the 640 needed for two separate processes.

29 It is easy to see that if the memory size would be increased say by the amount of 6000 characters, then the gaps would have negligible influence and the full saving of grouping the processes would be obtained.

30 It may be of interest to see what memory size corresponds to our assumptions. We had 5×2000 characters for program (including output data) and 450 characters for input data or 10450 characters in all but it is more common to have double the sizes for both total file volume and total program space, calling, of course, for twice the above memory size.

31 This example is another illustration of the fact that the design of the information handling system is inherently of an iterative character. Thus in a real situation similar to that of the example, we might have started with an assumed block length and on this basis have found it suitable to group the computations into one single process. After having done this we may find that we have to use a smaller block which then makes the grouping uneconomic and a new solution, with two separate processes, may instead have to be

chosen. It is also clearly exhibited by the example that a larger memory size not only increases computation speed and reduces file transport volume but also serves to reduce the systems design work, for instance, by removing the need for some iterations on the design structure.

32 Comparing Fig. 1 with Fig. 3, section 27.7, we find that Fig. 1, the system with consolidated files, looks nicer. It is analogous to the type of flow charts used commonly in data processing systems analysis, but contains, in addition, information about elementary files. It is important to note, however, that much of the information given in 27.7 or by E^{10} or P^{00} is lost in Fig. 1 and the corresponding precedence and incidence matrices. For instance it is not possible to see from Fig. 1 which information is actually used by a process. As in common flow charts also the information on elementary files is missing, such diagrams actually are very void of valuable information.

Chapter 10. System Design Computation Using Matrix Algebra.

210.1 Information System Design Computations[4]).

We have above[1]) discussed concepts associated with defining the needs for information within an organization. The set of all kinds of information needed, together with the interrelationships between them and the set of processes which "connect" them constitutes the "basic information system" for that organization. It was shown that the structure of this basic information system could be described by an "incidence matrix" E^{10} (see section 27.7), which has one row for each computation and one column for each elementary information set, or each "elementary file"[2]). E^{10} then gives information about the system, such as multiple file scan requirement, data origin, preceding and succeding processes etc. It was then shown how by grouping several elementary processes together into one composite process one could reduce the need for multiple input and output of files. It was also shown that such grouping of processes requires memory for storing the process programs. Hence memory space available had to be allocated to process grouping or other means for reducing total processing time had to be investigated. It was further shown that for different reasons, e.g. reduction of the number of tape handlers or better utilization of block space in mass memory, a consolidation of elementary files into composite ones has to be done. Such a consolidation may cause increased file input and output. A design problem for the information system was thus found to consist in finding a set of process groupings and file consolidation that would satisfy requirements of limited memory space and input-output units and would minimize "data transport" under these requirements. The grouping of processes was shown to correspond to joining the corresponding rows of the incidence matrix E^{10} in a certain way. We are going to show how this can be described as a generalized matrix operation.

We thereby use a way of defining a method for using generalized matrix operations introduced in "System Algebra"[3]).

---

[1]) See chapter 5, part 2.
[2]) See section 27.7.
[3]) See chapter 2, part 1.
[4]) The material in this Chapter was first published in 2 La 1965.

Similarly the consolidation of files is associated with joining columns of E^{10}. Again this can be done as a generalized matrix operation.

We also show that the changes (caused by process grouping or file consolidation) in data transport required by the structure of the information system, as defined by E^{10}, can be obtained by correlated matrix operations.

The matrix operations mentioned involve E^{10}, or the modified versions of it, which resulted through earlier operations, and also the vector defining file transport volumes as well as matrices which specify the process groupings and the file consolidations we wish to try out.

Any time that we have made a decision on how to group processes and consolidate files we can easily write down the matrices specifying this decision. Then a set of matrix routines will suffice for us to come to know what the resulting data transport and memory space will be. The matrix routines can easily be performed on a computer if a suitable generalized matrix program system is available. We have

thus achieved a convenient method for comparing different design alternatives. We still have the problem of choosing those design alternatives which we want to test. Because information systems commonly encountered contain hundreds of elementary files and processes, it appears that we are still left with a formidable task when we try to obtain a reasonable near-optimum design. We must limit the analysis to testing very few of the combinations possible. However, we often observe that information systems have many constraints which reduce very significantly both the number of processes or files that would profit from being joined with a specific process or file and the number of them that could be so joined without breaking system constraints. By carefully utilizing these system rationalization properties we can make the "manual" choice of design alternatives tractable. In that case the possibility to automatize the calculations made necessary by the matrix operations becomes a great advantage. Although we have no optimizing algorithm to offer at present, it is, of course, of great interest that our formalization of the design problem opens up the possibility of later automatization of the whole problem solution.

We give first a presentation of how rows and columns in E^{10} are to be joined in order to correspond to a grouping of processes (or consolidation of files, respectively) and how this can be done as generalized matrix operations. We then show how the number of feasible alternatives to try can be reduced and how this reduction can be made automatic as well.

210.2 Joining Rows in E^{10} to Represent Grouping of Processes.

Each row in the incidence matrix E^{10} (see, section 27.7) for an information system represents a process. Every element (column) in a row is associated with a specific file. If an element is equal to 1 this indicates that the corresponding file is required as an input to the process. If out of two processes to be grouped together either one or both has a 1 in a certain column, then the row of E^{10} for the system where these two processes have been grouped together is to have a 1 in that column position. Thus in combining rows of E^{10} to represent process grouping only such columns as have element values 0 or 1 obey the rules (which are of course well-known set operations)

1a $\quad 1 \cup 0 = 1$
1b $\quad 0 \cup 1 = 1$
1c $\quad 1 \cup 1 = 1$
1d $\quad 0 \cup 0 = 0$

However, some elements in a row E^{10} have a negative value. It is easy to see that if one row has -1 in a column position where the other row has 0 then the resulting row must have -1 in that column. When it happens that one row has -1 and the other row has 1, how should the combined row be formed then? In other words, what is the rule for determining the value of $-1 \cup 1$ in this problem type? Clearly, we have to distinguish between two different situations. If the file produced by the output operation indicated by -1 is only to be used with the process with which we are to group it, then obviously both the input indicated by 1 and the output indicated by -1 can be eliminated. Thus in this case we want to have $-1 \cup 1 = 0$. On the other hand, if the output file is also required for other purposes, then the output operation cannot be eliminated while still the input to the process to be joined is eliminated. In this situation we therefore shall have $-1 \cup 1 = -1$.

Normally it can be seen from E^{10} if a file which is output from one of the processes we consider for grouping is input also to processes

415

outside the group. This, simply, is then indicated by the existence of other 1-values in that column of E^{10}. (Note that several — 1-values cannot exist in one column of E^{10}) We can assume that when we order the joining of two rows of E^{10} according to our rules, as set out above which one of the alternatives to be used is uniquely defined within the system. Only if a file is to be output for use in other connections than as input to other processes represented in E^{10} then the operation will not be defined. Thus for a unique definition we require the E^{10} to contain all processes using any file indicated by — 1 in some row. This can be done by adding one row to E^{10} which represents "all other uses of files". The same effect can be obtained by tagging all files thus used. It follows that we can assume that all operations involved in this matrix operation, which have so far been discussed, can always be uniquely defined at the time of performing such operations. There remains the decision what to do in the cases when multiple input and output file scans are required by a process; for example when instead of 1 or — 1 we have k and — l, k and l being integers. It is reasonable to expect that if one process requires k input or output scans of a certain file and another process, to be grouped with the first one, requires l scans ($l<k$) then the grouped process requires k scans. However a combination of this kind is very strange and does not occur in normal systems. Therefore we find it most reasonable, at this stage not to require our procedure to handle such cases. If this is programmed for a computer the program will be supposed to print an alarm thus asking for a precise guidance on this point from the human analyst. (As we have seen we may come to use elements E^{10} which are different from 1 (and are not even integers) also when single scan operations are considered, in order to take care of different processing periods. In such cases we have, of course, to use the same logic as when only element values 1 or 0 occur. Again we have a reason to use some sort of tagging to be able to distinguish this case from multiple scan situations.)

Example.

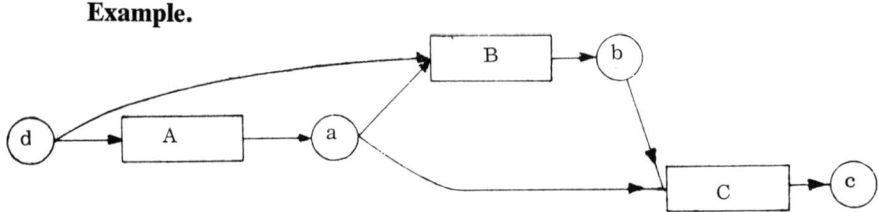

	files			
Processes	a	b	c	d
A	-1			1
B	1	-1		1
C	1	1	-1	

Total number of file scans: | 3 | 2 | 1 | 2 |

$A \cup B =$ | -1 | -1 | 0 | 1 | (this is the row for $A \cup B$ in the modified E^{10})

We have $(A \cup B)_a = -1 \cup 1 = -1$ because the grouped process $A \cup B$ needs to output a for use as input to C. Also $(A \cup B)_d = 1$ because d needs only to be input once to the combined process $A \cup B$.

$B \cup C =$ | 1 | 0 | -1 | 1 |

Here $(B \cup C)_2 = -1 \cup 1 = 0$ because when B and C are grouped the file b will not have to be output neither will it be input. If b would have to be used for other purposes than indicated in E^{10} this would have to be mentioned or tagged in some way. With the absence of such tagging, we will assume that no other use of b is called for.

210.3 Representing Process Grouping by a Generalized Matrix Operation.

We now introduce an operation ($\cup$) in such a way that it will lead to a modification of E^{10} as required by a specified grouping of processes. First we note that we want to operate on rows of E^{10} rather than on columns. We have to transpose so that we use E_T^{10}, instead of E^{10}, for the column selection procedure. Thus if "g" were a vector which selects those rows of E^{10} which we want to combine we shall obtain our desired result by the operation $E_T^{10}(\cup)g$. We shall find it convenient to write this instead as

1         $g_T(\cup)E^{10}$ (whereby the result comes out in transposed form)

which is common in matrix algebra. Thus if we write the selceting vector in transposed form to the left of a matrix we shall obtain a selection of rows, rather than columns.

As "g" selects rows associated with those processes which we want to group together, all elements of g will be 0 or 1. We shall take op_1 to be simple multiplication and thus after the operation op_1 we shall, in this case, have only the rows selected by unit elements in g. For op_2 we now take the operation $\cup$ as defined in section 210.2. As an example let us look at

$$g_T(\cup)E^{10} =$$

$$[011]\,(\cup)\,\begin{bmatrix} e_{11} & e_{12} \\ e_{21} & e_{22} \\ e_{31} & e_{32} \end{bmatrix} \to [e_{21}\ e_{22}] \cup [e_{31}\ e_{32}]$$

$$\to [e_{21} \cup e_{31},\ e_{22} \cup e_{32}]$$

Let us now do this operation on the example of section 2.
Suppose we want to group the processes A and B. This is defined by

$$g_T = [110]$$

	a	b	c	d			a	b	c	d
$g_T(\cup)E^{10} = A$	-1			1	$\cup$ B		1	-1		1

	a	b	c	d
$= A \cup B$	$-1 \cup 1$	-1		$1 \cup 1$

	a	b	c	d
$= A \cup B$	-1	-1	0	1

if we use the same procedure as in section 210.2 to define the result of $-1 \cup 1$. It is easy to see that the composition $B \cup C$ also is obtained as in section 210.2 by $g_T \cup E^{10}$.

210.4 Matrix Operations to Compute File Transport Reduction and Memory Space.

1 If we look at that part of two rows of E^{10} which contain only 0 or 1 (but not -1) then we find that the combination of rows, if done by $op_2 = \cap$ rather than $\cup$, ($\cap$ provides the intersection operation):

        1a $0 \cap 1 = 0$
        1b $1 \cap 0 = 0$
        1c $1 \cap 1 = 1$
        1d $0 \cap 0 = 0$

will result in a count of the file scans saved by grouping exactly two specific processes together. This fact suggests that "$\frown$" be used for an operation which gives the total, resulting saving of file scans if more than two processes are grouped and also when elements $=-1$ are contained in the rows (as is always the case, of course).

2 We find that we have to put

$$x_1 \frown x_2 \frown x_3 \ldots x_n = k - 1$$

if exactly k of the x_i's have value 1,
the others being $= 0$.

If one of the values in a column, among the rows to be combined, is -1 (there can only be one) then the result is well defined by the specification given in section 210.2.
Thus if in the sequence

3 $x_1 \frown x_2 \frown \ldots x_n$ one $x_i = -1$ and only one x_j ($j \neq i$) has value 1, all others being 0, then $x_1 \frown x_2 \frown \ldots x_n = 2$ if no other uses of file x are indicated (for both an output corresponding to -1 and an input corresponding to 1 are eliminated).

4 If $x_i = -1$ and k of the other x_j-values $= 1$ then we shall have $x_1 \frown x_2 \frown \ldots x_n = k+1$, if again no other uses of x are indicated. If the file x is also used in processes not covered by $x_1, x_2, \ldots x_n$, (that is if also other rows of E^{10} have a non-zero element in this column) then the saving is $= k$.

We find that if we define $g_T(\frown)E^{10}$ in a way that is analogous to the definition above for $g_T(\smile)E^{10}$, the only difference being $op_2 = \frown$ (as defined here instead of $op_2 = \smile$ as defined earlier) then $g_T(\frown)E^{10}$ will result in a row vector having an element for each file, showing the number of scans of that file that are saved by grouping the processes represented by unit elements in g.

Of course the number of scans saved can also be obtained by simply adding the absolute values of all elements in each column of E^{10} and doing the same for E^{10} of the grouped system, and then compute the difference between the vectors thus obtained, i.e.

$$1^T \cdot |E^{10}| - 1^T \cdot |E_g^{10}|$$

where $|E^{10}|$ is obtained from E^{10} by taking the absolute value of every element in E^{10}

and Eg^{10} is the incidence-matrix for the grouped system.

Example. If we take the example of section 210.2 and consider grouping the processes A and B we have

$$A_a \cap B_a = -1 \cap 1 = 1 \text{ (as file a has to be output (in } A_a\text{)}$$
because it is needed also in the process C.)

$$A_b \cap B_b = 0 \cap -1 = 0$$
$$A_c \cap B_c = 0 \cap 0 = 0$$
$$A_d \cap B_d = 1 \cap 1 = 1$$

hence $g_T(\cap)E^{10} =$

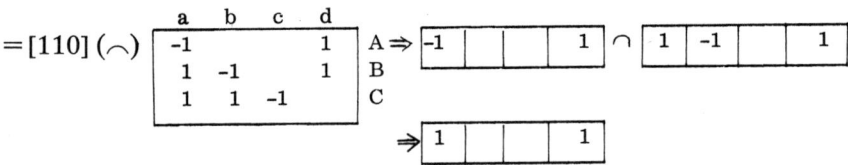

If instead we would group B and C we would have, for instance,

$$B_b \cap C_b = -1 \cap 1 = 2 \text{ (rather than 1)}$$

because b is not used elsewhere (hence both the input and output file scans are saved).

We have now defined the operations $g_T(\cup)E^{10}$ and $g_T(\cap)E^{10}$ and know that both result in one single row. It is easy to see that g can be obtained by forming the "logical sum" of those columns of the unit matrix I associated with the row numbers of E^{10} selected by g_T. It follows that if G is the matrix obtained from I by joining the rows in groups as selected by different g_T and for different, simultaneous groupings of process leaving the remainder of I unchanged, then

5      $G(\cup)E^{10} \to E^{10}$ for the modified system $\to Eg^{10}$

The row vector s obtained by the operation $s = g_T(\cap)E^{10}$ defines the multiplicity of scans saved for each file by the grouping g. Hence if

6          $v = [v_i], i = 1, 2, \ldots n$

is a vector of which element v_i is measure of the file transport volume for the file i, then the product

7          $s \cdot v = \sum\limits_{1}^{n} s_i v_i$

gives a measure of the total transport saving obtained by the process grouping defined by g.

8 **Remark.** Of course often it will be the case that a choice between several alternative processes it will be based on the effect of logical conditions upon certain values in an incoming transaction record. Then one may replace some units in matrix G above, by decision tables defining the conditions[1]).

9 **Example.** We take the same system as in the example of sections 210.2 and 210.5 and add one row to E^{10}, labelling it "D" and also add column d^1. We consider grouping (A and B) and also (C and D).

$$Eg^{10} = G(\cup)E^{10} = \begin{array}{c} \\ \end{array} \begin{array}{|cccc|} \hline A & B & C & D \\ \hline 1 & 1 & & \\ & & 1 & 1 \\ \hline \end{array} \ (\cup) \ \begin{array}{|cccc|c|} \hline a & b & c & d & d^1 \\ \hline -1 & & & 1 & \\ 1 & -1 & & 1 & \\ 1 & 1 & -1 & & \\ & & 1 & & -1 \\ \hline \end{array} \begin{array}{c} A \\ B \\ C \\ D \end{array}$$

or

$$Eg^{10} = \begin{array}{|ccccc|c|} \hline a & b & c & d & d^1 & \\ \hline -1 & -1 & 0 & 1 & 0 & A \cup B \\ 1 & 1 & 0 & 0 & -1 & C \cup D \\ \hline \end{array}$$

The multiplicity of file scans is given by

$$\mu^T = \begin{array}{|ccccc|} \hline a & b & c & d & d^1 \\ \hline 3 & 2 & 2 & 2 & 1 \\ \hline \end{array} \ \text{for the original } E^{10}$$

and

$$\mu_g^T = \begin{array}{|ccccc|} \hline 2 & 2 & 0 & 1 & 1 \\ \hline \end{array} \ \text{for the grouped system } Eg^{10}$$

---

[1]) Cf. 2 Sö 1968.

Let the file transport volumes be given by

$$v^T = \boxed{\begin{array}{ccccc} 1 & 2 & 3 & 4 & 1 \end{array}}$$

Then the system transport is

and
$$trp = 1 \cdot 3 + 2 \cdot 2 + 3 \cdot 2 + 4 \cdot 2 + 1 \cdot 1 = 22 \text{ for } E^{10}$$
$$trp_g = 1 \cdot 2 + 2 \cdot 2 + 3 \cdot 0 + 4 \cdot 1 + 1 \cdot 1 = 11 \text{ for } E_g^{10}$$

As an illustration let us draw diagrams showing the original system S (with E^{10}) and the modified system S_g (with E_g^{10}).

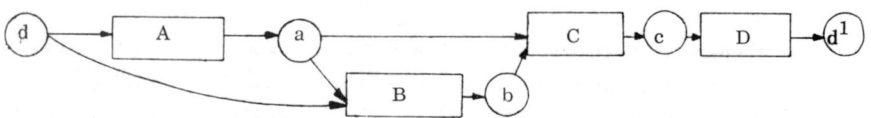

Fig. 1 System S.

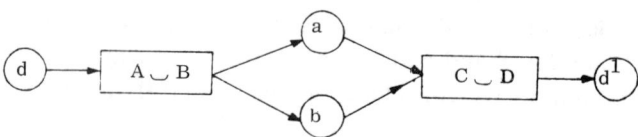

Fig. 2 System S_g.

It is seen from the results above that we saved a total of $22 - 11 = 11$ in system transport. We now compute this by the operation $g_T(\frown)E^{10}$. We have two groupings g_{T1} and g_{T2}

$$s_1 = g_{T1}(\frown)E^{10} = \begin{array}{|cccc|} \hline A & B & C & D \\ 1 & 1 & & \\ \hline \end{array} (\frown)E^{10}$$

$$s_2 = g_{T2}(\frown)E^{10} = \begin{array}{|cccc|} \hline & & 1 & 1 \\ \hline \end{array} (\frown)E^{10}$$

We get

$$s_1 = g_{T1}(\frown)E^{10} = \begin{array}{|ccccc|} \hline a & b & c & d & d^1 \\ 1 & & & 1 & \\ \hline \end{array}$$

$$s_2 = g_{T2}(\frown)E^{10} = \begin{array}{|ccccc|} \hline & & 2 & & \\ \hline \end{array}$$

The resulting saving is defined by the vector

$$s = s_1 + s_2 = \begin{array}{|ccccc|} \hline a & b & c & d & d^1 \\ 1 & & 2 & 1 & \\ \hline \end{array}$$

Hence, the total saving is

$$s \cdot v = 1 \cdot 1 + 2 \cdot 0 + 3 \cdot 2 + 4 \cdot 1 = 11$$

in agreement with the result above.

The grouping of processes does not only bring reduction of file scans. It also brings about increased memory requirement. This is because when several processes are to be performed in the same file scan the programs are in memory at the same time. The increased memory can be regarded as the price paid for reduced file scan multiplicity. This price could possibly buy other advantages, so the alternatives need separate analysis. It is thus seen that we want to be able to compute also the memory requirement induced by the grouping of processes. We assume here that we have solved the ("component") problem of determining the memory need for each simple process and we ask how this information can be used to compute the memory need of the grouped process (that is 'to solve the "systems problem").

As a very crude, first approximation one can assume that the memory space requirement for a grouped process can be represented as one space common to the whole group plus one additional space quantity for each simple process in the group. If then

$$m = [m_i]$$

is a vector (for the original system) such that m_i = the additional memory need for the simple process "i" then the corresponding vector for the system modified by the grouping of processes defined by G is obtained as

10    $$m_g = Gm$$

where conventional matrix multiplication is used.

In realistic situations the resulting memory need for a grouped process is somewhat more complicated but it can be defined in terms of G and a set of vectors $m^1, m^2, \ldots$

Then

11 $\quad m_g^1, m_g^2, \ldots$

are defined by G and m^1, m^2, ... by different kinds of generalized matrix multiplications. We do not take up this any further here as in most design situations we do not know more than could be represented by one vector. In fact, today not even that is known and our opinion differs from what seems to be the most widespread one today already in that we insist on defining at least one vector m before any design work is attempted at all.

210.5 Calculations for Minimum File Transport Design.

1 Up till now we have established a complete formalization (and hence made possible automatization) of computing of transport saving — or resulting transport amount — for any specified process grouping (if the number of multiple file scans of a process are defined). Thus if we have chosen a set of feasible (that is complying with memory space limitation, process ordering, and file sorting) process groupings and defined them by $g_1, g_2, \ldots g_l$, then G is defined and we can produce the modified system incidence matrix E_g^{10} (provided E^{10} is defined). If multiple file scan processes are to be involved in the grouping we also must have provided specifications for how the grouping influences them. We can then compute the system transport.

2 For the original system we get

$$\mathrm{trp} = 1^T \cdot |E^{10}| \cdot v$$

where $|E^{10}|$ is obtained from E^{10} by taking the absolute value of every element in E^{10} (if $d_{ij} \in |E^{10}|$ and $e_{ij} \in E^{10}$ then $d_{ij} = |e_{ij}|$

and 1^T is a transposed column-vector consisting of elements 1 only and for the grouped system we get

$$\mathrm{trp}_g = 1^T \cdot |E_g^{10}| \cdot v$$
where $E_g^{10} = G(\smile)E^{10}$

and finally compute the resulting saving,

$$\mathrm{trp} - \mathrm{trp}_g.$$

3 Hence we find the transport saving

$$(\underset{i}{\Sigma} g_i{}^T(\frown)E^{10}) \cdot v.$$

Thus if we perform this calculation for a set of different grouping designs, we can select as the best one that which makes

4 $\qquad (1_T \cdot G(\smile)E^{10})$ min.

or

5 $\qquad (\Sigma g_i{}^T(\frown)E^{10})$ max.

while g_i (or G) are such as to satisfy the constraint

6 $\qquad (G \cdot m)_i$ not greater than available memory space, for any i.

In order to develop this procedure into a fully automatic routine we still have to establish an algorithm for selecting the set of different groupings to be tested. In general such a procedure will have to find ways of eliminating most of the possible combinations as it is often impossible even for a fast computer to test all combinations. It appears that in many practical systems the number of feasible groupings is fairly small, although the total number of files and processes in the "un-grouped" system may be very large. A formalization of the selection of feasible groupings (that is groupings satisfying certain conditions of order, which the relations defined by E^{10} prescribe) may be in some cases adequately reduce the number of combinations enough to make possible a complete analysis of all of them. In such cases, then, we would have achieved a fully automatic solution of this design problem. For more complex systems, such full automatization may not be reached. Then such a procedure would still be useful, for it will reduce the amount of intuitive — or empirical — choice of the different designs to be tested. It also seems feasible to use a procedure where a set of random selections of the set of feasible groupings is made and then tested to define the best of them which, while not exactly optimal, may well be a better solution than would be obtained from a few intuitive choices.

We conclude this section by pointing out that for the design problem of minimizing process groupings we are by the present results in a situation which is very similar to what we have in many engineering problems; where a fully automatic design procedure is not yet available but computers can be of great help in reducing design analysis work and improving design quality.

We also point out, however, that in a real information system design we have to undertake a second kind of system modification since not only do we want to group processes in order to save file transport but also we want to consolidate files in order to keep input-output equipment within reasonable bounds. This problem will be studied below in section 210.7.

Notice that the arithmetic rules involved in operations upon E^{10} are of a special kind, especially with respect to negative elements of E^{10}. Cf. section 210.2 and also section 210.3.

210.6 Procedures for Aiding the Intuitive System Design Phases.

We have already made clear that we are not trying to obtain fully automated design of an information system in this book. Rather we are satisfied with obtaining a formalization which helps intuitive design in different ways[1]). One way it helps is by making possible automatic computer analysis of design alternatives. Another way would be to help in selecting different groups of processes which are worth considering for finding the design alternatives to test. In small systems, such as we may use as illustrations in a book like this — and in educational exercises — it may be easy to see directly which choices are worth trying, by looking at the graph or the incidence matrix E^{10} of the system. A real system will, in general, be much too big for this to be a feasible procedure. In such a situation it will be of great value to have a computer for help.

In section 210.5 we have already seen how by a calculation we can show whether or not a certain process "i" would be worth combining with another one, "j", in order to reduce file transport. Thus we found that if g_{ij} is the grouping vector defining the grouping of the processes "i" and "j" then

---

[1]) The usefulness of the formal analysis and the concepts introduced in this book have been demonstrated not only by applications in "manual systems design work" and computer-aided design work (cf. 2 Sc 1971). Even a totally automated "optimum design system" has been implemented, although resistricted to "linear files" (cf. 2 Nu 1971).
(Footnote added in the 1971 edition.)

$$(g_{ij} \,(\frown)\, E^{10}) \cdot v \quad (v = \text{file transport volume vector})^{2)}$$

would measure the transport saved. By letting j run through all values we will obtain a measure of the value of combining any process "j" with a certain process "i". In this way we obtain not only an indication of which processes are worth combining with any specific process, but also a possibility for comparison of the gain from any such pairing. While it is still quite a problem to establish algorithms for using this kind of information for optimization, it is obvious that this information, itself, will be a valuable aid for the human being who has to make the design.

We can display the result of the analysis described in the preceding paragraph in a matrix where we have one column and one row for each process and where each element in a column measures the transport saved by grouping the process for the column with that associated with the row position of the element. The procedure described will reduce the problem of choice for the system design to an extent which is dependent on the topological properties of the basic information system (or of E^{10}).

We now turn to another procedure for further reduction of the selected problem. The reduction is performed in order to simplify design analysis but also to determine which conditions must be satisfied in order that two processes may at all be grouped together. Such conditions can easily be seen to be associated with the ordering structure imposed upon the information system by the information precedence relations discussed in section 27.6—27.15. This precedence matrix should be sufficient for testing this condition.

1 If process "j" is a precedent to process "i" but is not an immediate (or 1st) precedent, then "i" and "j" cannot be grouped. If a process "k" is a 1st precedent of "i" (that is, $k \ll i$), this means that a file that is an output from "k" will be an input to "i". This, of course, is no hindrance for "k" to be grouped with "i". If however $j \ll k$ and $k \ll i$ then "j" is a 2nd precedent of "i". In this case "j" cannot be grouped with "i", for "i" cannot be run before "k" has been performed. Obviously it is impossible to group "i" and "j"

---

[2]) Notice the special rules for matrix algebraic operations involving E^{10} defined above.

if "j" is an n:th precedent of "i" (that is $j < i$ for any n-value greater than 1). We thus have the condition described in section 27.15 "the restriction rule for grouping".

2 Condition: Two processes "i" and "j" cannot be grouped together if "j" has a precedence relation with "i" which is of higher order than the 1st.

Notice that it may happen that j is simultaneously i 1st precedent and a higher order precedent. For instance the set

3
$$j \ll k$$
$$k \ll i$$
$$j \ll f$$

has the structure

$$j \rightarrow k \rightarrow i$$

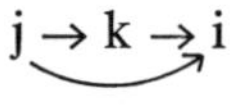

Fig. 1

which is quite feasible. In this case "j" has precedence relations with "i" of both 1st and 2nd order and, hence, the condition for not being groupable is fulfilled for the process pair i and j in this example.

4 Obviously, if the condition above is not satisfied, then "i" and "j" can be grouped, that is "i" and "j" can be grouped if no higher order precedence relation holds between "i" and "j".

It follows that we can test whether or not two processes "i" and "j" are "groupable" by computing the total precedence sets of both.

The set of all precedents of a file can be computed from the precedence matrix P^{00} or the incidence matrix E^{10} by search algorithms which search through the matrices[3]) like a person scans the corresponding network. It can also be computed by applying system algebra upon P^{00}. (This may be slower on a computer but can use "standard" system algebra software.)

---

[3]) Cf. 1 La 1961 and 2 Bg 1966 or 2 Nu 1971. Cf. also 2 Te 1969.

If P is the precedence matrix for the files in the system, then each column in P is associated with a file which is output from one process. Each row of P is associated with files which are input to a process. Hence each column in P is associated with a process and selects files which are immediate precedents of the column file. The processes which are 1st precedents of the process of that column are indicated. This is because each output file is produced by exactly one process.

5   It is easy to show[4]) that the squared (or "iterated") matrix $P \cdot P = P^2$ selects files which are 2nd precedents of the files associated with its respective columns. P^3 likewise selects 3rd precedents and so on. It follows that if the file produced by the process "j" (let us call it the file "j") is not selected by the ith column of P^2, P^3, ..., and vice versa, then "i" and "j" may be grouped. It can also be shown that for a certain value of the integer "l" $P^l \neq 0$ while $P^{l+k} = 0$ for any positive integer k. l is a topological constant for every feasible system. Thus we need only perform a limited number of matrix iterations (or equivalent procedures).

It is also easy to show that P can be computed from E^{10}. Let E^{10} be the matrix obtained from E^{10} by replacing all positive entries by 1 and all negative ones by -1. Then obviously we can write E^{10} as a difference of two matrices which have all their elements either equal to 1 or to 0.

6          $E^{10} = P_T{}^{01} - P^{10}$

where P^{10} is a matrix which for each file has a column which selects the processes contributing to its production (that is the processes preceding the file) and P^{01} has a column for each process, selecting the files preceding it (the input files of the process).

We have (see chapter 2, part 1)

7          $P = P^{00} = P^{01} \cdot P^{10}$.

This is easily seen because the ith column $P_i{}^{10}$ of P^{10} selects, by its elements, the processes contributing to "i", and in $P^{01} \cdot P^{10}$ these

---

[4]) Cf. chapter 2, part 1.

elements then select the columns of P^{01} associated with these processes. Finally these columns select the files which are inputs to the processes contributing to "i" and which are 1st precedents of "i". If all the files are elementary, then each file is produced by one single process only and each column in P^{10} selects one column only of P^{01}. During the design process, however, we group processes and consolidate files. (It is, of course, also easy to compute P^{00} from E^{10}, element by element as each element in E^{10} defines one precedence relation.)

Example. We take E^{10} of the example in section 210.4—9 and apply 6, that is we take all negative elements in E^{10} and move them to a second matrix:

$$E^{10} = P_T^{01} - P^{10} = \begin{array}{c|cccc} & a & b & c & d & d^1 \\ \hline A & & & & 1 & \\ B & 1 & & & 1 & \\ C & 1 & 1 & & & \\ D & 1 & & 1 & & \end{array} \quad - \quad \begin{array}{cccc} a & b & c & d & d^1 \\ \hline 1 & & & & \\ & 1 & & & \\ & & 1 & & \\ & & & & 1 \end{array}$$

We then obtain P by 7:

$$P = P^{00} = P^{01} \cdot P^{10} = \begin{array}{c|ccccc} & a & b & c & d & d^1 \\ \hline a & & 1 & 1 & & \\ b & & 1 & & & \\ c & & & & 1 & \\ d & 1 & 1 & & & \\ d^1 & & & & & \end{array} \quad ; (P^{00})^2 = \begin{array}{ccccc} a & b & c & d & d^1 \\ \hline & & & 1 & 1 \\ & & & & 1 \\ & & & & \\ & 1 & 1 & & \\ & & & & \end{array}$$

$$(P^{00})^3 = \begin{array}{c|ccccc} & a & b & c & d & d^1 \\ \hline a & & & & & 1 \\ b & & & & & \\ c & & & & & \\ d & & 1 & 1 & & \\ d^1 & & & & & \end{array} \quad ; (P^{00})^4 = \begin{array}{ccccc} a & b & c & d & d^1 \\ \hline & & & & \\ & & & & \\ & & & & \\ & & & & 1 \\ & & & & \end{array}$$

$(P^{00})^5 = 0;$

P can be checked against Fig. 1 of section 210.4. We now obtain by inspection of the columns of $(P^{00})^2$, $(P^{00})^3$, and $(P^{00})^4$ that for instance the c-column of these matrices select (a, d); d; Ø; respectively, that is "a" and "d". From E^{10} it is seen that c is produced by C, a by A, and d by no process. Consequently we have established that A and C cannot be grouped. In this way we find:

A cannot be grouped with C, D,
B — — — — D,
C — — — — A,
D — — — — B, A,

The result has been displayed in the matrix M below by shading all boxes corresponding to non-feasible groupings.

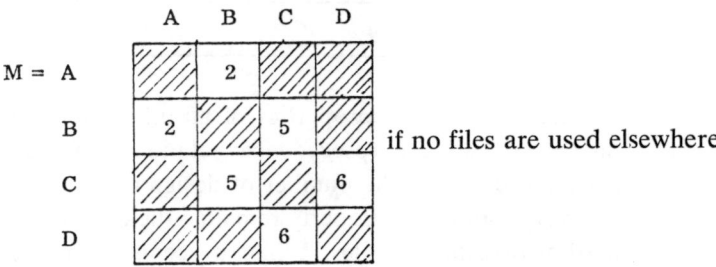

if no files are used elsewhere

In the boxes left open we have inserted the transport savings associated with the corresponding groupings. The ordering condition 2 is seen to have brought quite a reduction of the possibilities to be tested. On the other hand the calculation of transport quantities did not, in this example, bring any reduction as all the feasible combinations save some transport so that there is no one which is not worth-while. On the other hand the different amounts of saving to be achieved by the different pairings is of course information which can be used to guide the design.

It is easy to give an of a system in which the transport quantities would serve to reduce the number of groupings worth testing. Thus if we add to the system a process E, the output file of which is an input to process D, then we have

$$E \not< A$$
$$E \not< B$$
$$E \not< C$$
$$E \ll D$$

and hence E may be grouped with anyone of all the other processes. On the other hand only the grouping with D will save any transport.

If the file produced by E has a transport volume equal to 1 the saving to be obtained by grouping E with D would be 2. For this system we would have modified the M matrix to

	A	B	C	D	E
A		2			0
B	2		5		0
C		5		6	0
D			6		2
E	0	0	0	2	

In addition to those properties of an information system, which we have used so far (precedence relations and possible transport savings) to reduce the number of design configurations to be tested, one very significant property remains; the different sorting sequences used with different files. While it seems desirable that the design analysis should also contribute to an efficient solution of that problem and therefore the sorting strategy should be regarded as not fixed during the analysis, it appears to be most realistic at the present state of the art to regard file sequence to have been specified before the analysis starts. In that situation the sorting sequence of the different files will define also a partitioning of the set of processes into one subset for each set of file sequences. In other words, if a set of files a, b, c, d, e is such that a, b, and c have one file sequence (that i are sorted to the same key) and d and e have another sequence, then any process associated with any of the files a, b, and c cannot possibly be grouped with a process associated with d or e. In most practical systems this sorting condition will bring about a very significant subdivision of the system into much smaller subsystems, such that processes from distinct subsystems cannot be grouped because they handle files which have different sorting sequence.

It may be of interest to those familiar with abstract algebra that the property of having the same sorting sequence satisfies the axioms of an equivalence relation. From this follows that only processes belonging to the same equivalence class may be grouped. The problem of defining this partitioning of the set S of all processes then is the problem of defining the quotient set S/M, if M is a subset of S which defines all sorting sequences.

210.7 Defining File Consolidation by Matrix Operation on E^{10}.

As has been discussed before one of the basic problems in information processing system design is to consolidate the small elementary files into larger and fewer ones. This is necessary in order to keep input-output requirements within economic bounds, e.g. the number of tape handlers. If a direct access mass storage is used, this may not be a problem. Then instead we have block size built into the equipment. We may also have to make a combined design by using both kinds of storage. Thus the problem of efficient file consolidations is a problem of general importance for the information system design, whether it is built upon serial access memories, direct access memories, or both.

1 If two files, a and b for instance, are consolidated into one, then this consolidated file will have to be input to every process where either a or b are needed for input. Thus the corresponding combination of the columns a and b of E^{10} will result by the common union operation $1 \cup 0 = 1$, $0 \cup 1 = 1$, $1 \cup 1 = 1$, and $0 \cup 0 = 0$ for such parts of columns a and b which have elements equal to 0 or 1 only. Such elements which have value $= k$ ($k > 1$) will be supposed to obtain special treatment in analogy with section 210.4. The consolidated file will have to be output in one version from the process producing a and then in another version from the process producing b. In addition to this (if it is not a standing file) it may have to be input to that one of these processes which will be performed subsequent to the other one. (Notice that this may increase the demand for input equipment for that process and, hence, often may call for a further consolidation, which is then to be performed with another input for that process.) It must be recognized, however, that when the combined file is output from the first of the two processes, it does not yet have its final form and it must be given an identifier of its own.

For instance, let us assume that we have a system as shown in Fig. 1.

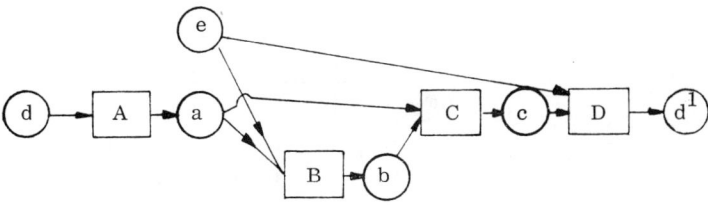

Fig. 1

We now want to see what happens if we decide to consolidate e with a, forming (ae). We assume that e is new information entering the system, d may either be new information or a standing file which is called "a" when updated. To consolidate, we may either have to insert an additional process a, e → (a, e) or we take e as an input to A. We decide to choose the latter alternative. Fig. 2 shows the modified system.

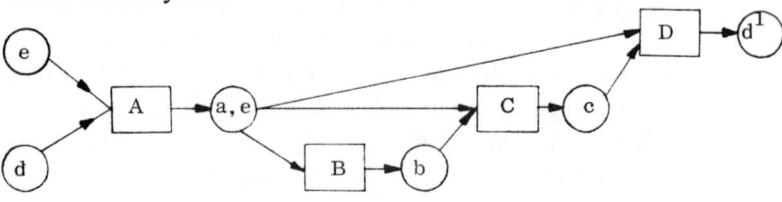

Fig. 2

If instead e and a would both be standing files, we would obtain the system of Fig. 3, and when a and e are consolidated Fig. 4 is the result.

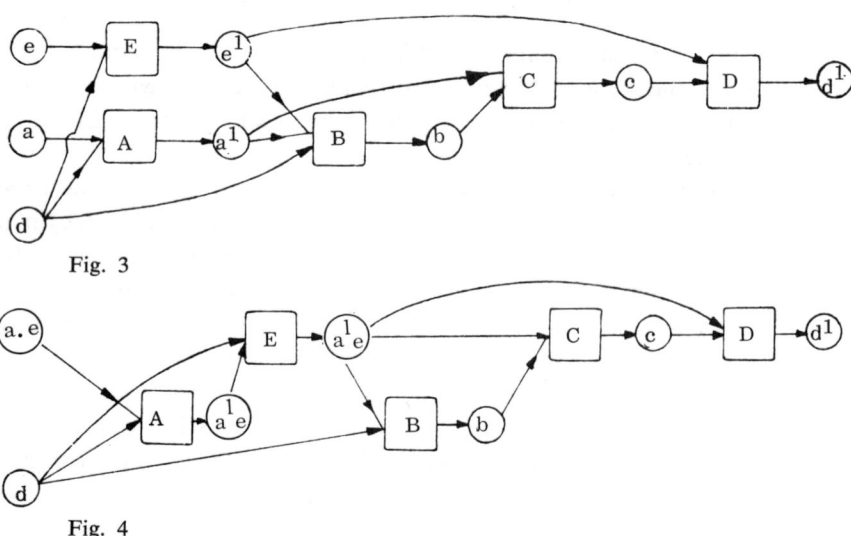

Fig. 3

Fig. 4

The incidence matrices corresponding to Fig. 1 and 2 are

		a	b	c	d	e	d¹
$E^{10} =$	A	-1			1		
	B	1	-1			1	
	C	1	1	-1			
	D			1		1	-1

and

2

$$E_c^{10} = \begin{array}{c|cccccc} & ae & b & c & d & e & d^1 \\ \hline A & -1 & & & 1 & 1 & \\ B & 1 & -1 & & & & \\ C & 1 & 1 & -1 & & & \\ D & 1 & & 1 & & & -1 \end{array}$$

It is seen that column (ae) in E_c^{10} is obtained as $e \cup a$ (from E^{10}) and that in addition a new column for e is introduced. This column simply assigns e to be input to that process which outputs the file with which e is to be consolidated. For the systems of Figs. 3 and 4 we obtain the following incidence matrices

3

$$E^{10} = \begin{array}{c|cccccccc} & a & b & c & d & d^1 & e & a^1 & e^1 \\ \hline A & 1 & & & 1 & & & -1 & \\ B & & -1 & & 1 & & & 1 & 1 \\ C & & 1 & -1 & & & & 1 & \\ D & & & 1 & & -1 & & & 1 \\ E & & & & 1 & & 1 & & -1 \end{array}$$

4

$$E_c^{10} = \begin{array}{c|ccccccc} & ae & b & c & d & d^1 & a^1e & a^1e^1 \\ \hline A & 1 & & & 1 & & -1 & \\ B & & -1 & & 1 & & 1 & 1 \\ C & & 1 & -1 & & & 1 & \\ D & & & 1 & & -1 & & 1 \\ E & & & & 1 & & 1 & -1 \end{array}$$

On comparing these two matrices we find some rules for constructing columns in E_c^{10} from those of E^{10} in accordance with a prescribed consolidation of two standing files. These rules are obviously of general validity. We see that the consolidated file (ae in this case) simply takes the place of that one of the original files which is chosen as the first one to be updated.

In the example this means that column ae of E_c^{10} is put equal to column a of E^{10}, corresponding to taking ae in place of a as input to A. Then the "half-updated" file a^1e is uniquely determined by its simple role of being output from one of the two updating processes and input to the other. Finally the fully updated file a^1e^1 gets its column by forming $a^1 \cup e^1$ with the modification that the process updating the first component of the consolidated file is not outputting the fully updated file. Thus in the example the -1 for process A in $a^1 \cup e^1$ has to be deleted. (Notice that this is a general rule for updating consolidated, standing files.)

We can describe the process of "consolidating" the "file columns" of E^{10} in a somewhat different way which better exhibits its close relation to the joint operation $\cup$. Thus, to form E_c^{10} which is to be obtained from E^{10} by consolidating two standing files a and e (for instance), we replace a^1 and e^1 with $a^1 \cup e^1$. (Here upper 1 denotes an updated version.) Let a be the name of that file which is first updated. Then in E^{10} replace the column name a by ae and replace the name e by a^1e. Finally move the — 1 which stands in the row of the first updating process (process a — or A in this case) from column a^1e^1 to column a^1e.

We can now conclude that by a somewhat specialized definition of the operation $(\cup)$ we can compute E_c^{10} from E^{10} by

$$E_c^{10} = E^{10} (\cup) C$$

C = a matrix which specifies the file consolidations considered.

The consolidation matrix C (or rather its transpose C_T) is defined in analogy with the definition of the grouping matrix G introduced before.

The incidence matrix for a system design after one or more operations of grouping and consolidation will be obtained as

$$E_{gc}^{10} = G (\cup) E^{10} (\cup) C$$

with the provision that the operations $(\cup)$ and $(\cup)$ have some different special features.

While the search for the best grouping (for a certain stage of consolidation of files) considers the maximization of transport reduction (plus maximization or "satisfaction" of file consolidation) any file consolidation tried has to be tested for maximum reduction of I/O equipment (plus minimization of transport increase).

Thus a procedure for aiding design in this stage would compute equipment reduction. This is easily seen to be obtained from the maximum value of the row-sums of $E_c^{10} = E^{10} (\cup) C$, counting all elements in E_c^{10} as units or zeros. Assistance in selecting candidate groups of files to be tested for possible consolidation can also be obtained from the computer, in analogy with the grouping phase. Thus groupings may enable consolidations to be made without increase in transport. Such consolidations can be found by scanning the incidence matrix and are searched, in fact, in the grouping phase. Further similarity of columns in E^{10} indicates feasibility for consolidation and can be pointed out by simple algorithms which analyze E^{10}.

210.8 Influence on Programming Language Development.

Even with programming languages which are designed for use in connection with information systems such as COBOL or ALGOL-GENIUS or PL/I a lot of programming work has to be done in addition to that necessary to define the processing proper. This comes from the fact that the grouping of processes introduces a set of logical relations between the different processes in a group and the different transaction records associated with these processes. These relations must be taken care of by a set of statements in the program which analyze the transaction identifiers and set up linkages to the appropriate processes.

The consolidation of files also introduces a need for statements in every associated program, in order to pass the unused file data from the old file to the new file[1]).

It follows from our analysis that the programs as described consist of a set of *elementary procedures* or *elementary subroutines*, each connected with a single, elementary process and, hence, with a single row of the incidence matrix E^{10} and a program part which is defined by the matrix G which describes how processes are grouped and by the matrix C which defines the set of file consolidations used in the system.

We may conclude that our study of information systems opens up a way to develop a new compiler technique which would be able to compile the programs from the matrices G, C, and E^{10} together with the set of elementary procedures. When using a compiler of this kind one would have the much simplified task of programming and testing only the set of elementary procedures and of writing the G and C matrices. The latter tasks will also usually be omitted as they will normally have been established in the process of designing the system.

---

[1]) See section 28.3.

It is obvious that a significant reduction of the programming work would result from the development of a compilation technique as described, and also that much of the more complicated programming would be eliminated. Also in this way a restructuring, caused for instance by replacement of equipment, would no longer necessitate any reprogramming. At most, a new compilation, using the new structure matrices G and C would be necessary. A programming sy- would reduce the memory area needed for I/O by a factor of f, of one or more elementary processes will be very easy and would nevertheless change the system functioning significantly[2]).

---

[2]) Recent "Generalized Data Base Management Systems" could be regarded as a first step toward this technique (remark added in the 1971 edition).

Chapter 11. File Storage Considerations.

211.1 Files in Systems Using Mass Memories of Pseudo Random Access Type.

1 While it should have come out clearly that the discussion of information system problems made in chapters 1 through 6, of part 2 and also in the sections 1 and 2 of chapter 7, part 2, is either completely independent of hardware or holds true for every kind of auxiliary file storage used, this may seem less obvious as regards section 27.3. For the rest of part 2 it will not always hold true. Much of the discussion in these latter portions of part 2 appears to be oriented towards the problems associated with serial access file storage (e.g. magnetic tapes). It is therefore of interest to find out the extent to which different results come out if other types of file storage are considered.

2 It is important to note that all auxiliary stores for large files are associated with an access time much longer than that of the central memory of the computer (s) used in the system. (That is we take this as an axiom, which means that to the extent it is true our conclusions will be believed to be true.) As a consequence any use of an auxiliary store will be connected with a data transport. Hence this is nothing unique to serial storage. Even if in the future mass memories would be as fast and randomly accessed as the present core memories, it seems probable that computers will again have still faster control memories so that the situation will become similar to the one we have today.

3 It is further important to note that all mass storages are of a *pseudo-random access* type rather than being truly "random access". This means that the time needed to retrieve data will depend on where these data are stored in relation to where the last retrieved data were stored. This fact is fundamental because most of the file organization problems have to do with organizing the files so as to take advantage of the quicker access associated with more "nearby" data. Thus many of the design problems would disappear if the storages were truly random access.

4 We conclude that the problem of trying to reduce transport volume is still with us when we use so-called direct access (or random access) file storage equipment. This was the topic of section 27.3. It also follows that the topological transport factor for an in-

formation system is one of the relevant parameters also when random access stores are used.

5 It follows from 2 that process grouping will still be a possible tool for reducing transport. A new form of process-grouping also enters with the direct access storage. This equipment makes direct processing or on-line processing possible. One then often activates all processes which are associated with a transaction upon the arrival of the transaction. This, of course, means that in effect one has grouped all these processes.

6 Likewise it follows from 3 that blocking file records to make for longer data blocks and to reduce the storage space in the backing store may be of value and thus may also need to be considered as an alternative to grouping processes, as is discussed in section 28.1.

7 We can now conclude that also the whole of chapter 8, part 2, is still relevant if we move from tape files to "random access" files.

8 When "random access" file storage is used exclusively the need to limit the number of file stations to a very low value (10 or less) disappears. Therefore one of the main arguments used in 29.1 and 29.6 and which leads to consolidation of files is no longer relevant. Thus we need not seek for the optimum consolidation of files to come down to a required maximum number of file stations, or find the most economical number. Hence one might expect to be using less complex files when random-access storage is used.

9 On the other hand there still remain hardware reasons for consolidating files. One reason for this is that a record of an elementary file may use only a small part of the physical block or cell made available at one access operation. Therefore if each elementary record is stored in its own block and if a process needs e elementary files and each block takes b memory positions we need to allocate at least $e \cdot b$ positions in memory for I/O-areas. If, for instance, f elementary file records could be stored in one block then a consolidation of the corresponding f elementary files into one file would reduce the memory area needed for I/O by a factor of f, that is to $e \cdot b/f$. If b is not too small then a reduction by some factor f may be a necessity thus forcing us to consider, again, the problem of file consolidation. It may be expected to be less of a requirement in this case, however.

Of course one could achieve similar results by blocking together f records of the same file. This, however, will cost more memory for buffer areas and processing for "un-blocking" records before they can be used.

10 A solution to this problem could be to have direct access file storage with smaller blocks (smaller b value). This may, however, result in more accesses becoming necessary for all required I/O. This could well be an inferior solution.

211.2 Direct Processing versus Batched Processing[1]).

1 When transactions are input data to a process which uses some files then, in general, the files have to be scanned in total during the process. This is almost always true when serial access file storage is used, but it may even be true for direct access storage if the file data are obtained through "retrieval by property"[2]) or "content addressing" as this type of access has come to be generally called now. This total file scan will introduce a considerable transport and this will be independent of the number of transactions in the batch of transactions taken as input to the process. As a consequence in these circumstances there will be a file transport volume per transaction which is in inverse proportion to the number of transactions in the input batch. Consequently a batching of transactions which approximates the optimum balance between reduction of file transport per transaction with larger batches and an increased delay of process results has to be found. Thus an optimization problem has to be solved.

2 Now if direct access file storage is used, and retrieval by name (direct addressing) is possible, then it appears that *direct processing* rather than batched processing should be used. It follows however from what has been said in section 211.1—3 that this is not necessarily true. Thus direct processing of transactions as they arrive in random order will call for frequent moving of process programs from the auxiliary store into the memory and, as was seen in section 28.3, will hence cause an increase in transport. Also a multiple transport of file data will still occur because of direct processing, as it often occurs that batching results in collecting several transactions associated with the same file record.

---

[1]) See also examples of section 24.1.
[2]) 3 La 1961.

3 Also it is not always true — perhaps it is only seldom true — that to let a transaction wait in a batch collecting queue before being processed is a drawback from the point-of-view of the managed system.

One fairly simple example of this is that one would not like to let the system produce several bills to the same customer in the same day because several input transactions have been processed directly. Rather a processing period of one day or one week will be more ideal in many cases. More precisely: there is in each system for each kind of processing a certain response time which determines the ideal processing period. Then another period, longer or shorter, would be used only if the balance of system response considerations and information processing costs makes this economically efficient[3]). However there are also principal reasons for using batch processing. For instance in a payroll calculation where "team incentive" is being paid, the records for all workers in the team must be available before the calculation can be finished.

4 Likewise when systems of equations have to be solved or, for instance, a linear programming calculation has to be performed as a part of the information processing, then the whole associated matrix, which may be made up from many transaction records or a significant part of it, must be available.

---

[3]) It is also known from industrial dynamics that too quick responses to changes will often call for dynamical instability which, of course, is exactly what information processing attempts to reduce, see 1 FO 1961.

Chapter 12. File Organization

212.1 Record Layouts.

It was shown in chapter 5, part 2, how information requirements were traced backwards in the precedence graph until it was defined in terms of what we shall now name *elementary files*.

An elementary file will consist of data from a minimum of two information classes so that each record in an elementary file (each *elementary* record) contains a minimum of two *terms*. One of these is the object identifier (or key) the other the value of some function of this key. Thus an elementary file might be defined by the pair: identification number, person name. Another might be: identification number, amount of salary. In many cases however it is not appropriate to use such small elementary files. Then the elementary file will contain the key and two or more information classes in a set that is in no case partitioned further. We may find that, to obtain a unique definition of all person identification numbers of the respective persons, the elementary record would, in this case, contain at least the three terms: identification number, name, address.

When elementary files are consolidated then the elementary records are assembled as *file records*, and these file records obtain a certain structure by the way the consolidation is done. It is in this way that the relatively complicated records of business data files come into being. It is seen that one might expect that the record formats are defined during this stage of the analysis. This is another kind of work that should be done well in advance of the actual, detailed programming.

Let us take the consolidated file $(i, g, h, f) = F_1$ (say). We find

$$i \text{ goes into } pr(b, i')$$
$$g \text{ goes into } pr(e, e')$$
$$h \text{ goes into } pr(a, e')$$
$$f \text{ goes into } pr(a, e')$$

It will be convenient to be able to move that part of the record F_1 (i, g, h, f) which is to be copied only during a process. If we look at Fig. 2, section 29—6, we see that in process (b, i') i', g is to be moved from F_1 to the output file (i', g) in the cases when a record from F_1 is not changed. Thus we find that the organization of the records of F_1 should be as shown in Fig. 1. We have introduced the name F_{11} for (i', g) and F_{12} for (h, f) as is seen in Fig. 1.

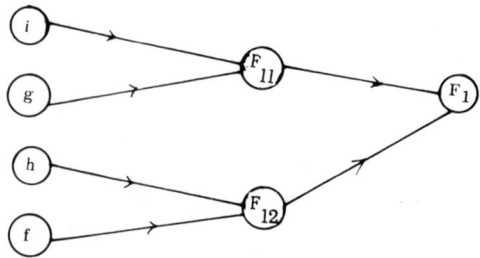

Fig. 1

We assume that the data sets i, g, h, f are consisting of elementary items in the following way:

$$i = i_1, i_2, i_3;$$
$$g = g_1, g_2;$$
$$h = h_1, h_2, h_3, h_4;$$
$$f = f_1, f_2, f_3;$$

where $i_1 = g_1 = h_1 = f_1 =$ the common sorting key which is also the key for the whole file F_1 and therefore will be denoted by F_{10}.

With this information we now have the record layout for F_1 as shown in Fig. 2.

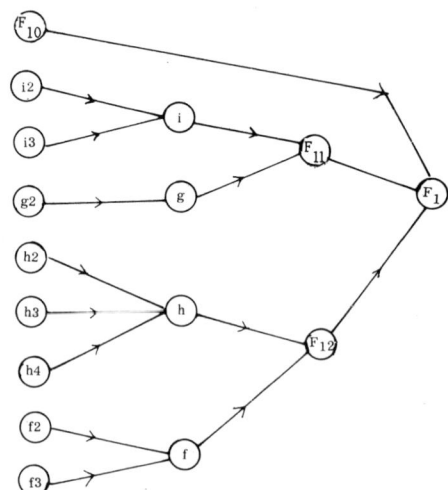

Fig. 2

This record organization can be described by the COBOL way of using level numbers with 01 for the record name, 02 for the data items or data sets on the highest level within the record and so forth.

```
01   F1
     02   F10
     02   F11
          03   i
               04   i2
               04   i3
          03   g2
     02   F12
          03   h
               04   h2
               04   h3
               04   h4
          03   f
               04   f2
               04   f3
```

We have seen how an organizational structure is imposed upon a record by the overall structure of the information system. More than this single influence determines the record format however. The way records are stored on tape affects data transport time and processing time in opposite ways. Thus the choice will depend on whether or not the file will be used in processing where transport time or processing time is the dominating factor. The decision in this respect may have to wait until programming is being done, although for some files the decision will be needed at the time the data structure analysis will be decisive.

The length of tape blocks will have to be decided at the same time, while the coding form may be open to special decision in some situations.

212.2 Record Organization.

Ideally the record of a file should be a function of the file only and not of the program. Therefore the record description should be made when the file organization is determined.

In any program using a file as input or output one should then, in the data description part of the program, only need to name the file or the record if the file has several record types.

Alternatively the file might itself carry with it its record descriptions.

In actual practice the problem is a little bit more complicated for it may be desirable to organize the record differently for different programs. This may be the reason for having normally new record descriptions for each COBOL program.

A better procedure would be to make use of the fact that the record is uniquely defined *to some extent by the file* and *to some extent by the actual process*. Thus one should have a *basic record description* which is defined by the file and an additional structural description which adds structure and "group names" to the basic record description. Only the latter then would have to be defined for the process[1]).

The basic record description would name all terms contained in the record, with type and size specification and a minimum of structure, for instance, as necessary by multiple occurrence of subrecords (arrays or "occurs declared groups").

The additional structure is defined by requirements for making simple term names unique by qualification by natural groups (or "elementary files"), or for reasons of enabling simple moving of record terms not used in the actual process.

Only the two last mentioned structure definitions should vary from one process to another. Only these should have to be defined with each program. It would even be possible to let the moving of unused data be done automatically on the call of a special move procedure, for instance "move unprocessed".

The advantage of limiting the individual program description only to describing additional structure is twofold. In the first place it

---

[1]) The distinction made here between the structure of the data as they exist in the file and their structure as seen by the user has also been made by T. W. Olle (2 Ia 1969). Its importance appears to have been widely recognized in the most recent work on generalized file systems (data bases). Remark added in the 1971 edition.

would reduce program work and reduce the need for reprogramming when the file organization is being changed. In the second place, and most important, it would guarantee that the correct basic record description is being used whenever the file is used in a process.

Chapter 13. System Reliability.

213.1 Reliability of an Information System.

1 In any system of not too small size the reliability of its functioning is a very important but also fairly difficult problem. This is so for at least two reasons.

2 The most obvious reason is that systems typically consist of a large number of components and any component is apt to be less than perfectly reliable. Therefore the total system reliability is dependent on the extent to which it has features which can counteract the effect of all individual component errors, or keep each of them so small in number that their total effect is tolerable.

3 This type of reliability problem has been well recognized in connection with military aeronautical systems and this has led to the establishing of reliability engineering as a main function in aircraft companies.

4 It has been found that reliability questions give rise to problems of an advanced mathematical-statistical nature. It is apparent that this reliability probiem is also very complicated in management information systems. It is therefore unfortunate that the systems staffs for business data processing analysis typically do not contain (at least not yet in influential position) mathematically well qualified people. Therefore there is a tendency in most present data processing systems for business to handle reliability questions in a rather arbitrary way. Thus it is common to find that error checks are utilized wherever this is easy to do — and often to an unreasonable extent — whereas important weak points are not satisfactorily checked.

5 The other important reason for the seriousness of reliability questions in systems design does not have to do with the reliability defects of the system components but is associated with the question of how reliable our understanding is of the systems problems and their true character.

Again the high number of components and their usually intricate relationships is the reason for making this a real problem.

6 While it is not too difficult to see at least along what lines the first reliability problem, 2, should be solvable, it is really difficult to see which principle could be used to safeguard against the second reliability problem, 5. This is a point worthy of much basic research.

7 It is clear that in information systems errors are generated or fed into the system at many different places, and that all errors cannot be detected and eliminated. It is therefore a central, system theoretical, problem how to organize the system so that it will produce useful results. An optimum distribution of error-checking efforts, considering the different error probabilities, has a central position in this connection. Again this is a problem which calls for extensive research.

213.2 Means for Checking Input Data.

In 1950 the author made an experiment to determine the frequency of errors in key-punching numeric punched-cards. It was found that 0.5 $^0/_{00}$ of the digits were in error. During a subsequent verifying operation about 90 % of these were detected leaving about 0.05 $^0/_{00}$ of erroneous digits. Unfortunately no other, and larger, statistics are available to the author. The publication of this subject does indeed need extension!

Some tests to determine the reliability of punched-tape numerically were reported recently[1]). About 1 % of errors punched were found, that is the order as mentioned above for cards. When a "check-digit" was used to control the numbers punched this detected about 99 % of the errors: thus this check is 10 times better than verifying, when feasible. This is not all, however, for the check digit will also detect the errors in the written material from which punching was done. As this is not true for card verifying, and as the error rate in written data probably is at least as large as in the punching operation, verifying actually takes only 50 % of all the errors.

These figures show clearly that it is necessary to have a better check on input data than that provided by verifying. We have come to estimate the number of errors done in punching to 1 %, and that in writing to likewise 1 %, and that after verifying still the 1 % of writing errors remain. If we input on the average as little as 10

---

[1]) 3 SI 1964.

digits per second we would still input about 3 errors per hour after verifying!

With this alarming figure for the quality of input errors that may be expected in a typical installation it should be obvious that it may not be too useful to spend increasing amounts of resources on improved checking facilities in the computer hardware. It is obviously orders of magnitude better than the input data stream. It also can be concluded that such means as using check digits in the input data where possible is a minimum requirement. Most important however seems to be firstly to do research to explain how the present systems can do useful work at all, in view of this high error input rate and how satisfactory this work really is at present correcting the errors in the original data. Obviously much work need to be done in this area.

Chapter 14. The problem of Optimum Grouping of Information Processes.

214.1 The Problem of Optimum Grouping of Information Processes.

The problem arises from the following assumptions:

Several processes use information from the same file. Therefore if such processes are grouped into one run the file information would only have to be transported once.

"Same file" here means that also the sorting order is the same.

Each process needs space in memory for process program, work areas, buffer areas and, perhaps, also for data preparation program. Therefore limitations on memory size will, generaliy, be a limit to the amount of grouping possible.

214.2 Special Case: Grouping Processes in Pairs.

The most simple grouping problem is, of course, when grouping is done only by pairs of processes.

1 Let S be the set of processes, i, j be the pair of processes i and j, $s(p_{i,j}^k)$ (k = 1, 2, ...) a sequence of pairs such that k is the ordinal number of a pair in the sequence and if $p_{i1, j1}^{k1} \ne p_{i2, j2}^{k2}$, then $i1 \ne i2$, $j1 \ne j2$,

v_{ij} be the transport volume saved by grouping i and j.

m_i be the memory space required by the process i.

2 Problem:

Find $sm = s(p_{ij}^k)_{max}$ such that

$$\sum_S v_{ij} = max$$

$$m_i + m_j \le Const$$

214.3 The Problem of Optimum Pairing Without Memory Constraint.

1 Let S be the set of elementary processes 1, 2, 3, ... The *pair saving* will be defined as the function v_{ij} over $S \times S = S^2$.

2 We order S^2 in decreasing values of v_{ij}, and then denote it by $\bar{S}^2$. We say that the pairs i, j and j, k (or k, j) are *connected* by j. Likewise way call v_{ij} connected with v_{kj} (by j).

Let $S^2_{max} \subset S^2$ be the set of pairs in S^2 which has the maximum value of $\sum_{S^2} v_{ij}$ (i and j uniquely occuring in Σ).

3 PROPOSITION. If $\bar{S}^2_{(1)}$ is the 1st element in $\bar{S}^2$ we have:

$$\text{Either } \bar{S}^2_{(1)} \in S^2_{max}$$

or $\bar{S}^2_{(1)}$ is connected with $\bar{S}^2_{(2)}$

4 **Conjecture.**

If both $\bar{S}^2_{(2)}$ and $\bar{S}^2_{(3)}$ are connected with $\bar{S}^2_{(1)}$ by j_2 and j_3 respectively, (i.e. $\bar{S}^2_{(1)} = j_2, j_3$), then we may take

$$S^2_{max} = \bar{S}^2_{(2)} + \bar{S}^2_{(3)} + S^2_{(2)(3)\ max}$$

where $S^2_{(2)(3)\ max}$ denotes S^2_{max} for the set $S(j_2, j_3)$.

5 A virtually more common simple special case is when different pairings cause the same reduction in transport volume but the memory requirement has to be considered. This might be the case when several transaction items are to be processed against the same master file.

This problem is not too difficult to handle even if no procedure is available and even for more general grouping than just paring. The reason is that we never have to handle a large number of different pairs. If the number of elements is high then it is easy to find pairs of equal size for almost all elements. Further if memory size permits many processes in each group it is easy to group combinations that fill the memory fairly well, just because in this situation there must be many "small" processes (in the sense of using but little memory).

Thus when many "small" processes are associated with many transaction items for one file it will be natural as a first approximation to take them together into much fewer groups which are still small enough to be feasible for further grouping by two or three, or four, in a final, more system oriented analysis. As an example we may consider the case[1] where each of the elementary files a, b, c, d and e could well consist of several smaller files. The natural objec-

---

[1] Example in section 28.4.

tion here would be that the first grouping might have been done in a more even way so that the large difference between for instance vol(a)=500 and vol(e)=1500 would not have occurred. Even this however is realistic because there will often be some connections between some of the initial elementary transaction items which makes only some grouping feasible at the first stage.

Part 3.
Some Data Processing Problems

Chapter 1. Relation between a Process and its Files.

31.1 Relation Between a Process and its Files.

The transport volume associated with a certain file and a process depends very significantly on whether or not the process will call for a single scan of a file or for a multiple scan. This depends on how intricate is the connection between the process and its files. As always this will be heavily dependent on the size of the main memory available to the process. More precisely the multiplicity of file scan will depend on how much of the file must be simultaneously accessible to the process and how this is related to the memory space available. This is a question that is intimately connected with the question of information precedence relations and does therefore belong to the information system analysis, rather than programming. The need for file sorting, in itself a multiple scan process, is also caused by relations that exist between the different data and their processes. The same is true for the need for complex data structures set up by pointers or directories in a direct-access file storage.

To be able to develop methods for handling this problem we first need to obtain a better understanding of the relation between a computing process and the sizes and structures of the files. Some aspects of this will be considered below.

31.2 Some Basic Problems of File Processing.

An electronic computing system, or computer for short, consists typically of a processor (or perhaps a set of them) and a set of memory positions with fast access, which we shall call the memory. When a computer works with its program and data stored in the memory, it is utilizing its highest possible speed.

When the data volumes and programs are too large to be stored entirely in the memory, then a back-up store or file store has to be used. We then talk about file processing. We have the problem here that this file store is slower than the memory. Hence the computer will lose time in transporting data between store and memory. The data and program then have to be organized in such a way as to minimize this loss of time.

The worst case, would be when the process requests all the time data in a random order, from the auxiliary storage. If this would happen for each individual instruction then the apparent memory speed of the computer would go down to that of the file storage. However quite such a bad case cannot happen. At most something like every fifth program step will ask for data in random order from out of a data set that is much larger than the memory space and with repeated access to most data[1]). In this case the effective operation speed of the computer goes down from an order of magnitude of the memory cycle time to that corresponding to about 1/5 of the average random access time in the store, which means, usually, a slow down by a factor of 100 to 100000. This is a problem type that is especially bad for magnetic tape stores. This "slow extreme", however, is almost impossible to occur in practice.

On the other extreme, "the fast extreme", — which does instead often occur — so often as to be typical for business data processing — each data item will only have to be moved once from store to memory (or from memory to store) whereupon it may be subject to several internal computer operations.

Further the items will in this extreme almost always be taken from (or put to) a part of the store to which access time is much smaller than the average one, because the file storage will have the "pseudo-direct access" character of accessing nearby areas faster than the average access speed and in the "fast extreme" case we always have the "next record" in a nearby position (whether on manetic tapes or discs). In this case the effective operation time of the computer retains its original order of magnitude. This type of problem is the ideal one for magnetic tape stores but will also give minimum time in other kinds of file store.

In most problems of engineering or scientific data processing, as well as in an increasing number of administrative problems, the

---

[1]) It is not possible, in normal processors, to have each program step call for access to the auxiliary store. This is because of the existence of "housekeeping" operations.

situation will be one that comes between the two extremes. All too often is it then hastily assumed to be a problem of the slow extreme, and supposed to be impossible for magnetic tapes. A careful organization of the processing and data will in many of these cases lead to reasonable process time and make tape systems as good as the other ones available. The new larger internal computer memories play an important rôle in this connection. It follows from what has been said that in connection with file processing applications it is important to be able to estimate, already on the basis of some few characteristics of the problem, the extent to which file storage will reduce the efficient processing speed.

1 **Linear file processing — the fast extreme.**

As has already been mentioned the least time loss from file store use arises when data can be transferred from (or to) consecutive positions of the store. This is true also for the so-called random access stores because they are in fact all of a pseudo serial type. We shall say that when a file is processed in this optimum way by a process always taking in consecutive data from the file then the file is *a linear file in this process*. When all files in a process are linear we shall say that we have *a linear file process*.

The simplest type of linear file processing is the one commonly encountered in business data processing, which is in fact the type generally referred to by the name file processing. In it the process takes one record from each of a set of input files and produces one record of each of a set of output files. Thus in fact the process is finished each time a set of records has been used up and another set produced so that this file processing is a sequence of separate processes. It is obvious that in this simple case the records can be taken in arbitrary sequence if only this sequence is the same for all files in the process. If the memory is large enough to take in and store an input record simultaneously from each file concerned, plus the program and its working area, the process is clearly a linear one.

2 We now ask whether or not there are other types of problems, of a less trivial character, in which the files still act as linear files. In order to answer this question we note first that one necessary condition for a file to be linear in a process is that it shall successively be given some memory space to fill with new data. This can of course only be the case when the process is able at some stage (r) to dismiss, once and for all, some of the previous data, or reduce

the volume of intermediate data, or both. We shall find it convenient to say that in such a case the *process produces a waste* Sw(r) (set of data). Sw(r) thus is the space made free by dismissed data plus space obtained from reducing the volume of internally stored intermediate data, including program space (or minus increase of such data).

Our definition of the waste set Sw(r) automatically implies the definition of a subdivision of the process P into *process stages* P(r), each stage being defined as a part of P large enough to produce a waste. We are now led to the definition of the current process set Sp(r) as the minimum set of data which must be made available to the process for it to produce a waste. In other words Sp(r) is the necessary data input to P(r).

The process data set Sp(r) may consist of one set of data left over from the previous stage P(r-1), which set we shall call the *kernel set Sm(r-1)*, and one set from each of the input files. This latter we shall call an increment set Sf(r) (where f will be a symbol for the file from which the set is taken).[1])

$$Sp(r) = Sm(r-1) + \sum^{F} Sf(r)$$

We note in passing that our assumptions about P(r) implies that it will in general be a triad of operators: *Pr(r)* which produces output, *Pm(r)* which produces intermediate results and *Pw(r)* which produces the waste set. All these operators operate upon Sp(r). Then the kernel set Sm(r) can be regarded as the kernel (in the common algebraic sense) of Sw(r) in that it is the part of Sp(r) not wasted (by the operation Sw(r)).

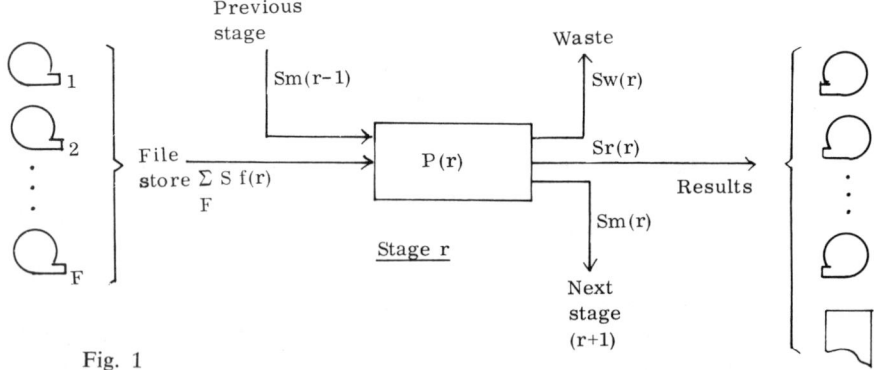

Fig. 1

3 Let So be the memory space available. Then $Sw(r) \leq$ So for all r.

---

[1]) Sp(r) is closely related to the concept of the "working set" of a program as used in recent works on real-time data processing systems (remark added in the 1972 edition).

31.3 K-Progressive Process.

It is easy to see that only if at each stage the memory space made available by the waste production is sufficient for taking in the increment set of a file for the next stage, can the file be linear in that process. In order to state this with more precision we define a concept which we shall call *K-progressive process*. A process shall be said to be K-progressive if for all process-stages R and all files F

1
$$\hat{S} = \sum_{r=1}^{R} Sw(r) - \sum_{r=1}^{R} Sm(r\text{-}1) - \sum_{r=1}^{R}\sum_{f=1}^{F} Sf(r) \geq K$$

(K a constant)

or $\quad \hat{S}_{min}(R) = K$

If the process is K-progressive it follows from 1 that after stage R-1, for instance, free memory space $\geq$ K is available for the next stage, that is for stage R. For all F files involved the space required is

$$\sum_{f=1}^{F} Sf(r).$$

Memory-covered. If the memory space available is $\geq$ K we shall say that the memory *covers* K and also: the K-progressive process is memory-covered. After each stage of a K-progressive process the memory covers K.

A sufficient condition for a K-progressive process to be linear is

$$\sum_{f=1}^{F} Sf(r) \leq K \text{ for each r, and } K \geq So$$

So = memory available for input at start.

for if the process is K-progressive then it follows that after any step R there has been made free a storage space which at least has a magnitude of K. (The condition is thus not a necessary one and sharper estimates might be obtained.)

In the common business data processing each stage corresponds to a complete process which means that then Sm(r)=0 for all r. (More precisely Sm(r)=const=memory space for some accumulated control totals. This, however, is trivial and may be taken into the working area of the program itself.) It also follows that at each stage

$$\sum_{f=1}^{F} Sf(r) = Sw(r)$$

so that we only have to choose $K \geq Sw(r)_{max}$ to make sure that we have a K-progressive file.

If $\Sigma\ Sf(r) > K$ a K-progressive file will not be linear. However, the smaller $\Sigma\ Sf(r) - K = dK$ the smaller will be the acces time to an auxiliary store. Further, the probability of an operation calling for data from the auxiliary store will also be smaller when dK becomes smaller.

31.4 Rectangular File Processing and Group Access.

1 In some situations the process requires access to the file data at several different occasions so that linear processing is not possible[1]) but still is such a special case that a far better situation is obtained than that encountered in the slow extreme. One common instance of this kind is what we call rectangular file processing. In this two files F_1 and F_2 are matched in the way that one of them, corresponding to the column F_2 of Fig. 1, is first run in a linear process together

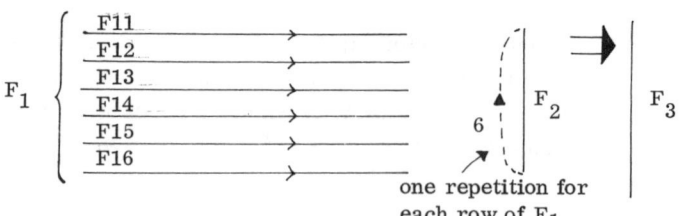

Fig. 1

with a part, F_{11}, of F_1. Then F_2 is rewound (perhaps while replaced by another copy of F_2 to save time) after which F_2 is run together with F_{12} and so forth until F_2 has run "linearly" with all parts of F_1, shown as lines in the rectangular array for F_1 in Fig. 1. Each linear process typically means that the records of F_2 are taken one at a time, in sequence, and the associated record of F_{1i} (for i=1, 2, 3, ... in sequence as described), if any, is retrieved. When the row number i) of F_1 has been processed against F_2 the result is put out onto F_3 as one or more records.

2 The rectangular process is seen to be linear with regard to the "rectangular file" F_1 and be repetitive for the "column" F_2. If r is

---

[1]) And we do not have, simply a retrieval situation. Cf. section 31.5 below.

the number of rows in F_1 (with respect to the process in question) then the latent need for repetition of F_2 is r times.

3 If memory space permits F_2 to be stored completely then the process

$$F_1; F_2 \to F_3$$

can be run as a linear process.

4 If F_2 cannot be held in memory one may find it possible to store instead several rows of F_1 simultaneously. Suppose a group of g rows of F_1 can be held in memory at the same time with space left for the computer program also. Then any time a record of F_2 is in memory it can retrieve associated records from all the g rows of F in the group. The result will be that each scan of F_2 handles g rows of F_1, rather than one. The number of scans of F_2 will then be reduced to r/g by *this group access technique*.

Notice that from a file processing point of view the rectangular file will have r/g rows rather than r rows, which is the "logical" number of rows.

5 If v_1 is the transport volume of F_1 and v_2 and v_3 are those of F_2 and F_3 then we see that the transport volume for the rectangular process, using group access with group size g, will be

$$t = v_1 + (r/g)v_2 + v_3$$

6 If instead we would store a part f_2 of F_2 in memory during a set of runs, and F_2 would consist of z such parts, it may in some cases be possible to run the process in z stages whereby the output may also have to be updated in each run. We would thus have the transport volume

$$t = zv_1 + v_2 + 2zv_3'$$
v_3' = the average size of the intermediate output which eventually becomes F

7 One example of a rectangular file processing is the multiplication of a rectangular matrix by a column if performed in the traditional way. If F_2 is very large a non-traditional multiplication scheme, "*the multiplication by column selection*", which calls for a linear process only followed by a sorting routine, will in general be better.

8 Another example of a rectangular process is a completely random retrieval operation as we shall see in section 31.5. It is interesting that such a completely random process can be done in such a relatively orderly fashion as by a rectangular process.

9 A matrix by matrix multiplication of the traditional type will correspond to a doubly rectangular process. In this r denotes the number of rows divided by g if group access is being used.

31.5 Retrieval of File Records for a Process.

We have mentioned[1]) that when a process is memory-covered then it can be run as linearly and will thus require only a single scan of the files involved. When the process is not memory-covered then the file information will have to be transported to the memory a number of times depending on how often such data are requested by the process. In addition the access time to these data will depend on whether the whole file or only a narrow band of it is active at each phase of the process. When file data from all over the file are requested in random at almost every operation we have the "slow extreme" case.

In many situations the process will request every datum only once. Even if then these requests are in completely random sequence we still have a much better situation than the slow extreme where each datum will be requested several times. It is requested only once and and as a rule several operations will be done between each such request. We shall call such a situation where file data are needed only once a *retrieval of information*[2]). Thus we shall say that when the process needs some file data it has the problem of how to retrieve these data.

2 The problem of retrieving data is associated with
      a identifying the group of data required
      b localizing these data
      c fetching the data and bringing them into the memory of the computer.

3 To identify the group of data is to specify which properties it is required to have. A group of data has properties defined by its

---

[1]) See section 31.2.
[2]) 3 La 1961—1.

structure (which terms are in the group[3]) and the values of its different terms. If data are stored in compact form, the structure cannot be sensed from its stored representation. Hence only the value associated with a specified part of a record — or set of parts — can be used in practice to check the data properly. As a result the "properties" of a record are identified with the values of its terms (elementary items). In the special case when the record is stored in an ordered sequence of the values of one term (or a set of terms) this will be said to be the (logical) *name* of the record[4]). The same will hold in any case when a record is stored in a cell which can be localized by a process using the term value as an input. Obviously when we want to retrieve a record specified by the value of its name we are in a best position. We shall say that we then have a *retrieval by name*[3]).

4 It may of course also happen that we want to retrieve records which are specified by the value of some of its other terms, that is by a property other than its name. One way of doing this might be to re-order the data file to make this property the new name. This is the reason for so often using sorting of file data as a prerequisite to (other) processing.

5 If we do not re-order before retrieving we are in the situation called *retrieval by property*[4]).

6 A third possibility is to use an auxiliary file (or to partition the file) such that the retrieval by property is performed on a much smaller file and gives as its result a retrieved record or set of records from which the names of all records having the desired property value is defined. This then enables the retrieval for the whole file record to be done as a retrieval by name. This may be of advantage if the retrieval by property is slower for a larger file. This we have seen to be the case not only for serial memories but also for direct access memories. A second condition which makes this advantageous is when retrieval by name is much faster than retrieval by property. This is true especially for random access or pseudo random access. This is the more so as memories are generally bad in connection with retrieval by property[5]).

---

[3]) 3 La 1961—1.
[4]) It is also often called the "key".
[5]) 3 La 1961—1.

7 **Example.** In a book giving surveys of computer application it was stated: "Another firm requirement... is random access type of storage... As an example, accounting may require 10000 or 20000 TV spots to be controlled alphabetically by cities. Media may require the same information by decreasing market value, ..." "We want to point out that in all of this re-use it is not a question of pulling out every third, fourth, or tenth item, but rather of using the material in a completely different sequence each time; complete dependency on tape stations would by a mistake." Comments, please.

Chapter 2. Influence of Word Structure

32.1 Influence of Word Length on Tape Recording Speed.

The numerical terms (elementary items) in common data files have a length that varies from 1 to about 45 binary digits (bits). Very roughly the statistical distribution of term lengths can be taken as rectangular that is all term lengths between 1 and 45 bits have roughly the same probability. From this we may conclude that the average term length may be taken as 23 bits. It also follows that if w is the word length of the computer used then the average number of unused word bits in a term storage is w/2. We say that the word boundary allowance is w/2, due to the non-uniform lengths of the different terms.

Data packing might be used to eliminate or reduce the boundary allowance. We see that complete omission of packing, i.e. complete carrying of boundary allowance, would increase the storage space from an average of 23 to $23 + \frac{w}{2}$ or by

$$\frac{w/2}{23+w/2} \cdot 100$$

per cent (very roughly giving an allowance of $100 \frac{w}{46}$ per cent) This would be the reduction of average tape length for the storage of one term if there would be no inter-record gap allowance.

If the inter-record gap has a length which corresponds to g words, and the record length is r words, then we have a "record gap allowance" of g/r words per data word or 100 g/r per cent of length allowance. When this is taken into account we obtain the reduced allowance,

$$= \frac{w/2}{(23+w/2)\ (1+g/r)}$$

By this rate then reading and writing speed is increased by taking care of the non-uniform length of packing. To do this on the other hand always calls for methods which require memory space and which decrease internal processing speed.

Table 1. $\dfrac{100w/2}{(23+w/2)(1+g/r)}$ max term length = 45 bits

w =		6	24	48
g/r =	2	4	11	17
	1	6	17	25
	0.2	10	29	43

Table 2. $\dfrac{100w/2}{(18+w/2)(1+g/r)}$ max term length = 38 bits

w =		6	24	48
g/r =	2	5	13	19
	1	7	20	29
	0.2	12	33	48

In addition to this allowance we also have, in non-binary machines, a *code allowance* caused by using coded forms for storage which take more space,

Thus for instance in 6-bit word machines (so-called variable word length machines) it is common to have one decimal digit in each word only, when using numeric data. As one digit corresponds to 3,3 bits or less this corresponds to a code allowance of (6—3,3)/6 = 45 %. This has been indicated in Diagram 1. Note that this allowance is equal to the word allowance even for as long words as 48 bits.

As is seen the gain in tape speed to be achieved by packing data, that is using non-uniform field length (a field being the space allocated to store one term) is rather small for a word length of 24 bits or less (even if we have used a rough estimate only). This is especially so when short records are used (small values or f/g).

For instance if r/g = 1 then the record gap allowance is 100 %, whereas if r/g = 5 the allowance is only 20 %, so that an increase of r/g from 1 to 5 would save 80 %. It is thus seen to be much more desirable to use memory space for reducing record gap allowance than to reduce word boundary allowance, that is to use term packing, if the words are not too long, for instance 24 bits

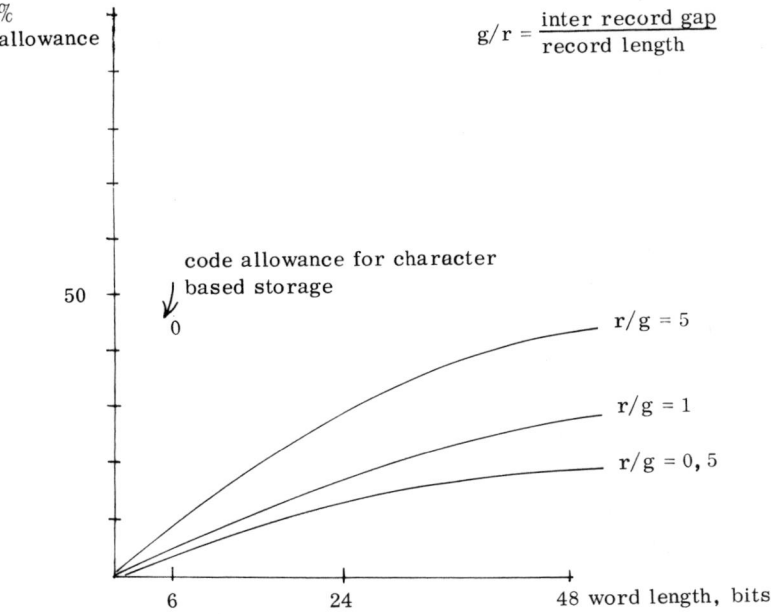

Diagram 1, max term length = 45 bits.

or less. When term packing is built into the computer hardware there is of course no choice, and term packing will be used whether advantageous or not. When term packing is by programming (software) it will often be wise not to use term packing for all terms. Still, if some groups of terms happen to be very short, or when some subrecords occur a number of times, the pay-off for memory space used for term packing these parts may be so high as to justify this packing, while the remaining terms of the record go unpacked.

REFERENCES

References marked x have direct relation to the content of the book or influenced it. Several references have been added afterwards, up to the date of printing.

Systems Theory

	1 Ax	1957	Alexandrov, P S: Combinatorial Topology, Vol 2, Graylock Press, Rochester NY
	1 Ba-H	1964	Bar-Hillel, Yehoshua: Language and Information, Selected Essays on their Theory and Application, Addison-Wesley Publ Co, London
	1 Be	1958	Berge, C, Theories des Graphes et Ses Applications, Donod, Paris
	1 BJ	1964	Bonini-Jaedicke-Wagner (editors): Management Controls, McGraw-Hill
	1 Br	1962	Brown, R G: Smoothing, Forecasting and Prediction . . ., Prentice-Hall
	1 Co	1964	Copi, I M: Symbolic Logic, McMillan, New York
	1 Cr	1965	Chorafas, D N: Systems and Simulation, Academic Press, London
	1 Da	1960	Danzig & Wolfe: Decomposition Principle for Linear Programming. Op. Research Society Am.
	1 Di	1968	Dijkstra, E W: Complexity Controlled by Hierarchical Ordering of Function and Variability (in Software Engineering, ed Naur and Randell, NATO, Scientific Affairs Division)
	1 Ei	1962	Eilon, Samuel: Elements of Production Planning and Control, McMillan, New York
	1 El	1966	Elmaghraby, Salah E: The Design of Production Systems, Reinhold Publ Corp, New York
	1 Fe	1964	Ferschel, F: Zufallsabhängige Wirtschaftsprozesse, Physica Verlag, Wien
	1 FF	1962	Ford, L R and Fulkerson, D R: Flows in Networks, Princeton University Press
x	1 Fo	1961	Forrester, J: Industrial Dynamics: M I T Press, Cambridge, Mass
	1 Ga	1960	Gale, David: The Theory of Linear Economic Models, McGraw-Hill
	1 Go	1957	Goode, H M and Machol, R E: Control Systems Engineering
	1 Hd	1963	Hadly, G and Whitin, T M: Analysis of Inventory-Systems, Prentice Hall
	1 Ha	1959	Haire, M: Modern Organization Theory, John Wiley
	1 Hl	1962	Hall, A D: A Methodology for Systems Engineering, van Nostrand
	1 Ht	1964	Hart, B L J: Dynamic Systems Design, Company Control for the Computer Era, Business Publications Ltd, London
	1 HW	1960	Hilton, P J and Wylie, S: Homology Theory, Cambridge University Press

1 Ij	1965	Ijiri, Yuji: Management Goals and Accounting for Control, North Holland Publ Co, Amsterdam
1 JK	1963	Johnson, Kast, Rosenzweig: Theory and Management of Systems
1 Kr	1942	Kron, Gabriel: Tensor Analysis, John Wiley and Sons, New York
1 Le	1962	Lange, Oscar: Wholes and Parts (A General Theory of Systems Behaviour), Pergamon
1 La	1956	Langefors, B: Algebraic Methods for the Numerical Analysis of Built-up Systems, Saab TN 38, Saab Aircraft Co, Linköping, Sweden
x 1 La	1959	Langefors, B: Algebraic Topology and Networks, Saab Ta 43, Saab Aircraft Co, Linköping, Sweden
x 1 La	1962—1	Langefors, B: Activity Network for Planning and Scheduling BIT, Bind 2, Hefte Nr 1
x 1 La	1962—2	Langefors, B: Computation of Parts Requirements for Production Scheduling, BIT, Bind 2, Hefte Nr 2
x 1 La	1961	Langefors, B: Algebraic Topology for Elastic Networks, Saab TN 49, Saab Aircraft Co, Linköping, Sweden
1 Ms	1961	March, James G and Simon, Herbert: Organizations, John Wiley, New York
1 Mi	1963	Miller, Robert W: Schedule, Cost and Profit Control with Pert, McGraw-Hill, New York
1 Po	1965	Porte, J: Recherches sur la theorie générale des systéms formels et sur les systémes connectifs, Gauthier-Villars, Paris
1 Ra	1968	Randell, B: Towards a Metholodogy of Computing System Design (in Software Engineering ed Naur-Randell, NATO, Scientifie Affairs Division), (Also Proc Congress 1968)
1 Ri	1962	Riordan, J: Stochastic Service Systems, John Wiley, New York
1 Sa	1962	Samuelson, A: Linear Analysis of Frame Structures. Dissertation, Chalmers, Göteborg, Sweden
1 Si	1960	Simon, Herbert A: The New Science of Management Decisions, Harper and Brother, New York 1960
1 Tu	1953	Tustin, A: The Mechanism of Economic Systems, Harward University Press, Cambridge, Mass
x 1 V	1958	Vaszonyi: Scientific Programming in Business and Industry, John Wiley, New York
1 Za	1963	Zadeh and Desoer: Linear System Theory, McGraw-Hill

Information Systems

2 Ac	1958	Ackoff, Russel L: Towards a Behavioral Theory of Communication Management Science, April 1958
2 Ad	1963	Adam, A: Systematische Datenverarbeitung bei der Auswertung von Versuchs- und Beobachtungsergebnissen, Physica-Verlag, Würzburg

2 Ad	1962	Adam, A and Roppert, J: Betriebliche Leistungsverrechnungen, Physica-Verlag, Würtzburg
2 Be	1967	Article by Becket, J A, se även 2 My 1967
2 Bg	1966	Briggs, R: A Mathematical Model for the Design of Information Management Systems, M S Thesis, Univ of Pittsburg, Pennsylvania
2 Br	1965	Brodda, B: Citation Index and Similar Devices in Mechanized Document Retrieval, Språkförlaget Scriptor, Fack, Stockholm 40, Sweden
2 Cd	1970	Codd, E F: A Relational Model of Data for Large Shared Data Banks, CACM Vol 13, June 1970
2 Co	1962	Language Structure Group of the Codasyl Development Comm: An Information Algebra, Phase I Report. Comm of the ACM, vol 5 No 4 (April 1962), pp 190—204, (1962 or 1963?)
2 Em	1969	Emery J C: Organizational Planning and Control Systems, MacMillan, New York
2 Fr	1969	Feldman J A and Rovner P D: An Algol-based Associative Language, CACM No 8, 1969
2 Gh	1963	Gregory and van Horn: Automatic Data Processing Systems, Wadsworth Publ. Co.
2 Ho	1960	Holt, Modigliani, Muth, Simon: Planning Production, Inventories and Work Force, Prentice Hall
2 Ia	1969	IAG: File Organization, Selected papers from FILE 68, An IAG Conferens, Swetz & Zeitlinger, Amsterdam
x 2 La	1959	Langefors, B: Flygtekniska Beräkningar (Aeronautical Engineering Calculations), Nordsam 1959, Proccedings, Swedish with English Summar
x 2 La	1963—1	Langefors, B: Some Approaches to the Theory of Information Systems BIT, Bind 3, Hefte Nr 4
x 2 La	1963—2	Langefors, B: Toward Integration of Engineering Data Processing and Automatization of Design. Chapter 10 in The Augumentation of Man's Intellect by Machine, Vol 1 of "Vistas in Information Handling, Spartan Books
x 2 La	1963—3	Langefors, B: The Problems of Education for ADP, IIC Bulletin, Vol 2, Nr 4 October
x 2 La	1964	Langefors, B: Automated Design, International Science and Technology, February
x 2 La		See also 1 La 1962—2 (and 2 La 1962 and 2 La 1960 below)
2 La	1965	Langefors, B: Information System Design Computations using Generalized Matrix Algebra, BIT Vol 15
2 La	1967	Langefors, B: Directive Information for Systems Control (in The Analysis of Business Systems, G Fisk ed), Gleerup Publ, Lund, Sweden
2 Lg	1963	Laden, H N and Gildersleeve, T R: Systems Design for Computer Applications, John Wiley, New York

2 Lu	1970	Lundeberg, Mats: On Information Systems Work. Thesis for technical lic. The Royal Institute of Technology. Inst Department Information Processing, Stockholm
2 Md	1963	McDonough: Information Economies: McGrav-Hill
2 Ms	1959	Marschak, J: Remarks on the Economics of Information Science Research in Management, University of California, Los Angeles 1959
2 Mr	1966	Martin, F: et con Optimale Planung und Führungsinformation, Mnemoton-Verlag, A G, Zürich
2 My	1967	Myers, Ch (ed): The Impact of Computers on Management, MIT Press
2 Ne	1960	Neuschel, R: Management by systems, McGraw-Hill
2 Nu	1971	Nunamaker, J F Jr: A Methodology for the Design and Optimization of Information Processing Systems, AFIPS SJCC 1971
x 2 Op	1960	Optner, Stanford: System Analysis for Bussiness Management, Prentice-Hall
x 2 Ra	1961	Raiffa, Howard and Schlaiffer, Robert: Applied Statistical Decision Theory, Harvard Univ Books
2 Sc	1971	Computer-Aided Information Systems Analysis and Design, Studentlitteratur, Lund, Sweden, 1971
x 2 Si	1960	Simon, H A: The New Science of Management Decision, Harper and Brothers Publishers, New York
2 Sr	1971	Schroder, H M: The Measurement and Development of Info Processing Systems, in Management Info. Systems, Grochla and Szyperski (eds) Betrieswirtsch. Verlag, Wiesbaden Germany
x 2 Su	1965	Sundström, L O: Automatiserade Informationssystem, Metodik för Blandad Transaktionsvis och Satsvis Bearbetning, Saab, Linköping, (Swedish)
2 Sv	1964	Sveistrup P: Systembegrebet og Administrativ Databehandling, Ehrvervsökonomisk Tidskrift nr 2, 1964
2 Sy	1970	Systemering 70, Studentlitteratur, Lund, Sweden
2 Sö	1968	Sem-Sandberg, Sverre, Ödmansson, Erik: File Organization by Pluto (in File Organisation). Svets & Zeitlinger, Amsterdam 1969
2 Te	1969	Teichroew, D: Methodology for the Design of Information Processing Systems, Proc Fourth Australian Comp Conf Adelaide, South Australia 1969
2 Vl	1965	Vlcek, J: Systems Analysis in an Economic Management Automation Design (in Economics of Aut. Data Proc., Frielink ed), North-Holland Publ, Amsterdam
x 2 Wi	1964	Williams, R: Basic Concepts for Production Controls as Applied to ob Shops, Ehrvervsökonomisk Tidskrift nr 1, 1964

Data Processing

2	Ba	1963	Bazilevskii, Yu UA: The theory of Mathematical Machines, Pergamon Press, New York
3	Be	1961	Belyakin, N V: The Universality of Computers with Potentially External Memory. Problems of Cybernetics, October 1964, Pergamon Press (Transl from "Problemy Kibernetiki")
3	Bi	1963	Brooks, F P and Iverson, K: Automatic Data Processing John Wiley and Sons, New York
3	Bu	1963	Buchholz, Werner: File Organization and Addressing, IBM Systems Journal
3	Er	1964	Elgot, Calvin C and Robinson, Abraham: Random-Access Stored-Program Machines, and Approach to Programming Languages Journ Assoc to Computing Machinery, October 1964
3	Fr	1965	A B Frielink (ed) Economics of Automatic Data Processing, North Holland Publ.
x 3	La	1961—1	Langefors, B: Information Retrieval in File Processing Nordisk Tidskrift för Informationshandling (BIT), Bind 1, Hefte Nr 1 and Hefte Nr 2
x 3	La		See also 2 La 1963—2; 2 La 1959
x 3	La	1964	Langefors, B: Algol Genius, A Programming Language for General Data Processing, BIT, Bind 4, Hefte 3
3	Pr	1965	Pritzler, Leon; Ogus, Jack; H-Hansen, Morris: Computer Editing Methods — Some Applications and Results, US Dept of Commerce, Bureau of the Census 35th Session Int Statist Inst, Belgrad, Yugoslavia 1965
3	St	1964	"Standardlön", Sammanslutning av Arbeidsgivere indenfor Jern- og Metalindustrien i Danmark, Konsulentavdelningen, Publ Nr 6401 UDK 518.5:331.2
3	Ma	1965	J Martin; Programming Real-Time Computer System, Prentice Hall
3	Mn	1965	E W Martin; Electronic Data Processing, Richard D Irwin
3	Wa	1961	Wallace E L: Management Influence on the Design of Data Processing Systems, Harvard University Press, Boston

Basic Theory

4	Ac	1961	Ackoff, Russel L: Progress in Operations Research, Vol 1, John Wiley, New York
4	Ba	1962	Banerji, R B: The Description List of Concepts, CACM
4	Ch	1964	Churchman W: Prediction and Optimal Decision, Prentice-Hall
4	Fo	1968	Forester: Statistical Selection of Business Strategies, Richard D Irwin
4	Ge	1962	Gebhardt-Seele, Peter: Rechnenmodelle für wirtschaftliches Lagern und Einkaufen, R Oldenburg, München

| 4 Ms | 1958 | March J G and Simon H A: Organizations, John Wiley and Sons, New York |
| 4 Ri | 1958 | Riordan, John: An Introduction to Combinatorial Analysis, John Wiley and Sons, New York |

Index

abstract operator   97
access   273—74, 345, 393—96, 398, 457
access operation   393, 396
access time   273, 345, 393—402, 439, 458
accounting   152
accounting system   154
acquisition of information   251
activity   128, 133
activity allocation   20
activity network   133
actual transport speed   342
administrative program   377
admittance   141—42
admittance matrix   142
algebraic description   47
algebraic topology   29, 145
ALGOL   310, 376
ALGOL GENIUS   310, 390, 437
algorithm   91—98, 103, 107, 111, 147, 233, 250—52
algorithm choise   252
algorithmic operator   97
alphabet   322
alphabetical representation   242
alphanumeric character   329
ambition degree   234
amount of information   243, 248
analog computer   22, 319
analog data   242
analysis by parts   29
analysis decomposition   267
analysis of information need   279
analysis of information precedence   303
approximation error   236
approximation of curve segment   235
approximation of optimum decision   254
arc   128—32, 136
arrow   89, 95, 146, 292
associated information system   224
attribute   94—95, 321
automatic design procedure   426

automatic information system   233
availability of information   242
axiom   31

back-up store   457
backward positioning   171
Bar-Hillel   231, 247
base set   98, 102
basic function   278—80
basic information   308
basic information system   413, 427
basic record description   446
basic scheduling operation   179, 183
basic topological system   361
basic topology   360
batch processing   361, 441
binary character   329
binary digit   243
bit   243, 322
block   243, 346, 351, 356, 365, 372, 392—96, 399, 411
block diagram   307
block gap   244
blocking factor   380
blocking of record   346, 352, 440—41
block size   393—94, 397—401, 433
block space   338, 346, 413
block transfer   402
Boolean addition   105
Boolean multiplication   106
boundary   56, 138, 141, 156—59
boundary allowance   467
boundary condition   56
boundary flow   138—42, 159, 161—63
boundary flow vector   140—41, 143
boundary mapping   157
boundary operation   137, 139—40, 152, 155, 158, 163, 188, 192
boundary operation matrix   146
boundary operator   62, 140, 143—45, 157—58, 163, 188—89, 192

477

boundary operator for flows   163
boundary operator matrix   144
boundary point   144—46
boundary position   322
boundary potential   159, 161
boundary to interior   159
boundary transference   157
boundary value   140
boundary variable   156, 158
boundary vector   142
branch   40—47, 90, 138—39, 141—48
branch boundary operator   145
branch element   144
branch-end-flow value   143
branch end point   146
branch flow   143
branch flow vector   142
branch operator   145
branch point   146
branch property   42, 143
bucket   392
buffer area   270, 375, 380, 441
built-up system   155
built-up system analysis   158
business data processing   23

capacity of system   39
capacity of work station   261
card file   345
cellular system   62—63
centralization   59
centralized control   260
chain   124, 149
chain of records   125
chain pointer   150
change of state   229
channel   38—41
character   329
character-based computer   331
check   450
check digit   333—35, 450
choise of algorithm   252
circle   89, 292
closed path   55, 167
COBOL   310, 376, 390, 437, 445—46
co-boundary   158—60
co-boundary mapping   158
co-boundary operation   141, 158
co-cycle   158
code allowance   346—47, 468—69
coincidence   44, 140, 148

coincidence matrix   143, 145, 147, 152, 163, 192—93
coincidence property   45
collecting   195
communication   204
compatibility   22, 24, 167
compiler   310, 437
complement   64
complete information   228—29, 249, 252
complexity   52, 196, 265
complex system   52
component   21—23, 28, 139, 196, 298
component(s) design   23
component problem   196—98
composite process   285
computation   295, 305, 307, 324—27, 336, 360, 363, 365—69, 376—78
computer   457
computer graphics   300
computer program   375
computer speed   270
concept of systems, see system concept
conceptual operator   97
condition for simplified timing   186
connection matrix   26, 28
connection property   42
consolidated file   265, 295, 391, 394, 396, 433, 435, 443
consolidated file record   410
consolidated masterfile   293
consolidated record   389, 392—93, 402
consolidating   324, 424
consolidation   367, 385, 388—92, 394, 399—401, 405, 413—15, 433, 435—37, 443
consolidation matrix   436
consolidation of elementary files   346—48
consolidation of files   292, 387—93, 398, 413, 430, 433, 436—37, 440
consolidation of records   389, 392
constant field length   322
constructibility   74
constructive   73
constructive subsystem structure   73
control   25, 200, 205, 208—09, 225, 228, 242, 245, 260, 280
control information   282
control of managed system   280
control quality   225, 241
control theory   200, 234
converse operator   157

conversion to mechanized form   252
Copi   33
correlation   35
cost   69—70, 221, 242, 249—53, 304, 399
cost analysis   255
cost balancing   260
cost curve   210, 226, 237
cost flow   249, 258, 262
cost of access   401
cost of error   236, 240
cost of information, see information cost
cost in information processing, see information processing cost
cost of memory space   401
cost of processing   258
cost of transport   401
CPU time   399, 402
criteria problem   34
criterion   22, 205, 399
curve segment approximation   235
cycle   158, 161—63, 193
cycle defining operator   160
cycle time   402

data   91—92, 105, 242, 319—20, 443, 457
data communication   245
data description   446
data file   391
data organization   277
data origin   413
data packing   371, 467—68
data processing system   292—93
data processing system analysis   198
data representation   97, 247, 322
data set   91, 93, 325, 367
data size   244, 389
data storage   245
data structure   91—94, 97—98, 102, 105—06, 111, 147, 149, 151—55, 277
data structure representation   94, 147
data term   400
data transport   270, 277, 287, 402, 404, 413, 439, 445
data volume   224, 228, 242
datum   243, 246, 322
deadweight transport   367, 388, 392, 401, 404
decentralization   34, 217
decentralized decision making   219
decimal digit   329, 468
decision   206—10, 228, 260, 282, 300

decision function   203, 207
decision information   260
decision maker   397
decision-making   204, 208—11
decision model   211
decision point   300
decision problem   302
decision process   211, 253
decision quality   253
decision rule   202, 218
decision situation   300
decision theory   200
decision value   209—10
deduction   33
definition of data   319
definition of elementary file   293
definition of information   319
definition of system   37, 47, 88
degree of ambition   234
degree of realism   226
delay   214
delay time, see time delay
delegation   59
demand quantity   213
demand time   213
demand vector   125, 173, 295
description of state   229
design analysis   427
design decision   339
diagonal matrix   27, 188—89
diagram   89—90
difficulty of forecasting   37
digit   320—22
digital form   319
digital representation   242
digraph   90
dimentioning of information system   221
direct access   274, 352, 402
direct-access file   392, 402
direct-access file storage   400, 441
direct-access memory   465
direct-access storage   272—74, 344, 349, 392, 402, 441
direct addressing   441
directed graph   90
directing center   216—19
directive   57, 59, 217—19, 253, 256
directive decision   208
directive decision making   255
directive information   200, 207—08, 215—17, 253—63

directive information processing   254
directive information system   206—07
directive information value   206
direct precedent   92
direct processing   274, 361, 441
direct store   346
disc   400
dismount time   352
displaying information   204
distributing   195
documentation   21, 299, 306, 308
downward specification   76, 79
dummy   131
dummy arc   131—32
dynamic batch determination   182—83
dynamic system   199

earliest position   169—70
echelon   50
economic analysis   253
economic balance   60
economic balance problem   58—60
economic batch size   183
edge   90
effective speed   269, 273, 359
effective tape speed   372
efficiency   205, 224, 253, 263
elastic network   27
elastic structure   25—27
electric network   25—26
element   90—91, 98—99, 101, 103, 142—43, 146, 192
elementary evolution   294, 305
elementary file   292—95, 298, 301—02, 304—06, 336, 348—49, 359—60, 376, 385, 387, 391—92, 410, 412—14, 433, 443, 454
elementary file consolidation, see consolidation of elementary files
elementary information   293, 413
elementary information class   293
elementary information set   293, 413
elementary item   304, 322
elementary message   130—32, 243, 248, 251, 320
elementary part   33, 156
elementary procedure   437
elementary process 283, 285, 292—94, 301, 374, 376, 385, 402, 413—14, 437, 453
elementary record   243, 251, 325, 333, 390, 400—02, 440, 443

elementary state   230
elementary subroutine   437
element boundary operator   143—44
element boundary matrix   146
element terminal   192
end point of branch   146
equivalence class   432
error   236, 309, 449—51
error cost   236, 240
error interval   240
event   90, 133
executive decision   209, 211, 252
executive decision situation   209—10
executive program   402
extensive information system   215
external data   252
external entity   156
external flow   41, 138, 163
external property   24, 42, 46

Falkenhainer   27
feasibility   22
feasibility study   78, 80—81
feasible subsystem   80
feed-back   58
fetching information   204, 228
field   322
field length   322, 468
file   269, 292, 301, 325, 330, 336, 371, 390—94, 396, 415—17, 420—21, 433, 457
file configuration   396, 398
file consolidation, see consolidation of files
file design   391
file label   389
file medium   388
file processing   457
file record   443
file scan   340, 350, 373, 417, 419, 423
file scan multiplicity, see multiplicity of file scans
file scan multiplicity vector   352
file size   269, 329, 332, 338, 342, 344, 350, 354—57, 359—60, 379
file sorting   424, 457
file storage   272, 330, 339, 401, 440, 459
file storage medium   269
file storage space   390
file storage unit   404
file transport   188, 341, 350, 352—56, 361, 375, 391—92, 422, 426

480

file transport handling   402
file transport reduction   418
file transport size   339, 342, 348, 353, 358, 363
file transport size vector   352, 370
file transport volume   339, 341—42, 346—49, 350—52, 361, 366, 369, 409, 441
file transport volume vector   352, 370, 427
file volume   338, 342, 346—49, 350, 360, 371, 379
firm function   278—80, 282—83, 285—87
firm model   206
first precedent   93, 101, 109
fixed batch production   183
fixed batch size production   180
fixed block size   338
fixed field   331
fixed production period   182—83
fixed record length   346
flip-flop   348—49, 358
flow   38—43, 45—47, 61—64, 138—39, 143, 158, 162
flow capacity   39
flow-chart   307, 412
flow component   162
flow of information   299
flow of material   137
flow value   139, 144, 163
fluctuation cost   260
forecasting   222, 224
formal description   91
forward positioning   169, 171
frequency of processing   255
function   287

gap   159—62, 170
gap-analysing operator   159
gap component   162
general positioning   171
general systems problem   53—55
general systems theory   55
generation   175, 177—79, 183, 185—88
global information   246
goal   20, 57, 207, 210, 279
graph   90—93, 128, 130—31, 134—36, 291, 368—70
gross analysis   33
gross diagram   64
gross property   31, 46, 89
gross system   155

gross system analysis   155, 158
gross systems property   32, 50
gross theory   31
group access   462—64
grouped process   270—71, 410—11, 416, 423
grouping   286, 296, 305, 363—65, 371, 374—75, 405, 409—11, 413—15, 419—25, 431, 436—37, 453—55
grouping computation   363
grouping matrix   436
grouping of computations   360, 365
grouping of processes   274, 371—75, 379, 413—14, 417, 423—27, 430, 437, 440, 453
grouping processes in pairs   453
grouping vector   426
group program   365

hardware cost   404
hardware design   404
hardware limitation   404
hardware system   404
hierarchical structure   79, 83
hierarchy   79—80

identification   230—32, 304—06, 391
identification by position   246
identification number   443
identifier   293
identifying part   232
identity of object   320
idleness cost   259
idleness cost flow   258
ill-conditioned computation   323
immediate precedent   92, 98, 101, 364, 428
immediate succedent   100, 167
imperceivable system   69, 73, 80, 83
incidence   136, 144—45, 148, 367
incidence matrix   136—41, 143—45, 147, 151—52, 155, 163, 190, 296, 326, 331, 360, 366—67, 369, 371, 387, 412—13, 415, 424, 434, 436—37
incidence number   137
incoming arc matrix   135
incompatibility   24, 37, 52, 159, 169, 307
increment set   460—61
inference   296
inference function   297
inference process   297

481

inflow   41, 43
information   91, 97, 199—201, 227—30, 231—32, 242—44, 247, 250, 258, 282, 298, 319
information acquisition   251
information amount   243, 247—48
information analysis   287
information availability   242
information center   213—14
information class   279, 292, 306
information cost   196, 205, 210, 217, 234, 240—41
information element   326
information flow   217—19
information free system   214
information need   199, 278—80, 287, 293, 303, 308
information precedence   298
information precedence graph   307
information precedence matrix   306
information precedence relation   307, 427
information precedent   283, 288
information processing   227, 251, 256, 288
information processing cost   210, 225—26, 237—38, 256—57, 263
information processing system   292—93
information processing systems analysis   196
information production   222
information quality   242
information quantity   221, 242
information relevance   242
information reliability   242
information representation   243
information set   279, 283, 285—88, 292, 306
information storage   251
information storing   203
information structure   302
information system   25, 195—96, 199—204, 215—17, 222, 224, 233, 249, 258, 265, 280—81, 83, 286, 414, 449
information system analysis   198, 457
information system design   195—96, 199, 222, 296, 426
information systems theory   200, 234
information timeliness   242
information value   196, 217, 221—25, 228, 233—35, 237—38, 242—44, 247—48
initial   286
initial element   80, 310

initial part   100
initial point   132, 171
initial position   169
initial record   332
initial set   286, 290
initial vertex matrix   134
inner boundary   50, 56, 293
input   156, 285, 329, 335, 359, 367—69, 371, 427
input data   325
input file   333, 343, 355, 362
input information   296
input junction   39
input operation   286
input/output   375—76
input/output requirement   433
input record   332—34, 337
input transport volume   361
input unit   387
input volume   411
intangible   60, 157
interconnection   51
interior   159
intermediary result   325
intermediate boundary   49—50, 56—58, 60, 358
intermediate transport   353
internal branch flow   140
internal branch flow vector   140
internal computer memory   459
internal computer operation   458
internal flow   41, 140, 142, 144, 159, 161, 163
internal flow value   189
internal flow vector   140, 163, 188
internal part   100
internal point   229
internal potential   159, 161
internal processing   371
internal processing speed   467
interrecord gap   346, 410—11, 467—69
intersection operation   105, 418
inventory   249, 256
inventory control   238
inventory cost   256—57
inventory economy   261
iteration   75—77, 79, 283

joint operation   436
junction point   40

kernel set   460
key   325, 389, 391—92, 401
key term   391
key value   325
key-word   306
kind of information   229, 250, 256, 299, 301
kind of property   320—22
kind of state variable   243
kind of variable   246
Kirchoff   40
K-progressive file   462
K-progressive process   461
Kron   26—29, 142

lead-time matrix   172
length of term   322
line   34, 66, 146, 149—50
linear file   459
linear file process   459
linear file processing   459
linear graph   90
linear process   462—63
line element   152, 368
line element boundary matrix   152
line record   150
link   95, 106, 109, 111, 125
linked data structure   106—09
linking address   125—27
local decision   218
local information   205, 262
logical addition   105
logical sum   420
lowest position value   169

machine instruction   377
machine-oriented program   377
magnetic disc   400
magnetic drum   375, 400
magnetic tape   272, 344—46, 391
magnetic tape store   458
main memory   404
making decision, see decision making
managed system   205, 208, 211, 224—25, 245, 253, 255, 263, 280
management (of) system   25, 207
mass memory   361, 388, 413, 439
master file   269, 375
material flow   137
material system   202
mathematical method   90

mathematical model   203
mathematical systems theory   30
mathematical tool   22
matrix   168, 286
matrix algebra   26—27
matrix-by-column multiplication   119
matrix-by-vector composition   165
matrix-by-vector multiplication   172
matrix-by-vector operation   105, 118
matrix multiplication   108, 140, 145—47, 290, 423—24
matrix of initial vertices   134
matrix of incoming arcs   135
matrix of responsive properties   142
matrix operation   118, 139, 148, 417—19, 433
matrix operation by computer   119—24
matrix representation   140—41
matrix structure   150
maximization of transport reduction   436
McKean   34
meaning of information   228—29
measurable property   320
measure part   232
measure of state variable   243
memory   457
memory area   440
memory cycle time   457
memory limitation   379
memory need   423
memory position   244, 457
memory requirement   271, 373—74, 378, 423
memory size   356, 360, 371, 380, 411—12, 453—54
memory space   339, 346, 350—51, 365, 371, 373, 375, 380, 404, 410, 413, 418, 423, 425, 457, 461—62, 467—69
memory space limitation   424
merging file   404
message   230—34, 241—45, 247, 319
message size   243, 245, 247
message value   243
minimizing process grouping   425
minimum file transport   424
minimum total cost   256
mixed precedence of arcs   130
model of a firm   206
mode of storage   352
modification   75
multiple file scan   359, 413, 424

multiple scan   416, 457
multiple scanning   326
multiple transport   358, 360, 363, 441
multiplication by column selection   463
multiplication of matrices, see matrix multiplication
multiplicity   341, 358, 361—62, 457
multiplicity factor   360
multiplicity of data   325
multiplicity of file scans   422—23
multiplicity of scans   420
multi-programming   402—03

name   389, 465
name link   95
negative slack   170
neighbor   62, 245, 291, 364
neighboring cell   62—63
neighbor relation   62
network   26, 28, 46, 61, 133, 137—39, 141
node   38—47, 90—93, 138—42, 144—50
node potential value vector   142
node property   148
node record   148—49
nominal speed   356
nominal transport speed   339, 342
non-feasible grouping   431
non-zero element   144
number of I/O-units   360
numeric(al) data   155, 346, 352—54, 468
numerical matrix   117

object   88—96, 101, 107, 304, 320, 401
object classification   304
object identifier   304, 443
objectives   278—80, 397
objectives of a firm   278
object system   224
object term   397
one-dimensional element   129
one-dimensional entity   368
one-dimensional object   147
on-line-real-time   361
on-line-real-time data processing   262
on-line-real-time equipment   262
operation frequency   256
operation of boundary, see boundary operation
operation of intersection   105
operation of union   105

operative action   203
operative control   202—03, 205
operative decision   208, 219, 253, 258, 261—62
operative frequency   255
operative functioning   205, 207
operative information   200—02, 205, 208, 215, 219, 253—55, 258, 260
operative information processing   253
operative information system   206—07
operative program system   375
operative system   206
operative transaction   253
operator   156
opportunity cost   60, 226
optimal error interval   240
optimization of information processing   224
optimum balance   59
optimum block size   398
optimum consolidation   398
optimum decision approximation   254
optimum design of system management   225
optimum efficiency   226
optimum executive decision   210
optimum grouping process   453
optimum pairing   453
order   260
ordering of a file   366
organizing the file information   329
originating information   286
outer boundary   50, 56—58, 66
outflow   41
output   156, 285, 329, 355, 359, 367—68, 371, 427
output data   325
output file   331, 344, 356
output information   296
output junction   39
output operation   286
output record   332—35, 337
output unit   387
out-terminal   192
overlap   170

packed data   346
packing data   371, 467—68
part   35, 51, 56, 101
part boundary operator   188
partitioning   64, 66, 188, 196, 432

part property   39, 41, 46, 89
path   109, 167, 169
perceivable set of subsystems   75
perceivable step   75, 80
perceivable subsystem   80
perceivable subsystem structure   81
period of processing, see processing period
Pert   133
physical connection   35
physical property   29
planning of programming   309
point   35, 65, 89, 100, 117, 145, 368
pointer   95, 106, 148—49, 152, 154, 394
point identification   247
point in time   230, 243, 320
point message   230—34, 244, 246—47
polygon   236—37
polygonal approximation of cost curve   237
polygon point   241
position   167, 170, 246
positional operator   164
positioning   168, 171
positioning operation   168
position vector   168
positive slack   170
potential   44—48, 141, 158
potential coincidence property   44
potential difference   45
potential drop   43—44, 46, 141
potential value   43—46, 141
precedence analysis   287
precedence graph   90, 116, 280, 291
precedence information   57, 213, 296, 306
precedence list   98, 106, 116, 297
precedence matrix   98—100, 102, 105, 107, 109, 117, 128—30, 132, 172, 214, 281, 285—88, 294—95, 305—06, 309—10, 326, 331, 356, 366—67, 387, 412, 427—29
precedence matrix for mixed dimension   134
precedence operation   174
precedence operator   97, 169, 192
precedence quantity   178
precedence relation   90—92, 128—32, 178, 280—81, 288—90, 297—98, 302, 308, 310, 359, 362, 364, 366—67, 428, 457
precedence set   289, 292, 324
precedence system   310

precedence vector   100, 116
precedent   90—93, 97—99, 101—03, 108, 111, 115, 117, 129, 171, 184—85, 192, 280—81, 283, 285—88, 290, 292, 297, 299, 305—07, 364, 367, 393, 427—30
precedent address   123
precedent information   280
precedent of set   102
precedent of set of parts   102
precedents list   92—94, 306
precision   229, 233, 244, 320, 322
predecessor   90
pressure drop   43
principle of systems work   51
problem-oriented program   376
procedure   324, 376
process   285—86, 324, 361, 364—68, 371, 373, 375—77, 380, 415—17, 419—21, 423, 427, 457
process data set   460
process grouping, see grouping of processes
processing   195, 269—70
processing cost   258
processing need   200
processing period   251, 253, 338, 353, 356, 360, 416, 442
processing time   413, 445
processor   457
process ordering   424
process program   375
process stage   460
process time   459
production of information   222
production system   249
program   437, 446, 457
program description   446
programming   406
programming language   437
program size   374
program space   373, 385
program switch   375
program transport   271—72, 274
program work   446
property   26, 28, 32, 38—44, 46, 51, 60, 71—76, 78—80, 98, 100, 129, 142, 155—58, 245, 320, 389
property of branch, see branch property
property of connection   41—42
property of node   148
property of part, see part property

485

property of system, see system property
property testing   71—72
property value   321—22
property value set   321—22
proposition   31—33, 67—69, 72—73, 403, 454
pseudo-direct-access storage   392
pseudo-multiplication   117
pseudo random access   439, 465
punched card   343—45
punched tape   343—45

quality of control   225, 241
quality of decision   253
quality of information   242
quantitative determination of information value   235
quantity of demand   213
quantity of information   221, 242

random access   439, 465
random access store   440, 459
random process   464
random processing   394
realism degree   226
realizable subsystem structure   72
record   91—95, 106, 111, 147, 242, 245, 270—72, 301, 325, 330, 336, 392—95, 400—02
record blocking, see blocking of records
record chain   124
record collection   387
record format   95, 443, 445
record gap   269—70, 273, 330, 347, 352, 354, 372
record gap allowance   467—68
recording density   348
record label   333—35
record lay-out   443—44
record length   352, 354, 372, 467, 469
record name   390
record organization   445
record size   246, 273, 329—32, 336—38, 345, 347, 379, 393, 398
record type   246, 446
rectangular element   368
rectangular file   462—63
rectangular file processing   462—63
rectangular matrix   463
rectangular process   462—64
reduction of file transport   188

redundancy   322
reference index   115
reference period   331, 340, 345, 350—53, 356, 361
reference point   232
reference system   340
relation   35, 46, 88—92, 94, 156, 292, 297
relativity principle for systems   36, 56
relevance of information   242
reliability   450
reliability of information   242
reliability problem   449—50
representation of information   243
reprogramming   447
requirement computation   172—88
requirement scheduling   172—88
resistance   47
resistance value   46
resource allocation   20
response matrix   142—43
response time   253, 442
response value   143
responsive property   43, 45, 141—42, 157
responsive property matrix   142
restriction rule for grouping   428
retrieval   464—65
retrieval by name   465
retrieval by property   441, 465
retrieval of information   464
reverse operator   141
rewind time   343, 348, 352
ring chain   149
rule for grouping   364

Saint-Venant's principle   63
Samuelson   29
satisficing   212
satisficing decision-making   212
scalar entity   30
scan   361, 363, 367, 380, 416, 457, 463
scanning speed   269, 273
scientific decision situation   209
second precedent   93, 101, 109, 111
second succedent   93
selecting column   103
selection column   99, 106
selection vector   99, 102—03, 105—06, 116, 136, 165
semantic content   231, 244
separator   330—32
serial access   272

serial access file   441
serial access storage   391, 402
serial memory   465
set intersection   88, 289
set of parts   101
set of precedents   101
set union   88
set-up time   266—67, 352, 354
Simon   212
simple path   166
simplification cost   239—40
simplification cost curve   226
simplification cost function   226
simplification of timing   186
simultaneous input/output   358, 372—73
simultaneous read/write   371—72
simultaneous transport   271
size   293
size of data term   320
size of message   246—47
solution by parts   29, 33
sorting key   444
sorting process   355—56
sorting sequence   432
special systems problem   53—55
speed factor   342, 345, 348
standard matrix multiplication   122
standard program   295
standing file   325, 333, 336, 344, 346, 352—53, 404, 434—36
standing file record   332, 338, 346
state change   229
state description   229
state information   216, 227
state measure   247
state of system   230
state variable   230—33, 243—46
state variable measure   243
stationary decision situation   211
storage   404
storage cost   249, 260
storage of information   251
storage space   467
storing   195
storing information   204
storing of term   322
structural information   155
structural property   91
subdiagram   64
subdivision by echelons   51, 60
subdivision of the system design   82

subgeneration   185
subgoal   34
subject of message   231
sub-optimization   20, 34, 183, 259
subrecord   95, 111, 149, 151, 155, 346
subroutine   295
subset   289
subset relation   289—91
subsystem   20, 24, 29, 48—50, 56—57, 60, 64, 72—74, 78—80, 159, 195—96, 204, 358
subsystem structure   72—76, 79
subsystem test   21
subtheory   32
succedence information   331
succedence matrix   112, 309
succedence operator   112, 169
succedence relation   128, 308
succedence set   324
succedence vector   100
succedent   90—91, 98, 107, 112, 171, 214, 290, 305, 307, 367, 401—02
succedent address   123
succedents computation   307
succedents list   94
successor   90, 133, 168
successor arc   131
system   21, 34—37, 46—50, 56, 75, 88, 92—95, 137, 199, 224, 227
system(s) analysis   20, 34, 47, 66, 75, 260, 267
system(s) analysis approach   48
system as a set of parts   51
system boundary flow vector   189
system branch   147
system capacity   39
system component   148
system(s) concept   23, 34
system connection   145, 163
system control   227
system(s) design   20, 47, 56, 66, 266—68, 412
system diagram   89
system efficiency   293
system element   98, 148
system(s) engineering   21—23, 25
system goal   205
system(s) graph   65, 90, 109, 164, 166
system incompatibility   23, 36
system matrix   147, 150
system node   45, 146—47, 192

487

system of connection   192
system part   25, 29, 36, 38, 45, 48, 51, 90, 103, 106—09, 111
system partitioning   64, 66
system point   31, 145, 216, 227, 229—33, 241, 243—45
system problem   38, 53—55, 196—98, 266—67
system property   38—43, 46, 51, 56, 88
system reliability   449
system structure   51, 60, 145, 155, 401
system(s) theory   21, 25, 34, 196—98
system topology   145, 190
system transport   341, 351, 354—55, 357, 359
system(s) work   47, 51, 53, 66, 82, 198, 299
system(s) work principle   51

take-down time   354
tape   388
tape length   348, 372, 467
tape recording speed   467
tape reel set-up   388
tape speed   372
temporary data   325
term   231, 243—44, 294, 304, 322, 389, 443, 446, 467
terminal   291
terminal part   100
terminal point   132, 152, 168, 171
terminal record   332
terminal set   287, 291
terminology problem   306
term length   322—23, 467
term packing   468—69
term storing   322
testing of property   72
testing program   309
testing subroutine   309
theorem   35, 69—70, 73, 75, 77, 80, 83, 312
theory of control, see control theory
theory of information system, see information systems theory
time delay   209—13, 223
timeliness of information   242
time of access   273
time of demand   213
time positioning matrix   214
time sharing   402—03

488

topological complexity   359
topological multiplicity   359
topological property   29, 143, 359, 427
topological system   362
topological transport factor   359—60, 362—63, 365, 439
topology   142, 359, 362
topology of information precedence system   340
total cost   251, 257
total cost curve   257
total optimization   20
total systems goal   24
total systems theory   32
total system transport   350
total test   21
transaction   272
transaction file   269
transaction frequency   269—72, 374
transaction record   269
transaction vector   153
transference   141
transference operation   141
transference property   43, 45, 156
transference relation   156
transfile   325
transient decision situation   211
transport   270—72, 329, 353, 360—66, 392—93, 396, 400, 404, 411, 421, 424—25, 427, 431, 437, 441
transport equipment   387
transport factor   351, 353—55, 358—60, 365, 370—71
transport factor statistics   360
transport limitation   408
transport size   343—46, 350—52
transport speed   270, 330, 350, 353, 356, 398, 400
transport time   270—74, 360, 396, 399—400
transport volume   339, 343—46, 349, 353, 355—56, 363, 365, 371, 373, 380, 404, 407—12, 439, 453—54, 457, 463
transport volume factor   343—45, 379
transport volume for program   373
transposed coincidence matrix   188
transposed incidence matrix   144
transposed matrix   27, 119
transposed positional operator   169
transput   387
transput file   404

transput unit 387, 404
type 293, 299, 301, 446
type code 389—90

underestimation 53, 69—70, 83, 234
union of precedents 102
union operation 105, 433
unit matrix 420
updated file 435
updating 204, 256, 259, 408, 435
updating frequency 256, 361
updating need 265
upward construction 76, 78—79

value 321
value curve 209—10
value of boundary 140
value of decision 209
value of directive information 205
value of information, see information value
value of message 243
value of property 320
value of variable 230
variable block size 338
variable word length 468
varying field 331
varying field length 331
vector 139

vector of boundary 142
vector of boundary flow, see boundary flow vector
vector of branch flow 142
vector of internal branch flow 140
vector of multiplicity 341
vector of node potential value 142
vector value 30
vertex 101, 129, 134, 136, 141
volume factor 342, 345—47, 356
volume of message 246

waste production 461
waste set 460
word 322
word allowance 346—47
word boundary allowance 467—68
word length 467—68
workable subsystem structure 72—75, 77
work area 376
work station 258—63
work station capacity 261

zero-dimensional entity 368
zero-dimensional object 147
zero-dimensional part 114
zero-sum flow 47
zero-sum law 40—43, 143
zero-sum property 41, 45, 138, 140, 142